Not long after the consumer and environmental movements in the United States became institutionalized in the early 1970s, the regulated industries began to advocate "regulatory reform." This regulatory reform countermovement reached its peak with the election of Ronald Reagan in 1980. Advocates of regulatory reform argued that regulatory agencies did not sufficiently analyze the costs and benefits of their rules. Rather, they claimed that the agencies adopted irrational "command and control" approaches to regulation that wasted scarce societal resources. The goal of this kind of regulatory reform movement was to "reinvent" bureaucratic rationality so that agencies would approach regulatory problems from the very different perspective of neoclassical microeconomics.

Using several case studies from the early Reagan years, this book examines and critiques the claims of the regulatory reformers that regulatory analysis will result in "better" decisionmaking. Drawing on hundreds of interviews with scientists, engineers, regulatory analysts, and upper-level personnel in six major federal agencies, the book examines the roles that regulatory analysts and their counterparts in the Office of Management and Budget play in the decisionmaking process. The book concludes with suggestions for enhancing the effectiveness of regulatory analysis while at the same time acknowledging its limitations.

Reinventing rationality

Reinventing rationality

The role of regulatory analysis in the federal bureaucracy

Thomas O. McGarity

University of Texas
School of Law

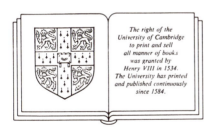

The right of the
University of Cambridge
to print and sell
all manner of books
was granted by
Henry VIII in 1534.
The University has printed
and published continuously
since 1584.

CAMBRIDGE UNIVERSITY PRESS

Cambridge
New York   Port Chester   Melbourne   Sydney

Published by the Press Syndicate of the University of Cambridge
The Pitt Building, Trumpington Street, Cambridge CB2 1RP
40 West 20th Street, New York, NY 10011, USA
10 Stamford Road, Oakleigh, Melbourne 3166, Australia

First published 1991

Printed in the United States of America

JK
901
M45
1991

Library of Congress Cataloging-in-Publication Data
McGarity, Thomas O.
Reinventing rationality : the role of regulatory analysis in the
federal bureaucracy / Thomas O. McGarity.
p.   cm.
Includes bibliographical references and index.
ISBN 0–521–40256–5
1. Independent regulatory commissions – United States.   2. Trade
regulation – United States – Cost effectiveness.   I. Title.
JK901.M45   1991
353.09′1 – dc20   90–2686
                                                       CIP

British Library Cataloging in Publication Data
McGarity, Thomas O.
Reinventing rationality : the role of regulatory analysis
in the federal bureaucracy.
1. United States. Public administration
I. Title
353

ISBN 0–521–40256–5 hardback

To my parents
Rev. Owen McGarity, Jr.
and
Lois Thomas McGarity

Contents

Acknowledgments

This book would not have been possible without large contributions from many people. First are the dozens of dedicated federal agency employees who generously donated their time to tedious interviews. Without their inside perspective the effort could have been little more than an unilluminating ivory tower exercise. The Administrative Conference of the United States supported the empirical research that forms the backbone of the book. With its customary courteousness and diligence, the Conference staff, particularly Michael Bowers and Jeff Lubbers, provided vital feedback during the early stages of the project. Later, the Rulemaking Committee of the Conference and especially its Chairman, Calvin Collier, provided useful comments and criticisms. The project's association with the Conference provided much needed access to high-level decisionmakers in the departments and agencies. A report prepared for the Conference in 1983 formed the basis for Recommendation 85–2 of the Conference, reprinted at 1 C.F.R. § 305.85–2.

The project profited greatly from the help of several research assistants, including Mary Sahs, Margot Brito, Janet Rasch, Raenell Silcox, and Jan Tierney. For this support, I thank the University of Texas Law School Foundation. I am especially grateful to the University of Texas University Research Fund for providing a semester's research leave during which I was able to turn mountains of notes into a first draft of a real book.

Finally, I am grateful to Cathy, Kristi, and Laurie for suffering through too many hours with a husband and father who was there, but not really there.

Abbreviations

APHIS Animal and Plant Health Inspection Service

AMS   Agricultural Marketing Service

ASCS   Agricultural Soil and Conservation Service

EIS   Environmental Impact Statement

EPA   Environmental Protection Agency

FAA   Federal Aviation Administration

FRFA   Final Regulatory Flexibility Analysis

FRIA   Final Regulatory Impact Analysis

FSIS   Food Safety and Inspection Service

NHTSA National Highway Traffic Safety Administration

OIRA   Office of Information and Regulatory Affairs

OMB   Office of Management and Budget

OSHA   Occupational Safety and Health Administration

PRFA   Preliminary Regulatory Flexibility Analysis

PRIA   Preliminary Regulatory Impact Analysis

RFA   Regulatory Flexibility Analysis

RIA   Regulatory Impact Analysis

Introduction

The history of the American political economy in the twentieth century is one of reform and reaction. During each wave of reform, an outraged public demanded legislation to cure past abuses. Sometimes Congress enacted direct legislation, such as antitrust laws, civil rights laws, and antiracketeering laws, that empowered courts to enforce vaguely articulated norms through private litigation. More often, Congress created regulatory agencies, which were supposed to be repositories of "neutral" expertise in public administration and other "scientific" disciplines, and charged them with advancing the "public interest."

One of the brightest stars in the firmament of the Progressive Era legislation was the Federal Trade Commission, the protector of consumers and small businesses from monopolistic and unfair trade practices. Other agencies of the Progressive Era included the Interstate Commerce Commission, the first modern independent federal agency, the Food and Drug Administration, and the precursors of the Food Safety and Inspection Service in the Department of Agriculture.[1] The New Deal reforms produced the Securities and Exchange Commission, the National Labor Relations Board, the Agricultural Marketing Service, the Agricultural Stabilization and Conservation Service, and the National Recovery Administration,[2] the most ambitious and shortest-lived agency of them all. Most recently, the consumer and environmental movement of the late 1960s and early 1970s brought us the Occupational Safety and Health Administration, the Consumer Product Safety Commission, a rejuvenated Federal Trade Commission (the old one had grown quite moribund), and (another very ambitious creation) the Environmental Protection Agency.[3] Although the earlier commissions engaged primarily in "economic" regulation (setting rates, eliminating "windfall profits," and overseeing public utilities), most of the newer agencies practiced "social" regulation (writing health and environmental standards, licensing potentially hazardous products and technologies, and ensuring fairness in employment, advertising, and other relationships).[4]

The institution builders of these three great reform movements were lawyers. Attorneys like Louis Brandeis, James Landis, Michael Pertschuk, and Douglas Costle wrote the statutes that created the agencies, and lawyers were usually appointed to head the agencies during their formative stages.[5] Felix Frankfurter sent a talented group of "happy hot dogs" from Harvard Law School to Washington, D.C. during the New Deal to remake society through the regulatory process. These young lawyers assumed a major role in implementing New Deal legislation before departing the agencies for judgeships and more lucrative private practices in Washington, leaving behind a corps of scientists, engineers, and less highly credentialed lawyers to carry out the nitty gritty day-to-day regulatory functions.[6]

The regulated industries did not sit idly by and accept the threats that regulatory agencies posed to their autonomy and, more importantly, to their economic and social power. In each era, regulatees fought back through trade associations, through industry-dominated private institutions such as the National Association of Manufacturers, the Chamber of Commerce, and the Liberty League, and through well-placed lawsuits challenging the constitutionality of the regulatory statutes and the legality of administrative actions taken pursuant to those laws. Although the regulated industries generally acknowledged the need for limited government intrusions into private relationships, most would have preferred to channel such intrusions through judicial application of the common law and broad statutory standards like those articulated in the antitrust laws.[7] The Progressive Era statutes were substantially undermined by Supreme Court decisions holding state and federal regulatory statutes unconstitutional under an expansive view of the contract clause and a judicially inspired notion of "substantive due process."[8] Two of the most important New Deal statutes fell to the nondelegation doctrine, which holds that Congress may not engage in standardless delegation of legislative power.[9] After Justice Owen Roberts' alleged "switch in time that serves nine,"[10] judicial thinking evolved rapidly and significantly from a grudging resistance to an open-armed acceptance of the activist regulatory state and a recognition that to a very large extent government intervention would take place at the federal level.[11]

Shifting from a substantive to a procedural attack, the regulated industries in 1947 secured the enactment of the Administrative Procedure Act, which judicialized much administrative practice and provided for substantive judicial review of the rationality of individual regulatory activities.[12] The industries hoped thereby to place the fate of the New Deal agencies in the hands of a judiciary that might be more sensitive to their economic concerns.

In reacting to the consumer and environmental statutes, the regulated industries for the most part abandoned the constitutional attack, although an occasional judicial utterance inspired renewed hope in a new generation of nondelegation doctrine proponents.[13] Because most of the newer statutes specified informal rulemaking as the preferred procedural mode, few courts were willing to find procedural irregularities in the activities of the consumer and environmental agencies. A modern judicial tradition of relatively lenient substantive review of administrative action, stemming from a Supreme Court dominated by Roosevelt appointees, made substantive judicial review a gamble. The industries therefore turned to Congress for help.

In a bold tactical stroke, the regulated industries and their allies in academia adopted the "reform" banner as their own, and during the 1980s they launched a new "regulatory reform" movement. The intellectual foundation for this enterprise was poured in the economics departments and the business and public policy schools of the nation's prestigious universities. It received a strong political, if less academically sophisticated, impetus from a constant flood of quasischolarly tracts written in privately sponsored "think tanks" like the American Enterprise Institute and the Brookings Institution.

Starting with a presumption that minimally regulated markets achieved the best distribution of goods and services, these scholars and essayists were pessimistic about the efficacy of regulation as an instrument of social change. They tended to rank liberty higher than equality in their scale of values, and they warned that too much safety or environmental protection could be inefficient. In those (presumably rare) instances in which they deemed governmental intervention into private arrangements to be justified, they expressed a strong preference for economic incentives, rather than the "command and control" regulations that typified the new consumer and environmental statutes. Finally, the regulatory reformers insisted that government should not act to achieve a particular social goal until it had thoroughly analyzed the impact of such intervention on other social goals. In particular, the new agencies should not promulgate new rules until they had analyzed their projected costs and benefits.

Riding the crest of popular dissatisfaction with regulatory agencies in the late 1970s, this new regulatory reform movement swept into Washington intent on changing the standard operating procedures of old-line agencies like the Interstate Commerce Commission and the newer agencies like the Environmental Protection Agency. By far the most successful reform tool was the nonstatutory "Regulatory Impact Analysis" requirement, under which executive agencies had to prepare written assessments of the costs and benefits of major regulations. Like the Environmental Impact Statement (EIS) requirement of the National Environmental Policy Act, from which it drew its inspiration, the Regulatory Impact Analysis (RIA) requirement created an institutional vacuum. The agencies needed a staff to write the regulatory analyses.

During the 1980s, a cadre of young economists and recent graduates of public policy schools, like the Kennedy School at Harvard and the LBJ School at the University of Texas, poured into Washington to fill the void. Like the "happy hot dogs" of an earlier era, these reformers were young, bright, ambitious, confident, impatient, and sometimes a bit arrogant. If the "happy hot dogs" went to Washington to save the world from the evils of big business, these young regulatory analysts made the pilgrimage to save the world from big government. Unlike the "happy hot dogs," their goal was not to oil the gears of government to hasten social change; rather, it was to resist precipitous governmental intrusion into the private economy. Conscious of limited resources, they were concerned about the wasteful side effects of regulation. They were skeptical about implementing high-sounding principles in the real world of greedy beneficiaries and opportunistic politicians. David Stockman, not Louis Brandeis or Ralph Nader, was their role model. They reveled in numbers, they rejoiced in keen "analysis" (which usually meant applying the paradigms of neoclassical economics to regulatory problems), and they relished a good bureaucratic fight. They were front-line guerrillas in the so-called Reagan revolution against regulation.

This book is about these skeptical young regulatory analysts and the roles that they have played and continue to play in modern regulatory agencies. It is also a book about analysis, its strengths and weaknesses. Although many bureaucratic battles during the Reagan years were noisy and contentious, it is difficult in the political arena to oppose the concept of analysis. Who can argue with the proposition that agencies ought to think before they act? Yet, the recent experience recounted in this book demonstrates that the matter is not so simple. Analysts perform a valuable service to regulatory decisionmakers when they lay out in a comprehensible fashion all of the realistic options and the advantages and disadvantages of each. But this function is not easily implemented. Creative alternatives are hard to find, data analysis is expensive, cost-and-benefit assessment models are inaccurate, biases can subtly creep into "objective" analyses, and the uncertainties are sometimes so huge and pervasive as to render the concept of objectivity virtually meaningless. More disturbing still is the frequent use of analysis to advance hidden policy agendas, providing a "scientific" veneer for decisions otherwise reached on political grounds. When examined in the real world, the virtues of regulatory analysis seem less obvious and its limitations more apparent.

An open-eyed view of analysis also reveals that it is many things to many people. A politically astute five-page briefing paper summarizing in layperson's terms the available information on a regulatory problem and outlining the pros and cons of three or four regulatory options can be a more useful analytical product than a three million dollar, five-hundred-page quantitative analysis of dozens of options replete with charts and tables. Although most advocates of regulatory analysis tend to view the latter format as the ideal, others recognize that heavy reliance on highly quantitative documents drafted by a small professional elite can threaten democratic values in regulatory decisionmaking.

Part I of this book briefly recounts the history of regulatory analysis in the federal government and explains how the new breed of regulatory analysts came to play a critical role in the rulemaking process of the executive agencies. It describes the two cultures that have evolved in the "program offices" and the "regulatory analysis offices" of modern regulatory agencies. In particular, it focuses on how the analysts see themselves and how they are perceived by their counterparts in the bureaucracy.

Several case studies in Part II provide examples of the clash of the two cultures in real-life bureaucratic contexts. The case studies pave the way for the more abstract discussion of the analytical enterprise. Part II presents an analysis of analysis itself. It examines some of the virtues of analysis, some practical impediments to good analysis, and some of the fundamental theoretical limitations that are inherent in the enterprise.

Part III suggests some roles that regulatory analysts can play in agency decisionmaking and proposes five models for structuring regulatory analysis into the bureaucratic process. The model one chooses depends on the roles that one wishes the analyst to play, and the roles that the analyst should be assigned in turn depend upon one's views about the virtues and limitations of the analytical enterprise. The discussion in Part III draws on the actual experience of regulatory analysts during the early and mid-1980s as captured in hundreds of interviews with low- and high-level agency employees in the following agencies: the Environmental Protection Agency, the Occupational Safety and Health Administration, the National Highway Traffic Safety Administration, the Federal Aviation Administration, the Food Safety and Inspection Service, the Animal and Plant Health Inspection Service, the Agricultural Marketing Service, and the Agricultural Stabilization and Conservation Service. Although changes have taken place in all of these agencies during the administration of President George Bush, the basic models remain available for future use.

Part IV examines two review mechanisms for regulatory analysis. First, and most importantly by far, agency regulatory analyses are reviewed by the Office of Management and Budget. That agency attempts to ensure that analyses prepared by the agencies meet accepted criteria for analysis. But it often goes beyond mere quality assurance and attempts to impose its own substantive views upon the executive agencies. A second reviewing institution, the federal judiciary, performs a much more limited review role. Although the courts have had little impact on the evolution of the regulatory analysis requirement, the influence of the Office of Management and Budget has been profound.

Finally, Part V draws some conclusions about the role that regulatory analysis should play in modern federal regulatory agencies. In brief, the book concludes that regulatory analysis is a useful tool for regulation if it is not applied too ambitiously and if it is not used merely as an excuse to slow down or eliminate regulation. Although the book takes a critical view of regulatory analysis, it is not intended to "trash" the analytical enterprise. On the other hand, the book cannot be read as a strong endorsement of regulatory analysis. The discussion of the proper roles for the regulatory analyst is intentionally left open-ended, partly out of the author's own ambivalence and partly out of a desire to allow the reader to draw his or her own conclusions.

PART I

The clash of regulatory cultures

CHAPTER 1

Rational analysis as regulatory reform

In the late 1960s and early 1970s, astute observers of federal regulation concluded that the cumbersome adjudicatory procedures with which agencies implemented most regulatory actions were ineffectual.[1] Responding to this criticism, many agencies began to use informal procedures to promulgate rules of general applicability. Rather than "put on a case" before an Administrative Law Judge using expert testimony subject to cross-examination and various evidentiary limitations, agencies began to experiment with "paper" rulemaking hearings in which the agency offered a proposed rule and supporting data and analysis for broad public comment. At roughly the same time, Congress enacted a new generation of safety and environmental statutes that empowered, and often required, agencies to govern through informal rulemaking. The "rulemaking revolution" that resulted had the potential to expand enormously the federal government's regulatory powers.

Three themes of regulatory reform

The rulemaking revolution had been under way for less than a decade when regulated industries and some academics began to complain that the federal agencies were going too far. Operating beyond the range of effective political control, they were irrationally imposing burdensome requirements on companies without taking into account their costs or assessing their corresponding benefits. These criticisms and their associated prescriptions for change paraded under the broad banner of regulatory reform.

Some of the critics longed for less burdensome times when administrative agencies were more sympathetic to regulated industries. Unconvinced of the social desirability of government intervention into the marketplace, these critics argued that the only effective solution to the regulatory morass was to remove the dead weight of government regulation from the back of American industry. In this view, regulatory reform meant "regulatory relief."[2] To some proponents relief meant retrenchment from the Progressive and New Deal

3

innovations, which had by now become quite commonplace. To others, it meant a less ambitious change in focus from a rules-oriented, or command-and-control, outlook to a less intrusive goals-oriented, or performanced-based, approach in which the agency allowed regulatees maximum flexibility to meet broad government-specified goals.[3] Although the natural targets of these criticisms were the statutes that empowered the agencies to promulgate burdensome rules, attempts to persuade Congress to ease the substantive regulatory burden or to redirect the regulatory focus proved largely unavailing.

Most critics of the new social regulation, however, agreed that regulation in some form was necessary to a properly functioning society. They argued that bureaucrats made bad decisions because they were not sufficiently accountable to the President, to Congress, and ultimately to the public. These critics offered various prescriptions, including heightened presidential scrutiny, regulatory budgets, legislative vetoes of final rules, and broadened public participation in the rulemaking process. For them, regulatory reform meant bureaucratic accountability.

Still other critics believed that agency personnel were not sufficiently analytical in thinking about regulation and its impacts on society. If internal agency decisionmaking procedures incorporated rational thinking analysts into the decisionmaking process, agencies would inevitably reach sounder results.[4]

By the beginning of the 1980s, the regulatory reform movement had achieved a high political profile, but it did not carry a unifying theme. To some, regulatory reform meant regulatory relief; to others, it meant bureaucratic accountability; to still others, it meant rational analysis. Whereas a thorough implementation of any one of these themes might predictably complement the others, they do not easily converge, and they can be at odds with one another in practice. For example, a rational analysis of an existing regulation might indicate that the agency should increase its stringency, rather than repeal it. But this analysis would run counter to the regulatory relief theme and might defy the desires of a White House bent on reducing the role of the federal government.

Executive Order 12,291, promulgated in early 1981, attempted to weave all three themes together by imposing extensive regulatory analysis requirements on agencies, vesting the Office of Management and Budget (OMB) with extensive review powers to ensure political accountability, and imposing substantive decisionmaking criteria on agencies (where not prohibited by statute) designed to provide regulatory relief for regulated industries. Although this book will draw upon all three regulatory reform themes, it will focus primarily upon the rational analysis theme, because it has been more successfully implemented than the others.

Rational analysis and the two rulemaking cultures

Although the goal of rational agency decisionmaking seems unexceptional, its proponents had in mind a very ambitious agenda. They meant to interject a new and very different way of thinking into a firmly entrenched bureaucratic culture.[5] Following the conventional nomenclature, we may label this new kind of thinking "comprehensive analytical rationality."[6] The term "comprehensive" suggests that this kind of thinking ideally explores all possible routes to the solution of a problem. The term "analytical" implies that it attempts to sort out, break down, and analyze (quantitatively, if possible) all of the relevant components of a problem and its possible solutions. The term "rationality" captures the pride that its proponents take in its objectivity and the dispassion with which it debates the pros and cons of alternative solutions without regard to whose ox is being gored. In practice, comprehensive analytical rationality has been dominated by the paradigms of neoclassical microeconomics.

This kind of rationality contrasts sharply with the thinking that has traditionally dominated the rulemaking process in most regulatory agencies, which I shall refer to as "techno-bureaucratic rationality." I use the term techno-bureaucratic to distinguish the thinking that dominates highly technical rulemaking activities from bureaucratic thinking in general.[7] Techno-bureaucratic rationality is a special brand of bureaucratic thinking that arises in the context of regulatory activities that must grapple with highly complex (and often unresolvable) issues of science, engineering, and public policy. Some of the existing models of bureaucratic thinking, such as Lindblom's perceptive "muddling through" model, are relevant to techno-bureaucratic thinking, but do not capture the essence of bureaucratic programs that have highly technical, scientific, and engineering components. I use the word "rationality" because, unlike many students of regulation, I do not believe that this kind of thinking is irrational per se. Techno-bureaucratic rationality is a rationality built on a unique understanding of the regulatory universe that is born out of frustrating hands-on experience with unanswerable questions of extraordinary complexity. It is, in a sense, a "second best" rationality that recognizes the limitations that inadequate data, unquantifiable values, mixed societal goals, and political realities place on the capacity of structured rational thinking, and it does the best that it can with what it has.

Techno-bureaucratic thinking in the traditional rulemaking culture

Under the traditional model of the rulemaking process that arose out of the rulemaking revolution of the early 1970s, a statute, an external petition, public pressure, or the agency's own discovery of a problem provides the initial stimulus for rulemaking. An office within the regulatory agency (the "program office") is assigned responsibility for determining the agency's initial response. At this point the issue loses whatever high-level visibility it ever had and becomes submerged within the bureaucracy while the program office generates a solution to the problem.

The program office is staffed largely by persons with technical training in the field or fields with which the office generally deals. Although most program office professionals have graduate degrees, they generally would not be classed at the top of their fields. Their primary responsibilities consist of gathering technical information, evaluating its quality, assembling it into a coherent whole, participating in intra-agency working group meetings, drafting rulemaking documents for publication in the *Federal Register*, reading and analyzing public comments, and drafting memoranda summarizing the contents of various documents for upper-lever decisionmakers. Their goal is to shepherd the rulemaking process along in a timely fashion to produce rules that will survive judicial and political review.

Under the traditional model, the program office has many sources of information. The agency might have a research office that supports research aimed at producing information in a usable form for rulemaking. The program office itself might contract with independent consulting companies to study technical issues and prepare reports suitable for rulemaking initiatives. Finally, program office staffers interact routinely with their professional counterparts, and these interchanges can yield useful data and information.

The studies available to the program office invariably prove inconclusive, and the office encounters the dilemma of regulating in the face of substantial uncertainty or doing nothing pending further research. The natural tendency of the program office is to forge ahead. Program office officials believe that they are judged by their superiors on the basis of the number of rules that they produce over time. It can be difficult for a program office staffer to explain to a superior that he or she has spent the last two years studying a problem only to conclude that it needs further study. An employee who reaches this conclusion too many times may not get fired, but it is not likely to put him on the fast track to promotion. On a personal level, it is probably more rewarding to a program office staffer to bring about a concrete resolution to a problem than to conclude that the problem cannot yet be solved.

The solutions to regulatory problems under the traditional model depend heavily upon professional judgment. Because the existing data rarely compel a particular result, a lot of techno-bureaucratic thinking is really grounded in a kind of intuition that is informed by technical training and experience. The technical experts do not analyze the problem and derive a solution so much as they "feel" their way through to an answer, accommodating as many affected interests as possible along the way to reduce the external resistance to their ultimate resolution of the problem.

The experts in the program office are not likely to look for just the right mix of governmental intervention and regulatory expense to optimize society's scarce resources. Given the uncertainties that confound their assessments of the pertinent issues, the suggestion that a solution could be arrived at through a careful balancing of costs and benefits is farcical to program office staffers, who are inclined to regard economics as a soft science. Nor will the program office attempt to define the problem in innovative ways or probe for radically different solutions. At any given point in the gradual evolution of a solution to a regulatory problem, the program office considers only a very limited range of options. In the program office view, the primary institutional goal is to produce rules that have a reasonable chance of surviving the inevitable political and legal attacks and that are capable to a tolerable degree of effective implementation in the real world; it is a matter of secondary importance that the benefits of the rule can somehow be shown to exceed its costs.

Once the program office has hit upon a solution to the problem, it resists suggestions that it consider different alternatives to the same regulatory ends. Because the problem-solving effort requires substantial time and resources, the program office is especially reluctant to consider any options that would require it to go back to the drawing board. This institutional resistance to change solidifies as the agency's proposal progresses up the agency chain of command.

The program office typically drafts a "decision memorandum" for the upper-level politically appointed decisionmakers. The memo lists three options, discusses the first and last options in a cursory fashion, discusses the second option in great detail, and recommends that the agency adopt option number two. Unless the upper-level decisionmakers are willing to devote substantial time to studying the problem and the program office's proposed solution, they will usually agree to option number two or some minor variation thereof.

At this point the proposal is published in the *Federal Register* for comment. If the public comments reveal flaws in the staff's technical work or produce relevant technical data that the staff has not yet examined, the program office will consider the comments, amend the rationale, and perhaps even change the content of the rule. If the comments are especially damaging, the staff may have to repropose the rule with a new solution and rationale. However, for the same reasons that the staff opposes internal suggestions for change, it resists such suggestions in the public comments. Therefore, drastic overhauls, although not unheard of, are rare.

There have always been exceptions to the techno-bureaucratic model. Some program office officials have enough respect for economics that they occasionally use marginal analysis in choosing options. Some agency heads demand that the program office consider a broader range of options, whether or not it is so inclined. And, undeniably, program offices on many occasions have elected to study regulatory problems further, rather than attempting to solve them immediately. Still, the foregoing description of the internal rulemaking culture prior to the mid-1970s bears a reasonable resemblance to reality, and it is a fairly accurate description of the decisionmaking processes in many agencies today.

The internal agency culture that the techno-bureaucratic model describes has, to a greater or lesser degree, the following defining characteristics:

Mission orientation. Unlike the vague "public interest" standard that dominated early regulatory statutes, the newer statutes (and recent amendments to older statutes) are often quite precise in defining regulatory goals. And the people who gravitate toward the newer agencies are often attracted to those goals. For example, one study of scientists in industry, academia and regulatory agencies found that those in regulatory agencies like EPA and OSHA were significantly more risk averse than the others and tended to be liberal politically.[8] The general perception that the agency has a mission helps build morale and attract fresh talent to jobs that rarely pay talented professionals as well as in the private sector. Although most sensible bureaucrats recognize that society will not tolerate the unrestrained pursuit of a single statutory goal, they are nevertheless willing to elevate some goals over other competing considerations.

Action orientation. The program office staff perceives that it is evaluated in part on the quantity of rules and regulations that it produces, and it can therefore become impatient with delays. Although program office officials not infrequently encounter difficulties in establishing and adhering[9] to priority schedules, once a deadline has been established (either at the behest of upper-level management working under statutory or self-imposed deadlines or as a result of a "bureaucracy forcing" lawsuit filed by an impatient beneficiary group)[10] the program office believes its job is to get the regulation on the books in a timely fashion. Its tendency is to move forward with rulemaking efforts, even when more study might enhance the understanding of the problem.

Restricted planning horizons. Like many private institutions, the program office cannot afford to spend much time studying the long-range implications of its activities. Its action orientation and perennial resource shortages focus its attention narrowly on the present. The office is always too busy resolving today's problems to think about tomorrow's.

Bounded options. Techno-bureaucratic rationality is inclined to narrow options early in the decisionmaking process and to be unreceptive to new options that come to light later on. The very definition of the problem may eliminate options. After the program office has defined the problem, it quickly forecloses less attractive approaches, and the technical staff rapidly heads down a fairly straight path to a single solution. If that path ultimately proves unrewarding, the staff backs up and heads down another likely path.

Turf consciousness. Perhaps the most powerful tendency of any program in a regulatory bureaucracy is to protect and, if possible, expand its "turf." An office's turf consists of the regulatory issues that come within its domain and the discretion it has to decide those issues. Turf is defined in the first instance by an agency's organizational structure. Second, it is defined by the nature of the review that an office's decisions must endure. The program office whose recommendations move straight up the chain of command to the head of the agency has more turf than the one whose recommendations must receive "sign-off" review by several other offices within the agency. Finally, turf is defined in other subtle ways, as by who chairs intra-agency working groups and who has direct access to upper-level decisionmakers. Obviously, turf can depend heavily on personalities and upper-level decisionmakers' perceptions of the capabilities of particular program offices, but it can also be a matter of relatively permanent institutional arrangements. During transitional periods, turf battles absorb an agency's institutional energies to a surprising degree. It is not uncommon for a program office to become so preoccupied with turf considerations that it loses some of its sense of mission.

Engineer's professional perspective. The program offices are inhabited largely by professionals: scientists, engineers, economists, lawyers, and the like. A professional brings to the job a particular perspective that defines the way duties are performed. The observation that engineers in an agency think more like engineers in the private sector than like agency economists is both trite and true.[11]

Comprehensive analytical thinking in regulatory reform

The foregoing descriptions of techno-bureaucratic rationality draw upon observations of the real-world decisionmaking process in regulatory agencies. It has never been an especially attractive brand of rationality to detached thinkers in academia who craft ideal models of rational decisionmaking. The regulatory reformers of the mid-1970s who called for more rational decisionmaking had these highly analytical models of rationality in mind. The term "comprehensive analytical rationality" has been used in other contexts to describe this sort of approach to regulatory decisionmaking.[12] Edwards and Sharkansky, for example, list the following essential elements of rational policymaking: (1) identify a problem and its cause(s); (2) clarify and rank goals; (3) collect all relevant options for meeting each goal and all available information on them; (4) predict the consequences of each alternative and assess them according to standards such as efficiency and equity; and (5) select the alternative that comes closest to achieving the goal and is most consistent with the standard of evaluation.[13]

The ideal regulatory bureaucracy, under this model, would react to a petition for rulemaking, a statutory command, or public pressure by assigning the matter to a regulatory analyst – a professional with training in policy analysis or economics who knows how to analyze a regulatory problem. The analyst would first define the problem as carefully as possible. Because comprehensive analytical thinking depends so heavily upon the paradigms of neoclassical microeconomics, the analyst would probably define the problem as one of market failure. If no market failure could be identified, the analyst would conclude that there was no problem and recommend that the market be allowed to function unimpeded.

Having identified the problem, the regulatory analyst would next clarify and rank the agency's goals. This may have already been done by Congress, but very often Congress articulates several somewhat inconsistent goals for a particular regulatory regime, in which case the analyst would seek the guidance of upper-level policymakers.

The analyst would next call upon the agency's scientists and engineers to identify as many technical options for addressing the problem as possible. The analyst also might suggest some alternatives from the economist's arsenal, which includes performance-oriented standards and assorted indirect incentives. The regulatory analysis office would then "cost out" the options, an operation that would yield an assessment of both the primary costs of the regulation to the regulated industry and the secondary costs in terms of increased prices to consumers, lost jobs, and foreign trade deficits. Agency scientists and engineers would at the same time predict the benefits of the various alternatives. If these calculations could be reduced to monetary terms, then the costs and benefits of each option would be computed, and the analysts would recommend that the agency adopt the option for which the benefits exceeded costs by the greatest amount. If benefits could not be stated in monetary terms, then the analyst would attempt to state them in equivalent units, so that the cost-effectiveness of different options could be assessed.

The defining characteristics of comprehensive analytical rationality are very different from those of techno-bureaucratic rationality. It should be noted, however, that although the preceding list of characteristics of techno-bureaucratic rationality was derived from a generalized description of the actual decisionmaking process, the following description of the characteristics of comprehensive analytical rationality is based upon an abstract ideal that can never be achieved in the real world.[14]

Neutrality. Comprehensive analytical rationality is first and foremost neutral. Regulatory analysts are never advocates of particular policy goals, not even the congressional goals articulated in the agency's statute, and they do not care whose oxen are gored. The mission orientation of the program office is foreign to the regulatory analysis office. Regulatory analysis is grounded in facts and analysis. It is up to the upper-level decisionmaker to rank goals; the analyst merely informs the decisionmaker how the options stack up against those goals.

Objectivity. The analyst's assessment of the pros and cons of policy options must rely upon hard facts and verifiable theories. It cannot be based upon soft quasiempirical observations of the sort that sustain editorial writers and motivate legislators. Most importantly, the analyst's work product should not reflect his own subjective personal views about how the regulatory universe is or ought to be structured. Although the scientists and engineers in the program office readily acknowledge the virtues of objectivity, they are more inclined to accept the limitations that poor or nonexistent data, inadequate models and general lack of resources place on objective decisionmaking.

Quantitative orientation. The analyst prefers to quantify the considerations that go into a policy decision to the fullest extent possible. Analysts are therefore inveterate model-builders, constantly striving to reduce nuance to numbers through statistical analysis, game theory, and other sophisticated mathematical techniques.

Comprehensiveness. The regulatory analyst views problems comprehensively and is reluctant to abandon options until they are thoroughly analyzed and compared to other alternatives. Ideally, the analyst is constantly on the lookout for fresh options that may have escaped the attention of other agency officials. Program office staffers believe in comprehensively analyzing the data relevant to the single option being pursued at the moment, but they are reluctant to spend resources comprehensively analyzing options that probably will not be adopted in the end.

Thoroughness. The regulatory analyst scours every source of data and information relevant to the policy choice. No datum is too insignificant and no piece of objective information too trivial to be factored into the analyst's equations. The analyst has a decided preference for undertaking more research and sponsoring further studies, rather than moving ahead simply to meet a deadline, as the program office is inclined to do.

Consistency. Inconsistency is the analyst's hobgoblin. The policies that an agency invokes to solve one problem should be the same policies that it invokes to solve identical problems in the future. The hierarchy of goals for policy analysis should not vary from problem to problem, absent an explicit change in agency policies. Agency decisions should not blow with the political winds. Consistency is also a virtue for techno-bureaucratic rationality, but it is the less abstract sort of consistency that adopts a regulatory approach "because that's the way we did it last time," without exploring in detail whether consistency with more abstract policy principles calls for a different approach this time.

Open-endedness. To the analyst, no decision is ever really final. Recognizing that previous decisions were based upon incomplete information, the agency should undertake retroactive studies to assess the accuracy of those decisions. New information may reveal that previous assumptions were bad, thereby undermining prior decisions based on those assumptions. The reranking of policy goals that can occur with changes in administrations can mean that old decisions are no longer optimal. Although the program office staffers are always willing to take a new look at old regulations, they are skeptical about the usefulness of opening old wounds and about the effectiveness of spending agency resources reinventing the wheel.

Openness. The regulatory analyst believes that agency decisionmakers should be willing to articulate publicly their decisionmaking criteria. In addition, the analytical process itself should be open to public scrutiny so that facts can be probed and assumptions challenged. The element of openness inherent in the concept of peer review is well-ingrained in the program office scientists and engineers, but they are sometimes leery of exposing technical analysis to review by persons lacking professional credentials, such as curious citizens who might be directly affected by a regulatory decision. At the same time, although openness is the regulatory analysts' ideal, they are at times hesitant to open up to public debate the psychological and political assumptions inherent in economic analysis of regulatory issues.

Economist's professional perspective. The analyst's professional perspective derives to a very large degree from neoclassical microeconomics.[15] This perspective gives the analyst a preference for market-oriented solutions to regulatory problems and a distaste for "command and control" solutions that substitute bureaucratic guidance for functioning markets. The regulatory analysts' commitment to neoclassical economics represents to some extent a departure from neutrality, because it adopts certain assumptions about human behavior about which reasonable minds can differ. It also leads to a turf consciousness of sorts on the part of an agency's regulatory analysts as they struggle with other offices in the agency to bring to the attention of upper-level decisionmakers the special insights inherent in that discipline.

The clash of rulemaking cultures

The two patterns of thinking described above represent two very different approaches to solving regulatory problems. At first glance, comprehensive analytical rationality may appear to be the more attractive alternative. Techno-bureaucratic rationality has come to terms with reality – the reality of poor and nonexistent data, resource limitations, and time constraints. When forced to come to terms with those same realities, comprehensive analytical rationality must compromise some of its lofty ambitions. Nevertheless, most analysts would argue that even substantially compromised, the comprehensive analytical paradigm represents the better approach to decisionmaking. And herein lies the rub of a clash between two dissimilar rulemaking cultures.

Perhaps the stubbornest sticking point concerns the nature of neutrality and objectivity. Techno-bureaucratic rationality does not admit to subjectivity in its approach to regulatory decisionmaking. Program office staffers maintain that their enthusiasm for objectivity is at least as ardent as that of the regulatory analysts. When they have the luxury of hinging their recommendations on verifiable facts, they are thrilled to do so. Unfortunately, in complex rulemaking proceedings, facts are few and far between. The existing data are sparse and always subject to varying interpretations. Because decisionmaking cannot await the completion of all the studies that are necessary to secure agreement, the agency must rely upon an informed intuition often called "scientific" or "engineering judgment." This judgment rests on training and experience, not subjectivity or bias, and it is an acceptable alternative to doing nothing.

The program office further argues that the highly touted "neutrality" and "objectivity" of the regulatory analysis office is in reality neither neutral nor objective, because comprehensive analytical rationality is so thoroughly dominated by neoclassical economics, which is as much a moral philosophy as a science.[16] The starting point of the regulatory analysts – that the sole rationale for regulation is to cure market defects – represents a bias against regulation, because it implicitly recognizes efficiency as the only goal for regulation. Fairness, equality, autonomy and other social goals have no place in the analyst's cost-benefit calculus. Analysts assign the burden of proof to the person advocating regulation. Because this burden can rarely be met in a world dominated by uncertainties, this represents a built-in bias against governmental solutions to society's problems. This is the stuff of politics, not science.

A second battleground concerns the role of time constraints in decisionmaking. Analysts generally prefer to engage in a thorough data-gathering and options-identification effort before making any decisions that would have the effect of eliminating options. They like to do research, build mathematical models, and make detailed projections concerning the primary and secondary impacts of as many options as possible. Indeed, analysts would have the agency continue to study the problem even after the rule has been promulgated to determine whether the predictions and projections were accurate, always with an eye toward changing the rule in light of new facts and theories.

Program office officials respond that there will never be enough time and money to consider all of the options that the human mind can imagine. To place too many options on the regulatory menu invites "paralysis by analysis." The program office simply cannot do its job if it must "study the problem to death"; nor can it spend significant resources "reinventing the wheel" when new evidence about an old regulation comes to light. There are simply too many pressing new problems to deal with, without reopening old wounds.

A third point of disputation concerns the extent to which the agency should subject its reasoning process to intense public scrutiny. Although both the program office and the regulatory analysis office advocate public participation in agency decisionmaking, they invite it for somewhat different reasons. The program office seeks public participation for the technical information that it can provide to the engineers and scientists. Sophisticated participants can perform their own studies and gather data that the program office may have missed. Program office staffers have little use for broad, nontechnical comments directed toward the policy implications of the agency's action.

Although the regulatory analysts share the program office's desire to receive technical comments on the agency's scientific, engineering, and economic analyses, they also value policy-oriented comments. One of the primary purposes of regulatory analysis is to relate factual conclusions in a straightforward way to an explicit preexisting policy framework. The public should be aware of the way that the agency brings policy considerations to bear on regulatory problems, so that the agency may ultimately be held accountable for its actions in the political review process.

If the goal of regulatory reform is to bring comprehensive analytical rationality to bear on a preexisting rulemaking process that has been dominated by techno-bureaucratic rationality, then the regulatory reformer must accomplish one of two objectives. The reformer must either purge the agency of techno-bureaucratic thinking and replace the existing bureaucrats with analysts or erect a decision-making structure that includes both modes of thought and harnesses the inevitable clash. The first option is unrealistic. An agency that is required to make decisions involving highly technical subjects within a reasonable time frame simply cannot avoid techno-bureaucratic thinking. Part IV of this book is therefore devoted to a search for procedural vehicles that are capable of avoiding the destructive tendencies of the clash between the two cultures, while at the same time inducing a creative tension that brings out the best of both cultures in a way that enhances the quality of agency decisionmaking.

CHAPTER 2

Evolution of the regulatory analysis program

Although agencies were never free to disregard the impact of their rules on regulatees and the public, formal requirements that agencies prepare documents detailing those impacts have existed for about two decades. The idea probably originated with the National Environmental Policy Act of 1969 (NEPA).[1] NEPA's real bite was in its requirement that agencies prepare an Environmental Impact Statement (EIS) for every proposal for legislation or other major federal action significantly affecting the quality of the human environment. The EIS was required to describe: (1) the environmental impact of the proposed action; (2) any unavoidable adverse environmental effects; (3) alternatives to the proposed action; (4) the relationship between local short-term uses of environmental resources and the maintenance and enhancement of long-term productivity; and (5) any irreversible and irretrievable commitments of resources.[2] Although agencies initially regarded NEPA as a wasteful impediment to the attainment of their programmatic goals,[3] the courts demanded strict adherence to NEPA's analytical requirements, and the agencies soon began to hire employees with expertise in environmental impact analysis.

As the agencies began to write NEPA into their standard operating procedures, observers noted that compliance with NEPA's analytical requirements did not ensure that agency action comported with NEPA's substantive goals.[4] Indeed, cynics suggested that agency staff often drafted lengthy EISs in excruciating detail to ensure that busy decisionmakers would not read them and therefore would not be influenced by them.[5] Perhaps the most cogent criticism of the environmental impact assessment process was that it presumed an unrealistic decisionmaking process "characterized by abstract rationality and focused on a single responsible decision-maker who, even if he did exist, could hardly be expected to undertake the investigation of alternatives that the Act requires."[6] Less pessimistic observers pointed to numerous instances in which agency actions were modified or abandoned in light of the environmental analysis contained in an EIS.[7] Some argued that the environmental impact assessment process forced agencies to do a better job of explaining their decisions,[8] and the agencies themselves frequently testified to the value of NEPA analysis.[9]

Observing NEPA's power to enlighten and, perhaps more importantly, to delay agency initiatives, the Office of Management and Budget (OMB) persuaded President Nixon to require the newly created Environmental Protection Agency (EPA) and Occupational Safety and Health Administration (OSHA) to send their proposed regulations through an interagency "Quality of Life" review. The agencies were required to prepare a summary of the costs of each proposed regulation and its alternatives to accompany it through the review process.[10] According to a former Deputy Administrator of EPA, interagency comments contributed important off-the-record input into the decisionmaking process without public review.[11] In retrospect it appears that the Quality of Life review was intended more as a vehicle for allowing other governmental agencies (and their constituents in the regulated industries) to have greater private access to EPA and OSHA decisionmakers than as a mechanism for forcing those agencies to regulate rationally.

President Ford expanded the intragency review process to include all executive agencies when he signed Executive Order 11,821, which mandated that an Inflation Impact Statement (IIS) accompany all "major federal proposals for legislation, rules and regulations."[12] Responsibility for implementing the new program was delegated to the Council on Wage and Price Stability (COWPS),[13] a new agency that was empowered by statute to review proposed rules and comment upon them in rulemaking proceedings.[14] In addition, OMB promulgated a circular that specified in broad outline the proper elements of an IIS. Although detailed operating procedures were left to individual agencies, OMB's criteria reflected its determination that the inflationary impact of a proposed rule could best be ascertained by comparing in a quantitative fashion the proposal's costs and benefits in light of the costs and benefits of its alternatives.[15] During the two-year period between the IIS program's inception and a major reevaluation at the end of 1976, COWPS commented on 23 of 41 IISs on regulations. Eleven of these comments were made on the public record; the other twelve were made privately by interagency memoranda.[16]

Once again, observers noted that agencies seemed to view the program as an unavoidable paperwork hurdle to be negotiated, rather than an analytical tool to be incorporated into the decisionmaking process. Too many IISs were prepared after the fact as post hoc justifications for decisions previously reached on other grounds.[17] The antagonistic relationships that often developed between COWPS and the agencies delayed rulemaking initiatives and discouraged meaningful dialogue.[18] Most observers agreed, however, that the program added to the agencies' analytical capabilities. Moreover, in the minds of some, the program had a positive impact on public participation in the rulemaking process, because it gave regulatees ammunition with which to attack rulemaking proposals.[19] On balance, the commentators, both inside and outside of government, concluded that the program was worth pursuing.

President Carter expanded the Ford Administration's IIS program and changed its direction somewhat in Executive Order 12,044.[20] The new Executive Order broke regulations down into three broad categories. A "significant" regulation could not be proposed until the agency made eight specific findings concerning the need for the rule, the burdens it would impose, and the absence of less burdensome alternatives.[21] The Executive Order further subdivided the significant rules category into "major" significant rules, which required a Regulatory Analysis (RA) and "nonmajor" significant rules, which did not. The RA for a major significant rule was to contain a succinct statement of the problem, a description of the major alternatives, an analysis of the economic consequences of each of these alternatives, and a detailed explanation for choosing one alternative over the others.[22] Significantly, Executive Order 12,044 did not explicitly require a cost-benefit analysis. COWPS retained its role as critical analyst and commentator. In addition, President Carter created the Regulatory Analysis Review Group (RARG), composed of fifteen agencies (including COWPS) and chaired by the Council of Economic Advisors, to review RAs and comment through COWPS in agency proceedings.[23] Although the RA requirement lacked the IIS program's emphasis on quantitative cost-benefit analysis, the Carter Administration did not retreat from the basic thrust of the Ford Administration program.

Within a month after assuming office, President Reagan rescinded the Carter Executive Order and replaced it with Executive Order 12,291, which mandated an even more comprehensive program of regulatory analysis.[24] The purpose of the new Executive Order was "to reduce the burdens of existing and future regulations, increase agency accountability for regulatory actions, provide for presidential oversight of the regulatory process, minimize duplication and conflict of regulations, and insure well-reasoned regulations. . . . "[25]

Unlike its predecessors, Executive Order 12,291 was intended to impose substantive restrictions on agency rulemaking as well as analytical requirements. Specifically, regulations were, "to the extent permitted by law," to adhere to the following requirements:

(1) Administrative decisions shall be based on adequate information concerning the need for and consequences of proposed government action;

(2) Regulatory action shall not be undertaken unless the potential benefits to society for the regulation outweigh the potential costs to society;

(3) Regulatory objectives shall be chosen to maximize the net benefits to society;

(4) Among alternative approaches to any given regulatory objective, the alternative involving the least net cost to society shall be chosen; and

(5) Agencies shall set regulatory priorities with the aim of maximizing the aggregate net benefits to society, taking into account the condition of the particular industries affected by regulations, the condition of the national economy, and other regulatory actions contemplated for the future.[26]

The analytical tool was renamed Regulatory Impact Analysis (RIA). An agency was required to prepare a Preliminary Regulatory Impact Analysis (PRIA) for proposed "major" rules and a Final Regulatory Impact Analysis (FRIA) for final major rules.[27] The RIA had to contain:

(1) A description of the potential benefits of the rule, including any beneficial effects that cannot be quantified in monetary terms, and the identification of those likely to receive the benefits;

(2) A description of the potential costs of the rule, including any adverse effects that cannot be quantified in monetary terms, and the identification of those likely to bear the costs;

(3) A determination of the potential net benefits of the rule, including an evaluation of effects that cannot be quantified in monetary terms;

(4) A description of alternative approaches that could substantially achieve the same regulatory goal at lower cost, together with an analysis of this potential benefit and costs and a brief explanation of the legal reasons why such alternatives, if proposed, could not be adopted; and

(5) Unless covered by the description required under paragraph (4), . . . an explanation of any legal reasons why the rule cannot be based on the requirements [quoted above].[28]

Like the Carter Administration RA, the Reagan Administration RIA required an analysis of alternatives, but the RIA more closely resembled the Ford Administration IIS in its specification of cost-benefit analysis as the preferred form of analysis. Although Executive Order 12,291 explicitly required benefit analysis, it recognized that not all benefits could be quantified in monetary terms. In addition, it added a new requirement that the agency identify the beneficiaries and losers of the regulation. If the agency was unable to reach the Executive Order's substantive goals – for example, if its statute dictated a different result – the RIA had to explain why it could not do so. This marked a major institutional departure from the Carter Administration program under which the burden was on the COWPS or RARG to demonstrate that a regulation was *not* cost-effective.[29]

The threshold definition of "major" rule paralleled the definition of "major significant" rule in Executive Order 12,044. A "major rule" was any regulation that was likely to result in:

(1) An annual effect on the economy of $100 million or more;
(2) A major increase in costs or prices for consumers, individual industries, Federal, State, or local government agencies, or geographic regions; or
(3) Significant adverse effects on competition, employment, investment, productivity, innovation, or on the ability of United States-based enterprises to compete with foreign-based enterprises in domestic or export markets.[30]

OMB was given complete discretion to designate any rule as major[31] and to waive the RIA requirement for any major rule.[32] OMB was required to prescribe detailed threshold criteria,[33] and it was responsible for determining the adequacy of the contents of RIAs.[34] An agency could not go forward with a proposed or final rule until disputes with OMB were resolved.[35]

Soon after President Reagan signed Executive Order 12,291, OMB issued a memorandum entitled Interim Regulatory Impact Analysis Guidance (Interim Guidance),[36] to help the agencies in RIA preparation. Operating on the presumption that the unimpeded market should be the preferred norm, the Interim Guidance strongly invoked the economist's paradigm. It cautioned that regulatory programs rarely perform perfectly and suggested that Regulatory Impact Analyses should compare the presently existing imperfect market with an imperfectly functioning regulatory program. The Interim Guidance also required agencies to consider alternative levels of stringency, alternative effective dates, alternative methods of assuring compliance, alternative market-oriented regulatory approaches and alternatives beyond their statutory authority.[37]

Finally, the Interim Guidance expressed a strong preference for quantification and monetization, and it suggested a discount rate of ten percent for long-range effects. In cases where benefits were not easily quantified, agencies were required to analyze the cost effectiveness of proposals and their alternatives. Where uncertainties plagued the cost and benefit estimations the agencies were to use the "most likely assumptions" in quantitative modeling, but reasonable alternative assumptions also had to be examined to test the sensitivity of the results to changes in assumptions.[38] OMB waited several years to publish its Final Guidance, but it did not vary significantly from the Interim Guidance.[39]

OMB quickly began to exercise its review authority. During 1981, ninety-five regulations were either withdrawn by agencies or returned by OMB for reconsideration because of OMB's questions concerning their consistency with Executive Order 12,291.[40] In 1982, eighty-seven regulations were returned to or withdrawn by the agencies.[41] The rejection and withdrawal pace continued at about the same rate throughout the decade. In 1988, for example, eighty-five regulations were either withdrawn or rejected.[42] This represented only 3 to 4 percent of all of the rules that OMB reviewed, but we shall see in Chapter 18 that OMB has had a very significant impact on the relatively small universe of regulations that really matter.

The Bush Administration left the Reagan regulatory analysis framework substantially intact. As Vice-President, Mr. Bush was the titular head of the President's Task Force on Regulatory Relief, which was empowered by Executive Order 12,291 to resolve disputes between OMB and the executive agencies over the adequacy of RIAs. From that vantage point, Vice-President Bush had an opportunity to see the RIA process in action. He apparently liked what he saw, because President Bush has done little to change it.

All of the preceding analytical requirements were imposed on the executive agencies by the President. The Regulatory Flexibility Act of 1980[43] is the only law enacted by Congress that requires all agencies to engage in systematic regulatory analysis. That statute is, however, limited to regulations that affect small businesses, small organizations and small governmental jurisdictions, collectively referred to as "small entities."[44] Roughly, this category includes businesses with fewer than five hundred employees or less than $5 million in sales.[45] According to Professor Verkuil's comprehensive study of the act, its enactment represented "a stunning achievement for the small business community and its representatives because it requires virtually all government policymaking to be sensitive to small business concerns."[46]

The goal of the act is to insure that agencies "fit regulatory and informational requirements to the scale of the business, organizations, and governmental jurisdictions subject to regulation."[47] To achieve this goal, the act imposes several procedural requirements, many of which had already been imposed by Executive Orders 11,821, 12,044, and 12,291. First, each agency must publish, at least semiannually, a "regulatory flexibility agenda" of all proposed or pending rules that are "likely to have a significant economic impact on a substantial number of small entities."[48] The agency must give notice of the agenda to the Small Business Administration (SBA) and to affected "small entities" to "assure that small entities have been given an opportunity to participate in the rulemaking. . . . "[49]

At the time that it proposes a rule in the *Federal Register*, the agency must publish an Initial Regulatory Flexibility Analysis (IRFA) that describes the impact of the proposed rule on small entities.[50] A Final Regulatory Flexibility Analysis (FRFA) must be published upon adoption of the rule.[51] Finally, each agency is required to develop a ten-year plan to examine existing and proposed rules which might have a "significant economic impact" on "a substantial number of small entities."[52]

The act specifies in some detail the contents of the initial and final RFAs. The purpose of the IRFA is to "describe the impact of the proposed rule on small entities."[53] The analysis must contain:

(1) A description of the reasons why action by the agency is being considered;

(2) A succinct statement of the objectives of, and legal basis for, the proposed rule;

(3) A description of and, where feasible, an estimate of the number of small entities to which the proposed rule will apply;

(4) A description of the projected reporting, recordkeeping, and other compliance requirements of the proposed rule, including an estimate of the classes of small entities which will be subject to the requirement and the type of professional skills necessary for preparation of the report or record;

(5) An identification, to the extent practicable, of all relevant Federal rules which may duplicate, overlap or conflict with the proposed rule.[54]

In addition, the IRFA must analyze "significant" alternatives to the agency's proposed action such as:

(1) the establishment of differing compliance or reporting requirements or timetables that take into account the resources available to small entities;

(2) the clarification, consolidation, or simplification of compliance and reporting requirements under the rule for such small entities;

(3) the use of performance rather than design standards; and

(4) an exemption from coverage of the rule, or any part thereof, for such small entities.

The analysis of alternatives, however, need be undertaken only to the extent that it is "[c]onsistent with the stated objective of applicable statutes."[55]

When the agency promulgates its final rule, it must prepare a FRFA containing:

(1) a succinct statement of the need for, and the objectives of, the rule;

(2) a summary of the issues raised by the public comments in response to the initial regulatory flexibility analysis, a summary of the assessment of the agency of such issues, and a statement of any changes made in the proposed rule as a result of such comments; and

(3) a description of each of the significant alternatives to the rule consistent with the stated objectives of applicable statutes and designed to minimize any significant economic impact of the rule on small entities which was considered by the agency, and a statement of the reasons why each one of such alternatives was rejected.[56]

The agency is free to adopt either a quantitative or numerical description of the rule's effects or "more general descriptive statements" if quantification is not "practicable or reliable."[57]

Liberal reference throughout the act to the Chief Counsel for Advocacy of the Small Business Administration indicates that Congress expected that official to provide an oversight function. Executive Order 12,291, in addition, gave OMB a coordinating role with respect to the analysis, transmittal, review, and clearance provisions of the Executive Order, the Regulatory Flexibility Act, and the Paperwork Reduction Act.[58] OMB promulgated a document entitled "Incorporating Regulatory Flexibility into the Regulation Process: Interim Guidance," which offered general guidelines to agencies on the RFA program.[59]

The foregoing history of analytical requirements in the federal bureaucracy suggests a pattern of increasing commitment to comprehensive analytical rationality on the part of the President and, to a lesser extent, Congress. After almost two decades of experience with regulatory analysis, one would expect the agencies to have written comprehensive analytical rationality into their standard operating procedures. The case studies in Part II demonstrate that agencies have by and large adapted to regulatory analysis, but the "analysis of analysis" in Part II suggests strong reasons for doubting that the paradigm will ever come to dominate regulatory decisionmaking to the extent that its advocates envisioned. Part III explores five descriptive models of how regulatory analysis has in fact been incorporated into real-world decisionmaking.

Regulatory analysis in theory and practice

CHAPTER 3

Getting the lead out of gasoline: EPA's lead phasedown regulations

Petroleum refiners have used tetraethyl lead since 1923 as an additive to boost the octane rating of gasoline and reduce "knocking." By the mid-1970s, approximately 90 percent of all gasoline manufactured in the United States contained tetraethyl lead.[1] Although large gasoline refiners produced most leaded gasoline, a number of smaller companies refined leaded gasoline and supplied tetraethyl lead to large refineries.

Unfortunately, lead can be extremely toxic, especially to children, in high concentrations. At very high blood concentration levels of approximately 120 micrograms of lead per deciliter of blood (μg/dl), lead can cause severe and irreversible brain damage. Children with blood lead levels of over 80 to 100 μg/dl can suffer permanent cognitive impairment. Lead can also have reproductive effects on both men and women. At much lower blood levels of approximately 40 μg/dl, lead can impair the synthesis of hemoglobin and cause anemia.[2]

Lead is ubiquitous in the human environment. It is present in food, water, air, soil, dustfall, paint, and other materials with which humans come into contact. Human exposure to lead can come from a variety of sources, including ingestion of food grown in lead-contaminated soils, ingestion of lead-based paint, inhalation of airborne lead, and ingestion of dust contaminated with airborne lead, the latter route being common among infants with pica, an affliction which causes them to eat dust and dirt.[3] A major source of human exposure to lead is airborne lead, and approximately 90 percent of airborne lead comes from automobiles.[4]

Regulatory background

Congress enacted Section 211 of the Clean Air Act specifically to empower EPA to regulate fuel additives like tetraethyl lead.[5] Because tetraethyl lead "poisons" catalytic converters (Detroit's technology of choice for reducing conventional automobile pollutants),

EPA in 1973 promulgated regulations requiring that converter-equipped autos use only unleaded gas, defined to mean gasoline with less than 0.05 grams of lead per gallon (gpg).[6] These regulations alone ensured that the demand for leaded gasoline would decrease as consumers substituted new automobiles for older models.

Under prodding from environmental groups, EPA published an additional health-based lead phasedown rule in late 1973.[7] All refiners were required to limit the lead content of gasoline to 1.7 gpg by January 1, 1975 and to 0.5 gpg by January 1, 1979.[8] Because the agency believed that small refineries faced special lead-time problems, it exempted them from the 1.7 gpg standard, but not the 0.5 gpg standard.[9] Although EPA had originally proposed that the phasedown be measured in units of grams of lead per *leaded* gallon of gasoline (gplg), the final rule specified a "pooled" standard, in grams per pooled gallon (gppg) under which a refiner that produced both leaded and unleaded gasoline could raise the lead content in its leaded gas (and hence the octane rating of that gas) if it manufactured a correspondingly larger amount of unleaded gas. The intent of the "pooled" standard was to encourage refiners to produce unleaded gas. EPA worried that if motorists could not purchase unleaded gas, they might switch to leaded gas, even though this would violate the law and poison their catalytic converters.[10]

Reacting to the energy crises of the 1970s, EPA and the refiners negotiated a series of extensions of the phasedown deadlines. EPA gave refiners until October 1, 1980 to meet the 0.5 gppg standard, and by that date a substantial number of large refineries were in fact in compliance.[11] At roughly the same time, Congress amended the Clean Air Act to establish new limits for small refiners and to prevent EPA from regulating further until October 1, 1982.[12] EPA then issued final regulations requiring all refiners, large and small, to meet the 0.5 gppg standard by October 1, 1982.[13]

During this hiatus, small refiners flourished and a budding new subindustry of small "blenders" arose to take advantage of the exemptions.[14] A blender would purchase inexpensive low-octane fuel (often from foreign markets) and blend in enough high-octane leaded fuel to bring the octane rating up to required levels.[15] Although the drafters of the 1977 Clean Air Act amendments almost certainly did not anticipate this new subindustry, the blenders were not anxious to see their profitable arrangement come to a halt in October 1982.

The February 1982 Proposal

By mid-1981 it was apparent that many small refiners and virtually all blenders would not meet the October 1, 1982 deadline, but they argued that the pooled (gppg) standard unfairly allowed large refiners to add more lead to their leaded gas because they produced more unleaded gas.[16] They found a sympathetic ear in Vice-President Bush's Task Force on Regulatory Relief, which concluded that reexamination of the lead phasedown rule should be given high priority under Executive Order 12,291.[17] The lead phasedown rule was an odd choice for the task force. Virtually all of the politically potent major refineries complied with the rule, and EPA certainly had more expensive rules on the books. But the rule offered an ideal vehicle for demonstrating the Administration's concern for the plight of small business at the hands of overzealous regulators. Although EPA staffers cautioned that lead was a sensitive public health concern and that rescission would not save much money for the refining industry as a whole,[18] the task force prevailed.

The Field Operations and Support Division of EPA's Office of Air Quality Planning and Standards (the "program office") was given the primary responsibility for drafting the proposal. A work group, composed of representatives from that division, the Office of Policy Analysis (OPA, or the "policy office"), and the Office of General Counsel, was the relevant institutional unit.[19] Because of the Bush task force's interest, the rule received more than ordinary attention from high-level political appointees in EPA.[20]

Initially, the newly appointed leadership at EPA believed that the rule should be rescinded.[21] But in a meeting with Joseph Cannon, the head of the policy office, staffers predicted a political firestorm if the agency rescinded the rule and speculated that the National Association for the Advancement of Colored People would "come unglued," because studies suggested that lead exposure was responsible for lowering the IQs of ghetto youth. Shocked by this assessment, Cannon was persuaded that the agency should not attempt to rescind the rule.[22] The agency therefore proposed a variety of options, including rescission.[23]

Faced with severe time constraints, the staff decided not to prepare a Preliminary Regulatory Impact Analysis as required by Executive Order 12,291. The policy office instead hired a contractor to prepare analyses of the economic effects of several plausible regulatory options. The contractor's reports were based on a computer model derived from a Department of Energy gasoline consumption model.[24] The results are displayed in Tables 3.1 and 3.2a–c.

Several aspects of the Tables stand out. First, they illuminate very concisely the cost and lead reductions for a wide variety of options, giving the decisionmaker a great degree of information and latitude. Second, they clearly reveal the marginal costs for increasingly stringent controls. For example, Table 3.1 shows that the savings of relaxing the standard for large refiners from 0.5 to 0.65 ($73 million) is almost as much as repealing the standard altogether ($86 million). Yet, repealing the standard would send 29,600 additional tons per year into the air, while relaxing it to 0.65 would increase emissions by only 16,640 tons per year. Third, the tables display the distributional effects of the averaging option. For all alternatives, averaging reduces overall costs without increasing emissions, but small refiners acquire a disproportionate share of the benefits.

The policy office used the contractor reports to calculate the cost per ton of lead removed:

Large refiners

Current standard	$ 1,762/ton
0.65 gpg	$ 380/ton
0.8 gpg	$ 30/ton
Unlimited	

Small refiners

Current standard	$11,654/ton
0.65 gpg	$ 6,338/ton
0.65 gpg with averaging	$ 939/ton
0.8 gpg	$ 1,568/ton
0.8 gpg with averaging	$ 627/ton
1.0 gpg	$ 565/ton
No limit	

The policy office further compared these costs with the cost per ton of lead required to be removed under one of the agency's standards for lead acid battery plants, which was calculated to be $13,900 per ton for medium plants and $5,080 per ton for large plants.[25] These comparative figures demonstrated to the work group that most of the options were at least in the right ball park.

The policy office made no attempt to identify the environmental benefits of the existing protections. It may have been impossible to predict accurately the extent to which each option would increase lead blood levels and the extent to which mental impairment and

Table 3.1. *Potential operating cost savings from lead regulation modifications (in millions of dollars)*

Policy option	Savings 1982 Large refiners	Savings 1983			Future savings[a]		
		Large refiners	Small refiners	Total refiners	Large refiners	Small refiners	Total refiners
No lead limit	86	47	28	75	138	72	210
0.5 grams with averaging	0	(15)	21	6	(16)	44	28
0.65 grams, no averaging	73	38	13	51	114	39	153
0.65 grams with averaging	73	35	27	62	111	70	181
0.8 grams, no averaging	86	45	28	73	138	59	197
Large refiners at 0.5 grams, small refiners at 1981 level	0	0	28	28	0	72	72
Large refiners at 0.65 grams, small refiners at 0.8 grams	73	38	23	61	114	59	173
Large refiners at 0.65 grams, small refiners at 1.0 grams	73	38	27	65	114	70	184
Large refiners at 0.65 grams, small refiners at 1981 level	73	38	28	66	114	72	186
Large refiners at 0.65 grams, small refiners at 1981 level through 1983; thereafter at 1.0	73	38	28	65	114	72	186

[a] Present value of all future savings.

Table 3.2a. *1983 Refiner lead concentrations and resulting lead emissions*

	Gasoline lead concentration (g/gallon)			Lead emission (tons/year)		
	Large refiners	Small refiners	National average	Large refiners	Small refiners	Total
No lead limit	0.80	1.25	0.83	78,400	8,870	87,270
0.5 grams, no averaging	0.50	0.50	0.50	48,800	3,550	52,350
0.5 grams with averaging	0.48	0.76	0.50	46,900	5,450	52,350
0.65 grams, no averaging	0.65	0.65	0.65	63,440	4,610	68,050
0.65 grams with averaging	0.65	1.06	0.65	60,520	7,530	68,050
0.8 grams, no averaging	0.80	0.80	0.80	78,100	5,680	83,780
0.8 grams with averaging	0.76	1.25	0.80	74,910	8,870	83,780
Large refiners at 0.5 grams, small refiners at 1981 level	0.50	1.25	0.55	48,800	8,870	57,670
Large refiners at 0.65 grams, small refiners at 0.8 grams	0.65	0.80	0.66	63,440	5,680	69,120
Large refiners at 0.65 grams, small refiners at 1.0 grams	0.65	1.00	0.67	63,400	7,000	70,400
Large refiners at 0.65 grams, small refiners at 1981 level	0.65	1.25	0.69	63,440	8,870	72,310
Large refiners at 0.65 grams, small refiners at 1981 level thru 1983; thereafter at 1.0	0.65	1.25	0.69	63,440	8,870	72,310

reproductive effects would correspondingly increase if more lead was allowed into the environment. Still, the policy office made no explicit attempt to grapple with the magnitude of the tradeoffs. In addition, it paid very little attention to the distribution of costs and benefits beyond the discussion of the impact of the averaging option on large and small refiners.

The policy office representative searched for the "knee-of-the-curve" in describing various options. Under this approach, the agency examines the costs of increasingly stringent control technologies and mandates the technology just prior to the point at which the cost curve slopes dramatically upward.[26] The policy office representative located the knee-of-the-curve at 0.65 gppg for large re-

Table 3.2b. *Cost of proposed lead phasedown (1.1/2.5 grams per leaded gallon): Regulations versus current 0.5 grams per gallon pool standard*

Content year	Annual cost (million dollars)	Average gasoline lead content (g/gallon)	
		Leaded	Pool
1983	(11)	1.18	0.51
1984	36	1.20	0.46
1985	80	1.22	0.41
1986	116	1.24	0.36
1987	142	1.26	0.33
1988	156	1.28	0.31
1989	130	1.30	0.28
1990	94	1.33	0.25
	743[a]		

[a]Average annual 93; total present value 515.

Table 3.2c. *Cost of alternative lead standards versus 0.5 grams per gallon standard*

Year	1.0/2.5 grams per leaded gallon	1.2/2.5 grams per leaded gallon
1983	24	(23)
1984	74	4
1985	124	10
1986	148	88
1987	172	120
1988	180	136
1989	140	102
1990	110	80

finers, and then searched for a standard for small refiners that would cost about the same amount per ton of lead removed.[27]

The policy office's analysis revealed that the averaging option could produce considerable cost savings, regardless of the level of the standard. The averaging approach would allow large refiners to sell the "right" to add lead to small refiners and blenders that had little or no capacity to produce unleaded gas. Large refiners would therefore have an incentive to produce more unleaded gas so that they could sell more rights to small refiners and blenders. The total amount of lead in the atmosphere, however, would not increase.

The program office was initially opposed to the averaging concept,[28] because of difficulties in monitoring lead trades to avoid cheating. It also objected that lead emissions would not decrease as rapidly, because large refiners would sell lead emission rights to blenders and small refiners that otherwise would have gone unused.[29] Finally, program office officials were concerned that averaging would lead to geographic "hot spots" in localities where gasoline suppliers were predominantly small refiners and blenders. They feared that averaging would allow suppliers to sell leaded gasoline at such discounts in such communities that rampant illegal fuel switching would result. Nevertheless, the program office acquiesced in including the averaging option in the February 1982 Proposal.

After upper-level decisionmakers signed off on the noncommittal proposal, it went to the Office of Management and Budget's (OMB) Office of Information and Regulatory Affairs for determinations on whether the RIA was adequate and whether the rule was consistent with the Administration's policies. The Vice-President's task force and OMB had initially preferred the rescission option,[30] and this precipitated a major showdown between OMB and top-level EPA decisionmakers. The matter bounced back and forth between EPA and OMB several times, with both sides remaining relatively intransigent. Time was working in EPA's favor, however, because the Vice-President had promised that EPA would act by the end of the year and because the October 1982 deadline for small refiners was drawing near. In the end, OMB approved EPA's multioption proposal. OMB also acquiesced in EPA's failure to prepare a preliminary RIA for the February 1982 Proposal. EPA was prepared to "paperclip" its contractor's analyses together, add some "boilerplate," and call the result an RIA, but argued that this would not be useful.[31] Given the time pressure, OMB agreed that it would be impractical to prepare a formal RIA.

The February 1982 Proposal was surprisingly brief. EPA agreed to consider alternative levels for the standard, including the 0.5 gppg, 0.65 gppg, 0.08 gppg, 1.0 gppg, and rescission options, and it announced that it would also examine averaging schemes. The agency further stated its willingness to consider alternative ways to deal with small refiners, including deleting blenders from the definition of small refiner. Finally, EPA proposed to suspend the October 1, 1982 deadline for small refiners.

Reaction to the proposal was swift and negative. Public interest groups, public health professionals and an unusually large number of individuals joined many large refiners in opposing any changes in the 0.5 gppg standard.[32] Public health groups cited recent studies indicating that lead was toxic at lower levels than previously suspected and that leaded gasoline was a more important contributor to lead in blood.[33] Particularly revealing was a new Public Health Service survey of lead blood levels that detected a dramatic decrease in lead levels in urban dwellers between 1976 and 1980. Many argued that the best explanation for this phenomenon was the 1973 lead phasedown standard.[34] Environmental groups maintained that the new evidence required the agency to tighten the standard or ban leaded gasoline altogether, rather than relax restrictions. Even a representative for the major petroleum industry trade groups realized by April 1982 that rescission was not a politically viable option.[35] Many large refiners argued that it would not be fair to rescind the 0.5 gppg standard after they had already installed the technology for producing high-octane unleaded gasoline. But most lead producers, small refiners, and blenders still favored rescinding or relaxing the 0.5 gppg standard and continuing the small refiners exemption.[36]

The public interest groups opposed the averaging concept for the same reasons that initially motivated the program office's opposition. Many large refiners strongly supported averaging among all refineries owned by a single firm, but most opposed interrefinery averaging, fearing a complex entitlements scheme reminiscent of the Department of Energy's notorious crude oil allocation program. Some refiners and the Justice Department were concerned that large refiners might abuse the resulting system for anticompetitive purposes.[37]

Some commentators suggested that the agency convert the standard from a grams per *pooled* gallon to grams per *leaded* gallon (the "leaded-only" option). Small refiners had always considered the pooled standard unfair to refiners with little capacity to produce unleaded gasoline. Other commentators argued that a leaded-only standard would be easier to administer and would effectively close the blender "loophole." Environmental groups supported the leaded-only approach on the ground that it would reduce the risk of hot spots if averaging were allowed. The Department of Justice and the Small Business Administration also endorsed the leaded-only approach, arguing that it would enhance economic efficiency and reduce the perceived unfair advantages of large refiners. Large refiners, however, argued that it would reduce the incentive among small refiners to install unleaded gasoline capabilities.[38]

The August 1982 Proposal

The public reaction to the proposal convinced top EPA officials that the agency could not adopt the rescission option.[39] Yet, Vice-President Bush clearly wanted something done. The leaded-only option provided a vehicle for resolving the contending forces, because it addressed the strongest complaints from small refiners while giving the appearance of being an effective deregulatory tool.[40]

The leaded-only option, however, posed the difficult analytical problem of determining the appropriate level of lead in leaded gasoline. Dividing the total tonnage of lead added to gasoline under the 0.5 gppg standard by the number of gallons of leaded gasoline currently in production yielded a suggested standard of about 1.1 grams per *leaded* gallon (gplg). This would be much lower than the current standard for small refiners, but was better for them than the 0.5 gppg standard. Adopting the averaging approach would ameliorate economic disruption for small refiners that had no capacity to produce unleaded gasoline. Finally, converting to a leaded-only standard could reduce the total amount of airborne lead. As demand for leaded gas decreased as automobiles burning leaded gasoline were retired from the fleet, the total emissions of lead would also decrease.[41]

During ensuing months, the policy office representative to the work group commissioned several more economic impact studies. One of the documents calculated the economic effects of moving from a pooled standard to a leaded-only standard.[42] Another study examined the geographic hot spot question, identifying six urban areas in which small refineries were likely to represent major contributors of gasoline supplies.[43] Once again, however, no thought was given to fitting the information contained in the economic reports to the RIA format.[44]

The program office continued to have doubts about the averaging idea, but the policy office gradually persuaded that office that sufficient enforcement capability existed to prevent fuel switching and geographic hot spots. Moreover, because unleaded gasoline constituted more that 50 percent of all refined gasoline by mid-1982, the program office became convinced that shortages of unleaded gas and consequent fuel switching would not result.[45] Air office officials were impressed by the substantial cost savings to small refiners that would result from moving to a leaded-only standard.[46]

In August 1982, the agency withdrew the February Proposal and proposed a 1.1 grams per leaded gallon standard for most refiners and allowed averaging among all refiners.[47] The proposal also contained a separate standard for a narrow class of small refiners of 2.5 gplg.

Although the agency did not prepare a formal Regulatory Impact Analysis for the new proposal, it did prepare an Initial Regulatory Flexibility Analysis (IRFA). The IRFA listed and detailed the costs of four options: (1) 0.5 gppg; (2) 0.4 gppg; (3) 1.2 gplg; and (4) 1.1 gplg for large refiners with 2.5 gplg for small refineries. The analysis was concise, but unsophisticated, consisting of little more than one paragraph synopses of pros and cons. The IRFA noted that small refiners "were fully cognizant of the effective date of the 0.5 standard before they entered the business" and "should have been prepared to meet a 0.5 pooled average on October 1, 1982."[48]

At the same time that EPA transmitted its proposal to OMB, someone in EPA leaked the proposal to the press. This tactic made it impossible for OMB to effect changes in the proposal privately. One White House official complained that EPA "did not play by the rules. . . . They left us very little room for maneuver."[49] The Vice-President's task force was pleased to see the agency propose a leaded-only standard and a separate 2.5 gplg standard for a small class of small refiners.[50] OMB was attracted to the leaded-only standard,[51] but it objected to keeping the standard at a constant level, arguing that the standard should gradually be increased from 1.1 gplg to higher levels as the demand for leaded gasoline decreased.[52] Although OMB was also pleased with the averaging approach,[53] it did not favor giving small refiners special consideration. The policy office helped "broker" a deal between the agency's program office and OMB by persuading OMB to accept a constant standard in return for the Air office's acquiescence in the averaging concept.

The Final Rule

While the outside comments on the August 1982 Proposal were coming in, the policy office representative to the work group continued to commission economic studies.[54] The new economic documents convinced program office doubters that averaging was not likely to create geographic hot spots.[55] In addition, a new scheme for requiring a paper record of every trade would reduce the incentive to cheat.[56] Finally, EPA and OMB became convinced that, despite industry objections, averaging would not be abused in an anticompetitive fashion.[57]

The economic documents also demonstrated that although a 1.1 gplg standard would not be inexpensive (the total impact of the standard was more than one billion dollars), neither would it cause significant economic disruption. The cost curve below 1.1 gplg, however, became very steep with costs increasing dramatically with increasing stringency.[58] In other words, the standard was very near the "knee-of-the-curve."

The work group spent most of its time examining the desirability of a small refiner exception. Recognizing that the most important institutional proponent of special treatment for small refiners was the Vice-President's task force, large refiners launched an intensive and ultimately successful campaign to convince task force officials that small refiners should not be given a special break.[59] At this point the major institutional parties – EPA, OMB, the task force, the Small Business Administration, and representatives from the White House – met to discuss how the agency would write its final rule. The parties concluded that all refiners, large and small alike, should be required to meet the same standard. The group further concluded that a brief transition period would be appropriate to allow small refiners to install octane-boosting technology and to make deals under the averaging approach.[60]

The decision to eliminate the small refiner exception forced the agency to redo completely its Final Regulatory Flexibility Analysis (FRFA). The FRFA dismissed two of the options identified in the IRFA – 1.2 gplg uniform standard and 1.1/2.5 gplg for large and small refiners, and in their place added three additional options – (1) 1.1 gplg uniform standard; (2) 1.1/1.9 gplg for large/small refiners; and (3) 1.1 gplg uniform standard with a phase-in period for small refineries and interrefinery averaging.[61] The discussion of the 1.1 gplg uniform standard relied on the policy office's economic studies to suggest that immediate imposition of the standard on small refineries would put them at a competitive disadvantage for about two years, at which time both large and small refiners would face equal marginal costs. The document cautioned that an immediate switch to a uniform standard might cause some companies to go out of business, but suggested that averaging would reduce that risk. The brief discussion of the 1.1/1.9 gplg standard suggested that that option would enable small refiners to avoid large capital expenditures, but noted that it would give small refiners a cost advantage and result in increased lead emissions over the uniform standard. The discussion of the 1.1 gplg uniform standard with a phase-in and averaging indicated that this approach would allow small refiners to modify their operations or purchase lead rights from large refiners during the interim period in which small refiners and large refiners faced differing marginal costs.

The October 29, 1982 Final Rule adopted a uniform leaded-only standard of 1.1 gplg for large and small refiners, effective November 1, 1982.[62] Small refiners could meet a relaxed 1.9 gplg standard until July 1, 1983. Small refiners could purchase lead rights to meet the standard, but they could not sell unused lead capacity to others during the phase-in period. The definition of "small refiner" was amended one more time to eliminate ambiguities.

Despite the agency's careful analysis, the U.S. Court of Appeals for the D.C. Circuit struck down EPA's interim standard for small refineries on January 26, 1983.[63] The court held that EPA failed to give adequate notice to small refiners that it might immediately require them to reduce significantly the lead content of their gasoline. The opinion recounted EPA's assurances to these refiners that the agency would take into account the lead time required for the construction of additional equipment needed for compliance. Further, the agency was unwarranted, said the court, in concluding that an interrefiner averaging scheme would rapidly develop, thus permitting the small refineries to meet the interim standard by purchasing lead credits. Noting that its decision would leave EPA without a rule limiting small refinery lead use, the court held that EPA could promulgate a temporary emergency rule. EPA accepted the court's invitation and promulgated an emergency Final Rule reinstating the lead content standards for small refiners in effect prior to November 1, 1982.[64] The rule ultimately had a profound impact on the quantity of leaded gasoline burned in the United States. According to the American Petroleum Institute, leaded gasoline constituted only about 10 percent of the 1990 gasoline market.[65]

Evaluation and conclusions

Quality of analysis

Although the agency did not prepare a formal regulatory analysis on the lead phasedown regulations, the policy office provided the work group with detailed and well-organized information on the costs of a large variety of regulatory options. Because the policy office, through its contractor, had access to a very sophisticated Department of Energy model of gasoline usage, it could make fairly reliable predictions. The reports helped the work group locate the "knee-of-the-curve," assuaged program office fears about averaging and hot spots, and addressed head-on the possible effects of not allowing a small refiner exemption. The public comments on both sides failed to challenge seriously the accuracy of the cost projections or to suggest more accurate projections. Unfortunately, such accurate and uncontroversial cost projections are extremely rare for health and environmental regulations. The lead phasedown experience may not be transferable to other industries.

On the other side of the equation, the benefits information was very controversial. No one doubted that exposure to lead could cause adverse health effects in human beings, but there was considerable controversy over the definition of "health effect," the level of lead exposure necessary to cause health effects, and the extent to which lead from gasoline played a role in the total human exposure to lead. Much of the agency's information came from its Office of Research and Development, which was contemplating revisions to the ambient air quality standards for lead. Still other information came from a large National Academy of Sciences Report on lead and from the ten-year survey of the Center for Disease Control. The policy office took the survey data and, through mathematical modeling, related it to leaded gasoline usage to draw the connection between reduced usage of leaded gasoline and reduced lead blood levels in urban areas.

The policy office did not attempt, however, to quantify or monetize the health effects of lead. Rather, the agency decided as a policy matter that lead in gasoline should be reduced up to the point at which it became prohibitively expensive. The policy office reports helped the agency identify that knee-of-the-curve. Although the policy office's cost information helped the agency choose from among regulatory options, health considerations dominated the rulemaking process.

Impediments to analysis

The agency's chief analytical impediment was the highly uncertain state of existing information on the benefits of lead phasedown options. Because the agency was unable to resolve these uncertainties in a "scientific" way, it had to make a policy-dominated determination that the lead content of gasoline should be reduced to the knee-of-the-curve. This was not the sort of finely tuned analysis of regulatory options that comprehensive analytical rationality envisions, but it nevertheless helped to bring about an informed decision. The agency understandably concluded that the costs of more extensive analytical efforts outweighed the probable benefits.

Role of analysis

At first glance, one might conclude that the lead phasedown rule is a good example of a failure of the RIA process, because no formal RIA was ever prepared. Yet, if the goal is to bring comprehensive analytical rationality to bear on the regulatory decisionmaking process, then the lead phasedown experience represents some degree of success. The policy office's representative on the work group commissioned the relevant economic reports, worked on several of the important health studies, represented EPA in the deliberations with OMB and the Bush task force, and pressed the program office on the averaging idea. The policy office's documents also made agency decisionmakers aware of the distributional impacts of the various options by detailing the shifts in wealth between large and small refiners that would result. In brief, the policy office had a substantial impact on the decisionmaking process.

Yet, comprehensive analytical rationality did not drive the decisionmaking process, and it certainly did not dictate the outcome. The work group did not attempt to evaluate the monetary value of preventing a two-point decrease in the IQ of a ghetto child; nor did it attempt to quantify the other health and environmental benefits of decreased lead emissions. The policy office gave agency decisionmakers a fairly sophisticated understanding of the costs of various options, but costs ultimately played second fiddle to subjective public health concerns.

One major analytical breakdown was the failure of the IRFA to consider the option that the agency ultimately adopted in its Final Rule. This option may have been so far from the realm of possibility at the outset of the rulemaking that no reasonable attempt to identify options would have discovered it. This seems unlikely, however, because large refiners had been strong proponents of a uniform standard for years and had made their position quite clear in their comments on the February 1982 Proposal. A better explanation may be that the agency did not devote much attention to the IRFA, regarding it merely as a paperwork hurdle. Yet, had the agency devoted more attention to the uniform standard option in the IRFA, it may have avoided the reversal that it suffered in the court of appeals, which found that the agency had not given small refiners adequate notice of the possibility that it would adopt a uniform standard with a brief phase-in period.[66]

Finally, to the extent that the goal of regulatory analysis is regulatory relief, the lead phasedown experience represents an abject failure. Although regulatory relief was unquestionably the motivation for reopening the lead phasedown issue in 1981, the regulatory analyses did not support relaxing the standard, and one policy office study of the correlation between blood lead levels and previous reductions in the use of leaded gas supported rather strongly a more stringent standard. Ultimately, even OMB and the Bush task force acquiesced in a standard that was more stringent than the standard that the task force had originally wanted to repeal.

CHAPTER 4

Getting the dust out of the air: EPA's ambient air quality standard for particulate matter

One of EPA's most important functions under the Clean Air Act is to promulgate and revise National Ambient Air Quality Standards (NAAQSs) for ubiquitous air pollutants. The primary NAAQS for a pollutant specifies an ambient concentration of the pollutant (expressed as micrograms of pollutant per cubic meter of air ($\mu g/m^3$)) that will protect the public health (including the health of susceptible groups such as infants, asthmatics and the elderly) with an adequate margin of safety. A secondary NAAQS is set at a level sufficient to protect the public welfare. In setting the primary standards, EPA examines the human health effects of pollutants, while secondary standards focus on effects on wildlife, visibility, crops, man-made materials, and the general ecology. States must write State Implementation Plans (SIPs) that impose emissions limitations on individual sources sufficient to meet the NAAQSs by specified deadlines.

Regulatory background

One of the very first NAAQSs was for "total suspended particulates" (TSP), a generic term that refers to any particles that stay in suspension in the air long enough to be captured by a designated measuring device. This includes a wide variety of solid and liquid particles that vary widely in size, stability and toxicity. Particulate matter from coke ovens and diesel trucks contains highly carcinogenic polycyclic aromatic hydrocarbons; particulate matter from West Texas cotton fields is mostly composed of relatively harmless silicates. Congress in 1977 told EPA to reevaluate the TSP NAAQSs by 1980 and at five-year intervals thereafter.[1]

The March 20, 1984 Proposal

EPA's first step in revising the particulates NAAQS was to prepare a criteria document setting out the available health and welfare information about the pollutant. Late in the development of the criteria document, the staff in the Office of Air Quality Planning and Standards (the program office) began to draft a lengthy staff paper for the Administrator setting out the pros and cons of several options for possible standards. The staff paper concluded that the current standard based on TSP was inappropriate for the health-based primary standards, because approximately one-half of the particles included within the definition of TSP did not penetrate into the lungs and were therefore relatively harmless. The staff recommended that the basis for the primary standard be changed from TSP to particulates of less than 10 microns in diameter (PM_{10}), and this recommendation met very little resistance within the agency.[2]

Although the program office recommended that EPA continue to set separate 24-hour and annual standards for PM_{10}, determining the appropriate ambient concentrations of PM_{10} for those standards was much more controversial. First, virtually all of the available epidemiological studies had used TSP, or "British smoke" (an even less specific characterization of particulates than TSP), as the measure of exposure of affected individuals. The staff therefore had to translate the results of the studies from TSP and British smoke to PM_{10}. Because the proportion of TSP consisting of PM_{10} varies from source to source and because the health effects of the various constituents of TSP likewise vary, arriving at an adequate conversion factor was no easy matter.

Second, the studies themselves were "subject to a number of inherent difficulties involving confounding variables and somewhat limited sensitivity."[3] Instead of attempting to characterize the large uncertainties in detail, the staff paper took the novel approach of subjectively characterizing the staff's conclusions about the likelihood that persons exposed to various levels of PM_{10} would suffer health effects. For the 24-hour standard, the staff concluded that an increase in mortality or aggravation of bronchitis was "likely" at levels (expressed in PM_{10}) ranging from 350 to 600 $\mu g/m^3$ and "possible" at levels from 150 to 350 $\mu g/m^3$. For the annual standard, adverse respiratory effects were "likely" at concentrations ranging from 90 to 110 $\mu g/m^3$ and "possible" at concentrations ranging from 55 to 110 $\mu g/m^3$. No significant effects were noted at levels of 40 to 55 $\mu g/m^3$. The paper noted that due to the uncertainties in the studies, the high end of this range (110 $\mu g/m^3$) "may not include any margin of safety, and should not be considered as an appropriate standard alternative." The paper also noted that at the lower end of the range the effects were only "symptomatic" effects that were "uncertain and small in comparison to baseline rates."[4]

The staff paper was even more ambiguous with respect to the secondary (public welfare) standard. Although recognizing that fine particles caused visibility problems, the staff paper did not propose any quantitative limits. The staff paper also urged that the Administrator give consideration to "soiling and nuisance" effects in setting a secondary standard, but noted that the "available data base on such effects is . . . largely qualitative."[5]

While the program office was developing the criteria document and the staff paper, analysts in the program office and in the Office of Policy Analysis (the policy office), a suboffice at the Office of Policy, Planning and Evaluation described in Chapter 3, were drafting the preliminary RIA. Although EPA had never undertaken a benefits analysis for an ambient air quality standard, the policy office believed that Executive Order 12,291 required at least a rudimentary benefits assessment with respect to the range of options proposed in the staff paper. When one of the regulatory analysts, Bart Ostro, merged two sets of data to study lost work days due to particulates in the ambient air, the results were shocking. Even at current exposure levels, which in most cases were below or only slightly above the existing NAAQSs, exposure to particulates was "related in a positive and significant way" to lost work days.[6] Although this study did not confirm that current exposures to particulates caused any particular disease, it indicated that current exposures were making people sick enough to miss work. The study had not, however, undergone review by the Clean Air Scientific Advisory Committee (CASAC), a group of prominent outside experts, because it was not formally a part of the criteria document.

While the Ostro study was being peer reviewed for publication in a scientific journal, it came into the hands of a statistician for U.S. Steel Corporation. He called a statistician in the Office of Standards and Regulations (the statistics office) to complain about the study. This triggered a bitter exchange of memoranda within EPA. An agency statistician concluded that the study had "little, if any, value in clarifying the relationship of air pollution to health."[7] A detailed rebuttal by the policy office pointed out that the Ostro study had undergone peer review by knowledgeable experts who found no significant problems with it.[8] The policy office circulated the statistician's critique to an outside expert, who found the criticisms "extreme and unwarranted, laden with value judgements" and concluded that they "did not invalidate the overall approach used by Ostro."[9] The statistics office retaliated by commissioning a contractor (for

$70,000) to critique the Ostro study. The statisticians remained convinced that it was inappropriate to "hang a benefits analysis on the Ostro study."[10]

Despite the controversy, the Ostro study played a prominent role in a preliminary program office assessment of the costs and benefits of various options for the primary standards. Based upon an analysis prepared by Mathtech Corp. (which relied upon the Ostro study) and data on costs provided by Argonne National Laboratories, the assessment concluded that the most stringent extreme of the range suggested in the staff paper would produce $132 billion in benefits and only $1 billion in costs for a net benefit of $131 billion. None of the less stringent options produced net benefits that were nearly so large, even though the costs were reduced somewhat. Although the Mathtech study was revised after peer review, its overall conclusions were essentially unchanged. Benefits still greatly exceeded costs for every option identified in the staff paper. Yet, the report acknowledged that its "most likely" estimates could vary considerably, depending upon the assumptions that went into them, including the assumption that a human life was worth $1.59 million.[11] When the program office staffers expressed concern that the report relied upon studies that had not been reviewed by the scientific advisory committee, the policy office responded that studies rejected for use in the criteria document could still be used for the benefits analysis, which (unlike the criteria document) did not have to result in a single point estimate of a "no-effect" level.[12]

Sensing that the staff might be moving toward an even more stringent standard, the American Iron and Steel Institute threatened high-level officials with a lawsuit if EPA did not immediately promulgate a relaxed standard. The Institute questioned whether the agency should prepare an RIA at all for the revised standard, noting: "EPA has uniformly interpreted the Executive Order 12,291 as requiring an RIA only when there is an adverse impact on industry, which would not be true in this instance. Because a proper revised standard would be somewhat less stringent than the present standard, there would be no adverse impact on industry."[13] In other words, RIAs should be prepared only when they indicate that standards should be relaxed. After the Institute reportedly made several trips to the White House,[14] OMB asked EPA for a briefing on the preliminary benefits analysis, noting that the analysis "seems to reverse the logic of all experience to date" with RIAs.[15]

The Steel Institute also commissioned a review of the Mathtech report by the CONSAD Research Corp. The CONSAD review criticized Mathtech for relying upon studies that had been rejected by the scientific advisory committee, for applying the quantitative results of various scientific studies in "unacceptable" ways, and for applying inaccurate air quality data in "invalid" ways. Not surprisingly, the CONSAD review concluded that the Mathtech report was "critically deficient and [was] scientifically unacceptable for any purpose related to setting a revised air quality standard."[16]

As a result of these criticisms, the Mathtech report was substantially revised in December 1982 and January 1983 to address several different scenarios, including one using only studies that the scientific advisory committee had reviewed and approved. Interestingly, the calculations for this latter scenario showed that for one of the options, the most stringent standard did not have the highest net benefits.[17]

In February 1983, Administrator Anne Gorsuch, without being briefed on the Mathtech controversy, decided to propose relaxing the 24-hour standard by 18 percent to 180 $\mu g/m^3$ and relaxing the annual standard by 41 percent to 55 $\mu g/m^3$, both expressed as PM_{10}.[18] Reports of Gorsuch's decision precipitated an impassioned protest from environmental groups, who alleged that the revision would result in hundreds of deaths and thousands of extra illnesses each year. Relying upon the Mathtech report, the environmental groups urged EPA to propose even more stringent options.[19] If the Administrator had not previously known about the Mathtech study, she was now made aware of its contents, ironically by the very groups who had consistently insisted in court that such information could not be considered in setting NAAQSs. A Jack Anderson column, relating in a somewhat muddled fashion the Mathtech results, further ensured that the Administrator and the public were aware of its estimates.[20]

The Steel Institute responded with a report severely criticizing many of the studies that EPA had relied upon in preparing the criteria document and the staff paper. Among other things, the report pointed to one study that appeared to show that mortality decreased as pollution increased.[21] Even the steel industry scoffed at the notion that pollution makes people healthier. Several Congressmen from districts containing steel facilities also urged EPA not to set a stringent standard.[22]

An uninitiated observer of this furious exchange might well wonder whether the participants were reading the same studies and reports. In fact, they were, but the uncertainties in the cost and benefit projections were so large that the data could easily be manipulated to support virtually any conclusion within a very broad range of possibilities. The battle was a very familiar one in which numbers that nobody takes very seriously are tossed around like so many hand grenades to defend positions staked out for other reasons.

Events rapidly overtook the particulate standard, as Administrator Gorsuch resigned in March 1983 and was replaced by William Ruckelshaus. After a year-long hiatus, Ruckelshaus in mid-July 1983, held a six-hour Options Selection-Rejection meeting with more than twenty-five staff members on a Saturday morning. Ruckelshaus said that he was frustrated that he could not consider the cost and benefit information because of fears that the standard would be thrown out in court if it appeared that the Administrator had considered cost information. Ruckelshaus concluded that the agency should propose a range of levels (expressed as PM_{10}) for the primary standards to educate the public about the difficulty he faced in choosing a single-number standard based on public health considerations alone.[23]

EPA sent a draft of the proposal and the Preliminary RIA to OMB in mid-December 1983.[24] OMB initially took a hard-line position that the agency should use the particulate rulemaking to challenge the notion that costs could not be considered in setting ambient air quality standards. OMB threatened to take this argument to the "Meese level at the White House" if EPA did not agree. EPA, however, adhered to its position, amply supported by two D.C. Circuit court opinions,[25] that the agency could not consider costs in setting NAAQSs.[26] Apparently OMB acquiesced, because the proposed rule was published on March 20, 1984 without any indication that the agency had changed its position on that issue.[27]

OMB also expressed interest in the fact that the analyses indicated that the benefits exceeded costs by greater amounts as the standard got more stringent. Confident that at some level of stringency, the costs would begin to outweigh the benefits, one midlevel OMB analyst suggested that the agency examine even more stringent alternatives. This analyst was, however, reversed within OMB, and EPA was allowed to proceed ahead without complying with the directive in Executive Order 12,291 that agencies should set standards at the level at which net benefits are the highest.

In the March 20 Proposal, the Administrator noted that he had not relied on the Ostro study as a basis for the proposal; nor had he considered the Mathtech report[28] or the PRIA, which relied heavily upon the Mathtech study.[29] The PRIA examined in detail the fol-

Table 4.1. *PM$_{10}$ alternatives analyzed*

Annual arithmetic mean	24-hour
55 μg/m^3	
55 μg/m^3	150 μg/m^3
55 μg/m^3	200 μg/m^3
55 μg/m^3	250 μg/m^3
70 μg/m^3	250 μg/m^3
48 μg/m^3	183 μg/m^3

lowing options, the most stringent of which (48 μg/m^3 annual, 183 μg/m^3 24-hour) was intended to be roughly the equivalent of the current TSP standard expressed as PM$_{10}$.

The cost analysis consisted of the following steps, each of which contained enormous uncertainties due both to the absence of information and to the poor quality of much of the existing information. First, the agency estimated PM$_{10}$ emissions from existing emissions inventories, which were admittedly incomplete and inaccurate. Because the inventories used TSP units, the agency converted to PM$_{10}$ by using a conversion ratio of 0.55 (PM$_{10}$/TSP). The staff later decided that the better approximation for most areas of the country was 0.46. Because all of its calculations were based on the 0.55 conversion factor, the PRIA merely noted that using the 0.46 ratio would probably affect both cost and benefits analyses, but not the overall ranking of the options.

Second, the agency assembled air quality data from monitors in counties throughout the country.[30] Because valid air quality data were not available for all counties, regression equations were used where possible to obtain estimates from incomplete data, or the county was eliminated from the analysis. The analysis used the data only from the monitor in a county indicating the highest concentration for particulates, even if other monitors in the county showed much lower levels.

Third, EPA analysts used a "linear rollback" model to estimate future emissions growth and future air quality.[31] The analysis assumed that all sources of particulates in an area accounted for air quality in direct proportion to their emissions and inversely to stack heights. The model further assumed that emissions reductions from sources far away from a monitor in the monitored area would result in the same degree of improvement in air quality as emissions reductions from nearby sources, even though many particulates fall to the ground fairly rapidly. The model did not attempt to account for future economic booms or recessions that might have dramatically affected the linear projections.

Fourth, for all counties and subcounties determined to be in violation of the alternative at issue, a list of sources and control options was developed. In an amazingly complex calculation, the projected costs for coming into attainment were calculated for each plant on the basis of a "model plant," with adjustments made for differing sizes and operating parameters. This procedure was only good for the limited number of industries for which EPA could hypothesize model plants. Sources were not considered if control options were not available or if there were insufficient data on file to permit calculations, and the reduction load was apportioned among the remaining sources. The purpose of this exercise was to predict how a state would impose requirements on individual sources in state implementation plans. In reality, the states did not have to implement the control options that EPA's model identified. Moreover, EPA assumed that states would in fact force sources to meet the standards by the deadlines, despite a long history in some states of missing air quality deadlines.

Table 4.2 excerpts EPA's cost analysis.

Even larger uncertainties plagued the benefits analysis. Problems stemmed "from a variety of sources, which include[d] limited and sometimes conflicting scientific information, paucity of data, and analytic techniques which have not always been thoroughly tested." The result was a "relatively high degree of uncertainty regarding the magnitude and precision of the empirical economic benefit estimates."[32] Like the cost analysis, the benefits analysis consisted of several steps.[33]

First, a search of the literature (including the Ostro study) revealed several categories of health benefits, some of which were more clearly established than others. Second, the agency calculated the extent of reduced exposure to particulates attributable to the implementation of each of the alternative standards on a county-by-county basis, relying on the same air quality data that it used in the cost analysis. Third, agency analysts estimated the health and welfare improvements resulting from the air quality improvements, again on a county-by-county basis. Because these estimates were based upon epidemiological studies that were clouded by large uncertainties, they too were highly uncertain. Fourth, an economic value was imputed to the estimated changes in health and welfare.

Table 4.2. *Total estimated nationwide costs: Full attainment (in billions of dollars)* [a]

Scenario[b]	Capital	Annual cost[c]	Discounted present value[d]
PM_{10} (70,250)/89	2.2	0.4	1.4
PM_{10} (55,-)/89	5.8	1.0	3.8
PM_{10} (55,250)/89	5.9	1.0	3.9
PM_{10} (55,200)/89	5.8	1.0	3.8
PM_{10}'(55,150)/89	8.2	1.4	5.3
PM_{10} (48,183)/89	7.8	1.3	5.0
TSP (-,150)/89	14.0	2.3	9.0
TSP (-,150)/87	15.0	2.4	11.0

[a]Costs were calculated in 1980 dollars and do not include the cost of (1) pre-1979 controls and (2) New Source controls tied to meeting NSPS or PSD requirements.
[b]Key: TSP (x,y)/z − x = annual standard, y = 24-hour standard, z = attainment year.
[c]Annual costs include operation and maintenance costs and annualized capital charges. Annual capital charges were derived using an assumed 15-year equipment life and a 10% real discount rate.
[d]Discounted Present Value represents the summation of the stream of annual operation and maintenance and capital payments discounted back to 1982 using a 10% real discount rate.
[e]This PM_{10} alternative approximates the current primary TSP standards. The PM_{10} values were derived from the TSP values by applying the regression equations used to estimate missing values in the air quality file and by applying the PM_{10}/TSP conversion ratio of 0.55. The costs are lower than 55,150 alternative because the 24-hour standards are controlling in most counties.

For some effects, property value studies allowed fairly direct estimates. For mortality risks, the PRIA estimated the willingness of individuals to pay for the reductions in risk. For morbidity risks, the analysis used average daily wages and estimates of medical expenditures, but did not attempt to factor in pain, suffering and inconvenience. The agency relied on the Mathtech survey of the literature to derive two possible values for reduced mortality risk: a low value of $0.36 for a reduction of a risk of death by one in one million, and a high value of $2.80 for the same risk reduction. Fifth, the monetary results were discounted to present value using a very high discount rate of 10 percent, and the benefits within each category were then summed to obtain a national total.

Before the benefits from different categories could be aggregated, the analysts had to address the complaints of EPA's statisticians and industry groups that the analysis should not consider studies that

Table 4.3. *Incremental benefits for alternative* PM_{10} *and TSP standards[a]: Full attainment (in billions of dollars)*

Alternative Standard[b]	Aggregation Procedure[c]		
	A	B	C
PM_{10} (70,250)/89	.37/2.0	1.7/3.5	12/14
PM_{10} (55,-)/89	.51/3.1	2.9/5.3	20/24
PM_{10} (55,250)/89	.51/3.1	2.9/5.5	21/23
PM_{10} (55,200)/89	.51/3.1	2.9/5.7	21/25
PM_{10} (55,150)/89	.55/3.5	3.5/6.5	25/29
$PM_{10}{}^{d}$(48,183)/89	.57/3.6	3.7/6.7	27/31
TSP (-,150)/89	.65/4.2	4.6/8.2	34/38
TSP (-,150)/87	.87/5.7	6.4/11.4	48/52

[a]1982 discounted present values in billions of 1980 dollars at a 10% discount rate. The 7-year time horizon is 1989–95 and the 9-year horizon is 1987–95. Comparisons between PM_{10} and TSP standards are in terms of TSP stringency, not particle size.
[b]Key: PM (x,y)/z − x = annual standard, y = 24-hour standard, z = attainment year.
[c]For each aggregation procedure/standard combination, two values are reported. The first is based on a $0.36 for a unit reduction of 1.0×10^{-6} in annual mortality risk, while the second is based on $2.80 for the same unit reduction.
[d]This PM_{10} alternative approximates the current primary TSP standards. The PM_{10} values were derived from the TSP values by applying the regression equations used to estimate missing values in the air quality file and by applying the PM_{10}/TSP conversion ratio of 0.55. The costs are lower than 55,150 alternative because the 24-hour standards are controlling in most counties.

had not been approved by the scientific advisory committee. The analysts finessed this problem by separating the information into categories based upon the studies relied upon to calculate the benefits. In Category A, the analysis only considered mortality and chronic morbidity based upon two studies that had been approved by the scientific advisory committee. Category B relied upon the Category A studies plus an additional study on acute morbidity that was used in the staff paper. Category C added the Ostro study on acute morbidity.

The results for Categories A, B, and C are shown in Table 4.3.

Finally, the PRIA combined the cost analyses with the benefits analyses to derive overall cost-benefit comparisons for each of the alternatives and each of the information categories. The PRIA noted that the cost-benefit analysis was not sensitive to distributional considerations and transfers of wealth that might result from the

Table 4.4. *Incremental net benefits for alternative* PM_{10} *standards: Full attainment (in billions of dollars)[a]*

Alternative standard[b]	Aggregation procedure[c]		
	A	B	C
PM_{10} (70,250)/89	−.58/1.1	.75/2.6	11/13
PM_{10} (55,-)/89	−2.0/.58	.38/2.8	17/21
PM_{10} (55,250)/89[d]	−2.1/.53	.33/2.9	18/20
PM_{10} (55,200)/89	−2.0/.56	.36/3.2	18/22
PM_{10} (55,150)/89[d]	−3.0/−.03	−.03/3.0	21/25
PM_{10}[e] (48,183)/89[d]	−2.8/.24	.34/3.3	24/23
TSP (-.150)/89[f]	−5.3/−1.8	−1.4/2.2	28/32
TSP (-,150)/87	−8.1/−3.3	−2.6/2.5	39/43

[a] 1982 discounted present values in billions of 1980 dollars at a 10% discount rate. Time horizons for 7- and 9-year standards are, respectively, 1989–95 and 1987–95. Comparisons between PM_{10} and TSP standards are in terms of TSP stringency, not particle size.
[b] Key: PM (x,y)/z − x = annual standard; y = 24-hour standard; z = attainment year.
[c] For each aggregation procedure/standard combination, two values are reported. The first is based on a $0.36 for a unit reduction of 1.0×10^{-6} in annual mortality risk while the second is based on $2.80 for the same unit reduction.
[d] This alternative is dominated by another alternative with the same time horizon. An alternative is considered to be dominated when another alternative provides the same dollar benefits for smaller costs or greater dollar benefits for the same or smaller costs.
[e] This PM_{10} alternative approximates the current primary TSP standards. The PM_{10} values were derived from the TSP values by applying the regression equations used to estimate missing values in the air quality file and by applying the PM_{10}/TSP conversion ratio of 0.55. The costs are lower than 55,150 alternative because the 24-hour standards are controlling in most counties.
[f] This alternative is dominated by another alternative with a longer time horizon.

adoption of a particular alternative. It further cautioned that its use of "point estimates" might obscure the attendant uncertainties. The results for Categories A, B, and C are set out in Table 4.4.

Table 4.4 reveals that the PRIA agreed substantially with the earlier Mathtech reports: The benefits of the most stringent alternatives exceeded the costs by the greatest amounts for Category C, which relied on the Ostro study. Excluding the Ostro study resulted in a more ambiguous assessment. In Category B, the benefits of all alternatives outweighed the costs if the larger value for mortality risks were adopted, and the current primary standard without the current secondary standard appeared the most cost beneficial. Only if one relied upon Category A studies exclusively would a less stringent standard be indicated.

The relevant interest groups reacted predictably to the March 20, 1984 Proposal. A coalition of environmental groups was harshly critical of the proposal for even considering levels that would provide for no margin of safety. They also stressed that EPA should have used the 0.46 conversion factor from TSP to PM_{10}. They pointed out that California had set its 24-hour PM_{10} standard at $50\mu g/m^3$, far below the 150 $\mu g/m^3$ low end of EPA's proposed range. Interestingly, the California agency had relied upon the Ostro study.[34]

Industry groups were also dissatisfied with some aspects of the proposal. The Steel Institute urged EPA to adopt standards in the mid-to-upper end of the proposed ranges, arguing that to pick the standards from the bottom end of the ranges would be "totally unnecessary to protect the public health and would impose as much as \$4 billion in additional costs on the steel industry."[35] The American Mining Institute argued that an even smaller particle size (PM_6) should be used for the revised standard.[36]

The Final Rule

The agency held a public meeting in April 1984 to review the public comments on the proposed rule. Of the 312 written submissions, 153 came from industry or industry groups, 93 from state, local, and federal government agencies, 32 from environmental and public interest groups, and 34 from private citizens. Not surprisingly, most industry comments favored selecting a level from the upper end of the proposed ranges, while most of the remaining commentators favored levels at the lower bound of the ranges, and in some cases even lower than the ranges suggested by the proposed rule.

The program office staff in 1985 amended the criteria document and the staff paper to include the Ostro study and other studies that had come in during the comment process.[37] This time, however, the staff solicited the Clean Air Scientific Advisory Committee's comments on the Ostro study. Both the CASAC and the staff recommended to Administrator Thomas that the final standard be based on PM_{10} at the lowest end of the proposed range (150 $\mu g/m^3$ 24-hour, 50 $\mu g/m^3$ annual) for the primary standards.[38]

The Office of Air Quality Planning and Standards regulatory analysts prepared two addenda to the RIA, both of which drew upon

Table 4.5. *Estimated nationwide costs including reduction of residual non-attainment (Scenario B)*[a,b]

Scenario	BTAC (10^6 \$/yr)[c]			DPV (10^6)[d]			
	1989	1992	1995	1989	1992	1995	Total[e]
TSP (75,150)	1,375	1,385	1,430	776	587	456	4,193
TSP (75,260)	761	824	851	430	349	271	2,418
PM_{10} (50,150)	572	622	640	323	264	204	1,859
PM_{10} (65,250)	151	182	193	85	77	61	528
PM_{10} (50,150) TSP(90,-)	690	694	736	390	294	234	2,110
PM_{10} (65,250) TSP(90,-)	568	567	606	321	240	193	1,733

[a]All costs are in first-quarter 1984 dollars.
[b]Values were computed for each year from 1989 to 1995. Only three yearly values are tabulated.
[c]BTAC: Before tax annualized cost.
[d]DPV: 1983 discounted present value.
[e]Total for 7-year period, 1989–95.

further studies and analyses gathered during the comment period. The Second Addendum took roughly the same approach toward the cost analysis as the original PRIA, and it acknowledged that the "entire process contained many analytic assumptions and used data bases with known limitations."[39] EPA amended its cost assessment models in several ways to incorporate more sophisticated assumptions and better data. The new cost estimates, which are reproduced in Table 4.5, projected costs through 1995.

The agency analysts incorporated fewer changes into the benefits analysis. Perhaps the most important change was its more confident reliance upon the Ostro study. The Second Addendum stressed that since the publication of the PRIA, Ostro's work had been peer reviewed and published in two journals, and the agency considered the functions used in that study "more applicable to the general population than the ones used originally." Therefore, the benefits tables in the Second Addendum did not distinguish between estimates that relied on the Ostro study and those that did not. The net result was "to increase benefits by approximately 15 percent for the most stringent alternative examined."[40] Finally, the agency increased the value of a statistical life from \$0.36 to \$0.43 at the low end and from \$2.80 to \$7.46 at the high end. The results are set out in Table 4.6. Because of the agency's increased confidence in the Ostro study,

Table 4.6. *Incremental benefits for alternative PM$_{10}$ and TSP standards: Partial attainment (in billions of dollars)^a*

	Aggregation Procedure^b		
Alternative standard^c	A	B	D
TSP (75,150)	0.7/9.8	1.3/10.4	43.4/167.2
TSP (75,260)	0.7/8.8	1.1/9.3	35.8/139.1
PM$_{10}$ (50,150)	0.6/8.0	1.0/8.4	28.5/112.2
PM$_{10}$ (65,250)	0.4/4.7	0.6/4.9	15.8/65.5
PM$_{10}$ (50,150) TSP(90,-)	0.6/8.2	1.0/8.6	30.2/118.4
PM$_{10}$ (65,250) TSP(90,-)	0.6/7.5	1.0/7.8	26.7/105.9

^{a}1983 discounted present values in billions of 1984 dollars at a 10% discount rate. The time horizon is the 7 years from 1989 through 1995. Comparisons between PM$_{10}$ and TSP standards are in terms of TSP stringency, not particle size.
^{b}For each aggregation procedure/standard combination two values are reported. The first is based on a \$0.43 for a unit reduction of 1.0×10^{-6} in annual mortality risk while the second is based on \$7.46 for the same unit reduction.
^{c}Key: PM$_{10}$ or TSP (x,y) x = annual standard; y = 24-hour standard.

it was included in Category D, which is included in Table 4.6 instead of Category C.

Once again, the calculations revealed that for most scenarios, the benefits exceeded the costs by the largest amount at the most stringent end of the spectrum of alternatives. Nevertheless, the Second Addendum cautioned that "despite very significant improvements made, there remain fundamental questions regarding certain aspects of the methodology used." For this reason (and because of doubts about the legality of considering costs in setting NAAQSs), "the agency has not considered this RIA in the review of the PM NAAQS."[41]

On July 1, 1987, EPA published its final standards for particulates. As expected, the agency decided to convert from TSP to PM$_{10}$. The 24-hour standard was set at 150 μg/m^3 with no more than one expected exceedance per year. The annual standard was set at 50 μg/m^3 annual arithmetic mean. Finally, the agency decided not to set a separate secondary standard, but rather replaced the original secondary TSP standard with 24-hour and annual PM$_{10}$ standards that were identical in all respects to the primary standards.[42] Thus, the Administrator followed the advice of the staff and CASAC and set the standards at the low end of the available options, which roughly corresponded to the status quo.

Evaluation and conclusions

Type and quality of analysis

Because the ambient air quality standards are so critical to the Clean Air Act's regulatory scheme, EPA was willing to spend a lot of money on the particulates RIA. That document was also viewed throughout the agency as a test case for the use of regulatory analysis in the air quality standard-setting process. The analysis was especially interesting in its bottom-line conclusion that for most options within the relevant range, the benefits exceeded the costs, often by a considerable amount. Only by rejecting all but the most rock-solid scientific studies did it predict that costs outweighed benefits.

The regulated industry and some agency statisticians adopted a strict "yes-no" approach to the available studies. Either the studies were "scientifically adequate" and were therefore appropriately factored into the analysis, or they were "scientifically invalid" and therefore useless. The regulatory analysts in both the policy and program offices, on the other hand, believed that all relevant information was useful, although some of the studies might appropriately be discounted because of problems in their protocols or in their execution. Recognizing that the extent to which studies without scientific advisory committee approval should be discounted was not purely a "scientific" question, the analysts creatively drafted the RIA to allow the decisionmaker (and consequently the public) to see the impact on the cost and benefit predictions of rejecting certain studies.

The outcome of this dialogue is critical to the analytical enterprise. If a regulatory analysis may only rely upon studies that are determined to be "scientifically adequate" by a group of scientists applying roughly the same criteria that they would use in deciding whether to accept the study for publication in a scientific journal (or some other criteria known only to themselves), then the analytical effort is virtually useless. It is always possible for a well-paid consultant to poke holes in even the best conceived empirical study, because of the insuperable difficulties of obtaining and compiling information in the real world. For example, if strict notions of scientific adequacy governed the *cost* analysis, virtually none of the available information could be used, because most cost studies rely heavily upon telephone surveys and nonbinding estimates from pollution control equipment vendors. An experienced analyst knows this and attempts to convey to the decisionmaker a feel for the uncertainties that result from those inevitable imperfections in the available information. The EPA analysts had to choose between using some questionable data to explore an important aspect of a regulatory decision or leaving that aspect entirely out of the analysis. They understandably elected the former option.

Impediments to analysis

The chief impediment to the particulates analytical effort was once again uncertainty in the available information. The RIA for the particulates NAAQS was the culmination of an extremely ambitious intellectual enterprise. The task was filled with projection after projection, based on assumption after assumption, and undergirded by very few hard facts. Necessarily, it left large uncertainties in its wake.

The analysts made an admirable attempt to reveal critical uncertainties and to speculate as to how erroneous assumptions would affect the analysis. The document did not, however, attempt to characterize the uncertainties in any greater detail. More disturbingly, the analysis used "point" estimates in its charts and graphs without explicitly revealing the uncertainties in the projections, even though virtually all of the numbers could be "off" by orders of magnitude. The quick reader (and the press) would naturally focus on the numbers in the tables and thereby lose any appreciation for the confidence with which the agency projected those numbers. One of the air office analysts acknowledged that the RIA probably "overstated the certainties," but he was convinced that if it had adequately characterized the full range of uncertainties, the document "would not have gotten out of the agency."[43] This begs the question whether a disarmingly precise analysis *should* escape the agency confines.

Another place in which the RIA ventured onto treacherous terrain was its attempt to place explicit values on mortality risks. As we shall see in Chapter 9, the subject of valuing lives is extremely controversial, eliciting strong ideological reactions that cut across the political spectrum. More than any other topic, it tends to distinguish believers in comprehensive analytical rationality from others, irrespective of political beliefs or economic status. At this point it is sufficient to note that the choice between the "high end" and "low end" estimate for the value of reduced mortality risk in the PRIA made the difference between a standard with positive and negative net benefits for five of the eight alternatives using Category A data and for three of the eight using Category B data.

Role of analysis

To the great consternation of Administrator Ruckelshaus, the PRIA played no role whatsoever in his decisionmaking process prior to the March 20 Proposal, because he declined to read it. It seems clear, however, that the analysts themselves were quite influential. Although the range for the standards was dominated by "pure" scientific considerations, the knowledge among lower-level work group participants and midlevel managers that the benefits of even the most stringent of the possible standards outweighed the costs except under the most severe information limitations no doubt increased their comfort with recommending that the Administrator choose an option from the low end of the range.

The role of the "superanalysts" in OMB is less easy to assess. Staff economists in OMB were at first skeptical of EPA's cost and benefit projections because the analysis defied the conventional wisdom in that office that agencies are bent on promulgating needlessly expensive regulations that drain society's scarce resources. Given an opportunity to review the Mathtech report and the Ostro study, OMB found some aspects that could stand improvement, but it did not (like the petroleum and steel industries) insist that EPA ignore the study. Yet, neither did OMB insist (as one of its top staffers advised) that EPA extend its analysis to even more stringent standards to find the option with the greatest net benefits. Apparently, a conflict erupted in OMB between the purists who were devoted to analysis for its own sake and the "realists" who were keen on analysis so long as it signaled less burdensome regulation but were willing to ignore it when it argued for greater stringency. The realists carried the day.

CHAPTER 5

Getting obstructions out of the driver's view: NHTSA's field of direct view regulations

The National Highway Traffic Safety Administration (NHTSA) was created in the mid-1960s after Ralph Nader convinced the nation that traffic safety depended as much upon the "nut on the wheel" as the "nut behind the wheel." Although state highway safety agencies are responsible for ensuring visual acuity for the human half of the man-machine combination, NHTSA must ensure that the machine half does not unnecessarily obstruct the driver's view of the road and of approaching hazards. The long-studied, but never implemented "Field of Direct View" (FDV) standard was NHTSA's attempt to establish requirements for a minimum field of view for the driver, for light transmittance through windshields, and for the permissible size of obstructions (e.g. roof pillars and rear-view mirrors) in the driver's field of view.

Regulatory background

Shortly after its creation, a NHTSA contractor reported that automobile rear-view mirrors were a major obstruction to driver vision and that roof pillars in both the front and the rear of some automobiles created substantial "blind spots." The agency also became concerned that windshield tinting could cause night visibility problems. The agency in April 1972 proposed a standard that would set requirements for: (1) obstructions in the driver's fields of view; (2) light transmittance levels of windshields; (3) visibility of the vehicle's corners; (4) visibility of ground surface targets for trucks, buses, and other such passenger vehicles; and (5) view obstruction by sun visors.[1]

Comments on the proposal were "strong, critical and helpful." Manufacturers agreed "in principle" with some of the proposals, but they disagreed with the agency and among themselves as to how visibility requirements should be achieved. Glass manufacturers objected to rules that did not permit windshield tinting. Commercial vehicle manufacturers complained that the ground visibility target rules would require them to change substantially the front-end structure of their vehicles.[2]

Yielding to this uniform opposition, NHTSA commissioned four more research projects,[3] and the issue lay dormant for several years until a more activist Administrator in 1977 directed the staff to revive it.[4] NHTSA issued a second notice of proposed rulemaking in November 1978 that differed significantly from the 1972 proposal.[5] Among other things, NHTSA dropped commercial vehicle ground surface target tests, loosened the light transmission requirements, and reduced the stringency of the rearward visibility requirements.

The December 1980 Final Rule

NHTSA does not coordinate its branches into formal work groups to draft rules and rulemaking support documents. The Office of Rulemaking (program office) first prepares a Rulemaking Support Paper for an initiative. The support paper contains a technical analysis of the need for the rule and regulatory alternatives for meeting that need. It also contains a rudimentary cost-benefit analysis and, for Final Rules, an analysis of the outside comments on the rule. The Office of Plans and Programs (the policy office) and the Office of Chief Counsel review and critique the support paper. Then the policy office prepares a regulatory analysis document containing a more detailed and sophisticated assessment of the costs and benefits of the options suggested in the support paper. The regulatory analysis document draws heavily upon the information in the support paper, but the policy office also consults other sources of available information. The regulatory analysis document for major rules becomes the formal RIA.

The agency had drafted a regulatory analysis for an early version of the FDV standard in 1976 that concluded that the benefits of a standard would be very speculative and small in number (12,600 accidents avoided, 40 fatalities avoided). Although the costs would initially be high, they would not recur as auto manufacturers made design changes to comply with the standard. The policy office saw the issue at that time as "determining where the [newly elected Carter] Administration stands on issues . . . which have common sense linkage to accident reduction but no proven basis for benefits."[6] The policy office took the position that "a rule should not be issued where the benefits are extremely speculative and where a large number of assumptions are required to derive those benefits."[7]

The program office was also initially somewhat dubious about the standard. In 1978, it told the Administrator that the benefits of the draft proposed standard were not supported by accident data and "[were] based on many assumptions that can be questioned."[8] It calculated that the proposed standard as revised would annually eliminate 1,300 accidents with 17 fatalities at a cost of $45 million, but it noted that the costs would be reduced if auto manufacturers were allowed a longer lead time. The head of the program office concluded that: "If we were starting from scratch, I would not recommend initiating the fields of view rulemaking. However, there is international interest in it, the rule would be relatively inexpensive, and the NHTSA has invested manpower and research monies in developing this regulation."[9]

During 1978, the program office circulated a draft of the support paper and the policy office circulated copies of a draft regulatory analysis document. The policy office was initially not persuaded that the initiative should go forward, believing that the program office had not really examined the reasons for not issuing the rule. But in the early internal debates, the program office stuck by its guns. When the analysts pressed it to identify the benefits of the regulations, the program office responded that "seeing more is better than seeing less" and that the standards were "directionally correct." Undaunted, the regulatory analysts urged the program office to quantify the alleged benefits, demanding to know "how much safer."[10]

A lively internal debate between the Chief Counsel's office and the policy office erupted when the lawyers inquired about the basis for the analysts' benefits calculations. The analysis document estimated that of all accidents in which automobiles strike pedestrians, 50 percent could be avoided by providing improved direct vision and 50 percent resulted from pedestrian and driver negligence. The attorneys wanted to know how the analysts arrived at these figures: "If the assumption is totally arbitrary, the [document] should say so. If it is based on some data or some other objective or even reasonable intuitive basis, then say that."[11] The Chief Counsel's office queried: "What do the claimed benefit figures tell us or anyone if we can't demonstrate the reasonableness of our assumptions? There is no legal requirement anywhere for quantification based on sheer guess work. Why do we do it?"[12]

The regulatory analysis office responded that the 50 percent assumption was agreed to by the program office: "If Chief Counsel has a better analysis, then I invite you to suggest an appropriate number. This is not a pure world; everything cannot be proven by fact. I intend to retain this estimate unless I can be shown a better one."[13] To the more general question about the value of assumption-laden quantitative analysis, the policy office replied: "I think in certain cases, we owe it to the public to justify rulemaking through quantification whenever possible. I think this is one case where we would be negligent in not attempting to quantify the benefits, especially with the amount of research time and money spent."[14]

The agency spent most of 1979 trying to come up with better factual support for the standard. Ultimately, the Office of Research and Development (the research office) gave up the effort for five reasons: (1) the mass accident data files available to the agency could not be broken down into vehicle body styles and usage types; (2) even if they could be, only certain subsets of those categories would have direct visibility problems; (3) the comparatively small proportion of accidents attributable to direct view problems in cars within each subset would probably be too small to yield statistically significant results; (4) there were not sufficient data on the number of miles driven by cars within various subcategories to estimate the extent to which people were exposed to risks; and (5) data were highly subject to fleet fluctuation and variations in reporting thresholds. The research office concluded passively that "the getting of any meaningful accident rate data is nearly hopeless."[15]

In internal meetings during late 1980, agency analysts demanded more quantitative data for the regulatory analysis document. The program office responded that there would be no retooling costs and no recurring costs for the tinted windshields aspect of the regulation, but it did not attempt to quantify any remaining costs. It also declined to quantify expected benefits from tinted windshields, other than to note that fatalities were 30 percent higher at night and that older drivers, who are more adversely affected by tinting, constitute 12 percent of automobile drivers. With respect to the binocular obstruction standards, the program office found no recurring costs, and it noted that retooling costs "have been minimized by extending the effective date until 1985 model cars." It did not attempt to quantify benefits beyond noting that two studies had associated binocular obstruction in some cars with higher accident rates. The monocular obstruction standards would likewise entail no recurring costs and would minimize retooling costs by extending the effective date. Again, no attempt was made to quantify benefits.[16]

The policy office was not satisfied. To the analysts' primary criticism that it had not quantified how many models would be affected by the final standard, the program office responded that most of the models that had failed to meet the standards in the past would now meet the somewhat modified standards, because "industry has been considering the visibility requirements in recent years and designing new models accordingly."[17] This left the program office open to the analysts' countercharge that "[i]f about all models do meet the standard, then by definition, the benefits are almost nil because the standard would not require any vehicle to be modified." The program office responded that the rules would at least prevent backsliding, and it stressed that because many cars did not comply with the tinting requirements, compliance would produce some unquantifiable benefits. The policy office did not accept the backsliding argument as an appropriate basis for regulation, and its concerns about the lack of quantitative evidence on the benefits of the standard were never fully satisfied. Ultimately, the debate was resolved during the lame duck period between Administrations, when the Administrator sided with the program office and signed the Final Rule on December 22, 1980.[18]

The rule established procedures for measuring field of view obstructions in passenger cars within angular limits, and it set limits for the maximum size of the obstructions. The requirements were organized in terms of four zones that represented the four quarters of a car – left front (I), right front (II), left rear (III) and right rear (IV), respectively. "A" pillars (the forwardmost roof supports) are found in zones I and II. "B" pillars (middle supports) and "C" pillars (rear supports) are in zones III and IV. The agency measured the obstructions within these zones by means of a binocular test (which simulates the "ability of the eyes to 'look around' narrow objects") and a monocular test (which simulates "the obstruction that would be presented to one eye").[19]

The agency rule would have allowed passenger cars only one binocular obstruction of no more than 6 degrees horizontal width in each half of the driver's forward field of view. The agency believed that the 6 degree limit would give automobile manufacturers enough tolerance for production variations. For zones I and II, the sum of the monocular obstruction angles could not exceed 11 degrees in each zone. In zone IV the obstruction limit for individual obstructions was 17 degrees and the total monocular obstruction for the zone was 25 degrees. The rule dropped the proposed requirements for zone III. General Motors convinced NHTSA that the requirements were unnecessary, because a driver would normally look directly through the side windows or use a combination of peripheral vision and the left side mirror to view objects located by the left side of the car. Finally, the rule required that windshields transmit at least 70 percent of the light entering from outside the vehicle. NHTSA declared that this requirement would not ban the use of tinted windshields, but it would prevent the use of heavily tinted glass in windshields.

Despite its considerable doubts about the efficacy of the standard, the policy office drafted a document that supported the Administrator's decision. Relying upon information from Ford, General Motors and the National Bureau of Standards, the analysis first estimated that 65 percent of all cars manufactured in the United States would require improved windshield light transmission performance to comply with the Final Rules. This could be accomplished in four ways: (1) decreasing the amount of ferrous oxide, a tinting compound; (2) decreasing the angle of the windshield; (3) decreasing the thickness of the glass; and (4) decreasing the curvature of the glass. Since ferrous oxide tinting was responsible for the vast majority of noncomplying windshields, nearly all manufacturers could comply by electing the first option. No windshield or body redesign would be necessary, and compliance costs would be very nearly zero.

The analysis predicted that most vehicles would require "little or no modification" to meet the monocular and binocular limits. Any redesign costs would be minimized by the generous four years' lead time that the rule provided. Foreign manufacturer costs were further minimized by the fact that the binocular requirements were identical with those being drafted by the European Economic Community.

The benefits analysis began with the familiar observation that available data were insufficiently detailed to permit a "quantifiable estimate."[20] Observing that almost 90 percent of all automobiles had some form of tinted glass,[21] the analysis concluded that low light transmittance through tinted windshields could decrease driver seeing distances. Although other factors, such as alcohol consumption, contributed to a higher rate of nighttime fatalities, the analysis suggested that driver visibility was an important contributor to the fatality rate. The analysis also cited a study demonstrating that the nighttime rate of accidents involving the elderly was disproportionately higher than the daytime accident rate,[22] and it concluded that this was attributable to poorer vision among the elderly.[23] Accident statistics revealed that accidents in which a passenger car struck an unlighted object in unlighted areas accounted for about 5,500 fatalities per year. Predicting that about 65 percent of all passenger cars would be improved by the standard, NHTSA estimated the number of cases affected by the rule to be "a candidate population of roughly 3,500 fatalities."[24] The analysis did not specify how many of these lives would be saved by its standard.

NHTSA determined that about 4.8 percent and 19 percent of existing automobiles had "A" and "C" pillars that would violate the Final Rule. The analysis concluded that although the low percentage of nonconforming automobiles might indicate minimal benefits, the rule was necessary to prevent backsliding. (The document stressed the backsliding idea despite the analysts' internally expressed doubts about the validity of the argument.) In addition, the analysis noted that in small cars design obstructions were closer to the driver's eye, thus increasing the relative size of the obstruction.

The analysis did not attempt to assess either costs or benefits monetarily. Because it did not attempt to quantify the number of fatalities that might be avoided, it did not have to struggle with the difficult question of the monetary value of a human life. Although it rejected General Motors' excessive cost estimate, it did not provide a more realistic one, beyond suggesting that compliance costs would be very nearly zero. Although the program office would no doubt have preferred a stronger statement of the rule's benefits, the analysts were unwilling to write a ringing endorsement of the standard. The analysis concluded that both the costs and the benefits of the rule were "likely to be minimal."[25]

The June 1981 proposed revocation

The Reagan Administration placed the FDV standard on a "hit list" of regulations that it would reevaluate in light of the automobile industry's perceived need for regulatory relief.[26] Although most automobile manufacturers had previously failed to estimate redesign costs, they now hurled a barrage of cost information at the agency. On June 22, 1981, NHTSA revoked the FDV standard, effective immediately, in response to manufacturers' petitions for reconsideration.[27]

The program office initially expressed confidence that NHTSA could meet the most substantial industry objections by simply extending the compliance dates by an additional two years and by adopting three or four relatively minor changes in some of the requirements. But it concluded that "the best approach is to rescind the rule at this time and repropose it, or portions of it, when we are better able to defend it."[28] An eight-page summary of the petitions for reconsideration pointed out that adopting the suggested minor changes would mean that the rule would not require auto makers to do any more than they were currently doing. Rather than promulgating a rule mandating that auto manufacturers adhere to the status quo, the program office recommended that the agency rescind the rule and conduct further research. Thus, the program office now conceded the analysts' earlier point about backsliding.

The program office concluded, however, that the requirements for "monocular zone IV" (the zone to the right rear where a driver looks when changing lanes) could not be addressed by minor modification and that they could yield substantial benefits. It pointed out that the chief objection to the requirement was that it would significantly impact the design of "cars with 'sporty' images," but urged that it was "important that the requirement not be weakened by relaxing it based on manufacturers' objections." Yet, in a mystifying turn of logic, the program office concluded: "Therefore, it is recommended that this requirement be rescinded and that further research be conducted so that the requirement can be better defended."[29] It analyzed the windshield tinting requirements in a similar fashion.

The best explanation for the program office's changed attitude is that its staff knew that the Reagan Administration would be scouting around for rules to rescind, and the FDV standard, of which no one was especially fond, was a prime candidate. The program office was willing to concede defeat at the outset, rather than face the policy office in a battle it could not win.[30] The new cost data provided the face-saving excuse for switching gears within a relatively short period of time.

Responding to the program office memorandum and a draft notice of revocation, the analysts urged that the notice balance its heavy emphasis on costs with a discussion of some of the agency's findings on benefits. Rather than stating outright that the agency had found the benefits to be minor, they urged the program office to say that the agency had not identified quantifiable benefits.[31] It is fair to conclude that the revocation question was resolved on an expedited basis without much discussion or analysis.[32] All involved actors recognized that revocation was preordained for policy reasons.

Despite an NHTSA press release concluding optimistically that the revocation would save the auto industry $160 million, OMB did not require NHTSA to prepare an RIA for the action. Because the revocation came within one of OMB's frequently issued "waivers" for deregulatory rules, it sailed through OMB without delay.[33] This one-way approach to the regulatory analysis requirement lent credibility to frequent criticisms from beneficiaries of regulation that it was used as a roadblock to slow down regulation, rather than as a tool for making regulation more efficient and effective.

The Center for Auto Safety (CAS) claimed that NHTSA had not provided a "valid reasoned explanation" for the revocation.[34] The only new information upon which the agency relied was manufacturers' cost data which, according to CAS, was too "cursorily" reviewed by the agency to provide a sufficient basis for the revocation. CAS further noted that NHTSA had already responded to manufacturer concerns in the January 1981 rule, and it had incorporated manufacturers' comments into the standard. CAS expressed concern that without the standard in place, manufacturers could engage in backsliding. Nevertheless, on June 17, 1982, NHTSA denied CAS's request for reinstatement of the Safety Standard, and CAS did not challenge that decision.

Evaluation and conclusions

Impediments to analysis

The 1981 Regulatory Evaluation pulled together existing information from a wide variety of available sources. The cost analyses relied heavily upon industry-supplied information. Although agency analysts looked over the industry submissions for accuracy, "basically, we took their word for it."[35] The benefits analysis was typical in its reliance upon very debatable estimates based on skimpy data and bold assumptions. Even though the available information was insufficient to support quantitative predictions, it did at least come from independent sources, such as NHTSA contractors, agency data banks, and insurance industry statistics.

The abrupt reversal of position on the merits of the FDV rulemaking in 1981 demonstrates dramatically the manipulability of analysis. The cost figures that the auto companies submitted in connection with their motions for reconsideration were nothing new. The uncertainties were no larger in 1982 than they had been in 1981. But the uncertainties gave a much less activist NHTSA, serving a President who campaigned under the banner of regulatory relief, sufficient room to reverse its previous conclusions.

This was entirely proper. Analysts could offer important insights, but they could not dictate that decision. Policy had to drive the decision. The Carter NHTSA advanced a policy of erring on the side of safety; the Reagan NHTSA erred on the side of the ailing auto industry. Policy change is what elections are about.

Less defensible, perhaps, was NHTSA's treatment of the industry cost data, which reflected the assumption that the standard would force companies to redesign their models and retool production processes at a cost of hundreds of millions of dollars. In 1981, NHTSA met this argument head-on by amending the standard slightly and extending the compliance deadlines far enough into the future to allow design changes to be incorporated into new models. The program office was prepared to offer an identical solution in 1981, but instead recommended that the standard be rescinded pending further study. On this point, NHTSA is subject to legitimate criticism, because the legislative history of the Motor Vehicle Safety Act evidences a congressional preference for extending effective dates, rather than reducing the stringency of standards to ameliorate their economic impact on the auto industry.[36] If Congress has articulated a policy in favor of promulgating strict standards with extended compliance dates, it is not appropriate for the agency to follow a different policy. The agency's cost analysis could have given some indication as to how far the standard should have been extended to reduce costs by a given amount, but it could not dictate whether extension was the right approach.

Role of analysis

It is clear that there was substantial doubt in both the program office and the policy office about the wisdom of going forward with a proposed rule in 1978. The strongest arguments voiced internally for the rule were that it was relatively inexpensive as NHTSA rules go (an argument that was undercut somewhat by its equally modest benefits) and that the agency had already sunk a lot of institutional resources into the endeavor. This latter argument was just the sort of argument that grates most strongly against the training and sensibilities of a regulatory analyst. To an analyst, the "do nothing" option should always be on the table and it should not be discounted by the program office's reluctance to admit that its resources were not well-spent in developing the rule. Given a relatively activist Administrator (Joan Claybrook had worked for Ralph Nader before joining NHTSA and she left NHTSA in 1981 to head Nader's Public Citizen), the program office prevailed in 1978 and 1981. But the policy office ultimately carried the day in 1982.

Both offices were troubled by the lack of hard statistics on actual deaths caused by poor visibility. Unlike EPA's assessment of the effects of lead and particulates, NHTSA usually does not have to employ speculative assumptions in predicting the benefits of its rules. It can usually assume that past experience, which is documented in accident reports and insurance files, will repeat itself unless something is changed. NHTSA can also contract for studies with dummies to assess the reduction in harm attributable to various options for standards. Because "hard" data are usually available to NHTSA, it tends to be more timid about relying upon assumptions and speculative models than agencies that do not have the luxury of basing decisions on real world statistics. NHTSA may be less comfortable about moving forward when its benefits projections rely upon speculative assumptions.

It is fair to conclude that the policy office was always less convinced than the program office of the virtue of an FDV rule,[37] but the analysts maintained that their role was primarily one of ensuring that the decision was based upon the best information available. Along with the agency lawyers, the analysts attempted to poke holes in the program office's rationales, hoping to firm them up against later attack in the public comment process. At the same time, the policy office seemed to adopt the position that if the agency could not quantify a standard's benefits, then it lacked authority to promulgate it. The lawyers disagreed emphatically with this legal assessment and questioned the value of quantification based on essentially arbitrary assumptions. The analysts' response ("if you don't like our numbers, come up with better ones") was not especially satisfying. If the lawyers were correct that NHTSA had authority to promulgate standards without quantifying benefits (and the Office of Chief Counsel was the institutional entity in NHTSA authorized to decide that question), then the analysts' insistence on quantified benefits was political as well as analytical. The analysts were in essence suggesting that the Administrator could not exercise her judgment to issue rules on the basis of anecdotal evidence and other evidence that did not lend itself well to their quantitative techniques.[38] Yet, the attorneys insisted that the statute did not so limit the Administrator. Thus, the analysts' training and weltanschauung tended away from promulgating new rules and from protecting values that were not easily quantified. This predilection was not lost on regulated industries and beneficiaries of regulation.

CHAPTER 6

Getting the bone out of processed meat: FSIS's mechanically separated meat standard

Modern food processing technology has passed the corner butcher by. The human butcher, however careful, inevitably leaves some edible tissue on the bone. Mechanical processes can break up the parts of the carcass remaining after hand deboning, grind them up, and force them at very high pressure through a small aperture to produce a pasty product that can be used in meat spreads, lunchmeat, and sausages. While this process maximizes the amount of edible tissue, it is impossible to keep very fine bone particles out of the final product. Mechanically separated meat (MSM) also differs from hand deboned meat in that it has a highly comminuted spreadable consistency, contains bone marrow and other minerals not common to hand deboned meat, and contains more fat and less protein than hand separated meat.[1] Because MSM can be substituted for hand deboned meat in many products, without detection by most consumers, marketing MSM as "meat" or "meat product" might run afoul of consumer expectations.

Although the consumer protection aspect of MSM might by itself justify regulatory intervention, MSM also raises a health concern. The additional calcium in MSM due to pulverized bone can be quite harmful to a small population of "calcium hyperabsorbers" who take up calcium at a much higher rate than the normal population. Because this sensitive subpopulation must monitor the calcium content of food very carefully, regulatory intervention may be necessary to limit the amount of calcium in food containing MSM or to ensure that calcium hyperabsorbers can easily avoid such products.[2] Finally, MSM's slightly higher fluoride content poses some risk of contributing to mottled teeth in children.[3]

Regulatory background

The federal government's efforts to regulate MSM began in early 1976 when the Administrator of the Food Safety and Inspection Service (FSIS) in the Department of Agriculture (USDA) published a notice of proposed rulemaking specifying numerical requirements for maximum calcium and fat and minimum protein acids in each of three categories of MSM.[4] The proposal specified the products that could contain MSM and required their labels to include the phrase: "Tissue from Ground Bone Added." After a district court remanded an interim Final Rule for being insufficiently protective,[5] FSIS appointed a panel of government experts to report on MSM's health effects.

Following the panel's report,[6] the agency published a new proposal in October 1977 and promulgated a Final Rule on June 20, 1978.[7] The Final Rule changed the name of MSM to "Mechanically Processed (Species [e.g. beef, pork, etc.]) Product." The agency felt that this term accurately conveyed the information that the substance had been processed mechanically and was a "meat product" rather than "meat." The agency further reasoned that because MSM was not an expected ingredient in a product, the phrase should be added to the product's name. In addition, FSIS required that labels of products containing MSM contain a qualifying statement – "Contains up to ____ % Powdered Bone" – in letters at least one-fourth the size of the product name. The rule also established a 14 percent minimum limitation for protein and a maximum limitation for fat. Additional limitations included a 0.75 percent limitation on the percentage of calcium in MSM and a 20 percent limitation on the amount of MSM in meat product.

The 1978 final regulations went into effect without challenge. Within nine months, however, the Pacific Coast Meat Association, a regional association of meat-packing and processing companies, petitioned USDA to amend the regulations. The petition alleged that although $30 million had been spent on mechanical deboning equipment, only a minuscule amount of MSM had been produced and sold under the 1978 regulations. Competing poultry products, manufactured by similar mechanical deboning processes, were doing very well under separate FSIS rules that did not require labeling and fat and protein restrictions. Admitting that no red meat food processors had actually attempted to market MSM under the restrictions of the 1978 regulations, the petition contended that the reason for the producers' failure to market MSM was the refusal of meat food processors (e.g., manufacturers of frankfurters and bologna) to take the risk of market rejection.[8] The agency denied the petition in May 1979.

The July 1981 Proposal

The meat packers and the American Meat Institute (AMI) next hired two contractors to provide additional information, and they once again petitioned the agency to amend the regulations on February 11, 1981.[9] The first contractor study was a market analysis prepared by Marketing Research Services, Inc. (MRS), which consisted of a qualitative survey of sixty-nine middle-income women concerning their preferences and perceptions with respect to the existing label for MSM.[10] It concluded that: (1) the term "Mechanically Processed Beef Product" was confusing and uninformative to consumers; (2) consumers generally reacted negatively to the reference to powdered bone in the label; (3) consumers probably would not purchase products labeled in accordance with the 1978 regulations; (4) the term "Mechanically Deboned (Species)" was "a more favorable and informative term"; and (5) most consumers believed that it was unnecessary to emphasize the mechanical deboning process if, in fact, the product was safe and nutritious and the product ingredient statement listed all ingredients. The report emphasized that it was "exploratory in nature" and cautioned that its findings should be viewed as "hypotheses which are not intended to be projectable to any larger population."[11]

The second study, prepared by Dr. J. Bruce Bullock and Dr. Clement E. Ward, associate professors in the Department of Agricultural Economics at Oklahoma State University,[12] focused on the broader economic effects of the standard. Assuming that MSM had no harmful effects and that consumers would readily accept MSM as an ingredient in processed meat products, the study concluded that the 1978 regulations generated social costs of $513 million per year and produced very small benefits for persons who must restrict calcium intake. The study further concluded that the minimum protein and maximum fat requirements would substantially restrict demand even if the labeling restrictions were eased. Finally, the study concluded that limiting MSM to no more than 20 percent of a product had no economic justification, because the rigors of the marketplace would weed out products that contained too much MSM.

Preproposal internal deliberations

It had never been the agency's intent to ban the mechanical separation technology; yet its 1978 regulations apparently had that effect.

Even the former Assistant Secretary who signed the 1978 regulations agreed that the regulations should be reworked.[13] The issue "had never really subsided" within the agency,[14] and when the rule made the "hit list" of the Bush Task Force on Regulatory Relief, it acquired a very high profile in the agency.[15] The Administrator of FSIS, in early February 1981, asked his special assistant to assemble a high-level work group to reexamine the 1978 regulations.[16] Normally, the Standards and Regulations Office (the program office) drafted FSIS rules with technical help from the Science Office, and the Policy and Program Planning Staff (the policy office) prepared a regulatory analysis of the draft proposal before both documents went to the Administrator's staff. For this high visibility rule, however, the Administrator ordered his Special Assistant to draft the rulemaking documents with the aid of a high-level work group or team.[17] The MSM team included the directors of the various departments within the agency and their deputies, and work group meetings often included the Administrator himself.

The policy office became involved in the rulemaking process at a very early stage. In early February 1981, the Administrator asked it to suggest some options for changing the 1978 rule without giving any strong indications of his preferences.[18] The Deputy Director of the office formed an ad hoc group consisting of himself, his staff assistant, and a staff member from another division in USDA. The Deputy Director made a site visit to a slaughter house that was equipped with mechanical deboning equipment. He learned that meat food processors would not purchase MSM from slaughter houses, because they thought that products containing MSM would not sell under the existing label restrictions. In addition, the Deputy Director consulted frequently with Bullock and Ward, the authors of the economic study cited in the meat packers' petition. He also persuaded two economists in the Economics Research Service (a separate agency within USDA) to develop a more sophisticated model, but its predictions varied only slightly from the Bullock and Ward predictions. After some additional data gathering from the existing agency files, the ad hoc regulatory analysis group drafted an options paper that set out the advantages and disadvantages from an economic and policy perspective of three options: (1) leave the 1978 rule in place; (2) delete the powdered bone denotation and eliminate the fat and protein requirements; and (3) repeal the rule and treat mechanically separated meat in the same manner as mechanically separated poultry.[19]

The Administrator's special team viewed its task even more narrowly than that assumed by the options paper. Its perceived goal was to come up with a "friendlier" label that would not discourage use of MSM. The team focused on "millions of little issues" that arose in pursuit of this larger goal. For example, the team did not seriously consider the broad option of eliminating the disparity between the agency's treatment of meat and poultry by amending both rules in a single regulatory package, despite the conclusion of at least one of the participants that this was the very best option. The Administrator had in fact considered and rejected this option prior to appointing the work group.[20] To treat the meat and poultry regulations equivalently would almost certainly have necessitated making the poultry regulations more stringent, an option that was perceived to be politically infeasible in early 1981, when a new administration had just come into office pledging to *reduce* the burden of regulation on industry. Moreover, expanding the rulemaking to include mechanically separated poultry would have made the rulemaking process a great deal more complicated and controversial. The Administrator was convinced that if the agency treated both rules simultaneously, it would fail at both efforts.[21]

The team spent most of its time considering narrow and specific suboptions within the parameters set by the tacit a priori assumption that the agency would change the rule in ways roughly paralleling the meat packers' suggestions. According to the Administrator's Special Assistant: "This was not a matter of options for doing regulations and economic analysis of those options. We had a set of regulations and were asking did it go farther than necessary."[22] With this narrow definition of the team's task, it is not likely that it would have considered broader policy options, even if team members had identified some.

Although most team meetings included a core of regular attendees, the Special Assistant called on expertise from all quarters of the agency as help was needed. Agency staffers "would tune in and tune out in terms of intensity of involvement as the issues changed."[23] Because the Administrator's office directed the rulemaking effort, no individual office assumed a possessive attitude about the rule. No team members felt confined to their own particular area of expertise. The lawyers and scientists, for example, read and critiqued the economic studies. The group achieved consensus on virtually all important issues after disagreements were debated at team meetings. The Administrator was often present at work group meetings, participated actively in the debates, and attempted to resolve disputes on the spot.[24]

The team quickly agreed that the word "product" in the name "Mechanically Processed (Species) Product" was redundant, because it could only be marketed as an ingredient of food that was already labeled "product." Upon discovering that the fat and protein limitations in many meat food products might also be redundant, the regulatory analyst suggested separating MSM into two categories: (1) MSM used in products already subject to fat limitations for which separate MSM limitations would be unnecessary; and (2) MSM for use in all other products. The group further learned from the technical staff that the relationship between fat and protein in MSM was such that so long as processors engaged in good quality control procedures, the fat limitations for products in the first group would automatically ensure that they would contain sufficient protein. Therefore, the team decided to eliminate both the fat and protein requirements for products in the first category. But the group rejected the industry contention that the market would ensure that products in the second category contained sufficient protein and not too much fat.

The team decided that it could encourage processors to develop better bone removing technologies if it allowed products to contain more than 20 percent MSM when the MSM contained less than the existing 0.75 percent calcium limitation. The team devised a sliding scale that would allow greater amounts of MSM in products depending on the calcium content of the MSM. This innovative "technology forcing" approach was apparently a product of the team's brainstorming sessions, rather than of any one office.[25]

The team also decided to eliminate the requirement that products containing MSM use the words "powdered bone" on the label. The group concluded from the market research survey that the requirement was affirmatively misleading to the average consumer. The regulatory analyst, however, was nervous about the quality of the focus group research in that survey,[26] noting that the study itself warned that its findings were "not intended to be projectable to any larger population."[27] He also warned other members of the team against building a strong case on research that could be challenged as being biased.

The group felt that calcium hyperabsorbers were sufficiently well attuned to their particular problem that they would always read the ingredients statements of foods that they consumed. Hence, a statement of calcium content in the ingredients statement would be sufficient to protect them without a second reference to powdered bone on the label. This conclusion directly contradicted the conclusion that the agency had reached in 1978.

It may be that there was no option that could have indicated the presence of powdered bone without creating the misleading impression that the product was unhealthy for ordinary consumers. But there is no indication that the group even tried to arrive at a compromise position that could inform, but not mislead. According to the Administrator's Special Assistant the job of the work group was not to find the label that most accurately informed consumers; it was to prevent labeling that misinformed consumers.[28] The agency's statute did not require a general nutrition labeling for meat products, and several attempts to amend the statute to require nutrition labeling had failed. Hence, the Special Assistant "never really regarded this [amended] rule as taking information away from consumers. It was simply a matter of reducing burdensomeness."[29]

After the draft regulation and accompanying Preliminary Regulatory Impact Analysis (PRIA) were forwarded to OMB, several agency employees attended a meeting with OMB staffers. The agency analysts convinced the OMB analyst that the fat and protein limitations would not affect the market for MSM. Despite lingering concerns that the rule would have a large adverse impact on ranchers, the OMB liaison allowed the proposal to go forward.[30] The OMB analyst did not recall offering any useful suggestions to the agency.[31]

After the meeting, the FSIS analyst became the unofficial liaison to OMB. Following an extended discussion, the analyst agreed to explain the proposal's distributional impacts more carefully in the PRIA. The analyst also assured the OMB staff that the meat industry had not dictated the list of options or the choices among the options. As a result of the OMB comments, the agency analyst spent a weekend redrafting the PRIA, but no substantive changes were made in the rule's basic approach.[32]

Not surprisingly, the July 1981 Proposal adopted the team's recommendations. It proposed to change the name of the product from "Mechanically Processed (Species) Product" to some other name that would "provide a less cumbersome and more meaningful description of its characteristics."[33] The agency announced that it was willing to accept arguments that a term that was technically correct might nevertheless be misleading or at least sufficiently confusing to dissuade consumers from trying products with which they might otherwise be satisfied.[34] The agency also proposed to delete the requirement that the name of a product containing MSM indicate its presence, leaving that function to the ingredient statement. The preamble to the proposal explained that in an era of rapidly changing food technology, it would not be "feasible" to change a product's name every time an unexpected and unique ingredient was added.[35] Citing the marketing research study, the agency suggested that consumers might think that the fact that the government required such prominent labeling indicated that there must be something wrong with MSM. It did not explain, however, how consumers would know that such prominence resulted from a government requirement.

Similarly, the requirement that the names of products containing MSM indicate the amount of powdered bone would be changed to a requirement that calcium content be listed as part of the nutrition labeling information or in the ingredient list. The agency argued that this approach "would more directly and effectively notify persons on calcium restricted diets . . . without the negative effects that the current language appears to have on the evaluation of such products by the general population."[36]

The proposal adopted the team's two category approach to fat and protein limitations and amended the agency's requirements for plant quality control to ensure that protein levels remained sufficiently high. Finally, the proposal adopted the team's sliding scale approach to use limitations, allowing greater amounts of MSM in meat food products to the extent that calcium amounts in MSM decreased.

The PRIA supporting the proposal relied almost exclusively on the industry-funded Bullock and Ward study.[37] The PRIA's calculations, therefore, reflected Bullock and Ward's assumptions that MSM was not harmful, that the ingredients statement would contain adequate information to allow calcium hyperabsorbers to avoid MSM, and that consumers would readily accept MSM in processed meat at prices that would provide an adequate incentive for its production and use.

Quoting the Bullock and Ward figures, the PRIA stated that had the proposed labeling changes been made in the 1978 regulations, the changes would have resulted in the production and consumption of an additional 85 million pounds of MSM during 1979 and a corresponding net economic gain of $110.7 million. The changes would have resulted in a transfer of wealth of $106 million from meat producers to processors and consumers, because beef and pork prices would decrease as MSM production increased. Because the agency found the food processing industry to be competitive, it predicted that most of the transfer would go to consumers.

Next, the PRIA assessed the benefits of deleting the fat and protein limitations. The PRIA adopted the Bullock and Ward hypothesis that changing the labeling requirements without changing the fat and protein requirements would only partially remove the existing impediments to full utilization of the industry's capacity to produce MSM. Adopting both of the proposed changes in 1979 would have resulted in an increase of over 350.4 million pounds of beef and pork over actual 1979 production and a corresponding net economic gain of $495 million. Wealth would again be transferred from producers to processors and consumers, with most of the transfer (approximately $493 million) going to consumers.

The only significant cost identified by the PRIA was the modest expense of changing a few labels. The document did not identify as a "cost" of the proposed rule the loss of information to consumers attributable to the label change.

Public reaction to the proposal was predictable. The Community Nutrition Institute and other consumer groups opposed virtually all of the changes, arguing that consumers had a "right" to information on the presence of MSM in products and that it should not be buried in the fine print of the ingredient statement. While industry commentators were by and large pleased with the direction of the proposed rule, many believed that the agency should have gone even farther. The most ambitious commentators urged the agency to deregulate MSM entirely and classify it as "meat," rather than as a "meat product." Agency analysts were surprised that the explicit prediction of a shift of millions of dollars from the cattle industry to consumers did not induce much comment from ranchers, who apparently believed that anything that encouraged consumption of beef was a good thing.[38] The public comments did not significantly change the agency's thinking, because most important arguments had already been aired in previous proceedings.

The Final Rule

The Administrator's special team evaluated the public comments and formulated the agency's final position. Responsibility for responding to particular comments was delegated to the office with the appropriate expertise. Again, the high-level team was able to reach consensus on all important issues. The agency commissioned a special study on the cholesterol content of MSM in light of suggestions from within the program office that the sliding scale approach might result in substantial increases of cholesterol in MSM-containing products. When the studies bore this prediction out, the team decided to abandon the proposed sliding scale and replace it with a flat requirement that no more than 20 percent of a product consist of MSM.

In addition, the regulatory analyst's office commissioned a review of the controversial marketing research survey by Arthur D. Little, Inc., and that review was quite critical. For example, the Little review of the transcripts of the focus group sessions noted a tendency of the questioner to lead the witness and pointed out that the order of exhibits was never rotated to minimize "order bias." Nevertheless, the regulatory analysts concluded that information from the report could be used "to illustrate the potentially confusing and misleading effects of the powdered bone content statement on the general public,"[39] and the group continued to rely fairly heavily upon the survey.

Interaction with OMB on the Final Rule was very brief. The OMB analyst had received a telephone call from the American Meat Institute urging OMB to hurry up its consideration of the rule so that the industry could begin processing MSM under the new regulations. OMB obliged and confined its comments to suggesting that the final RIA include a brief analysis of the no action option. The only element of disagreement concerned how to "pitch" the rule to the public. With the 1982 congressional elections near at hand, OMB wanted FSIS to portray the amended rule as one intended to benefit consumers, rather than as one intended to provide relief for the regulated industry. The FSIS analysts, however, refused to do this, and OMB did not press the point.

The Final Rule changed the name of MSM to "Mechanically Separated (Species)." Relying upon the marketing research survey, but acknowledging some of its weaknesses, the agency decided that consumers might be confused into thinking that the word "product" implied that it contained nonmeat components, such as ears, lips, and hooves. The preamble did not mention the fact that MSM did in fact contain some nonmeat components, such as bone and marrow. The agency also rejected the industry contention that MSM should be called "deboned," because MSM was not in fact deboned.

The Final Rule also rescinded the requirement that the presence of MSM and powdered bone be indicated in the name of the product containing it, arguing that an indication of the presence of MSM and extra calcium in the ingredient statement would suffice. The preamble noted that the ingredient statement "is the very place that consumers should look, not ignore, if they are interested in the contents of the foods they purchase. . . . "[40] Consumers who wanted to avoid or to pay less for products containing MSM could do so by examining the ingredient statement. The agency thus allowed the sale of products containing MSM without any indication that they contained powdered bone other than the reference to "Mechanically Separated (Species)" in the ingredient statement.

The Final Rule adhered to the proposed two-category approach to fat and protein content requirements. Relying upon the Bullock and Ward study and comments at the hearing, the preamble concluded that eliminating all fat and protein restrictions for MSM to be used in products already subject to fat limitations would "expand food supplies significantly by taking advantage of the full range of materials available for mechanical deboning. . . . "[41] The agency rejected industry contentions that fat and protein restrictions should also be eliminated entirely, citing a thirty-year-old experience with watered down hot dogs as an example of the failure of the market to ensure appropriate fat limitations.

Finally, FSIS withdrew its proposed sliding scale approach to use limitations, finding that it might result in significant unexpected increases of cholesterol in such products. Therefore, for reasons unrelated to the merits of the sliding scale approach, this innovative technology-inducing technique had to be abandoned.

The Final Regulatory Impact Analysis (FRIA) accompanying the Final Rule tracked the PRIA closely, and stated that its conclusions were "substantially the same as those" of the PRIA.[42] At OMB's behest, the FRIA considered the additional option of rescinding the 1978 rules altogether, but found that this would violate the agency's statutory obligation to prevent adulteration and misbranding. Like the PRIA, the FRIA did not attempt to quantify the loss of information to consumers resulting from amending the 1978 regulations as a cost of the amendments. Consequently the cost of the amended regulations ($1.9 million) was calculated to be relatively trivial compared to the projected benefits ($495 million).

Not surprisingly, the Community Nutrition Institute was disappointed with the revisions to the 1978 rules, and it challenged the agency in the District of Columbia Circuit Court of Appeals.[43] That court, in an opinion written by future Justice Antonin Scalia, upheld the agency in all respects. Judge Scalia observed tongue in cheek that the case "afford[ed] a rare opportunity to explore simultaneously both parts of Bismarck's aphorism that 'No man should see how laws or sausages are made'."[44] The court found no fault with the agency's reliance on the MRS consumer study, and it seemed to place the burden on consumers to produce a survey that would indicate that the term "Mechanically Separated (Species)" was affirmatively misleading. The court relied heavily on the fact that the presence of mechanically separated meat was indicated in the ingredient statement. Thus, after a six-year battle, the industry was finally allowed to place mechanically separated meat on the grocery shelves.

The agency's attempt to help the industry expand the market for MSM, however, failed in the marketplace. The vast market for MSM that the RIA had promised did not, in fact, materialize. Apparently food processors were still reluctant to put MSM in meat products as long as its presence was indicated anywhere on the label, even if only in the ingredients statement. In November 1986, several sausage companies petitioned FSIS to amend the 1982 rule to allow companies to delete all reference to MSM in the ingredients statements so long as the calcium content of the product was stated on the label as part of the nutrition information and so long as MSM constituted no more than 10 percent of the livestock and poultry product portion of the meat food product. In a by now familiar refrain, the petitioners asserted that no meat processor was commercially producing MSM because of "unwarranted negative connotations of the term Mechanically Separated (Species) which . . . would cause consumers to refrain from purchasing such products."[45]

FSIS published the petition in the *Federal Register* on April 3, 1987 and solicited public comments. The agency received 134 written comments: 95 from consumers, 20 from industry representatives, 9 from trade associations, 1 from a consumer advocacy group, and the rest from various other sources. Most of the comments argued that the same rules should apply to MSM as applied to mechanically separated poultry. Thus, the petition effectively combined the two issues that the Administrator of FSIS was reluctant to combine in the early 1980s.

The agency agreed with the petitioners that MSM was as safe and wholesome as the species from which it was derived, that granting the petition would result in more food being made available, and that the small amount of calcium contributed to a meat food product by MSM would benefit American diets, particularly diets of women. Most of the consumers, however, argued that they should at least be permitted to know what products contained MSM, so that they could avoid purchasing those products. FSIS tersely responded that the labeling scheme outlined in the petition was "neither false nor misleading" and therefore was acceptable to the agency. On September 9, 1988, FSIS published a proposed rule that deleted the requirement that the presence of MSM in meat food products be included in the ingredients statement.

Interestingly, OMB vehemently objected to the proposed rule on the ground that it would deprive consumers of information. The Director of the Office of Information and Regulatory Affairs wrote to FSIS: "If one accepts the assertion that some consumers would be reluctant to purchase a product that they know to contain [MSM], why should this information be omitted from the label?"[46] When USDA went ahead with the rule despite OMB's objections, OMB Director James Miller said that he would complain to Vice-President Bush that FSIS had violated Executive Order 12,291 by promulgating the rule over OMB's objection. Miller phoned Secretary of Agriculture Lyng personally to object that the department ignored OMB's recommendation to reconsider the rule.[47] Although FSIS did not withdraw the proposal, it has failed to finalize it. The outcome of this lengthy proceeding is still uncertain.

Evaluation and conclusions

Type and quality of analysis

The regulatory analysis documents for the MSM proceeding were the agency's first full-scale attempts to meet the cost-benefit requirements of Executive Order 12,291. They were, however, written in the absence of any data about how fully informed consumers in the real world would react to MSM. The documents therefore depended heavily upon a marketing research survey that was filled with indications of bias. For example, the fact that the survey's Washington, D.C. focus session screened out present and former members of the Virginia Citizens Consumer Council[48] suggested a bias against well-informed consumers. More importantly, the questions seemed carefully designed to elicit particular responses to questions that uniquely characterized the positions of the petitioners. For example, focus group members were asked if a label subject to the 1978 restrictions was "misleading," but were asked if the proposed industry substitute was "confusing." Yet, despite considerable doubts on the part of its analysts, the agency concluded that the survey constituted "substantial new evidence" sufficient to warrant reexamining the 1978 regulations.

The RIAs also relied heavily on an unpublished study by two academic economists undertaken at the behest of one of the industry petitioners. This subjected the agency to the justifiable criticism that it had not undertaken an independent examination of the economic issues. The agency's cost calculations depended upon the assumption that no consumers would find any differences in taste or texture of products containing MSM that would lead them to prefer products that did not contain MSM. There was some support in the agency files for this proposition, but it had not been tested in the real world. Indeed, one agency employee who had sampled products containing MSM was of the opinion that such products acquired a "gritty" texture that would be noticeable to an average consumer.[49]

The agency apparently made the much less explicit further assumption that the choices of consumers who could not physically distinguish between products with and without MSM would not be affected by the knowledge that products containing MSM also contained powdered bone. The absence of detectable health effects alone cannot support this assumption. For example, consumers might not trust the agency's health effects determination. Consumers might for reasons known only to themselves decide to pay a few more cents per pound for alternatives that did not contain bone, however irrational that might have appeared to FSIS analysts. Indeed, it was almost certainly the fear that consumers would shun products containing MSM that caused producers to refrain from attempting to market products containing MSM under the 1978 and 1982 labeling requirements. The essence of a free market is that consumers are free to make informed choices with a minimum of government supervision. Yet, by eliminating any indication of the presence of powdered bone from the label of products containing MSM, the work group proposed to take information away from consumers, information that by all accounts was crucial to actual consumer choice.

An independent review of the marketing research survey by an independent contractor concluded that "a sizeable minority [of the focus group participants] felt that consumers had a right to know about the powdered bone and felt that since many consumers are not ingredient readers, this information should be on the front of the package."[50] If many consumers are of the opinion that they have a "right" to powdered bone indications on the label, then surely they would consider themselves harmed by a regulation that took this "right" away from them. Therefore, taking away that information may have constituted a significant cost to consumers. Three officials from FSIS (including the primary draftsman of the PRIA) and the OMB representative who had responsibility for reviewing the rule acknowledged that the regulation would impose this cost on consumers.[51] They also acknowledged that no one on the team or in OMB initially identified this as a cost of the amended regulation.[52] In reviewing the agency's response to the 1986 petition, however, OMB recognized this significant cost to consumers, but its efforts to forestall publication of the proposed rule failed. Perhaps because it tracked so closely the industry-sponsored Bullock and Ward study, the PRIA simply missed an important cost of amending the rule. The RIAs therefore gave the decisionmaker and the public a very narrow view of the costs and benefits of the amendments, a view that made the proposed changes appear to be the obvious course.

On the positive side, the RIA did a very fine job of identifying the distributional effects of the revisions, stating clearly that virtually all of the monetary benefits of amending the rule would fall on consumers at the expense of meat producers. Cattle ranchers faced reduced prices for their herds because more meat could be extracted from each animal. The MSM RIAs were rare in the explicitness with which they described this redistributional effect.

Impediments to analysis

Three impediments to the preparation and use of analysis stand out in the MSM experience. First, FSIS depended very heavily upon industry-financed cost studies. This apparent bias provided ammunition to opponents of the new rule. Second, FSIS lacked data on consumer preferences with respect to the presence of powdered bone in products containing MSM. The industry-financed marketing research survey was seriously flawed, but it was the only nonanecdotal evidence available to the agency. Because of its quasi-objectivity, the agency tended to rely too heavily upon its tentative conclusions and to ignore its self-acknowledged limitations. Although FSIS cannot be faulted for using the survey, it could have explained with greater clarity the study's limitations and the uncertainties that plagued the agency's confident predictions that the 1978 requirements would have misled consumers. Finally, the agency analysts may have been blinkered by a relatively narrow reading of the agency's statutory mandate, which, in the view of some agency officials, precluded the agency from requiring consumer information for reasons other than safety. In any event, the statute clearly did not preclude agency analysts from considering the repeal of a consumer information requirement as a "cost" to society.

Role of analysis

The PRIA itself was not at all useful to the members of the team that was charged with drafting the rule, because the document did not exist prior to the important decisionmaking meetings.[53] The PRIA was meant to be an explanation for the decisions that the agency had already reached. FSIS did not use the RIA process as a tool for structuring the decisionmaking process; rather, it was primarily viewed as a vehicle for forcing lower-level employees to give reasons and analyses for their recommended actions.

Even though the formal document did not play a large role, the personnel who prepared the document were important institutional players. The policy office was intimately involved in agency deliberations about the MSM rule. Its director, a member of the Administrator's special team, participated frequently. Although the agency analysts apparently did not originate the innovative, but ultimately abandoned, sliding scale option, the idea of categorizing MSM into MSM for use in products already subject to fat limitations and MSM for other purposes was the brainchild of the policy office.[54] That office did not, however, play a key role in identifying the other options that the agency considered. The realistic options had been around for quite a while, and they were apparent to all team members without the help of the regulatory analysts.

The analysts were not often major participants at the meetings. The program office representative recalled that in the "master meetings" in the Administrator's office, where the most important issues were discussed, the analysts took a passive role, sitting back on a couch rather than around the table with the other work group members. Their substantial misgivings about relying heavily upon the marketing research survey were essentially ignored as the agency rulemaking documents made frequent references to that study at critical junctures with only passing references to the analysts' doubts. The head of the policy office recalled that "in the end . . . there was no substantive change that reflected our concerns about the quality of the marketing research."[55] Yet, despite its failure to exert a strong influence on the direction of the MSM proceeding, the experience with the MSM rule was in the opinion of several agency employees a strong factor in convincing the Administrator to expand the regulatory analysis office and to include it on a more regular basis in agency rulemaking activities.[56]

CHAPTER 7

Getting information into hazardous workplaces: OSHA's hazard identification regulations

For many decades worker exposure to toxic substances in the workplace has taken a heavy toll. Despite the efforts of the Occupational Safety and Health Administration (OSHA) to force employers to control workplace exposure to toxic chemicals, workers still played a guinea pig role for the rest of society. As science yielded more information about chemical risks, workers began to insist that they be apprised of the risks they faced at work.

Without information about risks, workers lack the freedom to make informed career choices. They also undervalue their services in wage negotiations, because they fail to attach a risk premium to unsafe workplaces.[1] On the other hand, evaluating and communicating risks is quite expensive, and employers are naturally reluctant to spend money informing employees when the predictable consequence will be attempts by employees to bid up wages.

Regulatory background

In 1974, the National Institute for Occupational Safety and Health (OSHA's sister agency in the Department of Health and Human Services) published a "criteria document" urging OSHA to promulgate a hazard communication standard.[2] After an OSHA-appointed advisory committee made similar recommendations, Ralph Nader's Health Research Group in 1975 petitioned the agency to issue a standard. Two years later, OSHA published an Advance Notice of Proposed Rulemaking (ANPR) discussing some of the important issues and soliciting public comment on whether it should mandate risk communication.[3] After spending four more years studying the responses to the ANPR, OSHA published a Notice of Proposed Rulemaking for a generic hazard identification standard as one of the many "midnight regulations" issued in the waning moments of the Carter Administration.

The 1981 Proposal was applicable only to employers in the manufacturing sector; other sectors, such as agriculture and construction, were exempted. Employers within the manufacturing sector

89

were further divided into "manufacturers" of chemicals and "industrial users." A single employer could, of course, be a manufacturer of one chemical and an industrial user of another at the same time. The proposal limited the rule to "hazardous" chemicals and mixtures, but it covered a broad range of health hazards, including physical hazards, acute health hazards and chronic health hazards. The manufacturer of a chemical substance was required to assemble existing scientific data from specified sources on the hazards of its chemicals, but it was not required to undertake additional tests of its own. Similarly, manufacturers were obliged to provide downstream users with available Material Safety Data Sheets (MSDSs), setting out the material health effects of chemicals, but the proposed rule did not specify any particular format or content for the MSDS.

Industrial users of hazardous chemicals had to label containers and pipes with the common name of the hazardous substance contained therein and to give appropriate warnings. A lengthy appendix to the proposal specified detailed elements of hazard warnings. Employers were also required to make the MSDSs available to employees upon request, but they had no obligation to make them generally available in the workplace. Worried about the political viability of a rule that might cost more than $1 billion,[4] the staff concluded that adding a training program to the preceding items would be too expensive.[5]

The March 1982 Proposal

The Reagan Administration did not feel bound by the last-minute activities of the outgoing administration, and OSHA quickly withdrew the notice of proposed rulemaking "for further consideration of regulatory alternatives" only one month after it was issued.[6] The labor unions were enraged by the withdrawal, accusing the Reagan Administration of caving in to industry for political reasons.[7] Shifting their attention away from Washington, D.C., the unions persuaded several state legislatures to enact "worker-right-to-know" laws.[8] The effort proved quite successful and in some cases state and local requirements were more burdensome than the proposed OSHA standard. Even worse for the chemical industry, many state and local requirements were inconsistent with one another. In a surprising shift in strategy the industry began to pressure OSHA to promulgate a new standard that would preempt state and local laws.[9]

The January 1981 Proposal had been the product of a team composed of the Deputy to the head of OSHA, three or four high-level career staffers and an academic consultant. The career staffers from the previous team formed the nucleus for the team that wrote the Reagan Administration's March 1982 Proposal. The chairperson of the team was a young career staffer in the Health Standards Directorate (the program office). The other two primary participants were an attorney from the Office of the Solicitor and an analyst from the Policy Directorate (the policy office). Upper-level management instructed the team to consider fresh alternatives within the broad parameters that the rule would continue to take a generic approach and that it would be limited to the manufacturing sector. The team's ultimate goal was to come up with a more cost-effective rule.[10] Upper-level political appointees also defined the broad policy contours of the effort: (1) performance-oriented approaches were to be favored over specific commands; and (2) the cost of the new proposal could not exceed that of the Carter Administration proposal. Otherwise, the team was allowed to go about its business with little upper-level intervention.

Although each team member had individual responsibilities, the quality of the final product was a joint responsibility, and no member was afraid to invade the "turf" of others. The program office technical staff, with some input from the agency's enforcement staff, suggested a number of alternatives. The regulatory analyst "costed out" these options along with several industry-suggested alternatives. The analyst also derived an innovative list of ten broad alternatives by mixing combinations of more and less stringent requirements for five or six basic regulatory functions. This list and the cost factors associated with it became the heart of the PRIA for the rule.

The team attempted to reach consensus on every important issue before taking a product to upper-level decisionmakers, and on nearly all important issues they were successful.[11] Members of the team would talk out the inevitable disputes that arose over the quality of information, the validity of assumptions, and the direction that the rule should take.[12] Occasionally, when the team encountered a particularly policy-laden issue and the available information did not dictate a particular result, a meeting would be scheduled with upper-level decisionmakers for a policy call.[13] Frequently, the team drafted issue papers in advance of these meetings. Because of this frequent high-level involvement, the team's final proposal was accepted by upper-level decisionmakers with few changes.

After the head of OSHA signed-off on the proposal, it went to the Department of Labor's Policy Review Coordinating Committee

(PRCC) for further review, and the RIA went to the Departmental Office of Policy for review. The PRCC suggested no significant changes. A senior economist in the Office of Policy went over the RIA in detail and rewrote the summary chapter, but could offer little advice on how to reduce its reliance on highly debatable assumptions.[14]

Although the March 1982 Proposal[15] departed in some important regards from the Carter Administration's proposal, they shared many basic similarities. Both accepted the fundamental tenet that workers had a right to be informed about the nature of workplace hazards, and both applied only to the manufacturing sector. But the March 1982 Proposal reflected the Reagan Administration's preference for the performance-oriented approach. Instead of specifying with particularity the substances that it deemed hazardous, the March 1982 Proposal gave employers a great deal of discretion to find that chemicals in their workplaces were or were not hazardous by considering "scientifically well-established evidence."[16] Although a brief Appendix suggested sources that manufacturers might consult, the proposal did not provide an explicit vehicle for challenging an employer's hazard determination.[17] The proposal required employers to label all containers (but not pipes) with labels displaying the "identity" of the substances contained therein, and identity was defined to mean "any chemical or common name." The proposal also required labels to contain warnings, but defined the term "hazard warning" very broadly to include "any words, pictures, symbols, or combination thereof which convey the hazards of the chemical(s) in the container."[18]

The 1982 Proposal went beyond the 1981 Proposal in requiring manufacturers to obtain or develop Material Safety Data Sheets (MSDSs) for each hazardous product that they produced or used. The proposal listed specific items that were to be included on every MSDS. The manufacturer would be required to search the relevant literature for information to meet each of the specific criteria, but if the search did not reveal such information, the manufacturer would not have to produce such information itself. MSDSs had to be updated with each new shipment. Employers were required to maintain copies of current MSDSs in the workplace and to ensure that they were readily accessible. The 1982 Proposal thus made the MSDS, rather than the label, the primary vehicle for conveying information to workers.

Perhaps the greatest innovation of the 1982 Proposal was its requirement that employers undertake training programs. The rule required employers to provide employees with information and training on hazardous chemicals "at the time of their initial assignment, and whenever a new hazardous chemical is introduced into the workplace." In addition to information about the requirements of the hazard communication regulation and the location and availability of the list of hazardous chemicals and the MSDSs, the training efforts were to include at least: (1) ways to detect the presence or release of a hazardous chemical in the workplace; (2) the hazards of the chemicals in the workplace; and (3) measures that employees could take to protect themselves from the hazards.[19]

The agency published a 381-page Draft Regulatory Impact Analysis and Regulatory Flexibility Analysis (DRIA) to accompany the 1982 Proposal. The document optimistically opened with the observation that informing workers would be a market-based approach to reducing workplace risks that could substitute for the agency's previous case-by-case regulation of individual industrial chemicals.[20] After recounting the basic structure of the Carter Administration proposal, the DRIA proceeded to trash it, voicing serious concerns about the "excessive costs and paperwork burdens" that it would have imposed. Other objectionable aspects included its specification orientation, the inflexibility of its labeling provisions, and "its focus on *identification* of chemicals rather than on *communicating* hazards to employees and employers."[21] According to the DRIA, the 1982 Proposal would reduce the initial implementation costs by 78 to 81 percent, from $2.6 billion (or $185 per employee) to $582 million (or $41 per employee). Total annual costs would be reduced from $1.25 billion (or $89 per employee) to $227.92 million (or $16 per employee). The DRIA attributed this cost savings to changes in key areas which "substantially improve its cost-effectiveness."[22]

The DRIA also identified several benefits of the 1982 Proposal. The proposal would increase employee awareness, which would increase the use of personal protective devices, improve work practices, and inspire other precautionary measures. Improved hazard communication would result in early job transfers and early treatment of chronic diseases, thereby lowering future health care costs and reducing disability and social security payments. Increased employer knowledge of workplace risks would result in more "safety enhancing investments – in new control technology, process redesign and perhaps most importantly, in product substitution." The DRIA also postulated that improved information would lead to "better matches between the risk preferences of workers and true job risks, thus improving labor market allocation."[23]

Chapter 2 of the DRIA described a simple model for evaluating how employees use hazard information to reduce workplace risks. Recognizing that all available information sources severely underreported workplace illnesses and injuries, the agency suggested an "underreporting factor" of fifty. This yielded an estimate of 8.5 million annual workdays lost due to chemically induced illnesses. For comparison, the agency also used an underreporting factor of ten, thereby yielding 1.8 million lost days.[24] Agency analysts emphasized that no one knew what the real underreporting factor really was.[25]

Chapter 3 of the DRIA examined the benefits of ten broad alternative standards. Citing workplace accident studies, OSHA concluded that "worker safety may be enhanced substantially through increased care."[26] Without attempting to quantify the proportion of workers in covered industries that would avoid exposure to chemicals, the agency simply assumed that a hazard communication program would reduce chemically induced injuries and illnesses by 1 percent per year throughout a twenty-year period, and then stabilize at 20 percent. These numbers originated in informal brainstorming sessions among team members in the summer of 1980.[27] According to an agency analyst, it was based on a "what if" scenario.[28] According to another participant, it was "cooked up by the policy people."[29] Using the total number of workplace-induced illnesses and injuries estimated in Chapter 2, the agency calculated (under the "intermediate" assumption that workplace injuries are underreported by a factor of ten) the reduction in chemical-related risk injuries and illnesses. The DRIA then monetized these benefits using the "human capital" approach to valuing human life.

Recognizing that the human capital approach was not the only permissible approach to valuing risks, the DRIA also very briefly examined the "willingness-to-pay" approach. Relying exclusively upon a study by Professor W. Kip Viscusi of Duke University, the DRIA used a figure of $30,000 per lost workday as the measure of the average employee's willingness to pay to avoid losing a workday. Because the DRIA's calculated cost for a lost workday avoided was only $14,000, the standard appeared to be justified under the willingness-to-pay approach.

These extremely rough calculations depended heavily on two striking assumptions: (1) worker injuries are currently underreported by a factor of 10; and (2) a hazard identification standard will reduce chemically caused injuries and illnesses by one percent per year for twenty years. The DRIA cited no hard evidence to support either assumption. Indeed, the calculations were of such a gross nature that the agency did not even attempt to distinguish among the ten regulatory alternatives with respect to the workplace illness that would be avoided.

The above calculations did not include any estimate of the workplace cancers that might be avoided as a result of the standard, because reports of workplace deaths and injuries rarely included cancers. To account for reduced workplace cancers the DRIA estimated the annual value of medical resources devoted to cancer treatment and adjusted that figure to account for the fraction of cancers that were estimated to be work-related. Unfortunately, estimates of work-related cancers were extremely controversial, ranging from 1 percent to 40 percent. Without explaining why, the DRIA adopted a conservative range of 5 to 20 percent. Next, the agency calculated that the percentage of total exposures to workplace carcinogens that occurred in the manufacturing sector was approximately 48.4 percent. This yielded annual values for reduced medical costs of all cancers in the manufacturing sector of $175.4 million, $350.8 million, or $701.6 million respectively, corresponding to the assumptions that 5, 10, and 20 percent of all cancers were work-related. Similar calculations were employed to estimate production losses due to premature deaths of $459.5, $919.0, and $11,838.1 million. Finally, the DRIA assumed that a hazard identification standard would reduce cancer cases by 2 percent in 10 years and by an additional 2 percent per year until year 20, at which time the effect would stabilize at 20 percent. The DRIA did not attempt to place a dollar value on the deaths due to cancer beyond the lost production costs. The results of all of these calculations are displayed in Table 7.1.

In addition to health and increased productivity benefits, OSHA believed that the standard would benefit employers by preempting inconsistent state laws.[30] For example, Massachusetts required that warning labels be composed of red ink on a white background, but Oregon required fluorescent orange on a contrasting background. The quantitative analysis used the following precise-looking formula:

$C = (TW) (A) (B)$

where:

C = cost of providing and filing sheets and label containers

T = chemical shipments (in tons)

W = number of state and local jurisdictions affected

A = average cost per transaction

B = average number of transactions per ton

Table 7.1. *Summary of some of the monetizable benefits – discounted and undiscounted 1980 (in millions of dollars)*

	Undiscounted benefits			Present discounted value[a]	
Type of benefit	1st year	20th year	40th year	20-year stream	40-year stream
Nonlost workday cases					
Lost production	0.03	1.36	3.60	2.92	5.48
First-aid costs	0.02	1.00	2.80	2.20	4.20
Lost workday cases					
Lost production	0.61	30.69	81.42	66.01	124.02
Medical costs	0.11	5.42	14.39	11.66	21.91
Disabling illness					
Lost production	13.40	667.80	1,798.30	1,357.80	2,739.00
Cancer illness					
Lost production	—	487.70	1,293.90	751.70	1,673.60
Medical costs	—	186.20	493.90	286.90	638.80
Turnover costs	0.04	2.32	6.16	5.00	9.39
Chemical fire costs	1.00	1.80	3.30	10.80	13.70
Total	15.21	1,384.29	3,697.77	2,494.99	5,230.10

[a]A discount rate of 10% is used.
Source: U.S. Department of Labor, Occupational Safety and Health Administration, Office of Regulatory Analysis.

OSHA calculated W by assuming that shipments traveling less than 200 miles stayed in one state, shipments of 200 to 500 miles crossed one state line, and shipments of greater than 500 miles crossed two state lines. Department of Transportation data yielded the percentage of all shipments in each category.

The DRIA then calculated A (the average cost per transaction) by adding its estimate of the total cost of information sheets and labeling and dividing by its estimate of the number of containers containing hazardous materials shipped in the manufacturing sector. OSHA next estimated the cost of complying with information and labeling requirements under various assumptions about the number of labels or information sheets (transactions) that would be required per ton of material. An assumption of one hundred transactions per ton yielded a forty-year discounted cost of complying with state and local information and labeling requirements of $15.275 billion; for 200 transactions per ton the cost was $30.549 billion; and for 300 transactions per ton the cost was $45.824 billion.

Finally, the DRIA also noted that, unlike any of the proposed OSHA options, some state laws required testing of chemical substances. Assuming that a chemical manufacturer was required to test only 1 percent for just acute hazards, state and local regulation would yield additional costs of $1.041 billion.

The agency's state preemption analysis was highly debatable. First, it failed to consider the benefits to workers of the more stringent state standards that would be replaced by the federal standard. Second, the DRIA simply assumed that state requirements would be so utterly inconsistent as to require label changes whenever an item crossed state borders. Third, the analysis assumed that state enforcement officials would be entirely inflexible. Finally, the DRIA assessment rested on the unarticulated assumption that no state standard could be more effective than the federal standard. Clearly, the state legislatures and agencies that imposed additional requirements thought that they would produce benefits that would outweigh the additional costs. OSHA apparently disagreed.

Chapter 4 of the DRIA examined the costs of complying with ten alternative proposed standards. For the most part, the agency relied on best estimates for the costs of preparing MSDSs, labeling containers, conducting training sessions, hiring a health and safety officer, and educating and training workers. Although these estimates were necessarily soft, OSHA had a good deal more confidence that they were in the right ball park than it had with respect to the benefits analyses. The red herring in the cost calculations was the fact that OSHA did not know the extent to which companies were already in compliance with the proposed requirements. Therefore, the DRIA calculated the costs based on estimates ranging from zero to 90 percent compliance, and selected 60 percent as a reasonable estimate. The DRIA's best estimate of the direct forty-year economic costs of the alternatives ranged from $3.2 billion to $33.7 billion, depending upon the initial assumptions.

Because OSHA's proposal was the first major new regulation of the Reagan Administration, it precipitated a two-month tug-of-war between the agency and OMB before the Bush Task Force on Regulatory Relief. OMB staffers drafted a fourteen-page "Administratively Confidential" memorandum to the task force "in the spirit of lively internal debate."[31] A summary offered three principle arguments against OSHA's proposal: (1) there was "no direct evidence of a need for universal labeling of chemicals" and "much indirect evidence that it is not needed"; (2) hazard identification was "not an appropriate area for federal preemption of state and local regulation"; and (3) "the potential costs of the proposal far exceed the benefits."[32] OMB disputed OSHA's characterization of the proposal as "largely performance-oriented," arguing instead that it was "in fact highly prescriptive and detailed in the obligations that it imposed on manufacturers."[33] OMB concluded that OSHA was "proposing a very costly and comprehensive regulatory scheme to address a problem whose extent is a matter of speculation rather than concrete evidence."[34]

OMB called OSHA's one-percent-per-year-for-20-years projection "completely arbitrary" and "implausibly high."[35] OMB's equally arbitrary prediction was that the standard might result in a 5 percent overall reduction in workplace illnesses.[36] OMB also challenged OSHA's assumption that workplace disease and injury was underreported by a factor of ten. OMB maintained that OSHA's analysis otherwise sufficiently accounted for any underreporting, and OSHA should therefore use no underreporting factor. OMB therefore reduced OSHA's estimate from $156 million to $16 million. OSHA's additional estimate that 25 percent of all chronic occupational illnesses were due to chemical exposure was called "quite arbitrary." OMB substituted its estimate of 2.5 percent, thus reducing OSHA's estimate from $2.7 billion to $270 million. Finally, OMB challenged OSHA's estimate for the number of occupationally induced cancers as "wildly optimistic."[37] OMB relied on a study estimating that only 4 percent of all cancers were workplace related. Finding that three-quarters of those were already taken care of by existing EPA and OSHA regulations, OMB estimated that at most 1 percent of cancers would be affected by the hazard identification standard. Because OSHA's best estimate was 10 percent, OMB reduced OSHA's prediction from $2.3 billion to $230 million. For the same reasons, OSHA estimates for losses due to employee turnover were also reduced by a factor of ten. By the time OMB's analysts had finished, OSHA's benefits estimates had dropped from $5.2 billion to $65 million, which was only 2.5 percent of the estimated $2.6 billion in compliance costs.

OSHA responded in kind. According to OSHA, OMB's tiny benefits estimates "flow[ed] directly from misinterpretation of the OSHA methodology and data sources."[38] OSHA contended that its benefits analysis "matches up the available data sources with reasonable, but consistently *conservative* assumptions in developing estimates in order to leave little doubt as to the validity of the 'bottom line' conclusion," and it noted that the DRIA analyzed all of the assumptions and possible sources of data error. OSHA accused OMB of relying upon "shaky arithmetic and faulty assumptions."[39] A point-by-point rebuttal of OMB's critique challenged the factual basis for OMB's substituted assumptions and questioned the technical competence of OMB's assessment of the scientific evidence.

After the task force failed to resolve the dispute,[40] OSHA contracted with a prominent academic economist, W. Kip Viscusi, to evaluate the RIA and OMB's critique and to prepare his own estimate of the standard's benefits. OSHA analysts picked Viscusi because he was a "good American Enterprise Institute-type economist" and because he had previously expressed views favoring informational solutions as an alternative to command and control regulation.[41]

Viscusi's report took pains to find some merit in the positions of both agencies. He correctly observed that the crux of the OSHA–OMB debate was over the "magnitudes of the key parameters": (1) the effectiveness of hazard communication in reducing job risks; and (2) the overall level of health risks that are to be reduced.[42] Noting that the "novelty" of the hazard communication approach "by its very nature makes the benefits necessarily speculative,"[43] he found it "inappropriate to criticize a relatively new approach to job safety as being based on speculation since all new approaches of this kind could be subjected to similar criticism."[44] Viscusi admitted that his own judgments as to the magnitude of these two critical parameters was likewise "necessarily quite subjective," but argued that the "inability to resolve these substantive issues is an inherent problem whenever one is dealing with the regulation of dimly understood health risks."[45] Viscusi was also perplexed by OMB's apparent position that "workers will not respond at all to hazard information."[46]

The primary difficulty that Viscusi had with OSHA's "one-percent-per-year-for-20-years" assumption was that he did not think that it would take twenty years for the standard to have this effect. Viscusi suggested that the standard would have an immediate and permanent effect of a 10 percent reduction annually, which would have a comparable overall impact on the benefits estimation as OSHA's assumption for all effects other than cancer. On the issue of underreporting, Viscusi found that OSHA's assumptions "do not seem clearly out of line." Likewise, Viscusi believed that OSHA was "on relatively solid ground" in imputing a fairly substantial portion of chronic and disabling illnesses to the workplace. Noting the great uncertainty surrounding calculations about workplace-induced cancer, Viscusi believed that either OSHA's 5 percent or OMB's 1 percent estimates were both quite reasonable. He adopted a conservative 2 percent estimate in his calculations.[47]

For the most part, Viscusi sided with OSHA on the big disputes with OMB, but adopted assumptions that were somewhere in between those of the two agencies. On the critical question of the value of a lost workday, Viscusi applied the "willingness to pay" test. From previous work, Viscusi had derived that the average worker was willing to pay $30,000 to avoid a lost workday. Using this number and the other assumptions, Viscusi arrived at a bottom line figure of $2.6 billion for the standard's benefits, compared with OSHA's $5.2 billion figure and OMB's $65 million estimate.[48] Perhaps not so coincidentally, Viscusi's figure just about equaled OSHA's cost estimate of $2.6 billion.

Ultimately, Vice-President Bush sided with OSHA, and the proposal went out without significant change. There are several possible explanations for the Vice-President's decision. First, it is possible that after reading Viscusi's report the Vice-President was persuaded that OSHA was right on the merits. A prominent economist with conservative credentials took much of the wind out of OMB's sails by writing an "independent" analysis that sided to a large extent with OSHA. Because OMB's institutional role was ostensibly only to ensure that the RIA was consistent with the requirements of the Executive Order, the independent assessment significantly reduced OMB's leverage in the internal policy debates. If true, this explanation suggests that OMB's critique of OSHA's DRIA was an ideologically motivated "shot from the hip" that could not withstand independent scrutiny.

An alternative explanation, which gives analysis a less prominent role, is that OSHA won a significant policy battle within the Administration over the institutional locus of decisionmaking power. The atmosphere surrounding the hazard identification rule was highly charged politically. The materials from the interagency debate had been leaked to Congress, and the Administration was receiving criticism from unions and Democrats in the House of Representatives for not allowing OSHA to perform its statutory role.[49] An OSHA memorandum for the task force captured the essence of the political situation:

> Labor and other groups have criticized the Administration for "gutting" environmental and safety and health laws. . . . Superimposing OMB over the regulatory process in a manner where they became the de facto regulator will lend credence to those criti-

cisms. This, in turn, portends significant political problems. . . . For 11 months organized labor has been saying that we were not coming out with a new proposal, and we have been saying that we are. . . . Labor has not yet been given a cudgel with which to beat this Administration. Failure to act on this matter will provide one. . . . Recent articles point to the Democratic party's efforts to rebuild its ties to the labor movement by painting this Administration as anti-worker. Let us not ignore political reality.[50]

It is probably not without significance that the regulations were released by OMB on the evening before the heads of OSHA and OIRA were to testify before a hostile House Subcommittee.[51] In the final analysis, it may be that in the context of a political battle that it was not likely to win, OMB, like any good bureaucratic actor, threw in the towel.

Reactions to the 1982 Proposal were highly critical and highly polarized. Most of the comments were directed to the merits of the proposal, and comparatively few discussed the RIA or the analysis contained therein.[52] Some of the industry comments addressed the "softness" of the RIA's numbers, but none came up with hard numbers to justify different quantitative predictions.[53] The unions opposed the performance-oriented hazard determination procedures, stressing that giving employers discretion to use "scientific judgment" to determine whether "scientifically well established evidence" supported a hazard determination ensured that too few substances would come within the ambit of the rule. The unions urged OSHA to adopt "specific definitions" of what constituted a health hazard with specific written hazard determination procedures and specific requirements for the contents of MSDSs.

The November 1983 Final Rule

After the public hearings closed, the team began the tedious task of evaluating the weight of the evidence supporting alternative resolutions of the issues raised by the proposal. All three primary team members read all of the written submissions. The chief disagreements now concerned the strength of the evidence on particular points, and most arguments were between the representative from the Solicitor's Office and the other team members.[54]

One large debate concerned the extent to which the final standard should adhere to the proposal's performance-oriented approach to the hazard determination question. The outside comments revealed a wide disparity in industry practice. According to the program office representative: "We did not get from the companies a common source of information that they could draw on."[55] The policy office representative's preference for retaining the performance-oriented approach was therefore rejected in favor of an approach that specified some of the chemicals for which hazard assessments would have to be undertaken.

The regulatory analyst, however, prevailed on the question whether the standard should be extended beyond the manufacturing sector. Although many commentators had argued that it was logical to concentrate on the manufacturing sector first, because it had a higher number of injuries, the evidence on this point was not very strong. The policy office's concern that extending the standard to other sectors would dramatically increase its costs ultimately carried the day with the team and upper-level decisionmakers.

The Final Rule significantly departed from the March 1982 Proposal in only a few regards. The agency continued to limit the coverage of the rule to hazardous chemicals or mixtures, but it amended the definition of that term to adopt the American National Standards Institute's standard for precautionary labeling of acutely toxic substances and to state explicit criteria for determining whether or not a substance was a carcinogen. Rejecting the performance-oriented approach, the agency decided to specify a chemical as a carcinogen when the National Toxicology Program, the International Agency for Research on Cancer, or OSHA published a finding that the substance was a carcinogen. The Final Rule also departed from the performance-oriented approach in requiring manufacturers and employers to consider as hazardous any chemicals for which OSHA had promulgated standards or the American Council of Governmental Industrial Hygienists had published threshold limit values. The Final Rule further reduced employer discretion by mandating that any substance that caused hazardous effects at a statistically significant level in a single species of laboratory animal in a study conducted in accordance with established scientific principles must be regarded as hazardous.[56]

The agency followed the 1982 Proposal for determining the content of labels, adhering to its position that the primary information conveying device was the MSDS.[57] The Final Rule also retained the 1982 Proposal's performance-oriented warning requirement.[58] Like the 1982 Proposal, the Final Rule required manufacturers to develop and transmit MSDSs to employers, and it required employers to keep MSDSs in a readily available spot in the workplace and to update them as appropriate within a reasonable period of time.

Table 7.2. *A cost comparison of the January 1981 and March 1982 proposals and the final standard (totals in millions of dollars)*

Cost	January 1981 proposal	March 1982 proposal	Final standard
Initial cost			
Total	2,600.000	591.440	603.926
Average per employee	185.00	42.00	43.00
Annual cost			
Total	1,254.000	158.490	158.870
Average per employee	89.00	11.00	11.00
Total present value			
(40-year period)	22,864.000	3,368.000	3,374.000

Finally, OSHA adopted without significant change the employee training portions of the 1982 Proposal.[59]

Surprisingly, the Final Rule and its Final Regulatory Impact Analysis (FRIA) sailed through OMB review unscathed. During the review period, OMB had three or four relatively minor questions that OSHA easily addressed. One explanation for OMB's subdued stance is that it did not believe that anything would be gained by reopening old wounds in a repeat of a battle that it had previously lost. Another explanation is that the regulatory analyst who drafted OSHA's RIAs was now employed as a desk officer at OMB.

The 287-page FRIA was organized very much like the DRIA.[60] In light of testimony presented at the hearings, the costs of the 1982 proposed standard were adjusted slightly downward, but the costs of the more burdensome final standard were somewhat higher. Table 7.2 compares the estimated costs of the two proposals and the final standard. Table 7.3 contains the agency's final benefits analysis.

The FRIA continued to rely upon the two critical assumptions that workplace-induced diseases and injuries were underreported by a factor of ten and that the standard would reduce chemically induced acute injuries and illnesses by 1 percent per year for twenty years before stabilizing at 20 percent. Unlike the DRIA, the FRIA could point to studies submitted during the hearing demonstrating rather dramatic decreases in injuries in companies that had already implemented some kind of hazard identification program. The FRIA also continued to assume that reduced cancer incidence would be zero for the first ten years and then 2 percent per year for the next ten years to an equilibrium level of 20 percent after twenty years.

Table 7.3. *Summary of quantified benefits 1982 (in millions of dollars)*

Source	Undiscounted			Discounted
	1st year	20th year	40th year	40-year period[a]
Reduced search costs	211.971	381.066	691.445	3092.445
Nonlost workday cases				
Lost production	0.030	1.360	3.600	5.660
Medical costs	0.020	1.000	2.800	4.200
Lost workday cases				
Lost production	0.720	30.600	81.400	147.200
Medical costs	0.130	4.533	12.000	25.490
Disabling illness				
Production lost	1.410	70.170	189.220	301.420
Medical costs	0.004	0.199	9.536	0.726
Cancer illness				
Production lost		305.144	808.680	1047.500
Medical cost		115.440	306.220	393.200
Turnover cost	0.070	4.060	10.780	16.400
Chemical fire	1.000	1.800	3.300	13.700
Uniform standard	74.800	135.410	244.580	1093.880
Total	290.155	1050.782	2354.561	6141.821

[a]The discount rate is 10%.
Source: U.S. Department of Labor, Occupational Safety and Health Administration, Office of Regulatory Analysis.

The FRIA took the same approach as the DRIA to monetizing the losses attributable to lost workday injuries, nonlost workday injuries, medical expenses, turnover costs, and fires. The extremely large difference between the estimates of forty-year discounted production losses due to permanent disabilities ($2,739 million in the DRIA compared to $301.426 million in the FRIA) is apparently attributable to the fact that the DRIA neglected to reduce the benefit stream to present value using the OMB mandated 10 percent discount rate. This slipup demonstrates the dramatic impact of using such a high discount rate.

The FRIA added an additional category of medical costs attributable to permanent disabilities. Although the DRIA had not identified sufficient data upon which to base such an estimate, the FRIA used the average monthly cost of medical care in nursing homes for similar disabling diseases and multiplied by the average stay of seventy-five days as reported in the 1977 *National Nursing Home Survey.* This yielded a discounted forty-year benefit of $0.726 million.

The discrepancy between the DRIA and FRIA predictions for lost production and medical costs due to workplace-induced cancers ($1,673 million versus $1,047 million and $638 million versus $393 million respectively) is less easily explained. The written analyses were identical except for the fact that the use of 1982 dollars in the FRIA yielded slightly larger annual estimates. No explanation what-soever was given for the fact that the forty-year discounted estimates were lower in the FRIA.

The FRIA, like the DRIA, also made a brief comparison of the effectiveness of the standard, measured by the willingness of work-ers to pay to avoid a lost workday injury. The FRIA compared Pro-fessor Viscusi's $30,000 estimate to the newly calculated high estimate of the cost per lost workday avoided of $23,984 to conclude that the standard was justified.

The FRIA calculated the benefits of a uniform standard that pre-empted inconsistent state standards using the same formula that the DRIA had used. However, it dramatically reduced the assumed number of estimated transactions per ton from 100, 200, and 300 to 5, 10, and 15, yielding drastically reduced forty-year discounted costs of $1.09, $2.18, and $3.57 billion, instead of $15.2, $30.5, and $45.8 billion. Nowhere did the FRIA explain the change in assump-tions that led to these reduced predictions. On the other hand, the FRIA did take into account state required chronic testing costs of an estimated $17.78 billion that the DRIA (which had considered only acute testing requirements) had ignored.

The FRIA also adopted an alternative method for calculating the costs of complying with state laws. It simply took at face value one company's estimate of the additional costs of compliance with the more stringent state standards and extrapolated some of them to the entire chemical industry. One of these calculations yielded a cost of $6.3 billion for merely determining whether or not chemical manufacturers complied with a single state's standards. Another produced an estimate of $47.6 billion for complying with state label-ing requirements. Like the DRIA, it failed to subtract the value of the additional protection attributable to more stringent state stan-dards, and it did not factor state standards into its calculation of the medical and performance benefits of the OSHA standard.

The FRIA included as a benefit an item that had not been considered in the DRIA. By requiring the manufacturers to provide hazard information to their employees and to downstream users and their employees, the OSHA standard would reduce the costs of obtaining hazard information for those firms and employees who would otherwise be willing to undertake some efforts to obtain that information.[61] According to the FRIA, this reduced "search cost" would be a benefit of the standard. To calculate its magnitude OSHA began with Ford Motor Company's estimate that it spent approximately $25 per product updating information on 15 percent of its products per year. The International Chemical Workers Union estimated that it spent an average of $50 per product in search costs. From a General Services Administration (GSA) study of Material Safety Data Sheets OSHA extrapolated that 70 percent of all of the almost 27 million chemical products in manufacturing establishments "may be associated with incomplete chemical hazard information."[62] If all manufacturers follow Ford's example, then the forty-year discounted cost would be $1.03 billion. Using the $50 per search that employees were apparently willing to pay, the forty-year discounted cost would be $2.06 billion. Hence, the agency added $3.09 billion in avoided search costs to the total benefits of the standard. This constituted the largest single item of benefits in Table 7.3.

Clearly this $3 billion chunk of benefits was built upon the flimsiest of evidence. First, it drew upon the experiences of a single company and a single union official. Second, it extrapolated from a limited GSA study of MSDSs an estimate that inadequate searches had been performed for 70 percent of all chemicals. Third, it tacitly assumed that searches would be taken for all 27 million chemicals that could be found in manufacturing workplaces. Finally, it assumed that all of those search costs would disappear upon effective implementation of OSHA's standard. It did not allow for the possibility that an employer or employee might want more or better information than the OSHA standard would provide.

To calculate the costs of the standard, the FRIA identified seven separate activities, each of which consisted of two or more components, and then estimated the costs for each of the components. The testimony in the hearings seemed to bear out OSHA's earlier "best estimates."[63] Like the DRIA, the final calculations in the FRIA were based on the assumption of 60 percent prior compliance for most calculations. The FRIA calculated the total forty-year discounted direct costs of the final standard to be $3.37 billion. Although the breakdown of costs in the DRIA was very different, this total did not differ greatly from the $3.2 billion estimate of total forty-year discounted costs in the DRIA.

On May 24, 1985, the Third Circuit Court of Appeals upheld much of the hazard identification standard, but held that the agency was arbitrary and capricious in limiting the scope of the standard to employees in the manufacturing sector.[64] The court held that OSHA had not adequately addressed the petitioners' contention that the limitation ignored the high level of employee exposure in specific jobs outside the manufacturing sector. The court was also unpersuaded by OSHA's contention that the benefits of the communication standard would trickle down to uncovered workers because containers would be labeled. The court concluded:

> There is record evidence that workers in sectors other than manufacturing are exposed to the hazard associated with use of toxic materials or harmful physical agents. The Secretary has given no statement or reasons why it would not be feasible to require that those workers be given the same MSDS's in training as must be given to workers in a manufacturing sector. The Secretary has given reasons why the labeling, MSDS, and instruction requirements comply with [the OSHAct] for employees in the manufacturing sector, but no explanation why the same information is not needed for workers in other sectors exposed to industrial hazard.[65]

The court held that the standard could remain in effect in the manufacturing sector, but it directed OSHA to reconsider the application of the standard to employees in other sectors "and to order its application to other sectors unless [the agency] can state reasons why such application would not be feasible."[66]

After OSHA failed to respond to the court's remand, the United Steel Workers petitioned the Third Circuit to mandate that OSHA respond to the rule by a date certain. On May 29, 1987, the court ordered the agency to respond to the remand, and on August 24, 1987, OSHA published an expanded hazard communication standard applicable to all industries.[67] OSHA found that the rulemaking record on the whole supported its conclusion that compliance with that the hazard communication standard was feasible in all industries.

Evaluation and conclusions

Type and quality of analysis

Knowing that the hazard identification rule would be the first major Reagan Administration regulation to impose heavy costs on a regulated industry, OSHA attempted to draft a high-quality RIA.

The cost analysis was not the standard analysis of available technologies that typifies OSHA economic impact assessments, but it was based on a similar thought process. OSHA polled the industry and suppliers of relevant products and services for cost data and added a liberal sprinkling of assumptions about the extent to which industry was already in compliance and the techniques that companies would use to meet the standard. Because the standard contained several performance-oriented provisions, the predications about how individual firms would comply were a bit shakier than normal, but the agency's cost estimates were not seriously disputed.

The benefits assessment was unlike any assessment that OSHA had ever undertaken, because the whole concept of substituting hazard communication for command and control regulations was unique. OSHA therefore had to rely upon less defensible assumptions about the number of injuries that the standard might prevent. Its 10 percent underreporting factor and its "one-percent-per-year-for-twenty-years" efficacy assumption were especially questionable, and (as OMB's analysis demonstrated) the agency's predictions were very sensitive to those assumptions. Equally controversial was OSHA's attempt to reduce injury, disability and death to dollar amounts. OSHA had stated on numerous occasions that it would not attempt to place a dollar value on human life, and a Supreme Court holding appears to preclude OSHA's adoption of a cost-benefit approach to rulemaking.[68] But its RIAs displayed to the decisionmaker the policy office's monetary estimates of both the costs and benefits of the standard. Both the "human capital" and "willingness to pay" approaches to valuing risks of death and disease are controversial valuation techniques, as we shall see in Chapter 9.

Although the RIA was somewhat lengthy and at times contained perplexing gaps in logic (as, for example, the failure to credit the health benefits of state and local regulations), it was of comparatively high quality. The fact that an independent academic economist who was paid to critique the DRIA could find little fault with its basic premises suggests that the agency did about the best that could be done with the very limited information that was available on critical questions.

Impediments to analysis

The most significant analytical impediment was the lack of relevant benefits data. OSHA did not even obtain a ballpark idea of the number of injuries and diseases caused by workplace exposures to hazardous chemicals. The agency guessed that existing statistics might be off by a factor of 10, but admitted that it could be more like a factor of 50. One can readily sympathize with OMB's cynical conclusion that OSHA's assumptions were driven by the need to justify the standard. But one could also agree with the conclusion of some OSHA staffers that OMB had equally cynically substituted assumptions that would advance its own political agenda. Either set of assumptions may have been right. The dispute over the assumptions was really a dispute over the policies that determined the outcome of the rulemaking process.

The role of regulatory analysis

In the final analysis, the questions whether to issue the standard and what kind of standard it would be were political judgment calls; the benefits analysis was largely irrelevant. Given the absence of credible information on benefits, it should have been irrelevant. The real debate was over who had the power to decide whether the rule should go forward. The RIA was simply the vehicle for this contest between OSHA and OMB over institutional power. In the end, the Vice-President sided with OSHA, more for institutional and political reasons than because of the acuity of its analysis.

The cost analysis, by contrast, was critical to the substantive decisionmaking process in the indirect sense that any alternatives that cost too much were out of bounds. The team operated on the assumption that any standard it wrote would have to come with a price sticker substantially below that of the Carter Administration proposal. Even the Carter OSHA worked on the assumption that the cost of the proposal could not exceed $1 billion.[69] Thus, when the regulatory analyst costed out an option the other team members paid careful attention, and when the analyst turned thumbs down on an option, even before undertaking a careful cost analysis, on the ground that it would cost too much, the rest of the team generally did not press it further. Still, the cost analysis did not dictate decisions at the microlevel. The chairperson of the team observed that: "Costs did not drive the process; they just informed it."[70]

The team's regulatory analyst played a significant role in the rule's development. She was an active member of the team, and she participated fully in the upper-level discussions. She was solely responsible for preparing and defending the RIA. Other members of the team were uniformly impressed with the amount of effort that the analyst put into the analysis.

The analyst did not contribute any more than other members of the team to identifying innovative options. The ten alternatives analyzed in the DRIA were simply permutations of previously examined options. One member of the team observed:

> Part of the requirements of [Executive Order 12,291] are to consider various alternatives. This tends to be an exercise in creating strawmen. It is rarely a process of starting from square one and continuously thinking about different ways of achieving the same regulatory goal. The RIA process forces you to think about more cost-effective ways of accomplishing regulatory goals. But you never break out of the original framework. The economists helped concentrate OSHA's mind on economics issues like the coverage of the rule. It was less useful in coming up with creative solutions to the hazard determination procedure problem.[71]

The regulatory analyst was, nevertheless, an "active and influential" participant in the collective team effort.[72] She supported the front office desires to make the standard more performance-oriented. Consistent with the economist's worldview, she favored flexibility over specification. This sometimes put her at odds with the attorney from the Solicitor's Office, who was concerned about the enforceability of very flexible rules.

The regulatory analyst argued strongly for limiting the rule to the manufacturing sector to keep costs down. The Third Circuit Court of Appeals, perhaps reflecting the lawyer's view of rationality, later found this limitation to be arbitrary and capricious, and it ordered OSHA to expand the coverage of the rule to all sectors of the economy. The analyst also expressed a strong preference for putting the primary obligation to acquire information on the manufacturer of a chemical, rather than requiring employers to ask manufacturers for information. In addition, she was influential in persuading the team to adopt an employee training requirement.

The agency's policy office was especially helpful in the agency's debates with OMB. It was able to craft arguments for why the standard was necessary to address market imperfections. In doing so, it "phrased the debate in terms that OMB could understand."[73] According to one participant, "a lot of the momentum behind the rule was due to our ability to put it in free market terms," and that ability came from the analysts in the Policy Directorate.

CHAPTER 8

The virtues of regulatory analysis

The three regulatory reform themes described in Chapter 1 – rational decisionmaking, bureaucratic accountability, and regulatory relief – merged in the mandates of Executive Order 12,291 and the Regulatory Flexibility Act that agencies analyze the impacts of their regulations on the regulated entities. Many regulatory reformers believe that regulatory analysis will inspire agencies to promulgate more logical (and less burdensome) rules in a way that ensures accountability to the President, the Congress and the public. These are high expectations indeed for a conceptual framework, but to some extent they are warranted. Comprehensive analytical rationality has many virtues, and it has great potential for enhancing the quality of regulatory decisionmaking. This chapter will first examine the concept of regulatory analysis and attempt to place it in the context of a larger body of experience and thought devoted to the broader practice of policy analysis. Next, the chapter will discuss the virtues of analysis and suggest how regulatory analysis can advance the goals of rational decisionmaking, bureaucratic accountability, and regulatory relief. We will save for Chapter 9 the discussion of the impediments to using regulatory analysis and the inherent limitations in the conceptual framework that make it less useful and desirable in real-world decisionmaking contexts.

Essential aspects of regulatory analysis

The enormous expansion of government since World War II has precipitated many ambitious attempts to manage governmental decisionmaking. The success of quantitative techniques to manage the war effort made students and practitioners of government optimistic that similar techniques could aid policymakers in other large bureaucratic contexts. Born in an age of great technological optimism, policy analysis was touted by intellectuals in academia and think tanks as a rational approach to bringing expertise to bear on important decisions about how government should affect the lives of citizens.

Policy analysis, broadly defined, is the process of using compre-

111

hensive analytical rationality to solve social problems.[1] The analyst must (1) identify the problem; (2) break it down into its constituents; (3) clarify and rank preexisting goals; (4) identify alternative policies for resolving the problem; (5) investigate the consequences of each alternative, using available information and clearly specified assumptions; (6) measure the consequences against the goals; and (7) select the policy that best advances the goals.[2] Regulatory analysis is simply the process of applying the policy analysis paradigm to regulatory problems. Although not required by the paradigm, regulatory analysis usually employs the conceptual frameworks of neoclassical economics.[3]

Regulatory analysis is a process that consists of at least two functions.[4] First, the analyst must bring the regulatory analysis paradigm to bear upon a regulatory problem. Second, the analyst must communicate the results of the analytical exercise to decisionmakers. The analyst can communicate orally or in writing. The writing can be located in a separate document (hereinafter referred to as a regulatory analysis document) or it can be incorporated into the explanatory document that the agency prepares for publication in the *Federal Register* (hereinafter referred to as the rulemaking document). The communications function can be accomplished by making the analyst a part of the day-to-day decisionmaking process, or the analyst can communicate with the decisionmaker from a distance.

Although regulatory analysis can be useful to decisionmakers in reaching substantive decisions, it is thoroughly instrumental in concept.[5] It is not an appropriate vehicle for prescribing or evaluating regulatory goals. Nevertheless, to the extent that bringing comprehensive analytical rationality to bear upon regulatory problems results in less burdensome regulations, regulatory analysis can advance the substantive goal of regulatory relief. Advocates of regulatory analysis therefore may be motivated by instrumental concerns for better regulation, or they may see regulatory analysis as a vehicle for furthering the substantive goal of less regulation. Although it would probably be difficult to find anyone opposed to the first goal, the second goal is likely to brook strong opposition from those who perceive themselves to be beneficiaries of regulation.

The virtues of regulatory analysis

Bringing comprehensive analytical rationality to bear on regulatory decisionmaking

Rational analysis is essential to the integrity of the rulemaking process under the Administrative Procedure Act. Unless an agency can demonstrate both that a rule is rationally related to goals that Congress intended for the agency to consider and that it has support in the data, assumptions, and reasoning in the rulemaking record, a reviewing court is likely to find that the agency has been arbitrary and capricious in promulgating the rule.[6] Yet, the scientists, engineers and technical staff in the agencies are fully as capable of analyzing regulatory problems rationally as regulatory analysts; techno-bureaucratic rationality can yield regulatory decisions that survive the rationality requirements of judicial review. One of the fundamental tenets of the regulatory reform movement, however, is that crafting regulations capable of surviving the bare minimum requirements for judicial review is no longer sufficient. Congress (in enacting the Regulatory Flexibility Act) and the President (in promulgating Executive Order 12,291) wanted agencies to analyze regulatory problems in more detail, paying particular attention to the economic impact of regulations. In the minds of its proponents, regulatory analysis can provide "a basis for improving rational, efficient methods of policy formulation in order to maximize the outputs of public policy in accordance with the values of a democratic society."[7]

Asking the right questions. Defining a regulatory problem correctly is the first step toward solving it. Although the program office staff may be wedded to conventional approaches to problems, regulatory analysts can frame old questions in new ways that suggest novel solutions.[8] For example, an engineer in the Office of Air Quality Planning and Standards in EPA, upon discovering that an industry is emitting large quantities of a potent carcinogen, might define the regulatory problem as one of locating technologies for reducing emissions and requiring individual plants to install them. A regulatory analyst might view the problem as one of minimizing the interaction of people and the pollutant; thus, the analyst might seek ways to induce individual firms, through appropriate economic incentives, to use a different chemical in the manufacturing process. An even more ambitious regulatory analyst might attempt to induce residents near the plants, again through appropriate economic incentives, to move away from the plants. The example suggests that how one asks regulatory questions is not value-free. Indeed, there is not likely to be general agreement that any way of phrasing the question is the "right" way. But for a decisionmaker hungry for new solutions to old problems, the regulatory analyst's ability to reframe old questions may be a virtue.

Options identification. One of the most frequently articulated complaints about bureaucratic decisionmaking is that it becomes wedded to a single solution to a problem too early in the decisionmaking process.[9] Regulatory analysts often complain of a program office tendency to adopt a conveyer belt mind-set, focusing upon a single option early in a rule's germination and adhering to that option throughout.[10] If upper-level decisionmakers later insist upon considering more than one option, the technical staff dutifully sandwiches its preferred alternative between two post hoc red herrings. Executive Order 12,291, the Regulatory Flexibility Act, and the National Environmental Policy Act, however, all require agencies to consider a broad range of options before settling upon a single alternative.

Because comprehensive analytical rationality insists that policymakers examine all realistically available options, regulatory analysts by training should be able to identify fresh options and to pressure the program office staff to search harder for alternatives.[11] Relying upon their backgrounds in economics, regulatory analysts might search for less burdensome market-oriented solutions to regulatory problems (such as effluent charges, marketable permits, and voluntary standards) and explore alternative timing strategies that correspond more closely to production cycles. One government survey reported that "most agencies believe that the 'alternatives' element of [regulatory analysis] has had the single most important effect on improving their decision-making procedures."[12]

Gathering and analyzing information. Another frequently expressed virtue of regulatory analysis is its capacity to bring information on the beneficial and detrimental aspects of regulatory alternatives to the attention of the decisionmaker in a coherent and systematic fashion.[13] Indeed, it is possible that the mere "generation of such information, even if never introduced as a formal part of the decision process, tends to make decisions more rational."[14] The program office staff can, of course, make information available to decisionmakers, and in fact that office is the source of much of the information that the regulatory analysts use. But the analyst brings to the information-providing task a unique quantitative perspective[15] and an objective posture[16] that seeks out a broader range of information and nuance, especially on the detriment side of the ledger.[17] Moreover, the regulatory analyst often has training in techniques for displaying information (charts, tables, graphs, etc.) that can make existing data more accessible to the harried upper-level decisionmaker and the general public. Finally, regulatory analysis can reduce the incidence of cognitive illusions that sometimes plague a layperson's assessment of complicated fact situations.[18]

A well-prepared cost analysis can raise the consciousness of upper-level decisionmakers to the impacts that their rules have upon society.[19] Quantitative benefits analysis can make the decisionmaker aware of the positive impacts of its rules, thus facilitating a comparison between the costs and benefits of rulemaking. By explicitly probing the distributional impacts of a rule, regulatory analysis can inform the decisionmaker of the groups that are likely to support the rule and those that are likely to be opposed to it.[20] The net effect can be to raise the decisionmaker's comfort level with respect to the correctness of the agency's final decisions.[21]

Regulatory agency heads have testified to the value of regulatory analysis in helping them make informed decisions. The head of the Food Safety and Inspection Service stated: "Generally good information yields good decisions. Sometimes we have made poor decisions because we did not know there was information out there or because we relied on poor information. While the process today is more expensive, the public is getting better work from the government."[22] And a former head of the Occupational Safety and Health Administration (OSHA) testified:

> OSHA has found that the Regulatory Impact Analysis required by Executive Order and the Regulatory Flexibility Analyses, which are required by the Regulatory Flexibility Act, reveal important information about the capital and operating costs of compliance with various regulatory approaches as well as estimates of reduction in risk to workers. Lacking regulatory analysis, OSHA would not have adequate information on the costs its regulations impose on society or the amount of protection received by workers.[23]

Increased sensitivity to small business impacts. A primary purpose of the Regulatory Flexibility Act is to make regulatory agencies sensitive to the impacts of their regulations on small business entities. This reflects a legislative determination that small businesses bear a disproportionate share of regulatory compliance expenses,[24] a conclusion that has some basis in the academic literature.[25] If compliance costs do not vary greatly with product output (an assumption that has not been tested in many real-world situations), then large companies will be able to spread compliance costs over a larger number of products than small producers and thereby gain a competitive advantage.[26] Although economists may disagree over whether this is an inefficient result, information on disproportionate small business costs can be extremely relevant to upper-level agency decisionmakers who must make decisions in a political world in which small businesses can often have a disproportionate impact upon their representatives in Congress. A good regulatory analysis document can provide this information.

Justification by explicit reference to articulated policies. An agency's policy goals can easily get lost in the convenience of adherence to precedent and unarticulated bureaucratic folk wisdom. For example, a policy analyst in the Food Safety and Inspection Service referred to an instance in which a regulatory analysis document drafted by the program office stated that "it has always been agency policy that. . . ." In fact, the regulatory analysis document was the first time that the agency articulated the policy explicitly.[27] Regulatory analysis resists bureaucratic momentum by insisting that the analyst attempt to measure regulatory alternatives against expressly articulated policy goals.[28] This in turn induces upper- and lower-level decisionmakers to think periodically about the ultimate purposes of their rulemaking efforts. Explicit references to agency policy also enhance agency accountability and increase agency credibility.[29]

Explicit identification of information gaps and assumptions. Analysts rarely have enough information to undertake entirely objective analyses of all of the pros and cons of a range of regulatory alternatives. A good analysis, however, will identify the gaps in the available information, draw appropriate inferences from the existing data, and identify the assumptions that the analyst has relied upon in extrapolating across information gaps.[30] The techno-bureaucratic thinker also encounters information gaps and fills them with assumptions in an intellectual exercise that is often loosely referred to as professional judgment. Yet, although the technical staff's assumptions and inferences may be informed by experience and received professional wisdom, its predictions are often based upon an outcome-oriented policy judgment about how the world should be arranged.[31] Regulatory analysts believe that the program office too often hides policy judgment behind an outer veneer of technical expertise. The analysts believe that they are more likely to be explicit about the policy preferences that motivate their choice of assumptions.[32] Moreover, they can draw upon analytical techniques for showing how predictions depend upon particular assumptions. The upper-level decisionmaker (or the general public) will then have a better understanding of how the assumptions affect regulatory policy choices, and they will be aware of the particular policies that inform the choice of assumptions.

Identifying research needs. The analyst's propensity to identify information gaps has the additional advantage of revealing research needs.[33] Many questions that arise in rulemaking proceedings can be answered by further research. For example, more research on agency cost estimates, perhaps by monitoring the costs of implementing past rules, can enhance the accuracy of agency cost projections. Similarly, research into the benefits of regulations may reduce uncertainties, thereby allowing less stringent regulations in the future.[34] A regulatory analysis of an environmental rule may reveal that the agency is spending too many research dollars studying an environmental problem that is outside the agency's authority and not enough resources on problems that the agency can do something about.

Restraint upon inappropriate "political" considerations. Comprehensive analytical rationality rejects the pluralistic view that regulatory decisions should reflect the interplay among political forces.[35] Insisting that decisions must be based upon more than the exercise of raw political power, comprehensive analytical rationality distinguishes between politics and policy.[36] Regulatory analysts insist that facts do exist and can point to appropriate regulatory conclusions. Goals can be ranked, and alternatives can be measured against those goals. In sum, regulatory analysis "holds the promise of bringing more neatness, order, and precision out of the political and philosophical quagmire within which much regulatory policy now finds itself."[37]

The regulatory analyst believes that well-conducted regulatory analyses can guide agency decisionmakers to rational decisions that are more than mere political accommodations. A comprehensive Study on Federal Regulation for the United States Senate concluded: "The need for careful appraisal in impact evaluation is increased by the complexity of regulatory tasks and the forces which can divert regulators away from attainment of Congressional goals, and toward protection of regulated interests or pursuit of administrative convenience."[38] Moreover, a good regulatory analysis can shield rational decisions from parties who have only their own narrow interests in mind. Although a regulatory analysis document may not satisfy the losers of the regulatory battle, it can reassure remote decisionmakers in the White House and Congress and members of the general public that the decision was reached in a consistent and nonpartisan fashion.

Identifying "correct" results. Many proponents of regulatory analysis believe that it can go a long way toward specifying a result that is the "correct" solution to the regulatory problem. Executive Order 12,291 ambitiously adopts this position by requiring agencies to select, among the options identified in the regulatory analysis, the option for which the benefits most outweigh the costs.[39] Proponents argue that only by pursuing analysis to its bottom line conclusions can society efficiently use its scarce resources.[40] This perspective, of course, also presumes that the efficient result is the "correct" result. But whether analysis will yield efficient results depends upon the extent to which its underlying techniques and assumptions are capable of measuring efficiency, a question that we shall address in the next chapter.

Securing successful judicial review. Because substantive judicial review of administrative rulemaking focuses upon whether a rule is arbitrary and capricious, given the evidence in the record and the agency's explanation for its decision, a regulatory analysis that effectively states regulatory goals, identifies alternatives, provides information on the advantages and disadvantages of the alternatives, and measures each alternative against existing statutory goals could aid the agency substantially in its attempt to persuade a reviewing court of the rationality of its rulemaking exercise. Conversely, litigants before a reviewing court can rely upon a good regulatory analysis to undermine the support for a decision that the analysis does not support. This in turn forces the agency to explain its reasoning process-one of the important goals of judicial review-when it appears to depart from that of the regulatory analysis.

Facilitating policy management

Although rarely mentioned in the extensive literature on policy analysis, agencies can use analysis as a management tool to ensure bureaucratic accountability. The accountability at stake here is not of the personnel management variety typically associated with public administration—ensuring that lower-level officials do their jobs well and on time. Rather, regulatory analysis can become an instrument of policy management.

Because a good regulatory analysis will explicitly measure the anticipated consequences of alternatives against articulated policy goals, upper-level decisionmakers can use the regulatory analysis process to communicate policy preferences to analysts and technical staff at lower levels in the agencies. Politically appointed policymakers can thereby ensure that lower-level officials are not implementing some hidden agenda known only to themselves. One early observer of the regulatory analysis process concluded that it "will almost certainly increase the power of the President and OMB relative to the agencies, the Congress, and the victims and beneficiaries of particular regulations, it will slowly increase the power of upper-level administrators within the agencies over bureaus and other subunits, and the power of staff economists in Washington over line-managers in the field."[41]

Although policy management may appear at first glance to consist simply of hiring people of the correct policy persuasion and monitoring their efforts as proposed rules circulate through upper-level management for final clearance, the reality of bureaucratic decision-making is much more complicated. First, no upper-level policy-maker has sufficient time or technical skill to monitor every rule to see if the underlying rationale for the rule adheres to his or her view of appropriate agency policy. Even monitoring selected major rules would strain the personal resources of upper-level policymak-ers in many regulatory agencies. Second, civil service laws prevent policy managers from firing uncooperative lower-level and midman-agement officials, and only a limited number can be shunted to ir-relevant way stations off the primary rulemaking track. Third, even if they could be fired, the lower-level officials who can obstruct an upper-level political appointee's policy initiatives very often possess technical skills and experience that are indispensable to the rule-making enterprise. Fourth, the lower-level staff often has surpris-ingly powerful allies among the regulated industries, the beneficiary constituency groups, the media, and members of Congress. The upper-level policymaker can replace or avoid these subordinate pol-icymakers only at considerable risk to the agency's steady-state equi-librium. Fifth, policymaking is inextricably infused into almost every aspect of the rulemaking enterprise. When they resolve ambiguities in the technical data one way rather than another, when they adopt one untested assumption rather than another, when they draw one inference rather than another, and when they demand one level of certainty rather than another, members of the technical staff in the program offices are in fact making policy.

A particular policy perspective may be inherent in the very disci-pline that a professional practices. Because health scientists are likely to be more risk averse than economists, they often resolve am-biguities and uncertainties in favor of protecting public health, without as much regard for the economic consequences. Lawyers in the enforcement division generally prefer command and control standards, because they are easier to understand and enforce. Agency economists are likely to suggest taxes and performance stan-dards, because their training and experience teaches that such stan-dards are generally more efficient.

Upper-level policymakers cannot effectively manage policy through the traditional personnel management techniques. They need management tools capable of spotting policymaking as it happens at all levels in the agency hierarchy and of providing an effective opportunity to guide policy choices as they are being made. Regulatory analysis is an ideal candidate for this policy management function.

Policy management requires two-way communication between upper-level policymakers and lower-level staff. If the head of the agency could participate in all subordinate decisionmaking entities (e.g., work groups), the head could effectively communicate policy preferences to the staff orally at the meetings. But such hands-on participation is rarely feasible in a busy administrative agency. Periodic meetings with the staff at certain critical decision points in a rule's evolution can likewise facilitate policy communication between the agency policymakers and the agency staff, especially if they take place at crucial junctures when the staff is choosing among significant regulatory options. Yet, even this approach requires that busy decisionmakers be brought up to speed periodically.

Regulatory analysis can be the vehicle for bringing upper-level decisionmakers up to speed quickly on the policy aspects of important agency rulemaking initiatives. The regulatory analyst assigned to a subordinate decisionmaking unit should insist that the participants in the subordinate entity attempt to state explicitly the policies that they are implementing. This explicit attention to policy should facilitate policy communication between lower-level officials and upper-level policymakers in the much rarer meetings in which they are all participants. For major rules, the decisionmaker will also have available the Regulatory Impact Analyses and briefing documents summarizing their contents. Many agencies, in fact, are sufficiently convinced of the value of a written document that their internal regulations require analysts to prepare some kind of regulatory analysis document for many nonmajor rules. If the upper-level policymaker disagrees with lower-level policy determinations, the rule can be remanded to the subordinate unit with instructions to apply a different policy, thereby sending the lower-level personnel a very direct message about upper-level policy preferences.

Whether this policy communication function works depends heavily upon the management style of particular agency heads. For example, the Secretary of Transportation, during the deregulatory period of the early 1980s, was content to let the Operating Administrations within the department promulgate regulations in a relatively autonomous fashion, and rules were rarely remanded for consideration of fresh options or application of a different policy approach. With the advent of Secretary Elizabeth Dole in 1983 with stronger policy preferences toward safety regulations, departmental review became more important to the rulemaking process. When the regulatory analysis documents that accompanied individual rules revealed agency departures from her policy preferences, she began to return the rules to the Operating Administrations for further analysis, and the Operating Administrations began to request that the Office of the Secretary be involved earlier in the rulemaking process to avoid remands. The regulatory analysis document can thus become a fairly effective policy management tool in the hands of an upper-level decisionmaker who wants to use it.

In the same way that regulatory analysis can facilitate policy management within agencies, it can facilitate White House policy management of executive agencies. The RIA that accompanies major rules should inform White House and OMB personnel of the policy considerations that motivated the agency to make its regulatory choices. They can in turn communicate policy downward by remanding rulemaking efforts for being "inconsistent with Executive Order 12,291." Policy can also be communicated through more direct communications between policy managers at the White House or OMB and their counterparts at the agencies, a topic that we will take up in Chapter 18.

Informing Congress and the public

Although Congress is not technically a manager of the federal bureaucracy, it does have a very intense interest in how agencies make and implement regulatory policy. In this sense, Congress has a policy management function, and regulatory analysis can aid Congress in the same way that it helps upper-level agency policymakers and OMB. Oversight committees and individual congressmen want to be apprised of the impacts of important rulemaking efforts on their constituencies. They are especially interested in any distributional aspects of agency rules. Committees that write legislation for agencies have a similar obligation to oversee agency policy implementation to monitor agency fidelity to congressional intent. Written regulatory analysis documents can perform the important role of holding agencies accountable to Congress.

Written regulatory analysis documents can also be a vehicle for making agencies accountable to the public. These documents can inform members of the public who are interested in a particular rulemaking initiative of the ways in which the agency expects the rule to affect their interests. Deeply affected members of the public are thereby encouraged to participate further in the public rule-making process.[42]

At the same time, regulatory analysis documents can enhance the quality of public participation in the public rulemaking process.[43] Most agency employees are quite unimpressed with the quality of public participation in rulemaking proceedings.[44] The typical comment from the public is a tirade against the agency for imposing unnecessary costs on the regulated industry or for providing too little protection to the beneficiaries. Occasionally, a submission provides an estimate of the rule's anticipated costs, but public commentators rarely provide background information and analysis to justify cost estimates. Without its own analysis, the agency must either accept the estimates (and perhaps redraft the rule accordingly) or ignore them and risk imposing catastrophic economic losses.

Regulatory analysis documents give the agency some idea of the rule's costs. The estimates may not be precise, but they have presumptive validity. It is then incumbent upon the outside commentators to demonstrate that the agency's estimates are erroneous. Ideally, the regulatory analysis "will shape the outcome of the rulemaking because it will be the focal point of an orderly and structured dialogue between the agency and the persons who must live with the rule after its promulgation."[45] Indeed, for some especially important rulemakings, outside parties have gone to the extreme of hiring consultants to "trash" regulatory analysis documents, as we observed in Chapter 4.

Providing regulatory relief

Many proponents of regulatory analysis maintain that one of its primary virtues is that it will induce agencies to provide relief for regulated entities.[46] To the extent that regulatory analysis is an effective policy management tool and to the extent that policymakers in the White House and the upper reaches of the agencies desire to effectuate regulatory relief, regulatory analysis can be expected to yield that result.[47] Moreover, to the extent that the agency must expend time and resources in analysis, rather than in promulgating rules, the flow of rules can be expected to decrease accordingly.[48] Finally, some regulatory relief advocates suggest that better analysis will beget fewer rules, because analysis will more often reveal that a rule should not be promulgated than it will suggest that a rule should go forward.[49] In any event, many proponents of regulatory analysis are apparently convinced that this essentially instrumental process can advance particular substantive ends. Whether this is an appropriate use for analysis will be discussed in Chapter 9.

Conclusion

The foregoing summary of the virtues of regulatory analysis indicates that it can be a valuable component of regulatory decisionmaking. It has been endorsed by many past and present agency leaders and heralded by prominent students of the regulatory process. Indeed, many agencies have been so impressed with its effectiveness as a decisionmaking tool that they routinely prepare regulatory analyses for nonmajor rules, even when not required by statute or executive order. Yet, like any decisionmaking aid, regulatory analysis is not perfect. It has its flaws and inconsistencies, and practical problems will impede its usefulness in the real world. Nevertheless, its potential is very large, and it should not be too easily dismissed, as many staffers in agency program offices are inclined to do, as merely another burdensome paperwork requirement for the bureaucracy.

CHAPTER 9

Limitations of regulatory analysis

The description in Chapter 8 of the virtues of regulatory analysis presents an ideal view of comprehensive analytical rationality. As might be expected, the ideal suffers considerably in the real world where values conflict, the available information is never adequate, and quantitative techniques encounter huge uncertainties.[1] Many students of government urge instead more realistic notions of "bounded rationality."[2] Because analysis is expensive and information-intensive, decisionmakers, in this view, can only muddle through by exploring a very limited range of options, relying heavily upon intuition and "back-of-the-envelope" predictions, and hoping for rapid feedback to meet limited short-term goals.[3] Critics maintain that politics is inseparable from bureaucratic decisionmaking, and purely instrumental techniques deprive it of an important democratic dimension.[4] One prominent student of the bureaucratic process has observed:

> The notion of some analysts that knowledge will carry the day is absurd. Knowledge does not and cannot govern. The diversity of our society and institutions sets the conditions for conflicting values to be maintained. Once we realize that problems of public policy are not solved but adjusted by policymakers, then it should be clear that the degree of trust within our society is equally as important as knowledge.[5]

Regulatory analysts react very negatively to such suggestions, arguing that an informed decision is always better than one made in ignorance. They argue that analysis enhances democratic accountability by forcing agencies to make explicit value choices.[6] Yet, as a purely descriptive matter, the muddling through model often appears to fit the decisionmaking process better than the comprehensive analytical rationality paradigm. This chapter attempts to explain the failure of comprehensive analytical rationality to transform the regulatory decisionmaking process in spite of forceful efforts by the last four Presidents. It probes the limitations of regulatory analysis and explores the impediments to the implementation of the comprehensive analytical rationality paradigm in the real-world bureaucratic context.

124

Some limitations are inherent in the paradigm itself. It is, frankly, too ambitious, and, pushed to the purest extreme of formalized cost-benefit analysis, it demonstrates many of the theoretical limitations that plague utilitarianism as a theory of political economy. As we have seen in Chapter 8, less ambitious versions of regulatory analysis have important theoretical and practical virtues. Yet, even attempts at regulatory analysis that stop short of formal cost-benefit analysis face numerous practical impediments. Although the theoretical limitations of formal cost-benefit analysis will probably prevent it from playing a large role in regulatory policymaking, less ambitious varieties of regulatory analysis can significantly improve regulatory decisionmaking if some of the practical impediments can be overcome.

Practical impediments to preparing regulatory analysis

Conflicting goals

In this pluralistic society, no ranking of regulatory goals is likely to command a consensus.[7] Absent agreement, someone must decide which goals will prevail over others in particular regulatory contexts. Although the regulatory analyst can play a very useful role in clarifying the choices that must be made between inconsistent goals, comprehensive analytical rationality offers no legitimate criteria for ranking goals.[8]

Regulatory policymakers are no more willing to destroy consensus-building ambiguities with explicit policy choices than the politicians who drafted the vague statutes that agencies must implement. Overt goal ranking inevitably antagonizes interest groups and constrains administrative flexibility.[9] Even so, the analyst can measure the available options against each of several goals, leaving the decision-maker to rank the goals either explicitly, in written or oral communications, or implicitly as similar regulatory questions are decided over time.

Identifying options

Although regulatory analysts insist that decisionmakers explore a wide range of options before settling upon a single solution, there are "inherent limitations on the capacity of a complex bureaucracy to explore alternatives."[10] Expanding the range of relevant choice can quickly press agency analytical resources to their limits and ultimately delay important rulemaking initiatives.[11] Perhaps more importantly, upper-level decisionmakers have only a limited capacity to consider widely ranging options.

Although regulatory analysts can bring a fresh perspective to the options-identification effort, experience suggests that they do not often do so. First, an agency's regulatory analysts do not always become a part of the decisionmaking process until after the program office has already limited the possible options to a considerable degree. Second, analysts often lack sufficient technical expertise to be of much practical use in real-world situations where experience, political feasibility and available technologies, not novel economic concepts, determine realistic regulatory alternatives. As one midlevel analyst observed: "What you can do now is very much limited by what you have done in the past."[12] Third, agency analysts are not immune to the tunnel vision that sometimes afflicts program office staffers.[13] For example, the Administrator of EPA once became so disturbed with the agency analysts' use of a $7.5 million per life saved cutoff that he wrote a memorandum to the agency staff telling it to consider a wider range of options for characterizing mortality rates.[14] Finally, many agency analysts do not list options identification as one of their primary duties, focusing instead on costing out options that have already been identified by others.

Nevertheless, the options' identification effort is very worthwhile. Even if only two or three realistic options emerge in subordinate decisionmaking units, the frequent differences of opinion between the program office and the regulatory analysis office about which option to pursue can illuminate the nature of the choices. Agency staffers can cast their nets broadly at early stages in the rulemaking process to identify a large pool of options that can be narrowed fairly rapidly as analytical resources are depleted. This "tiering" approach has been successfully incorporated into the environmental impact statement process,[15] and EPA's Office of Water Regulation and Standards has used it in writing industry-wide standards.[16] There is no reason why this modest options identification tool should not be extended to all rulemaking.

Inadequate information

By far the most frequently cited impediment to regulatory analysis is the lack of adequate information. Because agency regulatory analysts rarely have sufficient time and resources to undertake original research, they are perforce limited to using existing off-the-shelf studies that are rarely up to the task. Existing studies were usually undertaken for entirely different purposes and therefore often provide only tenuous answers to the questions that the analysts ask. Analysts piece together snatches of information from a government statistic here, a corporate report there, and add a liberal sprinkling of anecdotal evidence derived from frequent telephone calls and perhaps a site visit or two. They then attempt to "massage" the existing data to make it more usable, but in reality this often consists of little more than heroic efforts to gloss over glaring weaknesses in the data. The net result is an analysis that is laced with guesswork and plagued by large uncertainties. Nevertheless, because the agency can rarely avoid making a decision, it uses the best information that it can assemble and accepts the resulting uncertainties in its assessments and predictions.

Inadequate cost and economic impact studies. The agencies usually have sufficient resources to conduct or contract for primary cost studies, which consist of predicting how regulated industries will react to proposed regulatory alternatives and estimating the resulting costs. Cost estimates can be derived from vendors of compliance equipment, from attempts to simulate industry reactions, and from the industry's own estimates.[17] Although it is sometimes difficult to verify the accuracy of these assessments, especially when the extent to which the relevant industry is already in compliance is unknown,[18] they can usually be undertaken with some measure of objectivity. The accuracy of such studies, however, depends greatly on the resources that the agency wishes to devote to them. For example, EPA is generally satisfied with cost estimates that are correct to plus or minus 30 percent, believing that estimates that would yield more precise figures are generally not cost-effective.[19]

Even primary cost studies can be difficult for performance standards, which are intended to give regulated entities leeway in designing a compliance scheme. As we observed in Chapter 4 in connection with EPA's particulates standard, cost calculations can be very difficult when the agency cannot know in advance how individual entities will react to the standard.[20] Agency analysts also face great analytical difficulties in "sorting out various costs attributable to a specific regulation from those due to changing market demand, other regulatory requirements or broader-purpose redesign of production processes."[21] For example, although a certain amount of production process redesign was required by OSHA's cotton dust standard, foreign competition would have forced many companies to retool to reduce labor costs and other inefficiencies, even without the regulation, and several textile mills had already retooled by the time that OSHA promulgated the standard.[22] Finally, it is very difficult at the outset of a rulemaking initiative to "take into account the learning curve that makes compliance progressively cheaper."[23] Regulatory analysts nevertheless tend to use worst-case assumptions, which ultimately overestimate compliance costs, sometimes by orders of magnitude.[24]

Predicting the financial impact on regulated entities of government-imposed costs can also be extremely complicated. Companies are not always willing to share financial information with agencies, because many of them believe that financial records are trade secrets.[25] Although many agencies have authority to demand financial information, such requests must be approved by a rather niggardly OMB.[26] Even when the agency gains access to financial information, differing accounting systems can complicate analytical efforts.

An ideal regulatory analysis would go still further to predict indirect impacts, such as "effects on prices, productivity, employment, capital availability, research and innovation, balance of trade, and the supply of energy and other scarce natural resources."[27] These projections, however, depend upon an extraordinarily complicated array of unquantified and interrelated factors. For example, in order to project the number of firms that might be forced out of an industry as a result of a proposed regulation, an agency would have to investigate not only the direct capital, operating, maintenance and administrative costs, but also the competitive situation in the industry, the prevalent rate of return on investment and the availability of capital, just to mention a few of the more influential factors.[28] Given real-world resource constraints, agencies can make only the crudest of estimates based upon broad assumptions about economic behavior, few of which are subject to verification or rejection.

Inadequate benefit studies. The analytical difficulties of cost studies pale by comparison to the informational impediments to analyzing the benefits of many regulations.[29] The discussion that follows will focus upon three different kinds of regulation: (1) economic regulation; (2) civil-rights regulation; and (3) health, safety, and environmental regulation.

The benefits of economic regulation are perhaps the easiest to assess. The benefit of reducing monopoly or oligopoly power is simply the value of those goods that would have been produced in a free, unimpeded market. Although relatively sophisticated models exist for calculating these benefits, disagreement still exists over many of the assumptions that they employ.[30] The value to consumers of accurate information about products and investment securities is much harder to calculate. Estimates of the amount of consumer dollars lost to fraud, unfair trade practices and misleading advertising are very difficult to verify empirically, because the regulations are prophylactic in nature.[31] Similarly, the benefits of regulations aimed at maintaining adequate consumer services, such as obtaining a diversity of views in television programming, are very difficult to calculate. Even the benefits of deregulatory initiatives in the transportation and telecommunications industries that result in better service or lower prices are hard to quantify.[32]

The benefits of regulations aimed at providing equality of opportunity for victims of racial, religious, sexual, and national origin discrimination are not amenable to quantification. Quantitative analysis can illustrate the degree of existing discrimination by comparing the distribution of minorities (blacks, females, etc.) with the distribution that would exist absent discrimination. Predictive models might even be designed to project the impact of particular regulatory options on those distributions. But the benefits of regulation to persons who would otherwise be the victims of discrimination are captured in notions of justice, fairness and autonomy that are virtually immune to quantitative analysis.[33] There are no scales; there are no units of measurement; and there are no standards of comparison. Yet, these are precisely the tools that comprehensive analytical rationality requires if it is to be useful in guiding decisionmakers to rational regulatory results.

The analytical difficulties in assessing the benefits of health and environmental regulation have been treated at great length in the literature and will only be briefly summarized here. The complex interrelationships between pollutants and health and environmental effects are at present very poorly understood.[34] The benefits of standards for dangerous technologies, such as nuclear power plants, depend upon extremely complex interrelationships between humans and technology and between technologies and other technologies that overtax the capacities of the most brilliant minds and the most sophisticated computers.[35]

Direct evidence of environmental, health and safety risks is almost impossible to obtain. Ethical considerations preclude many kinds of experiments with human beings,[36] and experiments on disruptions of natural ecosystems are very difficult to design and conduct.[37] Epidemiological studies of groups of humans, such as workers, who have received greater than normal exposures to chemicals can provide some direct evidence of risk, but these studies are notoriously inconclusive.[38] As we observed in the EPA particulates case study, it is sometimes difficult to extrapolate the results of an epidemiological study conducted under one set of conditions to human exposures in different circumstances. Information on the causes of automobile accidents is similarly elusive and of varying quality.[39] Even information on relatively straightforward benefits, such as the effects of corrosive pollutants on metals, is very difficult to come by.[40]

Although tests in surrogate systems, such as animals and greenhouses, are often available, they are also expensive and inconclusive. They raise difficult questions concerning the appropriateness of particular species, validity of test designs, applicability of exposure routes, and a host of other technical considerations that cloak the analytical enterprise in huge uncertainties.[41] Information on the extent to which humans and the environment are exposed to hazards is also hard to find.[42] Pollutants move in unexplained ways through air, water and soil, and they even move back and forth between media.[43] Accidents follow strange and unpredictable causal paths from innocuous beginning to catastrophic end.[44]

Assessing the remote and indirect benefits of health and environmental regulations presents even greater analytical problems.[45] How does one calculate the emotional satisfaction of knowing that the Great Lakes are being protected from destruction by water pollution? The agencies have devoted little attention to these and other indirect benefits, such as pain and suffering prevented, worker absenteeism avoided, and the emotional well-being of family and friends of potential victims.[46]

Conclusions. Although many of the informational impediments to regulatory analysis are simply intractable, some initiatives can be undertaken to improve the quality of available information. For example, trade secrecy claims should not be allowed to hinder agency analytical efforts,[47] because agency analysts are capable of sanitizing financial information to reduce the risk of revealing trade secrets. Regulated companies should not be allowed to sit back and fire pot shots at agency economic impact assessments if they are unwilling to share accurate financial data with the agency's analysts. Similarly, OMB could enhance the quality of economic impact data available to the agencies by allowing agencies more leeway to acquire such information in industry surveys.

Agencies could further enhance the quality of analysis by coordinating research efforts with analytical needs. Although some agencies, such as the National Highway Traffic Safety Administration, carefully coordinate their research efforts with their rulemaking needs, others have been less adept. For example, the Occupational Safety and Health Administration has long had difficulty in coordinating research and rulemaking activities with the National Institute for Occupational Safety and Health, perhaps because the two entities are in entirely separate departments. Even within single agencies, such as EPA, coordination efforts are uneven. Employees in charge of agency research should be included in subordinate decisionmaking entities from a rule's inception, and agency analysts should play a substantial role in defining overall research priorities.

Bias in cost and benefit studies

Some observers of the regulatory process suggest that the information available to agency analysts may be biased toward particular regulatory results.[48] Regulatory analysts, out of necessity, rely heavily upon the regulated industry for information. For example, the Office of Toxic Substances in EPA relies almost exclusively upon manufacturers of chemicals for information on both the costs and the benefits of new and existing chemicals. EPA's other program offices also rely heavily upon industry surveys in identifying technologies for technology-based standards.

When a party with an interest in the outcome of the regulatory activity submits data and analysis, it is natural for that party to cast its submissions in the most favorable light.[49] It will hire experts who exercise their professional judgment in a way that reflects that party's view of the world.[50] Not surprisingly, retrospective studies reveal a pattern of consistent before-the-fact overestimation of compliance costs.[51] Yet, analysts do not have the luxury of ignoring studies simply because they come from sources with an interest in the outcome of the proceedings.[52]

Regulatory analysts in the agencies recognize the potential for bias in the cost information that they receive,[53] but many believe that they can independently verify industry-submitted cost estimates.[54] First, agencies can carefully scrutinize data and analyses that come from interested parties for indications of bias. Second, some (but not all) agencies have authority to require submission of raw data and to inspect or subpoena agency records.[55] Third, agencies can expose all submitted information to full public scrutiny so that outside commentators can point to sources of bias or identify additional information that might correct for bias. Fourth, agencies can reduce bias by collecting information from multiple sources.[56] Fifth, agencies can circulate potentially biased studies for peer review by expert advisory committees or independent scientists in academia.[57] The analysts would, however, have to avoid the valid-invalid dichotomy that plagued EPA's particulates RIA in Chapter 4. Outside peer reviewers should be charged with skeptically examining submitted information and probing assumptions for weak spots and policy biases, much like the role played by Professor Viscusi in OSHA's hazard identification RIA in Chapter 7. Sixth, in extreme cases, agencies can contract for independent studies to verify or refute studies from potentially biased sources.

Finally, agencies should experiment with cooperative regulatory impact assessments. Under this novel approach, representatives from the agency and all affected parties would review the available information, assess its strengths and weaknesses and agree upon the extent to which it should be relied upon in regulatory analysis documents. Cooperative regulatory analysis will probably not work for rules involving numerous affected parties because too many parties can interfere with the consensus-building that is vital to such an effort. More importantly, cooperative analysis can only work in an atmosphere of mutual trust, an atmosphere that is not likely to exist in a regulatory program that has historically been characterized by highly adversarial rulemaking proceedings. Finally, a cooperative regulatory impact assessment process will only work if there exists some mechanism for ensuring that the analysis is prepared in the absence of consensus. Cooperative regulatory analysis has the potential for assuring affected parties that the assessments are not systematically biased.

Inadequate models

When the analyst lacks adequate information, he or she can resort to mathematical approximations of reality. Mathematical models extrapolate existing data to areas where no data exist. For many natural phenomena, such as planetary motion, the available models are very good approximations of reality. For other phenomena, such as pollutant dispersion, low-dose effects of toxic chemicals and macroeconomic trends, the existing models are grossly inaccurate.[58] Analysts have made commendable attempts to create sophisticated computer models of reality, stretching available knowledge to its limits,[59] but the products of these efforts still leave much to be desired.

The predictions of mathematical models often depend heavily upon the assumptions that the modelers use.[60] For example, the predictions of cancer risk assessment models can vary over ten orders of magnitude.[61] Similarly, models that are used to estimate the likelihood of catastrophic failures of complex technological systems are subject to the limited ability of the human mind to imagine possible failure modes of safety technologies.[62] Once assumptions are programmed into a computer algorithm, they can easily become inaccessible to those who must rely upon the model's predictions. Regulatory analysis documents must, therefore, be very explicit about the assumptions that go into the models upon which they rely.[63]

Models simplify reality. Simplification begets inaccuracy, and inaccuracies grow as a model's projections get farther and farther from the real-world data.[64] Nevertheless, the results of the modeling effort are often stated with deceptive precision, leading decisionmakers to believe that the analysts know more than they really do. At their best, sophisticated models may be only marginally informative. Pushed past their considerable limitations they can work positive harm upon the decisionmaking process.

Inadequate tools for quantification

Numbers are the regulatory analyst's stock in trade.[65] Take away the ability to reduce complicated considerations to numbers, and the analyst becomes little more than a trusted advisor, broadly speculating on the pros and cons of various options with few standards for comparison. Yet, although quantification can greatly enhance the quality of regulatory decisionmaking by permitting comparisons and facilitating prioritization,[66] overly ambitious attempts at quantification can mislead decisionmakers and the public. We have already seen how inadequate data and imprecise models can befuddle the analyst's efforts to quantify the effects of particular regulatory activities. A more serious impediment to quantitative analysis is the immunity to quantification of some considerations that are essential to rational regulatory decisions.

An analyst who is excessively preoccupied with quantification may put to one side variables, such as historic, recreational and esthetic benefits, that are resistant to quantitative analysis. Former EPA Administrator Douglas Costle has noted that "[t]hat which can be measured tends to receive more weight than less tangible, though perhaps more important effects which cannot be quantified."[67] Former NHTSA Administrator Joan Claybrook opined that "economists habituated to number-crunching feel secure with the measurable, and indifferent to the immeasurable, though immense, benefits of avoided injuries and deaths."[68] Professor Laurence Tribe has identified three categories of values that are particularly "fragile" in this regard: (1) values, such as ecological balance, unspoiled wilderness, and species diversity, that are "intrinsically incommensurable, in at least some of their salient dimensions, with the human satisfactions that are bound to play a central role in any policy analysis"; (2) values, such as urban esthetics and community cohesion, "with inherently global, holistic, or structural features that cannot be reduced to any finite listing or combination of independent attributes"; and (3) values, such as the integrity of the body or the integrity of the community or neighborhood, that have "an 'on-off' character, and usually also a deeply evocative and emotional aspect."[69]

The tendency of regulatory analysis to "dwarf soft variables" can yield a unidimensional view of the world that in practice biases decisionmakers against crucial, but unquantifiable values.[70] Because unquantifiable effects may never show up in the regulatory analyst's calculations, quantitative analysis may unwittingly constrain the exercise of policy judgment by upper-level decisionmakers.[71] Professor Frances Rourke, a long-time student of policy analysis, has observed: "The greatest danger that these quantitative techniques of analysis present is the possibility that they may arm error with the seeming support of scientifically established fact, giving ill-advised policy greater credence. When this occurs, the finely honed rationalizing instruments of managerial science can become dispensers of irrationality measured out with mathematical precision."[72]

Regulatory analysts must therefore resist their natural tendency to dismiss soft variables and attempt to discuss them thoroughly in the text of regulatory analysis documents, even if the discussion tends to take away from their precision. Ironically, some effort at constraining the urge to quantify is essential to the credibility of the analytical process.

Characterizing uncertainties

Inadequate data, inaccurate models, and the infirmities of quantitative analysis all combine to leave regulatory analysis swimming in a sea of uncertainties.[73] Adequately characterizing these uncertainties is the greatest challenge to the regulatory analyst.[74] As we observed in Chapter 4, if analysts forthrightly confront the uncertainties inherent in their predictions and make the decisionmaker aware of the general lack of confidence with which they speak, they risk rejection. Analysts therefore face almost irresistible pressures to gloss over uncertainties and state quantitative predictions as "point estimates." Yet, if the analysts overstate their confidence in their predictions, they will inevitably mislead the decisionmaker, perhaps disastrously. The solution to this dilemma lies in locating tools for characterizing uncertainties in ways that retain the usefulness of analysis to decisionmakers without misleading them. Unfortunately, the majority of regulatory analysis documents that agencies currently prepare emphasize single-value estimates of costs and benefits and shun any serious attempt to characterize uncertainties.[75]

Perhaps the most effective method for characterizing uncertainties is the "confidence interval" that is typical of scientific reports.[76] The analyst makes a quantitative prediction that is his or her best estimate and at the same time predicts with some predetermined degree of confidence (usually 95 percent) that the result lies between two other points along the same spectrum. The "width" of this confidence margin can at times be more revealing than the best estimate prediction. For example, in one instance in the author's experience, an analyst in EPA's Office of Pesticide Programs predicted that registering a pesticide that had been shown to cause cancer in laboratory animals would cause twenty-seven cancers over a seventy-year period. When pressed for a 95 percent confidence interval the prediction was expressed as follows: $0 < 27 < 660,000$. The predicted cancers would be somewhere between 0 and 660,000. This vast interval spoke volumes about the confidence with which the analyst made his original prediction of twenty-seven cancers.

Strictly speaking, analysts can only rarely provide a confidence interval in its pure statistical sense, because analysts, unlike statisticians, rarely know with confidence the complete distribution of probabilities. Analysts can, however, use the confidence interval technique to display the uncertainties in their predictions if they base the interval upon their own subjective assessments of the distribution of probabilities. This, of course, requires that the analysts reveal their subjective probability statements to decisionmakers and the public and give the reasons for choosing them.[77] This is what OSHA analysts attempted to do in the hazard communication rulemaking when they estimated that workplace diseases were underreported by a factor ranging from 0 to 50 percent.

Analysts can also characterize uncertainties by applying two or more models to the same preexisting data.[78] For example, one survey of cancer risk assessment models discovered that from the same starting data, the risk predictions could vary over ten orders of magnitude, depending upon the model.[79] The analyst can tell the decisionmaker which model is preferred and why, but the decisionmaker must be free to base a decision on any or all of the models.

Still another technique for characterizing uncertainties is to subject a model's assumptions to sensitivity analysis. Very minor changes in critical assumptions can often have major effects on a model's predictions. And to a very large extent, the regulatory analysts are responsible for selecting the crucial assumptions that permeate the models that they use. In a sensitivity analysis the analyst performs the same analytical operation under several different sets of assumptions to determine how the predictions vary with different assumptions.[80] Once the decisionmaker is aware of the sensitivity of the analyst's predictions to particular assumptions, the decisionmaker can evaluate the assumptions themselves to determine how much credence to give any particular prediction.

If more sophisticated mechanisms for dealing with uncertainty fail, the analyst may prepare a worst case analysis of the costs and/or benefits of regulatory alternatives. This technique, which has achieved some prominence in the environmental impact statement context,[81] can be useful when margins of error cannot be calculated and when the regulated activity could have disastrous impacts.[82] In performing a worst case analysis, the analyst simply calculates the consequences of the worst credible scenarios and attaches a rough probability to each of those scenarios. One obvious drawback of this technique is that it tends to skew the analysis by focusing attention on the worst side effects of regulatory action or inaction,[83] even though the worst case scenarios are not likely to play themselves out in the real world. Nevertheless, as the Bhopal, India tragedy has shown, worst cases do sometimes happen, and it can be useful for the decisionmaker to know the most extreme downsides of regulatory alternatives.

Even though it may mean rejection of the analytical work product, analysts should forthrightly state the confidence with which they make quantitative predictions. If analysts continue to make unqualified predictions without confidence statements, the analytical effort is ultimately doomed to failure as decisionmakers realize that the analysts' point estimates have lulled them into a false sense of security.

Retrospective analysis

The regulatory analysis office can enhance the accuracy of its predictions if it obtains feedback from the real world through retrospective analysis of the actual impact of regulations on the regulated industry and the intended beneficiaries.[84] A good faith review of the effectiveness of existing regulations can loosen up the bureaucratic inertia that often plagues regulatory agencies. Over time, retrospective analysis can be useful in evaluating the entire regulatory analysis enterprise.

Interestingly, regulatory analysts, who are in the business of analyzing the work of others, rarely evaluate their own work.[85] Some of the program offices in EPA are required by statute to reevaluate rules periodically, but these evaluations do not focus upon the predictions made in past regulatory analysis documents. Of the agencies studied in detail in this book, only the National Highway Traffic Safety Administration undertakes routine retrospective analyses of its predictions in its past rulemaking efforts.[86]

Because uncertainties in the subject matter virtually guarantee inaccuracies in analytical projections, it is not surprising that regulatory analysts are hesitant to evaluate their own efforts. As one EPA analyst candidly observed: "How is my career going to be advanced by doing a study that shows that three years ago the agency made a wrong prediction? It is not in my best interest."[87] Although analytical resources in most agencies are strained by day-to-day responsibilities, existing retrospective analyses indicate that agencies could profit greatly from devoting some resources to evaluating the accuracy of past analytical efforts. Retrospective economic impact studies indicate a general trend toward overestimating compliance costs, sometimes to a fairly large degree.[88] For example, a retrospective look at the costs of complying with OSHA's vinyl chloride standard found the actual costs were only about 7 percent of predicted costs.[89] Retrospective benefit studies, however, are virtually nonexistent, in large part because very few benefit studies have been undertaken in the past.

One problem that has plagued retrospective efforts is the difficulty in determining after the fact exactly what monies regulatees expended in complying with a particular rule. Corporate accounting tools are not designed to facilitate the measurement of compliance costs. In addition, since performance-based regulations do not compel the adoption of any particular compliance scheme, industries do not always react in the way that the agency analysts expected, and it is sometimes difficult to attribute particular expenditures to particular regulatory requirements.[90] Finally, regulated firms are not always willing to cooperate with the preparation of retrospective studies that have little likelihood of reducing regulatory burdens.[91]

When these accounting problems can be overcome, retrospective analysis can be very useful in assessing the value of past uses of regulatory analysis and in avoiding the perpetuation of past analytical errors into the future. Although it would probably not be cost-effective for an agency to conduct extensive retrospective analysis for all of its major rules, it could set aside enough analytical resources to undertake retrospective analysis for one or two regulatory analyses each year. Most agencies devote some resources to program evaluation, and in recent years regulatory analysis has assumed an important role in the programs of most regulatory agencies. Agencies should follow NHTSA's example and fold retrospective analysis into their general program evaluation functions.

Deadlines and delay

For any decisionmaking body there is always a "tension between timeliness and analysis."[92] The time that it takes to draft a good regulatory analysis can mean delay for rulemaking managers in the program offices who then complain of "paralysis by analysis."[93] Hence, the potential for delay is another source of conflict between the policy staff and the program office staff. On the other hand, the need for further analysis can serve as a convenient conflict-avoidance device, as issues that cannot be amicably resolved are put off pending further analysis.[94]

Regulatory analysts sometimes complain that rulemaking deadlines force them to settle for cursory analysis. For some regulatory efforts, such as regulations accompanying quarantine activities of the Animal and Plant Health Inspection Service, time constraints render any significant analytical effort virtually impossible. Most timing problems, however, stem from the fact that analytical services are not requested until late in the process, after much of the technical work on the rule is completed. Structuring the decisionmaking process to involve regulatory analysts at very early stages so that they may play a role in setting research agendas and allocating resources could help alleviate this aspect of the timing problem. Suggestions for structuring analysis into the regulatory decisionmaking process are discussed in more detail in Part III.

Insufficient analytical resources

One of the most frequently identified impediments to analysis is the paucity of resources that agencies currently devote to that function.[95] This criticism must be taken with a grain of salt, because no analysis is as thorough as it could be. As Professor Lindblom has observed, "A policymaker, whether an individual or an organization, will become exhausted long before the analysis is exhausted."[96] The question whether regulatory analysis offices are receiving adequate resources is, like most resource issues, a matter of tradeoffs.

The federal executive agencies devote substantial resources to regulatory analysis. The most systematic attempt to determine the amount of resources regulatory analysis consumes was a questionnaire that the House Judiciary Committee in 1983 directed to fifteen agencies.[97] The questionnaire elicited responses of varying quality and precision from the agencies, and the results are summarized in Table 9.1. The Congressional Budget Office has estimated that the average Regulatory Impact Analysis for major rules costs $100,000.[98] A General Accounting Office survey, conducted in 1983, of the costs of RIA preparation in six major agencies yielded similar results.[99]

Whether the agencies are spending adequate amounts on their analytical efforts depends upon what society is getting in return for those resources and upon how society could otherwise be spending them. Some observers believe that a two million dollar regulatory analysis is worth the expense if it is instrumental in persuading an agency to adopt a standard that saves the regulated industry and, indirectly, consumers fifteen million dollars.[100] Others believe that resources are being wasted on gold-plated studies that can have very little real impact in a regulatory world that is dominated by the pulls and tugs of political forces. Many have therefore concluded that regulatory analysis requirements are not cost-effective.[101]

Although the Office of Management and Budget (OMB) has been responsible for increasing the analytical burdens upon the agencies in the last several years, that agency has not recommended that they be given additional resources to do the required analyses.[102] OMB has been especially parsimonious with funds for long-term research into the potential benefits of regulation. Reacting to OMB's resistance to funding research on the greenhouse effect and global warming, one EPA official observed that "OMB has taken a very dim view of long-range research of any kind at EPA," the rationale being "that 'we don't want EPA to go looking for anything because

Table 9.1. *The cost of regulatory analysis by agency (in thousands of dollars)*

	E.O. 12,044[a]		E.O. 12,291[b]		Both[c]	
	In-house[d]	Outside[e]	In-house	Outside	In-house	Outside
U.S.D.A.[f]						
Agricultural Marketing Service	45 (3)[g]					
Farmers Home Administration	44 (22)					
Federal Grain Inspection Service	25 (1)					
Food & Nutrition Service	11.9 (6)					
Food Safety & Inspection Service	208 (56)					
Foreign Agricultural Service	(3)[h]					
Forest Service	(7)[i]					
Office of Minority Affairs						
Packers & Stockyards Administration[j]	3.1 (2)					
E.P.A.						
Toxic Substances		667 (3)				
Air Programs	240 (4)	1,934 (3)		563 (2)		
Water Programs	20 (1)	100 (1)				
Radiation Programs				2,610 (2)		
Solid Waste Programs			40 (1)			
Pesticide Programs						
Miscellaneous						
Food & Drug Administration					290 (5)[k]	
Department of Health & Human Services (except FDA)					190 (11)[l]	25 (3)
Mine Safety & Health Administration[m]	8.4 (1)		4.2			
OSHA		454 (9)[n]	(7)	545.992 (3)[o]		
D.O.T.[p]						

NHTSA	288 (9)	435 (6)
Office of the Secretary	1,159 (1)	2,934 (1)
U.S. Coast Guard	359.1 (3)	
Federal Highway Administration	199.809 (20)	20.998 (1)
Federal Railroad Administration	101.049 (1)	312.768 (1)

[a] Rules proposed or promulgated between 1978 and 1980 – the total cost of regulatory analyses, under E.O. 12,044.

[b] Rules proposed or promulgated in 1981 and 1982 – the total cost of regulatory analyses under E.O. 12,291.

[c] When the agency fails to distinguish between the two specified time periods.

[d] The regulatory analyses were performed by in-house agency personnel.

[e] The regulatory analyses were performed by outside contractors.

[f] U.S.D.A. completed 198 regulatory analyses under E.O. 12,044 at an average cost of **$5,638**. The agency completed 46 regulatory analyses under E.O. 12,291 at an average cost of **$22,643**. The data for analyses under E.O. 12,044 is broken down among departments.

[g] Indicates number of regulatory analyses performed making up total cost.

[h] No dollar amount given – notation that analyses were performed by agency personnel.

[i] Analyses required under E.O. 12,044 were integrated into Environmental Assessments or Environmental Impact Statements. Therefore, data do not exist to compute their costs.

[j] Figures not given.

[k] FDA figures cover the period from 1976–82. Cost estimates are approximate, based on estimated professional person-months involved in preparation of each analysis, times assumed salary and overhead cost of **$5,000** per month.

[l] Department of Health and Human Services figures cover the period from 1976–82. Cost estimates are approximate, based on estimated professional person-months involved in preparation of each analysis, times assumed salary and overhead cost of **$5,000** per month.

[m] None of MSHA's rules were subjected to the requirements of E.O. 12,044 or 12,291; therefore no regulatory analyses were conducted. Economic assessments were prepared in-house and averaged **$8,400** (1978–80) and **$4,200** (1981–2).

[n] Time period used to answer was March 24, 1978 through February 17, 1981. The costs are those of the contract effort related primarily to data gathering. No separate estimate of the time spent by OSHA regulatory analysts or standards-development personnel was made.

[o] Time period used to answer was December 18, 1981 through April 26, 1983. The costs are those of the contract effort related primarily to data gathering. No separate estimate of the time spent by OSHA regulatory analysts or standards-development personnel was made.

[p] To compute costs of in-house analyses, DOT estimated the numbers of hours worked on each analysis by persons at various pay levels, multiplied that by 1983 hourly pay levels, and added 14% as an estimate of the value of Federal Civil Service fringe benefits. To the extent that pay increased since 1976, these estimates are overstated. To the extent they were unable to allocate to each analysis its share of overhead (rent, utilities, etc.) the cost estimates are understated. Additionally, the estimates do not include the required review by the Office of the Secretary and to that extent are understated.

Source: *Regulatory Reform Act: Hearings Before the Subcomm. on Administrative Law and Governmental Relations of the House Comm. on the Judiciary, Supplement*, 98th Cong., 1st Sess. (1983).

they might find something.' "[103] Many conclude that the real motivation behind existing analytical requirements is to force agencies to shift resources out of regulatory programs and into analysis, thereby stemming the flow of regulations.[104] This cynical motivation for the use of analysis, if true, does little to enhance the status of analysis among agency employees, regulatees and the general public.

Regulatory analysis and public values

One of the important lessons of the case studies in Chapters 3 to 7 is that regulatory decisions invoke fundamental public values. How an agency's decisions reflect important public values, especially those inherent in its statute, is an important measure of its institutional legitimacy. We learned in Chapter 1 that the regulatory analyst does not claim expertise in identifying the moral dimensions of regulatory problems; nor does the analyst overtly claim to know how to resolve the value conflicts that often arise in regulatory decision-making. Yet, we shall see that proponents of the highly formalized version of regulatory analysis called cost-benefit analysis do in fact tend to collapse important moral considerations into a unidimensional monetary measure of the utility of regulatory options.

As currently practiced, cost-benefit analysis is quite incapable of capturing the rich variety of moral concerns that regulatory decisions inevitably invoke. Indeed, some observers of the practice of formal cost-benefit analysis maintain that the technique itself is value laden, because it tends to regard the satisfaction of private preferences (as revealed in private markets) as a valuable public goal and even ranks that value above others, such as justice, fairness, and autonomy that are inherent in the United States Constitution and the statutes that the agencies have been created to administer. Although reducing analysis to monetary terms in a single cost-benefit comparison is not a requirement of a good regulatory analysis, the fact that Executive Order 12,291 and many of the strongest proponents of regulatory analysis advocate formalized cost-benefit analysis demands that some attention be given to the way that this special brand of regulatory analysis incorporates and expresses public values.

Values in cost-benefit analysis

For many proponents of comprehensive analytical rationality, the culmination of the analytical effort is the moment that the analyst reduces costs and benefits to a "common metric" and compares the two in a cost-benefit analysis.[105] Professor Andrews defines formal cost-benefit analysis as follows:

> A rigorous, quantitative, and data-intensive procedure, which requires identification of all nontrivial effects, categorization of these effects as benefits or costs, quantitative estimation of the extent of each benefit or cost associated with an action, translation of those elements into a common metric such as dollars, discounting of future costs and benefits into the terms of a given year, and summary of all the costs and all the benefits to see which is greater.[106]

Were a formal cost-benefit analysis possible in the real world, there would be very little remaining for a rational decisionmaker to do; the preferred alternative would be obvious. As we have seen, however, many practical impediments stand in the way of a simple application of cost-benefit analysis to regulatory decisionmaking. More importantly, cost-benefit analysis has a strong ideological component that belies the impression, carefully fostered by many analysts, that it is merely a neutral tool for guiding decisionmakers to the "best" result.[107] Indeed, cost-benefit analysis can lead the agency to the wrong result if the measure of "rightness" is the values inherent in the agency's statute, rather than a supervening concern for "allocative efficiency" or "wealth maximization."

Valuation problems. The most troublesome conundrum of cost-benefit analysis is placing a monetary value on the benefits of regulation. It is relatively easy to assign a monetary value to goods commonly traded in free markets. The analyst can assume that the market price is an adequate surrogate for value to society, even though some individual members of society would attribute a higher or lower value to the commodity. Thus, it is often possible to assign dollar values to the benefits of economic regulation,[108] and it is not conceptually difficult to value environmental damage to materials that are bought and sold in the marketplace.[109]

Attempts to place dollar values on civil rights, however, are much more controversial.[110] Although a theoretical literature exists on the inefficiencies of racial, sexual, religious and national origin discrimination, it has also been suggested that if there is in fact a preference for discrimination among some, then allocative efficiency may well decrease as a result of rules prohibiting such discrimination.[111] Obviously, in calculating the benefits of a regulation aimed at ensuring equality of opportunity, the "preference for discrimination" is entitled to no weight whatsoever, no matter how many dollars the bigots are willing to pay for the pleasure of discriminating. On the other hand, the value to society of rules against racial, ethnic, sex, and religious discrimination is not merely what the beneficiaries would be willing to pay to avoid the discrimination. Equality of opportunity is an important public value, and the marketplace cannot possibly provide a monetary measure for its worth. This is not merely because of some kind of market failure; it is because the market is the wrong place to look.

The heartiest debate centers on valuing the benefits of regulations that significantly reduce mortality and morbidity risks[112] or enhance important environmental, historical and esthetic benefits.[113] Proponents of cost-benefit analysis argue that, however distasteful it may appear to the uninitiated, valuing lives and other important amenities is unavoidable, and it is done implicitly in thousands of everyday decisions.[114] Explicit valuation techniques can help regulatory decisionmakers avoid the inconsistency of placing a high implicit value on life in one case and a low value in another.[115] Forcing decisionmakers to be explicit about valuation rids the analytical deck of a joker that can range from zero to infinity and thereby render any regulatory decision justifiable.[116]

Some early attempts to place a monetary value on natural ecosystems compared the ability of ecosystems to provide services (such as residuals disposal, nutrient cycling and soil binding of air pollutants) to the cost of installing man-made technologies for the same purpose. These studies yielded some surprisingly high sums (e.g., $205,000 per hectare for wetlands).[117] But most agree that the estimates are still low, because the operations of ecosystems are poorly understood.[118]

"Contingent valuation" techniques employ surveys in which hypothetical markets in nonmarket goods (such as uncertain risks) are described to interviewees and their willingness to pay for such goods is ascertained indirectly.[119] One such survey determined that consumers of electricity were willing to pay $6.2 billion per year for visibility in National Parks in the Southwest.[120] Contingent valuation techniques, however, are subject to manipulation. It is easy for a respondent to claim a willingness to pay vast amounts for a beautiful view when he or she does not actually have to part with the cash.[121]

Economists have also developed "shadow pricing" techniques for valuing objects and amenities that are not typically traded in markets.[122] For example, a shadow price for the value of a beautiful vista might be the difference between a home with the view and an equivalent home without the view. Shadow pricing techniques are unreliable, however, because the surrogate is not the real thing.[123]

First, more than a single family may enjoy a national park view; indeed, some who never take the trek to the mountaintop may value its very existence. Second, the technique draws its measure of value from a fairly narrow slice of society, viz, those who can afford mountaintop leisure homes. It may be that less affluent people (such as ardent backpackers or professional environmentalists) actually value the view more than wealthy second home buyers with money to spare and the need for a tax shelter. If dollars are the only measure of value that counts, then the value preferences of the poor count for less than those of the rich in the analysis.

The most acrimonious debates about cost-benefit analysis focus on the valuation of human morbidity and mortality risks. Perhaps the narrowest measure of the value of a human life is the cost of a contract killing, which varies from $5,000 to $10,000 and up, depending on the circumstances.[124] So far, no economists have advocated this low sum as the appropriate measure, but some techniques that they have suggested do not demonstrate much greater sensitivity to humanitarian values.

One frequently used measure of the value of human life – the "human capital" approach – simply adopts the discounted value of future earnings.[125] Indeed, some enthusiasts would subtract a person's living expenses or "maintenance costs" from this number to arrive at a "net" value for a life.[126] Although this approach is "rational" in the sense that it is free of moral sentiment, it nevertheless seems unacceptable, because a person's worth is obviously more than what he or she can earn in the marketplace. Even assuming that other intangibles, such as the love of family members, are taken into account, the human capital measure incorporates all of the arbitrary distinctions of the current labor market, including pay differentials between races, sexes, and religions.[127] Finally, it runs directly contrary to the egalitarian principle, with origins deep in Judeo-Christian faith and American democratic culture, that all persons are equal before the law and God. For these reasons, most serious students of policy analysis have discarded the human capital approach.[128] Nevertheless, most regulatory analyses (like the RIAs for particulates and hazard identification) still use values based on that approach, despite the fact that it yields consistently lower values for life than other techniques.[129]

Another approach for monetizing risks to life is to examine the implicit value that individuals and public policymakers give to such risks in day-to-day activities.[130] These valuation exercises, which have been especially prevalent in decisionmaking about nuclear power, often yield widely varying results, suggesting either that society is inconsistent in the implicit value that it places on life or that different values are implicitly invoked in different contexts. In either case, the wide variation argues against using any one (or even an average) for all future governmental decisionmaking, and few analysts have attempted to do so.[131]

Most economists prefer instead to use "willingness to pay" as the measure of life-preserving governmental actions. The focus here is not on willingness to pay for life, but rather upon willingness to pay for some unit of reduced risk to life.[132] Analysts can employ contingent valuation techniques to ask individuals how much they are willing to pay to reduce health risks,[133] but this approach encounters the manipulation problem discussed earlier. Economists can also examine labor markets for evidence of willingness to pay to avoid workplace risks,[134] but like other implicit valuation techniques this yields a fairly wide range of values. Early studies suggested a value of approximately $500,000 per life, while more recent studies range from $2.5 million to $5 million.[135]

Relying upon the willingness-to-pay measure, an appendix to a Department of Transportation (DOT) handbook suggests a value of $340,000 as the average monetary value for a human fatality. It further suggests $230,000 as the average monetary value for a critical injury, and $102,000 as the average monetary value for a severe injury.[136] The Occupational Safety and Health Administration has recently used a value of $3.5 million per life for one of its safety standards.[137] Other agencies, such as the National Highway Traffic Safety Administration and the Environmental Protection Agency, however, refuse to use explicit dollar values for human lives.[138] It has been suggested that the Office of Management and Budget, in performing its regulatory analysis review role, uses a de facto cutoff for the value of human life of about $3 to 5 million; regulations that implicitly value a life at more than $5 million "raise a red flag" at OMB.[139] The Administrator of EPA cautioned his staff, however, not to rule out options on the basis of "rules of thumb" of $7.5 million per life saved.[140]

Many opponents of cost-benefit analysis question the morality of placing a value on human life, arguing that the very process belittles life's intrinsic value.[141] Examples of morally repugnant uses of life valuation techniques are not hard to find. A study on the costs and benefits of treating handicapped infants concluded that for birth weights of less than 900 grams, the costs per survivor exceeded the child's potential average lifetime earnings discounted to present value.[142] In a like vein, the Consumer Product Safety Commission determined that eliminating a hazard to small children in reclining chairs would be cost beneficial only if it could be accomplished for less than twenty-five cents per chair. The study, which used a value of $1,000,000 per crushed child, prompted the chairman of a House subcommittee to declare the entire enterprise "not only stupid, but wrong,"[143] and it sparked an intense debate among the agency's staff.[144] The policy question of where to draw the line in preserving the lives of handicapped infants and young children is so dominated by moral considerations unrelated to their potential earning power that the added information provided by cost-benefit analysis is, to all but the most doggedly reductionist utilitarians, essentially irrelevant.

Other opponents, ranging across the political spectrum from the Chemical Manufacturers Association to labor unions and environmental groups,[145] argue that it is impossible to derive a useful number for the value of a human life, even if it were desirable.[146] The wide range in implicit values that emerge from studies of actual decisions involving risks to life suggests either that different populations value life very differently or that the studies are extremely imprecise.[147] But the problem goes deeper. "Shadow pricing" human lives by human capital techniques suggests that older people are less valuable than young people and that poor people are less valuable than rich people.[148] Moreover, the clear implication of this valuation analysis is that society should be indifferent to a choice between a live human being and a check payable to the public treasury in some amount, a notion that is morally repugnant in a society that purports to value human life.

Using studies of the "risk premiums" allegedly sought by workers in hazardous jobs assumes: (1) that past preferences are valid indicators of present and future preferences; (2) that people accurately perceive the magnitude of the risks that they accept; (3) that people make accurate decisions without being overwhelmed by their complexity and opting for suboptimal solutions; and (4) that the marketplace is an accurate measure of people's preferences.[149] All four assumptions are of dubious validity. It is probably true that all of us, including workers, tend to undervalue low-probability/high-consequence risks on the "it-can't-happen-to-me" theory, in which case risk premium measures of the value of small risks to life are generally too low.[150] More importantly, workers in hazardous industries who charge low risk premiums may be acting more out of desperation than choice.[151] Professor Kelman notes that "[t]o use the wage premium accorded hazardous work as a measure of the value of life is to accept as proxies for the rest of us the choices of people who do not have many choices or who are exceptionally risk-seeking."[152] Union representative Sheldon Samuels refers to the tendency of some regulatory analysts to rely upon hazard pay as the measure of workers' willingness to accept risks in the context of a "society that historically prides itself in a less than full employment economy" as "the conventional expression of cannibalism in America."[153] Dean Guido Calabrese of the Yale Law School cautions that "[t]he willingness of a poor man, confronting a tragic situation, to choose money rather than the tragically scarce resource [his health or safety] always represents an unquiet indictment of society's distribution of wealth."[154]

Echoing the industrialists of the early twentieth century, Zeckhauser & Shepard respond that "[w]e should not further reduce the welfare of the poor by denying them occupations just because middle-class individuals would not be willing to accept them." They suggest that "prohibiting the poor from taking such risks may be a way of salving the conscience of the middle-class at the expense of the welfare of the poor."[155] But this misses the critical point that poor workers' risk premiums are used by regulatory agencies to value the lives of rich and poor alike. A more appropriate technique might be to ascertain the premium that a rich person would demand to take a job in a coal mine and base health and safety decisions for poor workers on that measure.

The debate over valuing lives is indicative of a more general debate over techniques for monetizing highly prized or unique things, such as endangered species, wild and scenic rivers, friendship and loyalty, that are not frequently traded in markets. Critics argue that for these things cost-benefit analysis is ultimately incoherent[156] or schizophrenic[157] because it cannot yield a single numerical value. This incoherence derives from the dilemma that the value of a thing can be measured either by the willingness of the purchaser to pay for it or the willingness of the seller to sell it. In the typical market context, these two measures yield the same dollar amount – viz the price at which the parties are willing to exchange the item. For objects that are not traded in markets, however, the two measures need not yield the same result.[158] For example, the price at which a person might sell his or her heart (under the willingness-to-sell measure) probably exceeds the price at which the person is prepared to pay for it (under the willingness-to-buy criterion). The latter measure depends upon the resources available to the person; the former measure is limitless. Even for less valuable things, "evidence suggests that most people would insist on being paid far more to assent to a worsening of their situation than they would be willing to pay to improve their situation."[159]

Professor Thaler has proposed a mind game that vividly demonstrates the difference between the willingness-to-pay and willingness-to-sell measures of the value of small risks. He sets out three risk situations involving a one-in-a-thousand chance of contracting a fatal disease. His business students were willing to pay $800 to eliminate the risk and $250 for a one-in-four probability of eliminating a risk four times as great, but they would charge $100,000 to a laboratory experimenter who wanted to subject them to the same one-in-a-thousand risk. This author's own administration of the game to law students yields even greater disparities. Professor Thaler refers to this dramatic difference as the "endowment effect," which "stipulates that an individual will demand much more money to give something up than he would be willing to pay to acquire it."[160] He erroneously concludes, however, that such responses are "logically inconsistent." There is nothing illogical in the reaction of most persons to this "offer-asking" dichotomy. It is a rational reaction to the a priori assignment of rights.

Interestingly, virtually all regulatory analysts adopt the willingness-to-pay criterion,[161] which can seriously undervalue an object or amenity, and Carl Pope suggests that this is no accident. He believes that corporate interests in the late nineteenth century realized that recognition of Lockeian "rights" in bodily integrity (so that polluters would have to purchase the "right" to pollute from those affected by the pollution) would be a "severe blow to industrialization." Consequently, unlike their own rights to property (which the state would protect unless the owner was offered a price at which he was willing to sell), industrialists persuaded state legislatures and courts that protection of bodily integrity from toxic substances was an "interest," which would be valued at some hypothetical willingness to pay rather than a right, which would be protected absent a contract of sale.[162]

From this perspective, it appears that cost-benefit analysis using the willingness-to-pay measure is biased against governmental intervention, and the bias grows as the interest to be protected increases in value. The cost side of the ledger is calculated by reference to free markets where willingness to sell is the measure; the benefits side is calculated by reference to hypothetical markets where willingness to pay is the measure. Little wonder, then, that regulatees express a keen preference for cost-benefit analysis and regulatory beneficiaries uniformly oppose it.

Reducing values to lowest common denominators to facilitate tradeoffs is inconsistent with the notion, embedded in the United States Constitution, that individuals have inalienable rights.[163] One of the reasons that we do not have a good measure of the value of a heart is that our society does not tolerate markets in hearts. Nor do we allow people to sell themselves into slavery or indentured servitude. Although regulatory analysts have thus far declined to quantify the benefits of regulations designed to provide women and minorities equal employment opportunities, there is no reason in theory why they could not be calculated on the same willingness-to-pay terms as health and environmental protections. But a just society recognizes rights even when to do so is inefficient in economic terms.

Talk about rights has an important procedural component as well.[164] Even if a well-documented regulatory analysis could demonstrate beyond cavil that a televised drawing and quartering of an innocent person (which might top the Nielson charts) would discourage a minimum of ten future murders, we would not allow the ceremony to take place.[165]

Proponents of quantitative cost-benefit analysis often fail to draw a vital distinction between human beings as self-satisfying consumers and human beings as citizens in a polity or members of a community. They assume there is no difference between how people value certain things in private, individual transactions and how they would wish a social valuation of those same things to be made in public, collective decisions.[166] Professor Sagoff has observed that:

> We are not simply a group of consumers, nor are we bent on satisfying self-regarding preferences. Many of us advocate ideals and have a vision of what we should do or be like as a nation. And we would sacrifice some of our private interest for those public ends.... Why should we believe that the right policy goal is the one that satisfies only the self-interested preferences of consumers? Why should we not take into account the community-regarding values that individuals seek through the political process as well?[167]

Finally, cost-benefit analysis may rob regulatory decisionmaking of an important democratic dimension. Bollier & Claybrook point out that "cost benefit analysis . . . effectively disenfranchises citizens who cannot discuss regulation in a highly technical, economic manner. Only recognized 'experts' are given credibility in the regulatory process. The empirical judgments and anecdotal testimony of victims are considered unimportant." In this sense, cost-benefit analysis is profoundly antidemocratic.[168]

At the same time, cost-benefit analysis can substitute the analyst's valuation criteria for the ethical and political judgments that are embodied in the legislation that was enacted by a democratically elected legislative body.[169] It may well be that persons thoroughly trained in economics are less sensitive to some values than ordinary persons lacking such training. Steven Rhoads describes a revealing experiment in which students were given tokens to invest either in an exchange that would return 1 cent per token to the individual or in an exchange that would yield 2.2 cents per token to be shared by the entire group, regardless of how other members of the group invested. Most economists would predict that a rational person would choose the first option, because it would maximize his personal gain. In the experiment, however, most of the individuals devoted between 40 and 60 percent of their tokens to the group exchange, with one significant exception. A group of entering graduate students in economics contributed only 20 percent to the group exchange. According to Rhoads, they "found the concept of fairness alien, and were only half as likely to indicate that they were concerned with fairness in making their decision."[170] In a democracy, the legislature has the power to write values into legislation that do not accord with the values inherent in comprehensive analytical rationality.

One answer to this conundrum is to abandon regulatory analysis altogether. If "value neutral" regulatory analysis insists on specific normative techniques for quantitative cost-benefit analysis while ruling all other normative inquiries "out of order," then regulatory analysis has very little of importance to say about most regulatory policy choices, and cost conscious decisionmakers should seriously consider whether the enterprise is worth the considerable resources that it consumes. Another answer is to rely upon less ambitious versions of regulatory analysis that do not attempt to reduce all factual, political and ethical considerations into a single quantitative comparison.

Valuing the future. Another valuation problem that plagues cost-benefit analysis is the rate that the analyst uses to discount future costs and benefits. The discount rate is an estimate of how much more a dollar in hand is worth than the promise of a dollar in the future. Although most would agree with discounting future monetary costs, discounting benefits is more controversial.[171]

Many regulations are designed to benefit future generations, but a high discount rate biases the analysis against future benefits.[172] Even if future generations value regulatory benefits the same as the present generation, "it is not clear why the later born should have to pay interest to induce their predecessors not to exhaust [depletable resources]."[173]

Optimists suggest that we should trust future generations to look out for themselves; after all, they will no doubt be wiser and wealthier than us. Professor Sagoff replies that future generations will be shaped by the conditions of the future, conditions that the present will have a large role in determining. This, according to Sagoff, is a moral question, not a simple question of economic analysis.[174]

Without acknowledging this moral dimension of the discounting issue, OMB has traditionally insisted that agencies use a very high discount rate of 10 percent in calculating the benefits of health and environmental regulations. At a discount rate of 10 percent, a dollar's worth of benefits fifty years from now is worth slightly less than a penny today.[175] This means that the benefits of a regulation that would prevent catastrophic loss in fifty years are likely to be outweighed by even modest present costs. OMB's insistence upon this rate has been highly controversial. One regulatory official referred to the practice as "unethical," and a Congressman called it "ghoulish."[176]

Assuming that discounting is a useful tool for facilitating comparisons between present costs and future benefits, the actual rate used is entirely a policy question that should be left to upper-level decisionmakers in the agencies. Regulatory analysts could help ensure against misleading uses of discount rates by applying two or more discount rates in regulatory analysis documents, thereby revealing the sensitivity of the calculations to the discount rate. More importantly, the upper-level decisionmakers' choice from among several discount rates could reveal a great deal about how they value future generations.

Distributional impacts. Cost-benefit analysis is concerned with the efficient allocation of resources; it does not directly address the distribution of resources.[177] So long as a policy maximizes the total wealth to society, it matters not who the winners and losers are or how much wealth changes hands. Yet, regulatory decisions do have disproportionate impacts on different groups of people, and politically accountable decisionmakers must consider distributional impacts if they are to keep their jobs.[178] Analysts must therefore determine who pays the costs and who receives the benefits.[179]

Distributional considerations can be the primary rationale for economic regulatory programs such as price controls, transportation regulation, and commodity price support programs. Civil-rights regulations are obviously motivated by distributional concerns. Distributional concerns also inspire environmental regulators to establish stringent media quality standards to protect sensitive populations.[180] Health and environmental regulations can also have differential impacts on different age groups[181] and on the rich and poor.[182] The benefits of regulations can shift over time to different beneficiaries. For example, insurance companies ultimately receive part of the benefit of improved health and safety.[183] Finally, we saw in the lead phasedown case study in Chapter 3 that health and safety regulation can redistribute wealth among regulatees.

Unfortunately many RIAs do not address distributional considerations.[184] Even when distributional impacts are factored into an analysis, they tend to be treated as "side constraints," rather than as policy goals worthy of respect in their own right.[185] One reason for this ambivalence toward distributional concerns may be the relative immunity of distributional considerations to quantitative analysis. Yet, the regulatory analysts do their clients a disservice if they do not attempt to identify the winners and losers of a regulatory activity and the extent to which wealth shifts from one person to another.

Efficiency as a meta-value. Those proponents of cost-benefit analysis who maintain that it can lead decisionmakers to the correct result are in effect elevating economic efficiency to a meta-value that trumps all other conflicting values. Professor Sagoff, among others, has seriously questioned whether the "efficiency criterion" is an appropriate normative measure of the "goodness" of a society. Even if a "perfect" cost-benefit analysis could be crafted, it would not necessarily guide the decisionmaker to the "correct" regulatory result, because efficiency is not the only measure of correctness.[186] At its core, the efficiency criterion is about maximizing wealth. Yet, a society as richly diverse and steeped in Western culture as the United States hews to values other than material wealth. To the extent that regulatory analysis either ignores or cannot assimilate this basic fact, it can have little relevance to the real-world decisionmaking process.

Cost-effectiveness analysis. The considerable analytical deficiencies of cost-benefit analysis have led many observers to doubt its usefulness in guiding decisionmakers.[187] Cynics know that able economists can justify virtually any outcome under the efficiency criterion by strategically manipulating vague notions of free riders, fragile values, and transaction costs. Other observers wonder whether cost-benefit proponents do not have their own ideological axes to grind.[188] Although virtually no one seriously argues that cost-benefit analysis should be the exclusive source of guidance for social regulation,[189] less pessimistic observers urge that the structure be retained for decisionmakers to use as one of several factors in the decisionmaking process.[190] In this sense, cost-benefit analysis is "a kind of organized common sense"[191] – a useful tool in marshaling and analyzing information, but not a device for dictating precise regulatory results.[192] If cost-benefit analysis cannot identify the best option, it may at least be useful in screening out bad options. Others would limit it to the lesser role of aiding policymakers in defining priorities and structuring options.[193]

A less reductionist approach is cost-effectiveness analysis, under which the analyst simply compares the costs of different approaches to achieving a specified regulatory goal.[194] For example, when EPA analysts calculate the cost-per-ton-of-pollutant-removed for various technologies in promulgating technology-based standards, they are engaging in a cost-effectiveness analysis. Likewise, NHTSA uses cost-effectiveness analysis to calculate the cost-per-life-saved for various regulatory alternatives. The analysis allows the decisionmaker to compare different regulatory alternatives to the same goal in terms of their relative costs.

Cost-effectiveness analysis solves many of the problems of cost-benefit analysis by putting them to one side. In effect, the analyst tells the decisionmaker: "I will tell you the most cost-effective way to reach a particular goal, but I have nothing to say about whether it is a 'good' goal; nor do I have anything to say about how other values might be implicated by the goal itself or by alternative routes to achieving that goal." In many cases, this is an entirely appropriate response. In a democratic society, politically responsible officials – legislators and politically appointed administrators – should determine goals and weigh values, not unaccountable analysts. When regulatory analysts wade into the area of ethics and values they threaten the well-preserved positivist myth that policy analysts are professionals who provide only value neutral advice.[195]

Although cost-effectiveness analysis avoids many of the valuation pitfalls of cost-benefit analysis, it retains most of the other impediments discussed in this chapter. Moreover, it presumes that there is a single agreed upon goal for a particular regulatory effort, which, as we have seen, is rarely the case in the real world. Finally, cost-effectiveness analysis tends to focus the decisionmaker's attention too intensely upon regulatory costs, to the exclusion of other important considerations.[196] Hence, although cost-effectiveness analysis is more useful than cost-benefit analysis, it too should probably not be the exclusive determinant of regulatory action.

Still another alternative to cost-benefit analysis is "multiobjective" or "multiattribute" analysis, in which the extent to which a regulatory requirement advances each of several regulatory goals is analyzed and compared to a similar analysis of alternative regulatory requirements.[197] This approach preserves much of the richness of complex decisionmaking, while at the same time avoiding paralyzing attempts to reduce multiple societal goals to a common measure. But it does not avoid the problem of measurement itself. It will not be particularly useful for evaluating alternative regulatory approaches to reaching goals such as greater equality, greater autonomy or prettier views.

Depoliticizing regulatory decisionmaking

Proponents of comprehensive analytical rationality who applaud as a virtue its propensity to remove irrelevant political considerations from regulatory decisionmaking often fail to acknowledge the contradictory status of regulatory agencies as politically accountable repositories of expertise. If they must resolve regulatory problems through the application of technical and economic expertise, agencies cannot be entirely accountable to groups that seek only to advance their own economic interests.[198] Yet, as we have seen, very few regulatory problems are resolvable solely by reference to expertise – all retain essential policy components. Regulatory analysts tend to stress the role of scientific and economic input and denigrate the political component of regulatory decisionmaking.[199] This in part helps justify their claim to professional status. Few policy analysts would count Louis Howe, Sherman Adams, Hamilton Jordan, or Edwin Meese among their number. Yet, if policy analysis is no more than political analysis, the special status of a degree in economics or public administration from a prestigious school of public policy is substantially devalued.

It may be helpful here to distinguish between "appropriate political considerations," which contain the essence of the values that must drive regulatory decisionmaking in a democracy, and "inappropriate political considerations," which are narrow partisan objectives not tied to some notion of the public good. A strong public outcry (as reported in the media and reflected in pressure from Capitol Hill) against a hazardous waste dump is an appropriate political reason for requiring that it be cleaned up, even without a clear factual demonstration that leaking chemicals will cause any particular environmental harm. To exclude the public demand for action from the decisionmaking process and to focus exclusively upon "facts" and "analysis" is itself a value-laden enterprise with its own political connotations; indeed, it is to redefine the "problem."[200] Yet, just as it is appropriate to consider the political pressure to do something about the dump, it is inappropriate to consider the Administration's desire to have a Republican win a Senate seat from the state containing the dump in deciding the timing of the regulatory intervention.[201] Whether the Senate majority leader's promise to halt ratification of the Panama Canal treaty if a power plant standard is made too stringent is an appropriate consideration is a closer question, but it is probably inappropriate, because it is not directly related to the pollution problems that the standard addresses.[202]

In sum, regulatory analysis can have the virtue of restraining, or at least of exposing, inappropriate political considerations, but it should not remove all "political" considerations, because appropriate political considerations determine the goals that an agency pursues and, perhaps more importantly, inform the choice among competing goals when values collide, as they often do in regulatory decisionmaking.

Repoliticizing regulatory decisionmaking: Hidden policy agendas

Many regulatory analysts in the real world have very definite opinions about what goals agencies should pursue and the relative priorities of those goals.[203] To a very large degree regulatory analysts come to the enterprise with a value system and preconceptions shaped by their own professional training. In the words of Professor Laurence Tribe, the regulatory analysts' "intellectual and social heritage in the classical economics of unfettered contract, consumer sovereignty, and perfect markets both brings them within a paradigm of conscious choice guided by values and inclines them, within that paradigm, toward the exaltation of utilitarian and self-interested individualism, efficiency, and maximized production as against distributive ends, procedural and historical principles, and the values (often nonmonetizable, discontinuous, and of complex structure) associated with personal rights, public goods, and communitarian and ecological goals."[204]

When policy analysts seek to implement their ideas about the quintessential political question of "goal-ranking," they are behaving as political actors and not as objective analysts, and their input should be treated as such. Having ostensibly depoliticized regulatory decisionmaking by ridding it of unruly and emotional political discourse, they repoliticize it by injecting *sub silentio* their own political values. There is little virtue in the analyst's claim to be above the rough and tumble pulls and tugs of the political marketplace if the clandestine purpose of the exercise is to impose a single set of political values on the decisionmaking process. To the extent, however, that goal ranking becomes muddled in the instrumental operation of measuring alternative policies against preexisting goals, the political aspect of the regulatory analyst's participation can be hidden behind a false veneer of objectivity. As Professor Tribe has noted: "Ideology has often sought to masquerade as analysis, deriving a power it could never justly claim from the garb of neutrality it has at times contrived to wear."[205]

The large uncertainties that plague most attempts at regulatory analysis provide many opportunities for applying hidden policy agendas.[206] Analysts know that the choice between one assumption or inference and another, between a prediction at the high end or low end of a plausible range, and between a "liberal" or "conservative" mathematical model is usually a policy choice.[207] As one program office official in OSHA wryly lamented: "It is very difficult to know whether you have been 'zapped' by someone else's agenda."[208] This raises important questions about accountability for the policy choices that must necessarily guide the analytical effort.

Internal accountability. By manipulating assumptions to aim predictions at the high end or low end of the available range and by soft-peddling uncertainties, analysts can produce objective-looking analyses that considerably narrow the decisionmakers' effective range of choice. A good example is the well-publicized dispute between OMB and EPA in the mid-1980s over whether the Administration should seek acid rain legislation. In a meeting with the President, the Director of OMB, David Stockman, suggested that EPA's proposed legislation would carry a price tag of $6,000 per fish saved. In the minds of EPA analysts this was an absurdly high number that could only have been derived by erring on the high side of virtually every possible assumption.[209] Moreover, Stockman apparently did not attempt to characterize the uncertainties surrounding that number, and EPA had not prepared a "counter-prediction" for the meeting. Although President Reagan's own policy leanings may well have led him to kill the legislative initiative in any event, OMB's extremely slanted cost assessment, which reflected that agency's policy preferences, made the choice not to pursue the effort an easy one.

It should not, however, lightly be assumed that all agency regulatory analysts are Machiavellian manipulators intent upon foisting their policy preferences off on unsuspecting upper-level policymakers. Most regulatory analysts regard themselves as professionals without particular axes to grind. When upper-level policy preferences are accurately communicated, most regulatory analysts feel constrained to apply them, whatever their individual views or perspectives.[210]

Internal accountability can also be encouraged by structuring the decisionmaking process in a way that ensures that attempts by policy analysts to "fudge" or "cook" the analysis are detected in advance of the decision. For example, an adversarial process, whereby different institutional actors with different policy outlooks must confront each other throughout the decisionmaking process, could be a good tool for maximizing the upper-level decisionmaker's policy choices. Alternatively, the agency could structure the decisionmaking process so as to ensure frequent and effective policy communication between the lower-level policy analysts and the upper-level decisionmakers. These and other alternatives for structuring analysis into the decisionmaking process will be discussed in more detail in Part III.

External accountability. Decisionmakers can use regulatory analysts to avoid public accountability choices by exerting subtle pressure on them to hedge their predictions in one direction or another so that the decision appears better supported by facts and analysis than it really is. At the extreme, the analysis becomes merely a post hoc rationalization for decisions reached on unarticulated policy grounds.[211] This represents an abuse of policy analysis in two ways.

First, while it is altogether appropriate for policymakers to demand that the regulatory analysts use particular assumptions and models, there are limits to which honest analysis can be stretched to meet predetermined policy needs. In those cases in which the available information does permit some relatively confident projections, it would be inappropriate and unprofessional for the analyst to manipulate the analysis to suggest otherwise.

Second, and more importantly, because the source of the policy preferences that ordain the analysis remains hidden, the policymakers themselves are not accountable to the public and other reviewing agencies. Explicit references to the policies that inform regulatory analysis are especially important for regulatory agencies, because ultimately the policies that drive the analysis must find their source in a congressional grant of policymaking discretion.

Problems with communicating analysis

At least half of an analyst's job is to communicate effectively the results of the analysis to decisionmakers and the public. The starting point is obviously the analyst's personal communications skills, but this chapter will assume that analysts are effective communicators and focus exclusively upon institutional impediments to policy communication.

Intra-agency policy management

Because regulatory analysis is explicit about policy goals, upper-level decisionmakers can use the regulatory analysis process to monitor the recommendations of lower-level technical staff for adherence to management's correct policy views. Agency analysts, however, frequently complain that they do not always obtain a clear picture of policy preferences from upper-level decisionmakers. To the extent that this impediment to using regulatory analysis as a policy management tool stems from the inability or unwillingness of upper-level decisionmakers to be explicit about the way in which they rank competing policy goals, there are no easy procedural or structural solutions. Little can be done to force unwilling policymakers to make policy. But the fact that the problem seems to afflict large agencies, where communication must necessarily follow relatively formal paths, more than smaller agencies, where communication can occur frequently and informally, indicates that the failure of policy communication may be addressed by structural improvements in the decisionmaking process, a topic that will be discussed in Part III.

Communication with Congress and the public

No formal mechanisms exist for communicating regulatory analysis to Congress. Like any other member of the public, a congressperson can obtain a copy of the agency's RIA for a major rule, but unless the congressperson has some special reason to know about the rulemaking effort and the existence of the RIA, the communication is not likely to occur. The General Accounting Office has suggested that executive summaries of some RIAs should be routinely sent to appropriate congressional committees for review and comment.[212] Although full implementation of this suggestion might flood crowded congressional committee offices with unread regulatory analysis documents, it could be accomplished at little expense, and it might help to keep interested committees and subcommittees abreast of important rulemaking efforts.

Many regulatory analysts in the agencies believe that one of the most important benefits of regulatory analysis is its ability to enhance the quality of public participation in the rulemaking process. Yet, it can only perform this laudable function if it is accessible to the public, and it is accessible only to the extent that the sources of data that go into the analyses are clearly identified. Agency analysts should be careful to identify the sources of all information, including the identity of consultants who took part in the analytical effort. Although some sources of information, such as telephone surveys, may not have the respectability of a published scientific report, they should still be identified and made a part of the public record. Interested members of the public should be permitted to examine the entire technical and economic basis for a rule and form their own opinions about the validity of the conclusions that the regulatory analysts drew. These opinions can in turn be communicated to the agency during the public comment period.

Limitations on the use of analysis

After the analysts have prepared a regulatory analysis and communicated it to the agency decisionmakers, considerable institutional impediments to its effective use in the decisionmaking process still remain. For example, some agency statutes preclude explicit reliance on cost-benefit analysis. In some agencies program office officials and upper-level policymakers are still quite skeptical about the virtues of analysis. Finally, the fact that analysis can be used for purposes unrelated to bringing comprehensive analytical rationality to bear upon regulatory problems hinders its effective use.

Program office resistance

Many agency analysts view program office resistance as the single most important impediment to the effective use of regulatory analysis in regulatory decisionmaking.[213] Many program office staffers believe that regulatory analysis lacks scientific rigor. At the same time, program office staffers also feel threatened by analysis, because it can represent a direct challenge to status quo approaches to regulatory problem solving that they have historically established and dominated. This resistance of program office personnel to analysis is not unlike the resistance that the offices responsible for preparing Environmental Impact Statements (EISs) encountered in the early 1970s. Like the RIA, the EIS was meant to be a comprehensive analytical document, and it was intended to change fundamentally agency thinking processes. From its inception, observers of the EIS confidently predicted that resistance in the program offices would doom the analytical effort.[214] Although more recent reviews of that process are mixed, many current observers believe that NEPA has had a profound substantive impact on agency decisionmaking.[215] Whether regulatory analysis is capable of overcoming technical staff resistance probably depends on the inherent limitations of analysis discussed in this chapter, the commitment of upper-level decisionmakers to comprehensive analytical rationality, and the way that regulatory analysis is structured into the decisionmaking process, a topic to be discussed in Part III.

Resistance of upper-level decisionmakers

The frequent complaint of resistance on the part of upper-level decisionmakers is not easily analyzed.[216] The upper-level decisionmakers may be unfamiliar with analytical thinking or may have adopted a techno-bureaucratic approach to decisionmaking. On the other hand, an open-minded upper-level decisionmaker may over time grow skeptical of analysis due to the weaknesses of analysis itself. Finally, upper-level resistance may reflect concern for the political viability of agency decisions, a concern that is not always compatible with comprehensive analytical rationality.[217]

Although regulatory analysis has much to do with "policy," we have seen that it is in many ways antithetical to "politics." Regulatory analysis can do little to facilitate the inevitable compromises among competing interest groups that are fundamental to the successful implementation of any regulatory strategy, and it can even be counterproductive. Yet, it is entirely appropriate in a democracy that politics play a prominent role in administrative policymaking.[218] Indeed, the fact that regulatory analysis plays any role at all in controversial rulemaking actions should be counted as a victory for the analysts. The best decisionmaking may well reflect the interplay of comprehensive analytical rationality, techno-bureaucratic rationality and political rationality.

Statutory constraints on the use of analysis

The agencies' own statutes can erect two kinds of impediments to analysis. First, a statute can directly or by implication prohibit the use of one or more elements of regulatory analysis in the agency decisionmaking process. Second, an agency statute can so narrowly confine an agency's regulatory discretion that comprehensive analysis is essentially useless.

Limitations on the use of analysis. Several statutes preclude the use of some kinds of analysis in making regulatory decisions.[219] Congress, in these statutes, has determined that other considerations so outweigh economic efficiency that it is inappropriate for the agency even to consider the results of a cost-benefit analysis of regulatory options. In his important book on economic incentives for pollution control, for example, Professor Kelman surveyed congressional staffers who worked on environmental issues on a regular basis. The results of the survey indicated that the staffers tended to see the arguments in favor of and against incentive approaches to pollution control largely in ideological terms, and tended to rank environmental goals higher than the efficiency goals inherent in economic incentives.[220]

The Supreme Court has held that the Occupational Safety and Health Act precludes cost-benefit analysis in setting health standards,[221] and the D.C. Circuit has held that EPA may not consider costs in promulgating National Primary Ambient Air Quality Standards.[222] Obviously, such statutory constraints create a tension between Congress' statutory command and the President's desire that agencies factor regulatory analysis into the decisionmaking process.[223] In EPA, for example, regulatory analysts in the Office of Air and Radiation painstakingly calculate the costs and benefits of National Ambient Air Quality Standards, but (as we saw in the particulates case study) the Administrator refuses to read them.[224] The artificiality of this attempt to shield the decisionmaking process from analysis is apparent.

Even if an agency's statute precludes the use of analysis in decisionmaking, the exercise of preparing a regulatory analysis can be useful to the agency in setting long-range priorities and evaluating rules after they have been in effect for a time.[225] Second, regulatory analyses can be useful in designing alternative regulatory strategies and in educating agency employees generally about the costs of regulations and the existence of alternative decisionmaking criteria. Third, to the extent that Congress and the public become aware of the analysis, they can use it in overseeing and evaluating the statutes that preclude the analysis. Regulatory analysis can "rub everyone's nose in the senselessness of the statute."[226] Finally, even if the agency cannot consider analysis, a regulatory analysis document that reveals that the benefits of the agency's action outweigh its costs can make the decision more acceptable to the public.[227] On the other hand, regulatory analysis documents for major rules come at no small expense, and agencies must weigh the value of an analysis that cannot be used against its costs.

Alternatives beyond the agency's statutory authority. A good regulatory analysis will not necessarily stop at the agency's statutory boundaries. Brainstorming sessions among regulatory analysts and technical staff will often produce alternatives that the agency lacks authority to implement.[228] Because the agency cannot lawfully choose one of these alternatives, it arguably should not consume scarce resources analyzing them. Yet, considering such alternatives can advance the goal of educating Congress and the public about the effects of regulation; Congress might be persuaded to grant the agency more authority or more flexibility in implementing its existing authority. Agencies must already consider alternatives beyond their authority to comply with the environmental impact statement requirement of the National Environmental Policy Act.[229] As with the EIS requirement, agencies should follow a "rule of reason" in selecting the alternatives worthy of detailed study.[230]

Use of analysis to advance substantive goals

Many regulatory reformers believe that bringing comprehensive analytical rationality to bear on regulatory problems will ultimately result in relief to regulated entities, and they believe that this is the primary measure of its effectiveness.[231] Using regulatory analysis to bring about regulatory relief can run counter to declared congressional policy, and it will predictably encounter intense resistance from statutory beneficiaries.[232] Although some claim that regulatory analysis has stemmed the flow of rules,[233] in many cases it has done so by brute force, rather than through the persuasiveness of its reasoning.[234] For example, critics have complained about the long delays that RIA preparation and review entail,[235] and they have challenged OMB's practice of granting waivers from the regulatory analysis requirement to rules designed to provide regulatory relief.[236]

Perhaps an even more important objection to using regulatory analysis to further particular substantive goals is the threat that this use of analysis poses to the integrity of analysis itself. As we have seen, analysis is a tool for measuring regulatory options against pre-determined policy goals; it is not capable of serving as a meta-instrument for defining those goals. It may well be that thorough analysis will indirectly further regulatory relief goals, but an analysis of the costs and benefits of a proposed regulation may (as in the case of EPA's lead phasedown and particulates regulations) indicate that the regulatory response should be even more stringent. To rely upon regulatory analysis when it points toward one substantive end but to deny it when it points to another smacks of hypocrisy, and it will ultimately discredit the analytical enterprise. If analysis is broadly perceived by the beneficiaries of regulation as a tool for furthering regulatory relief goals, then they will object to the tool as well as to the goals. More importantly, they will not trust the products of regulatory analysis and they will condemn all decisions based upon regulatory analysis as politically motivated, thereby depriving analysis of its primary virtue – its perceived objectivity.[237]

Conclusions

Despite its considerable shortcomings, regulatory analysis has important virtues. Although regulatory analysis cannot fully inform and cannot precisely point to rational conclusions, it can help.[238] Perhaps more importantly, it can encourage the decisionmaker to articulate policy preferences and demonstrate to the public how they were applied in important rulemaking initiatives. If the public, and particularly the beneficiaries of regulation, become convinced that it is not being used cynically to reach particular substantive results, regulatory analysis can become an effective vehicle for enhancing public accountability. The creative tension between comprehensive analytical rationality and techno-bureaucratic rationality in the context of politically accountable institutions can, when used to its full potential, result in the kind of creative decisionmaking that is much needed in this complex and highly centralized society.[239]

CHAPTER 10

Regulatory analysis in the real world

Given the impressive array of debilitating limitations explored in Chapter 9, it should not surprise the reader to discover that analysis suffers considerably in its real world application. Despite the practical problems that plagued the analytical enterprise in the case studies examined in Chapters 3 to 7, they represent success stories; the agencies threw enough resources into the endeavor to give the analytical effort a fighting chance. The vast majority of regulatory analyses do not receive the kind of detailed attention that the agencies devoted to the analyses described in those chapters. Yet, most executive agencies attempt to honor the spirit of the analysis requirements, and some have devoted serious attention to beefing up their analytical capabilities.

This chapter will explore the commitment to analysis that executive agencies typically make on paper and in the real world. Its primary focus will be on EPA, OSHA, NHTSA, FAA, and four agencies in USDA. It will examine in a general way the analytical sophistication of agency regulatory analysis documents, paying particular attention to how they go about quantifying costs and benefits, stating assumptions, and characterizing uncertainties. It will also probe the extent to which regulatory analysts attempt to identify and evaluate innovative options that may go beyond the agency's statutory authority. Finally, it will examine briefly the impact of regulatory analysis on public participation in agency decisionmaking. We shall see wide variations among agencies, and even within agencies, in the level of analysis achieved in a typical rulemaking. None of the agencies, however, comes close to meeting the comprehensive analytical rationality ideal.

Analysis in the Department of Agriculture

In 1978, USDA's Office of Budget and Program Analysis prepared analytical guidelines for regulatory analyses, and with some modest revisions they remain in effect. USDA has not prepared extensive written operating procedures for preparing regulatory analyses; nor has it attempted to coordinate the regulatory analysis efforts of the many services with regulatory functions. USDA's budget office believes that the complexities of regulatory decisionmaking preclude detailed "cookbook" instructions for use throughout the department. Some USDA agencies have become more proficient with analysis than others, and they have acquired a credibility that has given them a degree of independence from the other bureaus in USDA with economic expertise.[1] This trend is consistent with the department's general tendency toward decentralized decisionmaking.

None of the USDA agencies studied here prepares a cost-benefit analysis for every rulemaking initiative. Although all of them quantify the regulatory costs, they rarely attempt to quantify benefits. This is partially attributable to a lack of adequate data and predictive models and partially due to an inability or unwillingness to monetize units of harm, such as disease or death. Most analyses do, however, attempt to explore alternatives and analyze which of the options could achieve the desired result at least cost.

The RIAs in the Agricultural Marketing Service and Agricultural Stabilization and Conservation Service are straightforward predictions of the impacts of agency regulations on the prices and supplies of commodities. The heart of these analyses, which typically do not exceed twenty pages, is the tables that summarize the predicted economic impacts. Rarely do such analyses examine nonobvious distributional impacts. Analysts in both agencies depend heavily upon other agencies in the department for the information that goes into the regulatory analysis documents. The extent to which public comment focuses on the regulatory impact analysis documents varies with the commodity.[2]

In the Animal and Plant Health Inspection Service, the analytical effort is devoted primarily to examining less expensive minor alternatives to program office recommendations. In the minds of program office officials it is always cheaper to nip pest infestations in the bud through quarantine programs, once they have crossed a certain damage threshold, than it is to allow pests and diseases to spread to other areas.[3] The regulatory analyses usually focus on cheaper ways to meet the objective of containing the pest or disease, and they are perhaps better characterized as cost-effectiveness analyses.[4] On the rare occasions when regulatory analysis documents are prepared, they rely primarily on government-generated data. Additional information on impacts on the farming industry is obtained by telephoning affected parties. The general public rarely has anything to say about the regulatory analysis documents.[5]

The Food Safety and Inspection Service has been the most conscientious of all the USDA agencies in implementing regulatory analysis requirements, and it has a reputation throughout the department for its high quality analytical work. Although the agency's statutes generally require it to give priority to safety concerns, cost considerations play a role in choosing the least cost route to particular statutory goals. Usually, the technological mechanisms available for compliance are not very numerous, and cost comparisons are obvious without quantitative cost analysis. In any event, the costs that the agency's largely performance-oriented requirements impose on the regulated industry are usually quite small, because the agency almost never requires the installation of a particular technology until nearly all of the regulated concerns have already installed it and because the agency typically gives regulated concerns long lead times for compliance.

The agency devotes even less effort to quantifying the benefits of its regulations, which by and large merely permit the use of new meat processing technologies. The agency can predict that the new technology will allow a new food product or more of an old food product to enter the market, but the agency does not attempt to predict quantitatively how much of the new product will in fact be desired and consumed. The Regulatory Impact Analysis (RIA) for the mechanically separated meat rulemaking, discussed in Chapter 6, was one of the agency's most ambitious regulatory analyses, and it did not contain an especially sophisticated analysis of the harm to consumers that might result from relaxing informational requirements.

The most common source of information on the costs of compliance is the regulated industry. Yet, agency analysts have found this to be an unsatisfactory source of information, and on rare occasions the agency has conducted its own empirical research.[6] Although public comments on routine rules have occasionally caused the agency to reconsider some substantive aspect of its proposal, they have rarely addressed the economic analyses in the regulatory analysis documents.[7]

Analysis in the Department of Transportation

The Department of Transportation's Office of Industry Policy has prepared a detailed handbook to guide regulatory analysts in the operating agencies within the department in preparing regulatory analyses. Beyond this, very little guidance on regulatory analysis is provided at the departmental level. Like USDA, DOT is highly decentralized, and the operating agencies are responsible for most of the details of regulatory analysis.

The Federal Aviation Administration

The Federal Aviation Agency (FAA) has published its own guidelines for regulatory analysis and FAA analysts rely heavily upon that document.[8] A second document sets out in great detail precisely how the agency's regulatory analysts should place monetary values on the costs and benefits of FAA regulations.[9] The "critical values" specified in the report include "the value of time of air travelers, the value of a statistical life, unit costs of statistical aviation injuries, unit replacement and restoration costs of damaged aircraft, and aircraft variable operating costs."[10]

FAA regulatory analysts go to numerous sources for cost and impact data. Although the agency does not conduct routine surveys of industry cost schedules, it does maintain contact with industry engineers and economists. The agency's analysts attempt to scrutinize cost and economic impact information submitted by outside sources for possible bias and exaggeration. They also examine carefully the economic information that the agency's engineers compile to ensure that the engineers do not underestimate the costs of FAA regulations.[11]

Over time, the agency has developed several in-house data bases. The agency frequently purchases data, such as scheduling models, from the same sources that provide the data to the industry. The office also hires consultants to conduct cost surveys. On one occasion the agency contracted with a consultant to design a "paper" airplane from scratch using the costs of parts purchased on the open market to meet the proposed regulation. Although this was a very expensive undertaking for the agency, the regulatory analysis office's input was outcome-determinative, because the data from the exercise demonstrated that the rule that the engineers had suggested was prohibitively expensive. In other cases, however, the cost information that the regulatory analysts assembled demonstrated that costs were trivial, and this information made it much easier for the rule to survive upper-level scrutiny.[12] Outside commentators address FAA regulatory analysis documents only extremely rarely.[13]

The National Highway Traffic Safety Administration

Although the National Highway Traffic Safety Administration (NHTSA) does not have its own guidelines, it prepares an analysis at least as sophisticated as that called for in the DOT Handbook for all of its important rules.[14] NHTSA does not, however, attempt to place a value on a statistical fatality or serious injury as the DOT Handbook recommends.[15] The agency usually estimates the benefits of life-saving rules in terms of lives saved and injuries avoided, and it occasionally combines these estimates with cost estimates to determine the estimated cost per life saved for each alternative.[16] Because its statutes require the agency to place safety considerations above costs, its leadership has not found it useful to reduce costs and benefits to dollar comparisons.

NHTSA relies upon data from the agency's own data center, and it often surveys the industry for relevant cost and engineering information. If necessary, the program office will conduct a "tear down" study soliciting cost estimates from independent designers and parts manufacturers to achieve a realistic cost estimate.[17] Although officials in the program office carefully review auto industry cost data, the policy office is not as skeptical of industry-generated information, and it often uses such data in preparing regulatory analysis documents. The agency prefers, however, to generate its own data or to rely upon independent contractors.[18] Contractor-generated information has occasionally proved controversial, because the agency has in the past done little to ensure against real and apparent conflicts of interest on the part of its contractors.[19]

NHTSA regulatory analysts do not attempt to place statistical confidence limits on uncertainties. Instead, they attempt to analyze carefully the assumptions that go into their predictions and to undertake sensitivity analyses to probe the extent to which the predictions depend upon the assumptions.[20]

Only the largest and most controversial regulations attract substantial public comment to the NHTSA's regulatory analysis documents. Comments are often blanket assertions without supporting data, and they rarely provide concrete information capable of filling data gaps.[21] External comments have sometimes suggested alternatives that the agency had not considered, and the agency has made an effort to address these alternatives in final rulemaking documents.[22]

Analysis in the Occupational Safety and Health Administration

The Occupational Safety and Health Administration (OSHA) has not drafted written guidelines for preparing RIAs. Since health rules must be economically feasible, OSHA has always undertaken detailed cost and financial analyses of the affected industries, irrespective of the requirements of the Executive Orders. Following a Supreme Court holding in 1979 that OSHA may not set a health standard unless it is necessary to address a significant risk to workers, OSHA has attempted to undertake a quantitative risk assessment for all of its health standards.[23]

OSHA's ability to rely upon formalized cost-benefit analysis in setting health standards is dubious in light of a second Supreme Court decision in the *Cotton Dust* case.[24] In that case the textile industry argued that the words "reasonably necessary and appropriate" in the definition of the word "standard" in OSHA's statute required the agency to base its decisions on a formal cost-benefit analysis. The unions argued that cost-benefit analysis was inappropriate because a separate section of the Act required that health standards be set, "to the extent feasible," at a level that ensures every working person a "safe" workplace. The Supreme Court held that once the agency determined that a significant risk to workers existed, it was obliged to set the standard at the lowest "feasible" level, even if the costs outweighed the benefits. The section of the statute devoted specifically to health standards, though not safety standards, elevated employee health to a higher status than economic efficiency. The Court noted that "Congress was fully aware that the Act would impose real and substantial costs of compliance on industry, and believed that such costs were part of the cost of doing business." Although the Court's holding represents a strong rejection of cost-benefit analysis in the context of OSHA health standards, it is limited to the specific language of the OSHA statute and has little relevance to other agencies. It does demonstrate, however, that the Court will give effect to congressional commands that other values trump economic efficiency.

Although OSHA is precluded by law from using formal cost-benefit analysis in promulgating health standards,[25] it has recently attempted to assess the cost-effectiveness of most health regulations by combining the cost analysis and the risk assessment to calculate the implicit cost-per-life-saved or cost-per-illness-avoided of the various regulatory alternatives, as we observed in Chapter 7. The cost-benefit analyses for safety regulations generally do examine monetized benefits.[26]

The agency staff usually consults a variety of sources of factual information, including "criteria documents" prepared by the National Institute of Occupational Safety and Health, industry-submitted information, the general toxicology literature, and informal contacts with personnel in other agencies. OSHA nearly always hires contractors to survey the relevant industry or industries, create an industry profile, and identify a range of feasible engineering controls. Most of the technologies that the contractors identify are further analyzed as potential alternatives for regulatory requirements.[27] Some of OSHA's regulatory analysis documents explore alternatives to regulation such as reliance on state administrative or tort remedies, over which the agency has no statutory authority, but it does not spend many resources examining options that it cannot implement.

The regulatory analysis documents attempt to characterize uncertainties in two ways. First, the OSHA analysts use "sensitivity analysis" to probe the sensitivity of the quantitative predictions to various assumptions in the quantitative models. Second, they attempt to "bound" the uncertainties in quantitative predictions by estimating the high and low extremes. At OMB's insistence, the agency usually attempts to predict a "best estimate" as well.

The regulatory analysts and some program office staffers believe that the regulatory analysis document plays a valuable role in the comment process by forcing the commentators to respond to explicit quantitative risk assessments and to the agency's analysis of the feasible alternatives for reducing those risks. It also makes the public aware of the probable effects of the agency's action in time to comment upon and take measures in anticipation of those effects.[28]

Analysis in the Environmental Protection Agency

After much internal debate, EPA promulgated "Guidelines for Performing Regulatory Impact Analysis" in late 1983. The Guidelines establish detailed criteria for sophisticated cost-benefit analyses of a broad range of alternatives, some of which can go beyond the agency's statutory authority. They recognize that environmental amenities can be difficult to quantify and monetize, but they express a strong preference for quantitative analysis. For example, the Guidelines suggest the analysis use a range of $400,000 to $7,000,000 for the value of a "statistical life saved."[29] The Guidelines also emphasize distributional effects, especially intergenerational effects, but they recognize that "[n]o entirely satisfactory method exists for evaluating intergenerational effects." When the benefits of an environmental regulation cannot easily be monetized or when the agency's statute articulates a specific regulatory objective, the regulatory analysis document must provide a cost-effectiveness analysis.

Some of the most successful regulatory analysis documents in EPA have been those, like the lead phasedown documents, that did not attempt to monetize health and environmental impacts. Many EPA analysts, especially in the program offices, seem to recognize that reducing complex health and environmental decisions to single dollar comparisons is fundamentally inconsistent with the policy judgments that Congress has made in many of the statutes that the agency must administer. Hence, they have been willing, as in the lead phasedown case study, to help the program office search for the "knee-of-the-curve," where the costs of additional health protection dramatically escalated, rather than insisting on monetizing health benefits to facilitate a search for the optimal, though perhaps not ethically justifiable, level of regulation.

In other aspects as well, agency practice only remotely approximates the Guidelines' ambitious goals. Since the early 1980s, EPA has installed regulatory analysts in a centralized agency-wide Office of Policy Analysis (the policy office) and in virtually all of the individual program offices as well. Despite the policy office's efforts at consistency, the level of analysis that goes into regulatory analysis documents varies from office to office and among programs within a single office.[30]

Although all of the program offices initially resisted the policy office's analytical efforts, the agency's experience with the particulates and lead phasedown rulemakings convinced some program office officials that analysis can be done in a neutral way that, at least sometimes, will support their efforts to promulgate protective rules.[31] Nevertheless, when the regulatory analysts in the program offices do prepare quantitative analyses they do not always attempt to provide a range of estimates, as required by the Guidelines, nor do the RIAs for major rules always undertake a full cost-benefit analysis for all relevant alternatives.[32]

The sophistication of analysis also depends upon whether the rule is characterized as major or nonmajor. The regulatory analysis documents that the agency prepares for significant nonmajor rules often contain a cost-benefit analysis of the preferred alternative, but many include only a cost-effectiveness analysis. Although not required by executive order, many programs prepare some kind of regulatory analysis document for virtually every substantive nonmajor regulation. These normally include only an analysis of the direct costs and economic impacts of the proposed option. The analyses that accompany the vast bulk of regulations that are neither significant nor major are not especially sophisticated.[33]

A very high proportion of the economic impact information that is used in regulatory analysis documents in EPA is produced by independent contractors working under the supervision of personnel in the regulatory analysis branches of the program offices.[34] The agency relies less extensively, but still heavily, upon independent contractors for benefits analysis, because "extramural dollars are easier to obtain than [full-time equivalent staff]."[35] The regulatory analysts in the program offices incorporate the information from the contractors' reports into the agency's regulatory analysis documents.

High-level agency analysts firmly believe that regulatory analysis documents should consider options beyond the agency's authority. One midlevel regulatory analyst in the policy office believes that public dissemination of regulatory analysis documents that consider alternatives beyond the agency's authority "has increased public awareness of the measured consequences of environmental regulations and has increased pressure on government officials to justify the efficiency of their decisions." As a consequence, he believes that "EPA decisionmakers now scrutinize each situation carefully to determine whether or not the law truly prohibits considerations of economic benefits and costs."[36]

Despite this strong preference of the regulatory analysis office, program office regulatory analysts very rarely include a discussion of extrastatutory options in regulatory analysis documents, even though such options do come up routinely in work group meetings and other internal agency discussions. Given the constant press of other business on the agency's analytical resources, it is not surprising that the program office analysts are not enthusiastic about discussing options that cannot be implemented without an Act of Congress.

Similarly, although the agency's Guidelines at many places suggest that the regulatory analysts should attempt to characterize the confidence with which they make their cost and benefit projections, the agency's regulatory analysis documents have not considered uncertainties in a sophisticated way.[37] After preliminary boilerplate statements about how risk analysis is hampered by uncertainties, the documents typically rely upon single number estimates that mask very large uncertainties.[38]

In most EPA programs the regulatory analysis documents attract some public comment,[39] but most comments go to the technical basis for the rule.[40] Most of the regulatory analysts in EPA believe that RIAs affect the quality of the comments.[41] Calculating the costs of a regulation, even when costs are by statute irrelevant to the final outcome of the proceeding, can enhance public understanding of the regulation. Because the regulatory analysis document lays out the agency's rationale and technical support, the commentators are obliged to explain why they are wrong, to suggest better rationales, and to come up with better technical data.[42] In some important rulemakings, the regulated industry has even hired outside consultants to critique the agency's regulatory analysis documents,[43] as we observed in Chapter 4. At the very least, the comments on the regulatory analysis documents can reveal places where the technical support for a rule is weak and suggest further studies that could be done to shore up the agency's technical case.[44]

Agency analysts feel that they are quite receptive to well-conceived critiques of their documents, and they frequently amend them to reflect outside criticism.[45] In one case, the agency even proposed a revised regulatory analysis and solicited public comment on it prior to promulgating the final rule.[46] Although EPA seldom amends its entire approach to a regulation as a result of public comment, it has on at least one occasion withdrawn a rule because changes in the agency's cost analysis precipitated by public comments indicated that the rule was no longer economically feasible.[47] Even when the agency rejects the public criticisms of its analyses, it attempts to demonstrate why the critics were wrong.[48] This requires the agency analysts to think more about their original analyses, and this ultimately increases the agency's confidence in the correctness of its decisions.

Conclusions

As the reader of Chapter 9 might have predicted, the comprehensive analytical rationality ideal has not been achieved in the real-world decisionmaking context of the agencies examined here. The commitment of some agencies to the articulation of the ideal is apparent from their ambitious attempts to write handbooks and guidelines. And some agencies have made heroic efforts in a few singular rulemaking proceedings to adhere scrupulously to those guidelines. Many programs do not pretend to comply with the ideal, and some departments, like USDA, make only halfhearted efforts to insist that agencies regularly use regulatory analysis. As we shall see in Chapter 19, the judiciary is not normally available to require agencies to comply with the spirit of the Executive Orders and the Regulatory Flexibility Act; therefore, agencies are generally free to go their own way. OMB is available to police adherence to the analytical requirements, but it is spread too thin to do so on a regular basis for all executive agencies. It must choose its battles carefully, and the fights it picks often are chosen for substantive, rather than analytical reasons.

Although agency devotion to the ideal has been uneven, all now have the capacity to undertake comprehensive analysis when they need to, and many appear to want to. That they all fail to achieve the ideal so often is as much due to its inherent limitations as to lack of commitment. Many agencies have demonstrated the capacity to produce a high level of analysis when necessary despite substantial legal, programmatic and practical impediments. None achieve a high level of analytical sophistication all (or even most) of the time, because analysis is very expensive. The high level of analysis that the Executive Orders demands is possible only for the most important rules. For the vast majority of rulemaking efforts, only a much less sophisticated effort is warranted. Although most agencies have the capability to produce one or two "Cadillac" analyses per year, the more frequent analyses for less important rules are clearly "Chevrolets."

The next phase in incorporating comprehensive analytical rationality into the decisionmaking process will consist of integrating the analysts themselves into the process without so much concern for their formal written product. We turn in the following chapters to an examination of the roles that analysts can play in agency decisionmaking and to the different models that exist for structuring analysts into the decisionmaking process.

PART III

Structuring regulatory analysis into the decisionmaking process

CHAPTER 11

Roles for the regulatory analyst

Because institutions lack a centralized nervous system steered by a single brain, institutional decisionmaking tends to be very different from individual decisionmaking. Most regulatory decisions are the products of numerous encounters between the various institutional entities that have roles to play in the decisionmaking process, and they therefore represent a synthesis of many views. A requirement that agencies prepare regulatory analysis documents does not by itself ensure that comprehensive analytical rationality will play a role in regulatory decisionmaking. Bulky analytical documents can be ignored by subordinate decisionmaking units, and upper-level decisionmakers in most agencies simply do not have time to absorb the contents of lengthy regulatory analysis documents. The documents themselves are likely to affect agency decisionmaking only to a very modest degree.

Yet, regulatory analysis requirements can influence agency decisionmaking in a more subtle fashion. Once the agency establishes a regulatory analysis office with an institutional stake in comprehensive analytical thinking, agency decisionmakers can adjust how that kind of thinking affects agency decisions by structuring the decisionmaking process to give that office greater or lesser prominence. Hence, to discover the real role that analysis plays in an agency, one must focus attention on the role of the regulatory analyst, rather than on the document that the analyst prepares. The role that the analyst plays will, to a very large extent, determine the degree to which analysis affects regulatory agency decisionmaking.

Chapter 11 describes several roles that regulatory analysts can play in the regulatory decisionmaking process and examines some of the advantages and disadvantages of each of those roles. Chapters 12 to 16 explore several models for structuring the internal agency decisionmaking process to include the regulatory analysis office. Each of these models is currently in use in at least one agency in the federal government. Finally, Chapter 17 suggests conditions under which each of the institutional structures may or may not be appropriate.

179

The extent of the regulatory analyst's impact on the bureaucracy depends upon the degree to which upper-level decisionmakers trust analysis. In some agencies, regulatory analysts are no more than glorified "gofers," tracking down relevant information for other agency employees to use in the decisionmaking process. In others, the analysts occupy an isolated niche in the organizational chart and speak only when spoken to.[1] In still others, the analysts are influential institutional actors with veto power over the products of agency program offices.

Although it is probably premature to characterize policy analysis as a full-fledged profession,[2] many regulatory analysts have received similar training and they share many common values. Yet, the agencies have not generally assigned these experts a well-defined role in the decisionmaking process.[3] Although regulatory analysts must constantly attempt to preserve the appearance of neutrality and objectivity, they can be important internal political actors, and occasionally their influence extends beyond the agency's confines.[4] As we have seen in Chapter 9, many of the ostensibly technical questions that arise in agency rulemakings can only be answered by applying a heavy dose of policy to sparse data. Determining the content of that policy is a value-laden enterprise, and the analytical output must inevitably reflect somebody's values. To the extent that a regulatory analysis reflects the analyst's values and to the extent that the analysis guides the decisionmaker, then the analyst can become an influential determinant of agency policy.

Some past efforts to explore the role of policy analysts in bureaucracies have followed Professor Downs' lead in focusing upon their personality characteristics.[5] For example, Professor Meltsner has divided policy analysts into four broad categories according to perceived political skills and analytical talents: (1) entrepreneurs have high political skills and high analytical skills; (2) politicians have high political skills and low analytical skills; (3) technicians have low political skills and high analytical skills; and (4) pretenders have low political skills and low analytical skills.[6] Jenkins-Smith similarly divides policy analysts into three categories: (1) the objective technician searches for programs that maximize net benefit to society; (2) the issue advocate attempts to advance particular views of appropriate public policy; and (3) the client advocate attempts to advance the interest of his or her client within the bureaucracy.[7]

Although these attempts to group policy analysts are useful in characterizing the role of individual policy analysts in bureaucracies, the more important question for our purposes is the institutional role that the unit containing regulatory analysts plays in a given bureaucracy. Once a regulatory analysis office is created, whether or not it is inhabited largely by entrepreneurs, politicians, technicians, or pretenders may depend upon happenstance, but it will more likely reflect conscious institutional choices. Entrepreneurs will soon depart an office that has been assigned a backwater institutional role, and pretenders will not last long in an office that has been assigned an important substantive role in the institutional decisionmaking process. In the real world, personalities and skills may often be more relevant to the assignment of institutional roles than more abstract considerations of professional outlook and style. Yet, over the long haul, the upper-level managers who are responsible for creating decisionmaking structures must look to the essential characteristics of the profession when assigning members of that profession to particular institutional roles. This chapter therefore assumes that upper-level decisionmakers make conscious choices about the roles that they want regulatory analysts to play in agency decisionmaking and that these decisions reflect an assessment of the general strengths and weaknesses of the budding policy analysis profession.

Seven roles for the regulatory analyst

When twelve regulatory analysts from three regulatory agencies were asked what their institutional "mission" was, they responded as follows:

> Help the agency: (1) to develop its policy into a policy framework; (2) to document its policy; and (3) to be accountable.

> Try (1) to be an independent voice to the Administrator, and (2) to be an institutional nay-sayer.

> Use economics to make sure that we do things that make sense first before we go chasing butterflies.

> Bring sound analytical and policy work to bear on the regulatory programs; improve decisionmaking through analysis.

> Attempt to (1) make sure that the Administrator has well-done and empirical analyses to base his or her decisions on; (2) provide unbiased analytical work; and (3) provide net benefits to society.

> Inform decisionmakers of tradeoffs among costs and environmental results, without prejudicing them about substance.

> Ensure that the environment is cleaner and healthier, but you could go crazy if you wanted to see every particular regulation go a certain way.

> Improve the quality of decisionmaking within the agency.

Improve the quality of decisionmaking about the environment.

Pursue maintenance and improvement of the environment within the bounds of good public policymaking.

Lay out for the decisionmaker the costs and benefits of an action.

One striking aspect of these responses is their strong commitment to decisionmaking of high "quality." Another is their desire to make good "public policy." Still another is their commitment to "objective" analysis. Underlying these broad concepts of the regulatory analyst's mission lie at least seven rather distinct roles that regulatory analysts can play in regulatory decisionmaking. Some analysts play only one or two of the roles; others play them all. Some play different roles at different times; others play two or more roles simultaneously.

Information analyst

Virtually all analysts believe that they play the role of provider and analyzer of information on the costs and benefits of particular regulatory options,[8] and several view it as their only appropriate role in the decisionmaking process. The analyst does not create knowledge but simply gathers existing information, culls the useful from the useless, organizes it to fit the agency's needs, and communicates it to the decisionmaker and the public in an understandable fashion.[9]

Because regulatory analysts have professional training in gathering, analyzing, quantifying, and displaying technical information, they may serve the information-providing function better than members of the technical staff in the program offices, who usually lack such training. In all of the case studies in Part II, the regulatory analysts played this basic role.

Justifier

Our society generally demands that regulatory agencies provide rational justifications for their decisions, and judicial and executive branch review processes tend to reinforce this commitment. Yet, many important issues that arise in regulatory decisionmaking cannot be resolved on the basis of existing information alone, and policy considerations must play a very large role in determining the outcome. Considerations that are irrelevant to a rational analysis of a regulatory problem, such as the predicted reaction of a political constituency, often dictate the choice among the available options.[10]

The external requirements for findings and reasons nevertheless create a strong institutional demand for justification on more appropriate grounds. Most of the program office staff and some upper-level decisionmakers prefer that the regulatory analysis staff play this justifier role.[11]

Most regulatory analysts, however, draw a sharp line between the role of information-provider and the role of justifier. It is one thing to provide information relevant to a decision that has yet to be made, and quite another to craft an analysis to justify a decision that has already been made. Although some regulatory analysts seem willing to assume the role of post hoc justifier,[12] most desire to play a more influential role in the agency decisionmaking process. They believe that allowing themselves to be used as pawns in larger power plays greatly damages the credibility of the newly emerging profession. Yet, so long as society is unwilling to accept erstwhile political considerations as an acceptable rationale for administrative decisionmaking, it will probably have to tolerate a certain amount of post hoc rationalization. To the extent that agencies are forced into this mode by various statutory requirements and the threat of judicial and executive review, there will continue to be a demand for regulatory analysts to play the justifier role.

Policy communicator

Many regulatory analysts believe that there is great value in measuring regulatory options against explicitly articulated policy goals and communicating that analysis to upper-level decisionmakers. First, as we saw in Chapter 8, this function is critical to the application of comprehensive analytical rationality to regulatory decisionmaking. Second, to the extent that the analysis is further communicated to reviewing institutions and the public, it enhances agency accountability. Third, it provides periodic opportunities for the agency, and other reviewing institutions, to review agency policies in light of changed conditions. Fourth, explicit analysis of agency policy can help screen out extraneous factors that are not relevant to a rational decision based upon a given statutory command. Finally, to the extent that upper-level decisionmakers carefully monitor the decisionmaking process, it helps ensure that lower-level staff continue to adhere to the policy preferences of politically appointed decisionmakers, rather than following their own hidden agenda.

Although upper-level decisionmakers generally agree that a policy communication function is needed in the regulatory decisionmaking process, assigning this function to a separate regulatory analysis staff has some disadvantages. First, upper-level decisionmakers often prefer that explicit analyses of agency policy not be publicized. The legitimate policies relevant to a given regulatory decision invariably conflict with one another, and they are not often easy to rank without alienating some important constituency. Second, the analysis itself can reflect hidden agendas that run counter to statutory or agency policy goals. Third, agencies operate in a political world, and upper-level decisionmakers will not last long if they entirely ignore political considerations, however rationally they steer the agencies toward previously articulated policy goals. To the extent that political considerations affect the future vitality of the bureaucratic entity, they cannot accurately be characterized as extraneous. Finally, even assuming the value of explicit attention to how regulatory options advance particular policy goals, it is not clear that this function must be performed by a separate professional staff.

Options identifier

Comprehensive analytical rationality has a strong preference for expanding the options available to the decisionmaker. This suggests that regulatory analysts could perhaps play the valuable role of options-identifier in the decisionmaking process. The EPA lead phasedown case study in Chapter 3 provides a good example of the effective use of the regulatory analyst's options-identifier role. In that proceeding, one of the primary reasons that EPA had not proceeded more rapidly toward phasing tetraethyl lead out of gasoline was the large financial burden that a rapid phasedown would impose upon many small refiners of leaded gasoline. The existing standard had been stated in terms of grams of lead per gallon of gasoline produced by a regulated refinery. As more and more older automobiles were replaced with new automobiles that, under a separate set of regulations, could not burn leaded gasoline, larger refineries began to convert much of their production capacity to unleaded gasoline and could therefore add more lead to a gallon of their leaded gas and still meet the same "pooled" standard. Agency analysts suggested an alternative that would allow large refiners to sell lead "rights" to small refiners, thereby greatly reducing the impact of a more stringent standard on small refiners. After some hesitancy, the program office accepted the innovative approach, and the agency adopted it in the final rule. In some of the other case studies (such as the FSIS standard for MSM in Chapter 6 and the NHSTA "Field of Direct View" standard in Chapter 5), however, the analysts did not seem to play a large role in identifying options.

Institutional skeptic

Although skepticism is not automatically programmed into a regulatory analyst during his education, many analysts have a strong perception of themselves as institutional skeptics. In this role the regulatory analyst is responsible for probing carefully the logic and the factual and policy bases for the agency's rulemaking activities. The analysts are expected to challenge the conventional wisdom and insist that the program office staff justify regulatory choices by explicit reference to facts and policy considerations.[13] Regulatory analysts can probe assumptions, question inferences, and challenge extrapolations. We saw this role played to the hilt in the Field of Direct View case study in Chapter 5.

It is probably a great tonic to the program office to know that its efforts will be reviewed by an institutional skeptic. The certainty of such review can provide an incentive for the technical staff to hone arguments and to anticipate and refute counterarguments prior to publicizing its position. A critical review of the technical work can also enhance accountability by helping upper-level decisionmakers identify instances in which the technical staff has substituted policy judgment for uncertainties. Finally, an institutional skeptic can in some instances prevent the agency from promulgating ill-considered rules that it may later have to withdraw, thereby conserving agency resources in the long run.

An agency's institutional skeptic, however, need not be the policy office. Persons with training in economics and policy analysis are not the only professionals capable of taking a skeptical look at the rationales for agency rulemaking efforts. The Office of General Counsel in many agencies has performed this role and continues to perform it quite apart from the policy office. Still, regulatory analysts bring a unique perspective that is antithetical to command and control rules, has a penchant for flexibility, and is unsympathetic to the rigidities that the Office of General Counsel often insists upon to ensure that agency rules are enforceable.

Employing the regulatory analysis office as institutional skeptic can give rise to acrimonious intra-agency disputes. No one likes for his work to be reviewed critically, and the technical staff in the program office can be expected to react defensively to outside criticisms, however legitimate they may be in reality. Another, more subtle, disadvantage of the institutional skeptic role derives from the fact that in a regulatory area that is fraught with uncertainty, virtually any technical analysis is vulnerable to devastating criticism from a determined critic. There may be limits to the usefulness of carping at a document that is admittedly based upon poor information and large assumptions. Regulatory analysts acknowledge that skepticism has its limits and, pressed too far, can be counterproductive. Nevertheless, they maintain that a healthy dose of skeptical review by an office that is not committed to a particular regulatory posture can help an agency promulgate rules that are capable of surviving political and judicial review.

Advocate for efficiency

Regulatory analysts in many agencies believe that their proper role extends to that of institutional advocate for efficiency.[14] In the context of regulatory decisionmaking, this role is often that of institutional advocate for the results that would attain in unimpeded markets.[15] As we observed in the EPA particulates rulemaking in Chapter 4 and the OSHA hazard identification rulemaking in Chapter 7, this is a role for which analysts in OMB have a particular fondness. In this role, which Lindblom defines broadly as "partisan analysis,"[16] the analyst has an obligation to advocate market-oriented solutions to regulatory problems. Assigning an institutional entity this role probably reflects a conclusion by upper-level decisionmakers that the rulemaking process is otherwise inclined to burden the regulated industries with inefficient rules. Agency heads may assign regulatory analysts an advocacy role out of a conviction that bureaucratic thinking can become so encrusted with conventional wisdom that it takes an effective advocate of a different point of view to produce noticeable changes in the way that their agencies go about making decisions.[17] To the extent that upper-level decisionmakers desire to have their decisions reflect a market-oriented perspective that is sensitive to the costs that regulations impose upon society and to the extent that they are not capable of monitoring the decisionmaking process carefully enough to ensure that staff recommendations are reflecting that perspective, assigning the regulatory analysis office an advocacy role in subordinate decisionmaking entities can help ensure that that point of view informs staff output.

Assigning an advocacy role to the regulatory analysis office, however, can clash with the analyst's other roles of impartial provider of information and institutional skeptic. If the regulatory analyst is an advocate of particular regulatory approaches or results, other participants in the decisionmaking process and the beneficiaries of the regulatory program are likely to question the neutrality of the information and analysis that the analyst provides.[18] The analyst cannot effectively play the role of institutional skeptic if other parties to the decisionmaking process perceive that the skepticism is not motivated by a detached concern for the integrity of the agency's reasoning process, but rather comes from a particular policy perspective. Assuming an advocacy role can also put the regulatory analyst at odds with the agency's attorneys when, as is often the case, allocative efficiency is not the primary goal of the regulatory program. The agency lawyers, alert to the possibility of judicial reversal, may indeed assume the role of advocate for nonmonetary policies and values inherent in the agency's statute against the regulatory analyst's advocacy of wealth maximization.

Yet, it is undeniable that many analysts in agencies come to their positions with a perceived mission, and they devote their energies toward accomplishing particular substantive ends. Although lacking formal training in advocacy, regulatory analysts can be very persuasive to upper-level decisionmakers. Indeed, it is fair to say that in many agencies, the analysts have become such effective advocates of substantive policies that their efforts have profoundly affected regulatory output. Whether one views this advocacy role as an encouraging or discouraging development depends upon one's views about the role of regulation in society and about the extent to which an agency's fidelity to its statute is important.

Influential determinant of agency policy

There can be little doubt that the recent Executive Orders have significantly enhanced the power of regulatory analysts in the agencies.[19] Although not all analysts aspire to a direct policymaking role,[20] the regulatory analysis office in many agencies has been structured into the decisionmaking process in such a way as to give that office an influential role in the determination of agency policy. When the regulatory analysis office must be represented on subordinate and upper-level decisionmaking entities, when the representative from that office is generally a strong advocate of particular regulatory policies, and when the agency implements those policies with some frequency, then the regulatory analysis office has in effect assumed the role of policymaker.

Yet, like the advocate role, the influential determinant role conflicts with the roles of information provider, institutional skeptic, and policy communicator. There is, indeed, something of a conflict of interest between the analyst as analyst and the analyst as decisionmaker. An institutional entity that controls information necessarily possesses institutional power. If the provider of information also participates in policymaking, the information-providing role can be manipulated to enhance the power of that office.[21] This enhanced institutional power can operate to further the policy goals of the upper-level decisionmakers and of Congress, but it can also be manipulated to further the individual goals of the individual regulatory analysts or the goals of persons or institutions outside the agency.[22]

Making the regulatory analysis office an influential determinant of agency policy may pose a serious threat to the integrity of the policy analysis "profession." So long as the profession practices neutral analysis, it has some distinct contours. When it expands its professional bailiwick into policymaking, it begins to lose definition. At some point in the growth of the regulatory analysis office's institutional power, analysis becomes indistinguishable from politics. Although many students in schools of public affairs no doubt aspire to careers in politics, analysis has attempted to set itself apart from politics as a distinct profession. When an analyst becomes a policymaker, he or she begins to lose that distinctive quality that defines the analyst as a professional. Spread throughout several agencies, this role dilution could pose a serious threat to the efforts of the fledgling profession to define itself with sufficient clarity to give it an enhanced status in society.

Timing of regulatory analysis

The effectiveness of the regulatory analysis office in playing an assigned role will depend upon the timing of the analysis, and the timing will in turn depend upon the role that upper-level decisionmakers assign to the analysts. If, for example, the agency plans to use its regulatory analysts primarily in a justifier role, then it is not important that the analysis be completed until after the decisionmaking process is done. Indeed, it is probably preferable that the analysts not begin to prepare a regulatory analysis until after the decisionmakers have arrived at a particular regulatory approach that needs justification. If, however, upper-level managers want regulatory analysts to play a more meaningful role in the internal decisionmaking process, they will have to pay some attention to the timing of analytical input in designing that process.

If an agency plans to use its regulatory analysts in an information-provider role, it faces a tradeoff between its informational needs and its limited analytical resources. The economic impact and benefits analyses that agency analysts typically provide should be available to subordinate decisionmaking units prior to the time that they begin active deliberations.[23] To the extent that the analysts have to hire contractors to produce original data, they should be involved even earlier in the rulemaking effort at the time that research needs are defined.

The desirability of gathering data at an early stage in the evolution of a rule must be tempered, however, by the need to conserve limited analytical resources. If, for example, the regulatory analysis office begins extensive information-gathering efforts prior to the time that the engineers in the program office have completed rudimentary feasibility studies, the analysts may wind up studying the economic impact of alternatives that are precluded on technological feasibility grounds. On the other hand, if the analysts wait too long, until after options have thoroughly crystallized, the rule development process may be delayed as the analysts attempt to gather information and perhaps contract for additional studies.[24] In practice, this tradeoff means that the regulatory analysis office must design a system that is capable of providing a relatively rapid response to a broad range of inquiries. This system may not be well suited for providing comprehensive analyses of particular options.[25]

The agencies might attempt to resolve this dilemma by "phasing" the analysis to reflect the seriousness with which subordinate decisionmaking entities are considering particular options at particular times. Under this approach, the regulatory analysis office could examine a large number of feasible options in a very cursory "back-of-the-envelope" fashion very early in the process, before very many alternatives have been eliminated. This early first-cut analysis, which would require very little information gathering, might eliminate several options on economic feasibility grounds. Later, as the subordinate decisionmaking unit rejects more options, the intensity of the analysis could increase. The phasing approach to timing regulatory analysis input would ensure that many options received at least some attention from the agency's regulatory analysts, while at the same time ensuring that serious alternatives received serious analysis.

Early access to the decisionmaking process is probably even more important if the analyst is to play an options-identification role. If upper-level decisionmakers expect agency regulatory analysts to identify innovative options for use in the decisionmaking process, the analysts must have access to subordinate decisionmaking entities very early on before the program office staff has set its research agenda. Yet, at some point in the almost infinite range of possible solutions to a regulatory problem, the agency must quit studying options. One possible solution to this dilemma is to structure the participation of the regulatory analysts into the process at a very early stage in the decisionmaking process while at the same time structuring the process to secure high-level input before any option is explored in great detail, a possibility that will be discussed in more detail in Chapter 16.

The regulatory analyst who is playing only a policy communication role need not become involved in the process much before the subordinate decisionmaking entities have completed their deliberations. In this role, the analyst's main function is to communicate to upper-level decisionmakers the extent to which regulatory options advance particular agency goals. Although the policy communication function could be helpful to subordinate groups in formulating their recommendations to upper-level decisionmakers, it is not essential to their function. Because the analyst who is assigned a policy communication role will likely also play an information-gathering role, the analyst will probably already be involved in the subordinate decisionmaking process at the time it becomes appropriate to analyze the regulatory options. Hence, for the regulatory analyst to play an effective policy communication role, the timing of the analytical input need not differ from the timing of the information-providing role.

The same is true of the roles of advocate and influential determinant of agency policy. Although it is not essential that either of these roles be structured into the decisionmaking process until just before upper-level decisionmakers are ready to choose from among the available options, as a practical matter the analysts will usually be involved long before then. Still, it is important that the analysts play their advocacy and policymaking roles while they are engaged in their information-providing role in subordinate decisionmaking units. If the regulatory analysts remain silent during internal discussions in subordinate decisionmaking units, they are subject to legitimate criticism when they take "late hits" at advanced stages where serious consideration of additional alternatives means returning to the drawing board.

CHAPTER 12

The hierarchical model

Many agencies did not modify existing institutional arrangements to meet the analytical requirements of the Executive Orders and the Regulatory Flexibility Act (RFA). Several simply added the task of preparing regulatory analysis documents to the responsibilities of the technical staff without creating a separate regulatory analysis office. The same employees who draft the rulemaking documents also draft the regulatory analysis documents. The regulatory analysis then winds its way up through the hierarchy of the program office along with the other rulemaking documents. Under this "hierarchical model" the technical staffers and their superiors at each level in the agency hierarchy can become aware of the relevant information and analysis, but there is no separate institutional entity to skeptically review rulemaking documents and otherwise carry the flag for comprehensive analytical rationality.

Both of the agencies chosen here as examples of the hierarchical model are lodged in the United States Department of Agriculture (USDA). USDA is so decentralized that in the words of one USDA employee, it is "like a supermarket."[1] As a practical matter, the individual services within USDA are relatively autonomous. All documents that are published in the *Federal Register*, however, must receive clearance for legal sufficiency from the centralized Office of the General Counsel.[2] USDA has a large staff of agricultural economists in the Economic Research Service, who assemble data relevant to the agricultural economy and make projections about future crop yields, prices, and exports. Although the Service plays a fairly small role in preparing regulatory analyses,[3] informal discussions between its economists and regulatory analysts in the agencies occur frequently.

The Office of Budget and Program Analysis (OBPA) in the Office of the Secretary has approximately twenty individuals with program management expertise who focus on departmental regulatory concerns in many contexts, including budget proposals, legislative proposals, and specific regulations.[4] OBPA performs a centralized

191

clearance function for all important agency rules, and it reviews the regulatory analysis documents for all major and many nonmajor rules. The extent to which OBPA personnel become involved in day-to-day regulatory activities depends a great deal on the importance that top USDA policymaking officials attach to particular issues. This, in turn, is sometimes determined by an issue's program and budget implications.[5] As regulatory analysis has become a more important function in agencies with regulatory responsibility, some services have become more proficient with regulatory analysis and have developed a credibility that has given them a degree of independence from OBPA.[6]

The hierarchical model in the Agricultural Marketing Service

The Agricultural Marketing Service (AMS) promulgates marketing orders for various commodities governing the terms and conditions under which they may be sold in interstate commerce. The primary purpose of these orders is to ensure price stability for the relevant commodities by regulating supplies. The regulatory staff is divided into six divisions, each of which regulates a separate activity or commodity. A seventh division, the Marketing Research and Development Division, houses a three-person Regulation Review Staff.[7] The various commodity divisions generate agency rules, and the staffs of those divisions draft both the rulemaking documents and the regulatory analysis documents. The Regulation Review Staff then reviews regulatory analysis documents for sufficiency.

The decisionmaking process

The AMS promulgates two kinds of substantive rules. First, the agency promulgates general marketing orders for commodities, using the formal rulemaking procedures of the Administrative Procedure Act.[8] Second, and more rarely, the agency promulgates informal rules using informal rulemaking procedures. The regulatory analysis documents for formal rules are submitted as testimony in the formal rulemaking hearings where they are subject to cross-examination and rebuttal.[9] Because the agency makes a special effort to encourage the participation of small businesses in the formal hearings, it takes the position that the opinion that concludes the formal rulemaking process is the equivalent to a final RIA and

RFA.[10] Regulatory analyses are performed only very rarely for informal rules.

The origin of most rules in AMS is a new statutory enactment or a petition from the regulated industry. A staff employee in the division dealing with the commodity that is the subject of the rule drafts a work plan for the rule and identifies options. When a rule is required by statute, the agency has little discretion to pursue other options, and it does not attempt to do so. A draft of the work plan for a rule is forwarded to the three-person Regulation Review Staff, which attempts to ensure that the work plan is readable and to determine whether the rule crosses the thresholds for preparing a formal RIA or RFA. The staff rarely suggests additional options.

An employee in the commodity division drafts both the rulemaking documents and the regulatory analysis documents, and introduces both documents and any supporting studies in the hearings. AMS does not assemble formal working groups. The commodity division employee simply forwards the rulemaking and regulatory analysis documents to the Regulation Review Staff, which performs the ministerial function of ensuring that the documents are suitable for publication in the *Federal Register*.[11] After approval by the AMS Administrator, they go to the Departmental Office of Budget and Program Analysis (OBPA) for review of the adequacy of the economic analysis and consistency with broad departmental policies.[12]

The AMS is unique among the agencies examined in this book in that public participation takes place in formal rulemaking proceedings where parties are entitled to submit competing analyses and to cross-examine the agency economic experts. The primary focus of the hearing is upon the predicted economic impacts of the agency's action. At the conclusion of the hearing, the staff prepares a recommended decision, and the parties address this recommendation in their briefs to the Administrator, who is the final decisionmaker.

The role of regulatory analysis

Regulatory analysis plays almost no role at all in the internal decisionmaking process at AMS. The regulatory analysis documents consist entirely of analyses of impacts on supplies and prices of agricultural products, and they do not probe the advantages and disadvantages from the consumer's perspective of broad options. Because most of the rules that AMS writes are intended to support commodity prices, their primary impact is to shift wealth from consumers to farmers, but the regulatory analysis documents do not analyze even this fundamental distributional effect. In the absence of any regulatory analysis requirements, AMS would assemble the very same information and subject it to the very same procedures.

Although AMS has a small staff of persons who review regulatory analysis documents for sufficiency, they can be classified as regulatory analysts in only the most rudimentary sense. They do not write the regulatory analysis documents, and they do not participate in important meetings where real decisions are made. Even the "super-analysts" in OMB play no role at all in AMS decisions, because Congress specifically excluded them from the process after several incidents in the early 1980s in which they challenged the fundamental precepts of the agency's programs.[13] It is fair to conclude AMS is an agency whose product, for political reasons, has so far been immune to careful analytical scrutiny.

The hierarchical model in the Agricultural Stabilization and Conservation Service

The Agricultural Stabilization and Conservation Service (ASCS) administers numerous grants and loan programs for farmers. Its primary functions are to stabilize commodity prices and conserve soil and other valuable agriculture resources. Although its regulations are for the most part merely conditions upon federal loans, they have the same practical effect as binding rules upon the farming industry, because few farmers in the regulated commodity areas can afford to opt out of the ASCS grant and loan programs. Because nearly all ASCS rules have a large impact on the relevant agricultural sector and because most farmers are small businesses, a regulatory analysis document is nearly always prepared for ASCS rulemaking initiatives. Most rules and regulatory analysis documents are drafted by commodity specialists in the relevant program areas. A three-person Regulatory Impact and Executive Correspondence Staff (Regulatory Impact Staff) performs a modest review function.[14]

The decisionmaking process

A rule in ASCS follows a route very similar to that of AMS. The most common source of rules in ASCS is a new statute, which gives the agency very little discretion.[15] After Congress enacts a new farm bill, a commodity specialist in the program office identifies the need for a regulation and fills out a work plan and forwards it to the Regulatory Impact Staff. That staff plays a review and advisory role.

Although all staff members have training in economics, a member participates in the preparation of a regulatory analysis document only when the commodity specialist is overburdened with other responsibilities.[16] The Regulatory Impact Staff does make threshold recommendations whether to prepare formal RIAs to the Under Secretary, who makes the final threshold determination with input from OBPA.[17]

The next stage in the process, the first "policy guidance session," is the most important step in the genesis of a rule at ASCS. A total of ten to twenty people usually attend such sessions, including the commodity specialist, the Administrator or one or two members of the Regulatory Impact Staff, representatives from the Office of General Counsel and OBPA, and other high-level officials. Prior to the meeting, the commodity specialist prepares a lengthy agenda that explains the reasons for the regulation, identifies several options, sets out the information and analysis supporting each of the options, and suggests a calendar for promulgating the rule.

The purpose of the session is to decide what options the agency will explore in its published proposal. The group attempts to identify a very broad range of options that "cover the waterfront." The agency even analyzes regulatory options beyond the scope of its current legislative authority on the theory that it might surface issues that could be appropriate for future legislative initiatives. Although any member of the group is encouraged to contribute options, the commodity specialist, who is the most familiar with the commodity and the statute, provides nearly all of them prior to the meeting. Additional options can arise out of the give and take of ideas and opinions during the meeting.[18] High-level decisionmakers become intimately involved in the options identification process at the policy guidance sessions and in the informal communications that precede those meetings. Yet, although upper-level input helps to narrow the range of options somewhat, the policymakers do not dictate choices among options at this point. The initial policy guidance session rarely precipitates disputes, because additional options can always be added to avoid disputes. Usually the participants' substantive questions can be answered by reference to the newly enacted statute or prior administrative practice. Things can get more contentious later, when the rulemaking and regulatory analysis documents are being circulated for review prior to publication.

After the policy guidance session, the commodity specialist writes a memorandum summarizing the need for the regulation, the options, and the advantages and disadvantages of the options. This gives upper-level decisionmakers a final opportunity to inquire about the direction that the agency is taking. The commodity specialist next drafts the rulemaking documents and any necessary regulatory analysis documents. Regulatory analysis documents vary from about ten to thirty pages in length, and they often contain tables detailing economic impacts. The commodity specialists in ASCS usually make a point of sending these tables to OBPA for review and comment.[19] ASCS staffers have a great deal of respect for their counterparts in OBPA, and they do not hesitate to take advantage of their advice. This receptivity to OBPA input makes ASCS unique among USDA regulatory agencies.

After the commodity specialist completes the proposed rule, which is really no more than a series of proposed options, and the regulatory analysis documents, the specialist forwards them to the relevant division and then to the Regulatory Impact Staff. A member of that staff reviews the regulatory analysis document for completeness and occasionally suggests editorial changes. The staffer also attempts to ensure that all of the options are reasonable and feasible.[20] One of the jobs of that staff is to find soft spots in the regulatory analyses. Disagreements are generally resolved in meetings between the staffer and the commodity specialist. Because not all of the commodity specialists are trained in economics, they usually accept the Regulatory Impact Staff's input. On occasion, however, the commodity specialist, who is intimately familiar with the particular commodity, must educate the economists in the realities of the relevant markets.[21]

The commodity specialists analyze all of the public comments and incorporate them into a position paper, which narrows down the options to the two or three most promising options and sets out the specialist's recommendations. The Regulatory Impact Staff does not review the public comments; nor does it participate in drafting the position paper. A second policy guidance session is held after the position paper is completed.[22] At this point the members of the policy guidance group pay particular attention to the regulatory analysis documents, because it is at this point that the group must make the hard choices. After the relevant agency personnel have agreed upon a preferred option, the analysis is updated and transmitted with a memorandum to the Under Secretary for a decision.

The role of regulatory analysis

Regulatory analysis plays only a slightly more important role in ASCS than in AMS. The charts and tables that form the core of the regulatory analysis documents detail the impact of various regulatory options on commodity supplies and prices. This information is critical to agency decisionmaking, but, as in AMS, it is clear that it would be forthcoming even in the absence of the regulatory analysis requirements. The regulatory analyses do not seriously probe the broad advantages and disadvantages of regulatory options.

The small regulatory analysis staff in ASCS seems to play a somewhat larger role than its counterpart in AMS. Although the commodity specialists in the program office draft the regulatory analysis documents, the analysts on the Regulatory Impact Staff seriously review them and often recommend modifications. The commodity specialists usually accept these recommendations. The AMS analysts also attend the all-important policy guidance sessions, although their role is quite limited. They do not seem to be the source of many innovative options. On the whole, regulatory analysts appear to have a very modest impact on ASCS decisionmaking.

Conclusions

When the program office can gather information and draft cost and benefits analyses, without the critical review of an independent regulatory analysis office, its task is relatively simple. For rules that raise predominantly economic concerns on both the cost and benefit sides of the ledger, a single program staffer is probably capable of performing the analysis with only minimal input from other trained economists. Upper-level review and the public comment process may provide a sufficient critical perspective on the work of the lower-level technical staff.

The hierarchical model, however, does not ensure that comprehensive analytical rationality is brought to bear upon regulatory decisions. First, the hierarchical model provides no assurance against bureaucratic tunnel vision. Yet, interjecting a broad range of perspectives into the hierarchical decisionmaking process at critical junctures, such as the ASCS's policy guidance sessions, can help alleviate this problem. Moreover, it is not clear that the input of a separate regulatory analysis office would necessarily result in making a broader range of options available to upper-level decisionmakers.

Second, the hierarchical model does not have an independent entity to insist that regulatory options be measured against articulated agency policy goals. The hierarchical model is therefore particularly susceptible to decisionmaking by precedent without periodic reexamination of first principles. Some measure of accountability is lost in a decisionmaking process that lacks effective policy communication, and the model may be less amenable to policy changes from politically appointed officials.

Third, the hierarchical model lacks a designated institutional skeptic. Although it is possible that the technical staffer charged with drafting the rulemaking and regulatory analysis documents for a rule is capable of independently analyzing the staff's own ideas and analyses, he or she is not as likely to see gaps in data or reasoning that may undermine the economic and technical rationale for a rule. There may also be a tendency to use regulatory analysis documents as vehicles to justify decisions reached on other grounds. Although upper-level decisionmakers and their staffs can bring independent perspectives to bear on the rationale for a rule, they may not have the time or the inclination to provide an effective critical perspective.

Fourth, the hierarchical model exerts little pressure on the technical staff to react substantively to criticisms of its reasoning. Ordinarily, the technical staff has received a clear indication of the result (or at least a very narrow range of options) that the upper-level decisionmakers would like to reach prior to drafting regulatory analysis documents. Once the staff has developed a rationale to support the favored result, to critique that rationale or to suggest a different result during the hierarchical review process is to force the staff back to the drawing board. Too many trips back to square one can waste staff resources and destroy staff morale.

Fifth, the rationale for a rule may become distorted as it moves up the hierarchy. Professors Edwards and Sharkansky observe:

> [M]ost bureaucracies have a hierarchical structure, and the information on which decisions are based usually passes from bottom to top. At each step in this ladder of communication personnel screen the information from the previous stage. This is necessary because decisionmakers cannot absorb all the detailed information that exists on an issue. . . . The longer the communication chain, the greater the chance that judgments will replace facts; nuances or caveats will be excluded; subordinates will paint a positive face on a situation to improve their own image or that of their organization; human error will distort the overall picture; and the speculations of "experts" will be reported as fact.[23]

The hierarchical model can thus impede the flow of innovative options and important information to upper-level decisionmakers.

Finally, the hierarchical model does not necessarily contain an institutional efficiency advocate. If one of the regulatory reform goals of the recent Executive Orders is to make rules more efficient and less burdensome, it may not be enough merely to send that message to the technical staff that has historically written and explained agency rules. On the other hand, as we have seen, it may be that the agency's regulatory mandate is sufficiently clear that the agency has little discretion to adopt less burdensome approaches.

CHAPTER 13

The outside advisor model

A second model of the regulatory analysis process casts the regulatory analyst in the role of outside advisor. In this model, the agency devotes a separate office at least in part to regulatory analysis, but it has no formal role in the decisionmaking process. It lacks institutional power, because it is not necessarily included in subordinate decisionmaking entities and because it does not have "sign-off" authority. The office is usually called in to provide information and analysis for large or controversial rulemaking efforts. Under this model, the regulatory analysis office speaks only when spoken to.

The outside advisor model in the Animal and Plant Health Inspection Service

The Animal and Plant Health Inspection Service (APHIS), one of the regulatory agencies in the highly decentralized USDA, is responsible for protecting domestic plants and animals from pestilence and disease. The quarantine statutes that it administers date back to the late nineteenth century. Under the more recent Federal Plant Pest Act, APHIS issues permits for the import and transport within the United States of plant pests and plants containing plant pests. In addition, APHIS licenses veterinary biological products, such as animal vaccines, to ensure that they meet agency standards for purity, safety and efficacy.

APHIS has two program offices: the Plant Protection and Quarantine Office and the Veterinary Services Office. The former deals with plant protection; the latter is responsible for animal protection. The agency's four regulatory analysts are lodged in the Policy Analysis and Program Evaluation Staff (the Policy Analysis Staff).[1] The Policy Analysis Staff has become actively involved in document drafting in only a very small percentage (less than 5 percent) of the agency's rulemaking efforts.[2] A separate Regulatory Coordination Staff, consisting almost entirely of lawyers, serves the Administrator directly. The two program offices generate rules and prepare most regulatory analysis documents: The Policy Analysis Staff prepares some regulatory analysis documents and reviews some others; and the Regulatory Coordination Staff coordinates the rulemaking efforts and drafts the *Federal Register* documents.

The decisionmaking process

A rule in APHIS typically comes from one or more of three sources. A staff employee in one of the two program offices may identify the need for a rule, and the proposal flows upward. Alternatively, a large pest outbreak may generate demands for action from the regulated farming and ranching community, and the Administrator directs a staffer in one of the program offices to work with the Regulatory Coordination Staff to initiate the rulemaking process. Finally, members of the affected industries may formally petition the agency to initiate a rulemaking effort. Because the agency's rules are designed to protect crops and animals from pest and disease outbreaks, they are not often very controversial. Disputes do erupt, however, over the amount that the agency will pay for animals and crops that it destroys in quarantine programs. Because APHIS rules are often promulgated in emergencies, regulatory analysis documents are often prepared on an expedited basis or after the fact.[3]

After one of the two program offices has drafted a work plan for a rulemaking initiative, it is sent to the Regulatory Coordination Staff and then to the Assistant Secretary for Marketing and Inspection Services. Few efforts are made to identify options in work plans, which usually consist of a broad articulation of a single proposal. The plans are rarely specific, and they almost never include analysis or regulatory impact data.[4] The program office occasionally consults with an analyst from the Policy Analysis Staff about whether a rule crosses the RIA thresholds. Interestingly, APHIS does not base its threshold determination on the benefit of the regulation to the agricultural sector or to consumers. Instead, the agency tends to rely upon the rule's cost to the agency; for example, the amount that the agency will have to devote to administering the program, purchasing pesticides, and paying for destroyed plants and animals in quarantine programs.[5] Under this approach, the agency rarely prepares a formal RIA for a major rule. The program offices are, however, responsible for preparing regulatory analysis documents for rules that the Assistant Secretary designates "reserved nonmajor" and for rules for which the attorneys on the Regulatory Coordination Staff request additional information on regulatory impacts.

An attorney on the Regulatory Coordination Staff has the primary responsibility for drafting rulemaking documents with the aid of staff from the program office.[6] After the documents are drafted, the attorney meets with program office staffers and representatives from any other programs that the rule may affect to critique and edit the drafts. A representative from the Policy Analysis Staff meets with this work group only if the program office or the Regulatory Coordination Staff explicitly requests its input.[7] Although an APHIS Directive assigns the Policy Analysis Staff responsibility for preparing regulatory analysis documents,[8] the program offices in reality prepare nearly all such documents. These documents are then reviewed by the Regulatory Coordination Staff.

Because the Policy Analysis Staff becomes involved in a rulemaking initiative only upon request, it usually enters the process after the program office has eliminated most alternatives. This leaves some staffers with the strong impression that they are only invited to meetings when the Regulatory Coordination Staff believes that the regulations are in need of further justification. The Policy Analysis Staff, however, resists the role of "justifier." On one occasion, when the Policy Analysis Staff was asked to help shore up a rulemaking effort, it prepared a regulatory analysis document, even though a separate document was not requested, that identified and examined alternatives to the program office's proposal and critiqued that proposal. If the regulatory analyst feels strongly enough about an alternative that the program office did not examine, the analyst may attempt to send an independent analysis through formal channels to the Deputy Administrator for Administration, thereby virtually ensuring that the document will find its way into the rulemaking record. The Policy Analysis Staff does not, however, have any authority to veto a rule with which it disagrees.[9]

The departmental OBPA, a potential ally to the regulatory analysis office in these matters, plays no role whatsoever in the internal agency decisionmaking process, because the agency promulgates so few major rules.[10] Another potential ally, the Office of Management and Budget, is only slightly more helpful. OMB occasionally asks the APHIS liaison why the Policy Analysis Staff did not prepare a regulatory analysis document on a rule when the OMB staffer has questions about its cost-effectiveness.[11] More often, however, OMB questions the substance of the rule, rather than the analysis supporting it.[12]

After the close of the comment period, the program officials meet with the Regulatory Coordination Staff to discuss the final rulemaking document. The Regulatory Coordination Staff then drafts the final document. The Policy Analysis Staff can be called in to participate in the preparation of the Final Rule and final regulatory analysis document, but this is not required by standard operating procedures, and it happens only very rarely.[13]

Role of regulatory analysis

In the opinion of the Director of the Regulatory Coordination Staff, regulatory analysis is not especially useful for APHIS efforts, because it is almost always cheaper to stop a pest infestation or disease at the border or limit its spread through quarantine than it is to allow the infestation or disease to spread. In the opinion of the director, "the benefits of our regulations so obviously outweigh the costs that it is not necessarily a good use of our resources to engage in detailed analysis." Although an important purpose of regulatory analysis is to force the agency to justify its rules by explicit reference to agency policy, the justification for most APHIS rules is, in the director's opinion, obvious. Finally, the director is of the opinion that the agency nearly always chooses the least-cost alternative for combating a pest or disease, although this is not always well documented.[14]

At least one former member of the Policy Analysis Staff, on the other hand, feels that agency decisions could be improved by devoting more resources to identifying less costly alternatives to current response mechanisms, citing the failure to search broadly for alternatives in the agency's response to the Mediterranean Fruit Fly outbreak in 1981 as an example of agency failure in this regard. Conceding that regulatory analysis is rarely determinative of the big "yes-no" decisions, the regulatory analyst nevertheless argued that analysis can be very helpful in identifying minor cost-effective suboptions and in discovering instances in which rules impact intensely in unintended ways upon small entities.[15]

The current agency decisionmaking procedures place the regulatory analysis office in the role of "outsiders looking in."[16] The vast majority of regulatory analysis work in APHIS is done by the program office staff. On those relatively rare occasions in which the Policy Analysis Staff becomes involved in the rulemaking process, the analyst becomes part of the work group that makes the preliminary regulatory decisions and the recommendations for final rules. However, the work group does not meet until after the program office has settled upon a single preferred alternative. The analysts are most effective when they suggest minor alternatives to options that the program office has proposed. This role can be important,[17] but it is obviously not very profound.

The Policy Analysis Staff can best be viewed as an independent consultant to the program and regulatory coordination staffs, who are the primary advisors to upper-level agency decisionmakers. Personnel on that staff do not attempt to advocate any particular position in the context of individual rulemaking proceedings, and they do not attempt to influence agency decisionmakers. When their input is requested, they attempt to analyze the available options without taking a position on which option is preferable.[18] This limited role may be inherent in the nature of the business that the agency conducts. When asked whether the regulatory analysis process has had an impact on the agency's decisionmaking process, the Director of the Regulatory Coordination Staff referred to the emergency nature of the agency's primary functions and replied, "I don't think it could."[19]

The outside advisor model in the Federal Aviation Administration

The Federal Aviation Administration (FAA) is one of the larger Operating Administrations in the Department of Transportation. Two of the agency's primary rulemaking functions are to promulgate operational rules for aircraft operations and to promulgate standards for certifying aircraft. The first function is performed largely by personnel in the agency's Washington, D.C. headquarters. The agency has adopted a "key region" approach for implementing much of the second function. Under this approach, rules are developed in the geographic regions that have primary expertise with particular aircraft.

The Associate Administrator for Aviation Standards is responsible for developing standards for aviation safety. The Office of Aviation Policy and Plans (the Aviation Policy Office), which serves the Associate Administrator for Policy and International Aviation, is the agency's regulatory analysis office. A branch of that office contains seven economists who prepare regulatory analysis documents for most of the rules that the agency generates. Most agency work groups include one of its analysts.[20]

The decisionmaking process

Most FAA rules arise out of the development of a new aviation technology, a petition from an outside party, National Transportation Safety Board recommendations, or a problem that one of the program offices has identified. The director of the responsible office must appoint a "team" to "work up" the idea into a concrete proposal. The team is composed of a representative from the technical office, an attorney, and (if requested) a regulatory analyst.[21] At the end of its initial deliberations, the team drafts a Project Report, which consists of a brief (approximately four pages) resume of the project's objectives, an estimate of resource and personnel requirements, and a proposed schedule. At this point, the Aviation Policy Office estimates whether the agency should hire a contractor to generate cost and benefit data.[22] The Project Report is updated periodically to reflect changes in the status of the action.

A high-level Regulatory Review Board, made up of personnel from headquarters and the relevant regions, meets approximately twice a year to go through new and existing rulemaking projects.[23] These meetings serve to keep headquarters personnel apprised of the status of rules and to give them input into the process of deciding which new actions ought to be pursued. As its nickname "murder board" implies, the board has the power to terminate projects.[24]

The agency prepares some kind of regulatory analysis document for virtually all of its important rules, although it sometimes incorporates the analysis directly into the preamble of the proposed regulation, rather than preparing a separate document.[25] The intensity of the analysis varies with the perceived importance of the regulation.

When the engineers in one of the directorates request the participation of the Aviation Policy Office, one of its staff economists becomes a member of the team that drafts the proposed rule and other rulemaking documents. The team meetings usually give rise to painstaking discussions among the engineers, the regulatory analysts, and agency attorneys about the merits of several alternatives for addressing the regulatory problem. The goal of the meetings is to reach a consensus on the content of the rule.[26]

Relying upon an extensive manual that the Aviation Policy Office drafted in 1982,[27] the regulatory analyst assigned to the team prepares a relatively formal cost-benefit analysis.[28] The regulatory analysts generally limit their cost-benefit analyses to alternatives that the program office has identified, which in many cases is but a single option.[29] The regulatory analysis office, however, is often a strong proponent of the "no action" alternative that the program office sometimes neglects.[30] The regulatory analysis documents never examine alternatives beyond the agency's statutory authority.

Disagreements between the Directorates and Aviation Policy Office occur very infrequently. Indeed, more disputes over regulations in FAA occur between parallel rulemaking offices (e.g. between aviation standards and air traffic control) than between the regulatory analysis office and any particular program office. The analysts regard themselves as providers of a service to the program offices; they do not regard themselves as coequal decisionmakers. In their opinion, the value of the office lies in providing neutral advice from the perspective of an entity with no vested interest in the rulemaking proceeding.[31] Although the program office nearly always accepts the analysts' advice, the decision is ultimately made by the Directorate.

Role of regulatory analysis

For most regulations of any consequence, the FAA Administrator reads a summary of the regulatory analysis document's contents. In many cases, the Administrator also reads the actual regulatory analysis document. The fact that the documents may be read by the Administrator probably enhances their quality.[32] Their primary impact stems from their costing out function, which allows upper-level decisionmakers to choose the least costly alternative to a given regulatory result.[33] Thus, although the regulatory analysts attempt to prepare full-blown cost-benefit analyses, the upper-level decisionmakers apparently employ them in a way more consistent with cost-effectiveness analysis.

The regulatory analysis office has a high profile in FAA, and it appears to be fairly influential in agency decisionmaking, even though the regulatory analysts consider themselves little more than consultants to the program offices. An analyst will be present on the work group only if the accountable Directorate requests that it participate. On the other hand, the Directorates know that it will be difficult to get an important rule through upper-level review without the kind of detailed analysis that the analysts can provide.[34] The analysts' contribution can be outcome-determinative in both directions. In one proceeding the Aviation Policy Office hired a contractor to design an aircraft from scratch, and the study demonstrated convincingly that the proposed rule was prohibitively expensive. Conversely, the office's cost studies frequently indicate that the burden of a rule will be trivial or that the cost of repealing an existing rule will be substantial. The Director of the Aviation Policy Office is confident that the agency's rules would not be as cost-effective if his office did not participate in rulemaking activities.[35] Officials in the Office of Chief Counsel agree that the regulatory analysts have played an important role in regulatory decisionmaking.[36]

The contribution of the Aviation Policy Office, however, is limited to the preparation of cost-benefit analyses of alternatives that the program office has already identified. There is little evidence that the analysts have suggested innovative new options that the technical specialists missed.[37] Their chief function, beyond preparing regulatory analysis documents, is to provide an economic perspective on issues that are discussed at team meetings. Their input can change the direction that a rule takes toward a less expensive option, but it rarely changes the broader outcome of a rulemaking proceeding.[38]

Conclusions

The primary advantage of the outside advisor model is that it allows the program office and upper-level decisionmakers to take advantage of the information and analysis that regulatory analysts can provide without allowing the analysts to dominate the decisionmaking process. The outside advisor model effectively prevents the regulatory analysts from playing an advocacy role and from becoming influential determinants of agency policy in the guise of neutral providers of information.

Upper-level decisionmakers who are sensitive to the limitations of regulatory analysis and who are willing to take responsibility for the policy aspects of their decisions may prefer the outside advisor model, because it allows the regulatory analyst to measure regulatory options against agency policy without delegating significant decisionmaking authority to the regulatory analysis office. The outside advisor model also conserves valuable analytical resources for rulemakings in which they are really needed. The program office is also likely to favor the outside advisor model, because it constrains the bureaucratic power of a competing organizational entity. Even some regulatory analysts may prefer this model, because it does not allow the program office to foist off unpopular policy choices on the regulatory analysis office.

Most regulatory analysts, however, resist being placed in the limited role of outside advisor. Many analysts have chosen their profession out of an attraction to the policymaking process. Like many program office staffers, regulatory analysts probably aspire to becoming influential within their bureaucracies. Perhaps more than the technical staff, regulatory analysts come to the enterprise with definite ideas about the role of regulation in society, and they would like to see those ideas implemented. The FAA experience indicates that outside advisors can become influential in particular cases, but some analysts may prefer a more systematic role in the day-to-day decisionmaking process.

Beyond frustrating the policymaking aspirations of the regulatory analysis staff, a significant disadvantage of the outside advisor model is the danger that regulatory analysis will be used merely to justify decisions previously reached on other grounds. This is apparently its primary use in APHIS. Analysis can provide acceptable rationales for decisions reached on impermissible grounds, but most analysts regard post hoc rationalization as an abuse of analysis and a threat to the integrity of the profession. Perhaps more importantly, it reduces the accountability of the politically appointed decisionmakers.

Another significant disadvantage of the outside advisor model is its failure to use the agency's regulatory analysts as options-identifiers. This disadvantage should not be pressed too far, however, in light of the absence of strong evidence that regulatory analysts with greater institutional power contribute significantly to the options-identification process. Moreover, upper-level decisionmakers in programs with little discretion to adopt market-oriented regulatory alternatives may not feel that this role is important enough to warrant making the regulatory analysis office a full-fledged participant in the decisionmaking process.

The outside advisor model may also reduce the extent to which the regulatory analysis office can play the role of institutional skeptic. If the regulatory analysts speak only when spoken to, they will probably not become sufficiently acquainted with the work of the program office to provide skeptical comment and review. The result may be that poorly reasoned regulations find their way into the *Federal Register*.

CHAPTER 14

The team model

The team approach is by far the most prevalent decisionmaking model in federal regulatory agencies. The primary subordinate decisionmaking entity in this model is a team, or work group, composed of representatives from all of the institutional subunits within the agency that have an interest in the outcome of the rulemaking process. Typically, a team is composed of representatives from the program office, the research and development office, the policy office, the Office of General Counsel (or Solicitor's Office), the enforcement office, and one of the agency's regional or field offices. The team meets periodically to discuss regulatory options, to examine problem areas, to respond to requests of upper-level decisionmakers, and to resolve disputes among team members. Although the program office usually has responsibility for the rulemaking effort, the group often delegates tasks to individual members of the team or to small subcommittees. Copies of memoranda, rulemaking and regulatory analysis documents, and other decisionmaking documents are circulated to team members for review and comment. All team members are regarded as coequal participants in the decisionmaking process, and there is usually strong pressure, deriving from both the group psychology of the effort and from upper-level decisionmakers, for the team to reach consensus on important questions.

Mechanisms for resolving disputes on teams vary. Sometimes disputes are resolved by votes, with the minority acquiescing in the majority's decision. Usually, dissenters are allowed to elevate disputes through formal or informal channels to higher levels for resolution. A team member, however, can only elevate dissents a limited number of times without fracturing the overall consensus necessary for the effective operation of the team.

In most agencies that employ the team model, the same approach is also employed at higher decisionmaking levels. After the low-level work group has completed its work, a steering committee, composed of the superiors of the team members, will review the initial team's efforts. This second-level team is often used as a quality control mechanism and as a vehicle for resolving disputes upon which the low-level team could not reach consensus.

Three of the agencies examined here employ the team model to a greater or lesser extent. Two of those agencies will be examined in this chapter. The unique hybrid model that has evolved in the Environmental Protection Agency (EPA) is examined in Chapter 16. The team model in the Food Safety and Inspection Service (FSIS) evolved from the hierarchical model. Prior to 1983, the hierarchical approach was employed for nearly all rules. After the success of the team approach in the mechanically separated meat (MSM) rulemaking, described in Chapter 6, the agency began to employ the team model for a larger universe of rules. In the early 1980s, the team model was written into the Occupational Safety and Health Administration's (OSHA's) standard operating procedures. Because it did not resolve crucial questions of accountability, OSHA abandoned the team model after the agency received severe criticism from unions and congressional committees. The model had such staying power, however, that lower-level staffers continued to use it on an informal basis, even after it had been officially abolished. Toward the end of the 1980s, OSHA once again formally adopted the team approach.

The team model in the Food Safety and Inspection Service

The Food Safety and Inspection Service (FSIS) is one of the more active regulatory agencies in the United States Department of Agriculture (USDA). FSIS has its origins in the progressive movement's reaction to the unsanitary practices in the meat-packing industry revealed in Upton Sinclair's *The Jungle*. In addition to maintaining inspectors in all meat slaughtering and processing plants, FSIS sets standards and labeling requirements to prevent the preparation and sale of adulterated and misbranded food.[1] The agency has a separate Policy and Program Planning Staff (the Policy Staff) that serves the Administrator directly. This staff devotes approximately twenty-five professionals to regulatory analysis. The agency undertakes an informal predecisional analysis for all of its rules,[2] but the agency has written very few full-fledged RIAs.[3]

The decisionmaking process

In FSIS, proposals for rulemaking can come from at least four sources: (1) a statutory requirement that the agency enact rules; (2)

outside petitions for rulemaking; (3) upper-level determinations that a rule is needed; and (4) recommendations from staff employees in the field. Most outside petitions come from the regulated industry, and the agency is often inclined to adopt industry proposals.[4] Over a period of seventy-five years the relationship between FSIS and the regulated industry has evolved into one in which there is a great deal of information-sharing.[5] Industry trade associations have technical committees that discuss ideas with agency personnel, and agency staff frequently speak at association meetings, thereby facilitating informal interchange. The agency and the industry can usually agree that a new rule is necessary, and the contents of a rule ordinarily become controversial only when the industry itself splits on an issue.

After initial approval, a rulemaking initiative in FSIS can follow one of two tracks. On rare occasions – not more than once a year – the Administrator decides to become involved personally in the rulemaking process, and designates a Special Assistant to draft the primary rulemaking documents and to coordinate rulemaking activities. As we observed in Chapter 6, these specially designated rules usually involve complex issues and significant resource commitments.

In normal cases, however, the agency follows a different and more systematic review process. A staff employee in the Office of Meat and Poultry Inspection Technical Services (the program office) drafts a proposed rule, supporting documents, and a one-page entry for the agency's Index of Pending Regulatory Actions.[6] The initiating staffer works together with a regulatory analyst to determine whether an RIA or Regulatory Flexibility Analysis should be prepared.[7] The agency generally prepares some kind of regulatory analysis document for all rules,[8] but the document for nonmajor rules need not fit the confines of the OMB guidance documents. The Policy Staff forwards a draft index entry and the threshold analysis to the Administrator, who then decides whether or not to pursue the rule and sends the package on to upper-level departmental officials. After the Administrator gives initial approval, he monitors periodic "docket development reports" to determine the extent to which the Administrator will become involved in the actual decisionmaking process.[9]

For the relatively rare specially designated rules, the Administrator forms a work group composed of the Special Assistant (who acts as the docket manager), the Deputy Administrator for the program office and one or more Division Directors, the Director of the regulatory analysis office, the Deputy Administrator for Science, and the

Administrator. The Special Assistant directs questions to persons with expertise in particular areas, develops and circulates information, and works with staff members to resolve outstanding issues. Numerous drafts of the rulemaking documents are reviewed during lengthy work group meetings. The members of the work group attempt to achieve consensus on the substance of the regulatory provisions, the preamble, and other documents. Any disputes that cannot be resolved prior to the work group meetings are usually resolved by the Administrator on the spot after the discussion has reached an impasse.[10]

These special rules invariably require regulatory analysis documents, which are the responsibility of the Policy Staff. A regulatory analysis document typically evolves as the high-level work group deliberates, and it is usually completed at about the same time that the work group has finished with the rulemaking documents. The agency analyst's chief function at the work group meetings is to provide information on the costs of various options. Occasionally the analyst identifies options that the group did not see, but such instances are relatively rare. The analyst hardly ever serves as an advocate at these high-level meetings.

Because regulatory analysis documents evolve as the rulemaking documents evolve, the time consumed in preparing them does not delay the decisionmaking process. For the same reason, however, the document itself plays no real role in the decisionmaking process. Whereas the information that is ultimately contained in the regulatory analysis document is usually available to the work group through the participation of the Policy Staff, the final document is not completed until after the work group's decisions are made.[11] Agency analysts feel that within broad limits their duty is to draft a document that makes the best analytical argument for what the agency proposes. The final regulatory analysis documents that the agency makes public therefore represent a "blend of analysis and advocacy." The Administrator usually reads the regulatory analysis document for special rules prior to forwarding the proposal to the Assistant Secretary.[12]

The FSIS Administrator was so pleased with the team concept that evolved in the MSM rulemaking that in 1984 the preexisting hierarchical process was replaced with a docket committee drawn from all relevant offices within the agency.[13] Once the Administrator approves a rulemaking initiative for an ordinary rule, the program office director asks each of the relevant offices to designate a member for the docket committee. The committee meets periodically and attempts to reach consensus on recommendations to the Administrator. Because a sign-off by a committee member generally binds the office the member represents, committee members stay in close contact with high-level officials in their offices. This reduces the number of disputes that arise at later stages in the decisionmaking process.[14]

The Policy Staff has the primary responsibility for drafting regulatory analysis documents. For routine regulations, the program office tends to assume that an elaborate regulatory impact analysis is unnecessary and perhaps undesirable. During the years in which the hierarchical model was in effect, program office staffers saw little value in burdening the process with a lot of external analysis.[15] Now that a regulatory analyst representative is on every docket committee, the program office staffer usually acquiesces in Policy Staff arguments that further analysis is necessary, even though this means that the regulation will inevitably suffer some delay. Because the program office staffer, who is responsible for producing a rule in a timely fashion, has no authority over other committee members, problems of accountability often arise.[16] To enforce a deadline, the program office representative must cajole the slaggard, ask his superior to speak to the head of the office responsible for the delay or do the job himself.

The intensity of the regulatory analysis varies with the importance of the rule. The analyst's chief concern is that the program office explicitly place the proposal within the agency's existing policy framework. The analyst attempts to ensure that either the rulemaking documents or the regulatory analysis documents state explicitly how the proposal will advance particular agency policy objectives, thereby rendering the agency accountable for its decisions. In the opinion of a past Director of the Policy Staff, the agency lacks a tradition of "going back to zero and explaining why we are doing what we are doing"; the job of the Policy Staff is to change that.[17]

The different perspectives of the regulatory analysis office and the program office inevitably breed tension between the two staffs. Once the program office is satisfied with the substance of a rule and its rationale, it would prefer that the analysts "roll over" and acquiesce in the program office's work product.[18] In the minds of some agency analysts, the program office becomes too management-oriented, and managers are reluctant to reexamine old assumptions. In this view, program office staffers are inclined over time to lose track of the reasons for why they do things in the convenience of adherence to ancient precedent.[19] To counter this tendency, directors of the Policy Staff have urged analysts to play an aggressive policy development role.[20]

Program office staffers respond that the Policy Staff has in recent years gone beyond analysis to assume a "traffic cop" role, refusing to allow rules to go forward when it disagrees with their substance. Whereas the program office in the past could often ignore the analysts and allow the rule to proceed up the hierarchy, under the team approach, the Policy Staff can indefinitely stall a rule until the program office acquiesces.[21] A former Director of the Policy Staff agrees that it has become more inclined to elevate matters to the Administrator and also agrees that more disputes arise over policy or values than over the content of analysis.[22] Thus, the switch from the hierarchical to the team approach has had the predictable effect of empowering agency analysts in substantive debates over agency policy, as well as of allowing greater analytical input. Although most substantive debates in the past were resolved in favor of the program office,[23] now the regulatory analysis office often wins.[24]

After the proposed rule has been published in the *Federal Register* and the public has commented on the proposal, FSIS must determine its response to those comments. For those rules receiving special treatment by a high-level agency work group, the Administrator's Special Assistant works with the program office staff to assemble and summarize the public comments. The Special Assistant also refers questions and information to persons within the agency with relevant expertise. For run-of-the-mill regulations, the official in the program office responsible for the regulation refers comments addressed to the regulatory analysis to the Policy Staff for response. Because the agency does not generally publish its regulatory analyses in the *Federal Register*,[25] the public comments rarely address them.

The role of regulatory analysis

FSIS probably makes more use of formal regulatory analysis documents than any other agency in USDA. But even in that agency, the formal documents have marginal impact on the decisionmaking process. The Administrator reads the documents for the rules that receive special high-level treatment. Yet, because the Administrator participates actively on the high-level work group that drafts the proposed and final rules and is therefore quite familiar with the issues, reading the formal document is not especially burdensome. The documents themselves do not affect the deliberations of the high-level work group, because they are not drafted until the work group has substantially completed its deliberations. The cost considerations that are raised at the meetings prior to the preparation of the formal document do, of course, affect the Administrator's thinking. It is probably more accurate to say that the content of a regulatory analysis document for a rule receiving special treatment reflects the input of the work group. For ordinary rules, the impact of the regulatory analysis document is not much greater, because it generally does not become available until the docket committee has made most of the important decisions.

The Policy Staff has a higher profile than its equivalents in other agencies within USDA. The agency's positive experience with the MSM rulemaking persuaded the Administrator to commit additional resources to strengthen the agency's regulatory analysis effort.[26] For example, the Policy Staff was provided resources for a series of seminars on regulatory analysis that featured prominent analysts from academia and government.[27] The Administrator became convinced that the presence of regulatory analysts in the decisionmaking process produced better decisions.[28] Consequently, the Administrator assigned the Policy Staff a larger role in the decisionmaking process for specially designated rules.

For ordinary rules the role of the policy office is somewhat more attenuated, but remains powerful after the recent adoption of the team approach. Although the agency prepares very few formal RIAs and RFAs, agency analysts prepare an analysis for all rules of any significance and they play a prominent role on the docket committees. The Director of the Policy Staff has a de facto veto that gives that staff substantial leverage in internal negotiations over the substance of rules. According to one of the program office directors, the Policy Staff is rarely a justifier of program office positions, and is almost always an influential determinant of agency policy. The change of institutional structure from the hierarchical model with the Policy Staff playing an occasional outside advisor role to the team model no doubt sealed the status of the Policy Staff as a powerful institutional player.

The team model in the Occupational Safety and Health Administration

The Occupational Safety and Health Administration (OSHA), one of several agencies in the Department of Labor (DOL), was established in 1970 to promulgate health and safety standards to protect workers and to ensure that employers comply with their general duty to provide a place of employment free from recognized hazards.[29] The Assistant Secretary for OSHA and two Deputy Assistant Secretaries head the agency. Of the seven Directorates that conduct the agency's day-to-day business, four – the Health Standards Directorate, the Safety Standards Directorate, the Policy Directorate, and the Technical Support Services Directorate – are usually involved in rulemaking activities. The Directorates of Health and Safety (the program offices) contain the scientists, engineers, and project managers who draft the agency's two or three proposed and final health and safety standards per year.[30] The Technical Support Services Directorate makes additional engineering and scientific expertise available to the program offices.[31] The Policy Directorate contains a small fifteen-person Office of Regulatory Analysis that has a budget of approximately three million dollars for preparing the regulatory analysis documents for the agency.[32]

Other offices within DOL also play a role in OSHA rulemaking. The Solicitor's Office provides lawyers who sit on rulemaking teams, represent the agency's position in the rulemaking hearings, and work with Justice Department attorneys on judicial appeals. The Solicitor's Office is also the designated departmental contact with OMB. The departmental Office of Regulatory Economics and Economic Policy Analysis under the Assistant Secretary for Policy plays a central review role for regulatory analysis documents.[33]

Like the other agencies within DOL, OSHA has a high degree of autonomy. The Department has, however, developed a detailed regulation management process, and it maintains a regulatory oversight function that is lodged in the Policy Review Board, which reviews all policy and regulatory initiatives.[34] The Secretary of Labor chairs the Board, and the Assistant Secretary for Policy serves as its Executive Director. Its purpose is to communicate policy prescriptions from the upper-level departmental decisionmakers to lower-level staff and to facilitate upper-level departmental input into the regulatory process.[35]

The decisionmaking process

In its early years, OSHA was a very loosely run organization, and especially so in its rulemaking functions. Rulemaking initiatives were launched in an ad hoc fashion. The Directors for Health and Safety Standards controlled the rulemaking process with substantial and continuing input from the Assistant Secretary. Loose internal work groups drafted rulemaking documents with the aid of outside consultants.[36] On at least one occasion, an outside consultant (a university professor) was the de facto head of the work group. The Directors themselves played very substantial roles in the drafting process, even to the point of typing the final version of a rule at 4:00 a.m. on the morning that it was due.[37] The entire agency would typically gear up for a single rulemaking effort, putting aside most other initiatives until the current effort reached a clear stopping point.[38] The result was a fairly low production of fairly stringent rules.

The 1982 Regulation Management System. In 1982, OSHA developed a formal Regulation Management System.[39] A Regulation Review Committee, composed of high-level OSHA officials, was charged with coordinating issues among the directorates, reviewing documents resulting from the standards development process, and recommending to the Assistant Secretary whether the agency should go forward with rulemaking initiatives. If the Assistant Secretary decided to pursue a topic, the Regulation Review Committee appointed a "Preliminary Team" to prepare a "Research and Analysis Plan" and "Part I of the Assistant Secretary's Summary."[40] The Research and Analysis Plan was "an outline of the facts to be documented and analyses to be made," and was to be based on "available or easily attainable information."[41] Part I of the Assistant Secretary's Summary set out the nature of the proposed action, the justification for that action, alternatives to the action, and groups with an interest in it.

If the Assistant Secretary decided to pursue the rulemaking effort further, the Review Committee would assemble a new Regulation Team to complete the agency's standard-setting process. Team leaders could come from any of the offices within the Health or Safety Directorates.[42] The team's first task was to prepare a "Workplan" and Part II of the Assistant Secretary's Summary. The Workplan described the resources that would be required to complete the rulemaking project and provided a schedule of activities. After the Review Committee and the Assistant Secretary approved the Workplan, the team prepared a risk analysis and an alternatives analysis. The team summarized these analyses and recommended a course of action in an Action Recommendation, which was intended to be the primary decision document within the agency.[43] Following approval of the Action Recommendation, the Regulation Team drafted the Notice of Proposed Rulemaking under the direction of the relevant Standards Director. The team leader would assign to a member or members of the team the task of incorporating all of the information that the team had considered into a Preamble for the Notice of Proposed Rulemaking. While the Regulation Team was deliberating over the contents of the proposed rule, the representative from the Office of Regulatory Analysis drafted the preliminary regulatory analysis documents.[44] The Notice of Proposed Rulemaking Package and related documents were finally reviewed by the Review Committee, the Assistant Secretary, and the Departmental Policy Review Board and sent to OMB for further review.[45]

Abandonment of the 1982 system. The above-described 1982 internal procedures for OSHA rulemaking are best described as Byzantine. Their excessive documentation requirements and their repetitive review procedures provided almost insuperable barriers to rulemaking, and in fact only one rule of any consequence (the hazard identification standard; see Chapter 7) was produced during the three to four years that the procedures were in place. The procedures were never closely observed for safety standards, which proceeded sequentially from the Safety Directorate to the Policy Office, to the Solicitor's Office and back to the Safety Directorate.[46] After a time, the 1982 procedures were abandoned for health standards as well. The Review Committee did not always come to closure, and some initiatives were effectively tabled indefinitely. The teams often bypassed that committee altogether and communicated directly with the Assistant Secretary.[47] The Research and Analysis Plan and the Assistant Secretary's Summaries were either ignored or treated in a very cursory fashion, and in many cases no Preliminary Team was ever appointed. High-level input was secured through informal meetings with the Assistant Secretary for which the members of the team prepared memoranda and charts to lay out the issues and options, and the Assistant Secretary often decided the important issues on the spot.

By late 1984, the 1982 procedures were as a practical matter irrelevant to the real-world rulemaking process. Not only had they effectively stymied rules aimed at enhancing workplace safety, they had also sidetracked efforts aimed at repealing or amending existing rules. Yet, although the formal processes were largely ignored, the teams remained in place as the agency's primary decisionmaking units. Indeed, teams would often make recommendations to agency leadership that ran against the policies of the current Administration. The recommendations were often leaked to the press, generating pressure on the agency's leadership to decide in accordance with the team's preferences.[48] By 1985, the Assistant Secretary was concerned that "renegade teams" had undermined the policy agenda of the agency's political appointees. In addition, OSHA was by 1985 receiving a great deal of congressional pressure to begin promulgating rules, and it had received several court orders to complete internal decision making by specific dates. With rulemaking projects increasingly subject to court-ordered deadlines, the agency was forced to abandon the 1982 procedures or face the threat of being held in contempt of court. The procedures were formally abolished in mid-1985.[49] The department procedures, establishing the Policy Review Board and requiring agencies to prepare a "Concept Analysis Paper" and an "Options Memorandum," however, remained in effect.

The current system. The 1982 procedures have not been replaced by any formal management regime.[50] The team concept was abolished along with the 1982 procedures, and responsibility for rulemaking devolved once again to the Health and Safety Standards Directorates. Yet, the project officers in those Directorates usually established informal teams made up of representatives from the Policy Office, the Solicitor's Office and other persons from the Health and Safety Standards Directorates with expertise in the subject area.[51] Although many of the subsidiary documentation requirements disappeared, a good deal of communication still occurred on a less formal basis between the Assistant Secretary's Office and the staff person with responsibility for the initiative.

Under the present informal team process, the initial impetus for an OSHA rule can come from several sources, including (1) recommendations of the National Institute for Occupational Safety and Health (NIOSH), (2) petitions from interested groups, (3) congressional investigations, (4) the agency's own staff, (5) periodic reviews of existing standards, and (6) media reports of widespread public concern. More recently, the agency's agenda has been set by outside groups that have sued the agency to require it to promulgate regulations by specific deadlines.[52] Although one purpose of the agency's 1982 procedures was to encourage more rational priority-setting, the agency has still not implemented an effective prioritization process.[53]

At the time that OSHA begins to devote staff or other resources to a rulemaking effort, departmental procedures require the staff to prepare a Concept Analysis Paper to inform key departmental units that the agency is planning to address an issue and to aid in the departmental tracking of pending regulatory developments.[54] By the time that the relevant directorate drafts that document, it usually has some idea of the direction that it wants to take. If the Assistant Secretary approves the Concept Analysis Paper, it is forwarded to the Departmental Policy Review Board. The Board does not engage in substantive debates about the Concept Analysis Papers, and it almost never disapproves them.[55]

After the Assistant Secretary and the Board have decided that a rulemaking initiative should go forward, the Director of the Policy Directorate and the Solicitor assign an analyst and an attorney to the effort. In many cases, staffers from those offices have already been working on the topic, and they are assigned the task of following it through to conclusion. These three lower-level officials form the nucleus for an informal team for drafting the rule. Whether the three function as a team or as three discrete actors who must coordinate their activities periodically depends on the nature of the topic and the personalities involved. This informal team calls on additional expertise from the Health and Safety Standards Directorates and from other sections of the agency as needed.

Deadlines are established informally, and project officers often reduce them to writing in Workplans, but these deadlines usually slip without serious penalty.[56] The time interval between when OSHA decides to examine a possible rulemaking topic and the time that it prepares a Notice of Proposed Rulemaking depends almost entirely upon the amount of outside pressure the agency receives.[57] The Workplan may also address the threshold question whether the agency will prepare an RIA or RFA for the rule at issue, but the agency's regulatory analysts feel obliged to prepare a comprehensive analytical document for all agency rules.[58]

After the demise of the 1982 procedures, there are no requirements for periodic team meetings, and the Policy Directorate is not required to sign off on proposed and final rules. Lacking a "consensus-forcing mechanism,"[59] the Policy Directorate representative must lobby his counterpart in the Health or Safety Standards Directorate. For very important issues, the Director of the Policy Directorate can, of course, raise the issue with the Assistant Secretary, but the policy office does not often prevail.

Although the project officer from the Health or Safety Standards Directorate who assembles the informal team is responsible for guiding the rule through the internal process, the officer does not have direct authority over any of the individual team members.[60] Indeed, it is not unusual for one of the members of a team to outrank the team leader in the bureaucratic hierarchy.[61] Thus, although the team leader gives assignments to various team members at various times, the leader has no authority to ensure that the assignments are completed on time. The team leader must therefore depend heavily upon the professionalism of individual team members and the commonality of interest that the team has in producing a high-quality product. Some team leaders have training in "conflict management."[62] Many team leaders simply complete the necessary tasks themselves when others do not perform in a timely fashion.[63] Most team leaders attempt to guide their teams to a consensus and to avoid unnecessary time-consuming conflicts.[64]

The team's first task is to assess the risks posed by the workplaces or work practices at issue and to analyze the available regulatory alternatives for addressing those risks. The risk analysis consists of researching the relevant industry, identifying situations posing risks, and determining the significance of those risks. For health standards, a written risk analysis is usually prepared by the Office of Risk Assessment in the Health Standards Directorate, sometimes with the aid of a contractor. The Policy Directorate can also play a role by identifying the affected industries for the "industry background" section of the risk analysis and in evaluating the statistical validity of conclusions drawn from accident data.[65] Finally, the Policy Directorate converts the risk assessment into a benefits analysis for purposes of drafting an RIA to satisfy OMB requirements. The agency, however, is not permitted to base its health standards on cost-benefit analysis.[66]

After the risk assessment is completed, the project officer in the Health or Safety Standards Directorate suggests two or three alternatives for economic and technological feasibility analysis.[67] The job of costing out alternatives is entirely the domain of the Office of Regulatory Analysis in the Policy Directorate.[68] That office usually hires a contractor to aid in this effort.[69] Although the analysts cannot cost out every conceivable regulatory alternative, they attempt to provide cost information on as many as possible.

The regulatory analysts from the Policy Directorate and the industrial hygienists and engineers from the program offices interact frequently as they attempt to achieve a consensus on the option that the group will recommend to the Assistant Secretary.[70] Although each member of the informal team has a special area of expertise, every member reads and has an opportunity to comment upon the work of every other member. In this way the rule is crafted in an interdisciplinary fashion.[71]

As the analyst compiles the contractors' reports and calculates the economic impact of the cost projections, preliminary analyses are made available to the project officer and to other members of the informal team.[72] The preliminary economic impact information can have an important impact on the team's choice of options long before the formal Preliminary Regulatory Impact Analysis is completed. If a particular option costs out to be very expensive compared to a slightly less protective rule, the program office may screen out the more expensive option.[73]

Disputes often arise over the effectiveness of engineering controls versus worker education and personal protective devices for protecting worker health and over performance-oriented approaches versus engineering standards.[74] In most cases, disputes are resolved at the staff level through negotiation and compromise.[75] The project officer, however, is ultimately responsible for the rulemaking effort, and his resolution of the dispute will prevail if no one seeks to elevate the dispute to a higher level.

The informal team is responsible for preparing an Options Memorandum for the Policy Review Board, prior to publishing a Notice of Proposed Rulemaking.[76] By the time of the board meeting, however, the agency has achieved consensus on the relevant technical and policy issues, and the agency staff is not inclined to make changes absent compelling reasons. Any significant demands from the board that the agency consider new options or undertake additional analysis requires a rescheduling of the entire effort.[77] Thus, as a practical matter, the board meeting is largely informational. Nevertheless, several proposed standards have had to be reexamined as a result of board meetings. In some cases the agency responded by providing additional analysis. In others, the agency altered the proposed regulatory provisions.[78]

The project officer's next responsibility is to draft a Notice of Proposed Rulemaking. The project officer sometimes drafts the Notice, and sometimes divides up the task among team members with expertise in the particular areas that the rule addresses.[79] The project officer then circulates the draft to OSHA technical experts, the Office of Information and Consumer Affairs, the Standards Director, State Programs, and external technical reviewers before submitting it to the Assistant Secretary for final approval.

While the team is deliberating over the contents of the proposed rule, the analyst drafts the preliminary regulatory analysis documents. Analysts begin to think about the contents of the preliminary regulatory analysis document early in the process, and they commission cost and economic impact studies during the team's deliberations. They do not, however, begin serious work on the actual document until after the team has narrowed down the regulatory options considerably, because the Policy Directorate lacks the resources to analyze marginal options.[80] The preliminary regulatory analysis document is generally written to support the option that the Assistant Secretary decides to propose.[81] This does not often pose professional difficulties for the analysts, because they are present at the team meetings and are therefore familiar with the arguments for and against the various options. Given the large uncertainties that often surround the analyses of the options, the analyst can usually craft an analysis that both supports the proposal and maintains the analyst's professional integrity.

Finally, the project officer drafts a second Options Memorandum to accompany the rulemaking package through departmental review. Because the Policy Review Board has already had an opportunity to examine the rulemaking effort, only minor changes to the rulemaking documents are usually necessary at this point. The Notice of Proposed Rulemaking package and related documents are then sent to OMB for further review.

After the Notice of Proposed Rulemaking appears in the *Federal Register*, OSHA allows a period for public comment, and it usually conducts one or more hearings at which interested parties may present expert testimony and conduct limited cross-examination of opposing experts. Because economic feasibility is a central issue in most rulemakings, comments routinely address the regulatory analysis documents.[82] Agency regulatory analysts frequently testify at the hearings and respond to questions about the content of the regulatory analysis.

The team then divides the comments up by issue. Comments directed toward the economic analysis in the RIA are routed to the regulatory analysts. Because the process of weighing the evidence in the record requires team members to reach conclusions about which facts, judgments, and assumptions have sufficient support in the record to survive judicial review, the attorney from the Solicitor's Office plays a large role at this stage.[83] The team again attempts to reach consensus on the content of the final rule. Any disputes may be elevated through the hierarchy on an ad hoc basis and may ultimately have to be resolved by the Assistant Secretary. Upper-level agency officials can and do interject policy considerations at any stage of the team's deliberations, but they rarely have much to say about the weight of evidence in the record.[84] Thus, to the extent that technical facts or scientific and engineering judgments dominate the rulemaking effort, the team absorbs a great deal of the agency's decisionmaking power.

The role of regulatory analysis

The formal regulatory analysis documents play a very minor role in OSHA's decisionmaking process, because the formal documents arrive too late to affect the team's deliberations. The documents are generally not changed much as a result of suggestions of team members.[85] The analysts themselves, however, play a significant role in OSHA decisionmaking.

Although most staffers agree that the 1982 procedures were terribly cumbersome and ultimately unworkable, agency analysts feel that something was lost when the agency abandoned the team concept altogether. Under the 1982 procedures, analysts were guaranteed input into the decisionmaking process, and they were usually among the more active of the team participants.[86] In addition, the analyst was guaranteed a say in planning early strategy and information-gathering activities. Although agency analysts can still participate actively from a very early stage in the process, much depends upon the managerial style of the project officers in the Health and Safety Standards Directorates. In the absence of a formal process, the project officers can treat the analysts as outside consultants. The analyst can be given a proposed rule in a virtually complete form and asked to cost out the options that the project officer has already identified. The analyst is free to suggest and cost out additional options, but the analyst may have to account for any delays that this causes.[87]

Most project officers, however, attempt to incorporate agency analysts more thoroughly into the regulation management process. Analysts who become part of informal rulemaking teams interact with the lawyer and project officer more frequently, sharing information and ideas. Analysts generally prefer this mode, because it gives them more influence and allows them to begin working at an early stage on analyzing the costs and feasibility of the alternatives that the group has identified.

It is unclear how important the regulatory analysts' options-identifying function is to the actual decisionmaking process. Staffers from the Health and Safety Directorates generally characterized the role of the regulatory analysts as one of providing information, rather than identifying options.[88] When asked to recall specific options that the regulatory analysts identified in particular rulemaking proceedings, agency analysts could think of few examples.[89] The most prominent example is the hazard identification standard (see Chapter 7) in which OSHA analysts played a major role in identifying the ten regulatory options listed in the agency's lengthy RIA.

Team members generally respect the regulatory analysts and attempt to take their ideas into account in selecting preferred alternatives.[90] Although program office staffers do not believe that the regulatory analysts have preconceived notions about how regulations should be crafted,[91] they do think that the analysts' role is "to put limits on what we do," and this sometimes creates a "chasm" between the analyst and the project officer.[92] Many agency analysts agree that the analyst has an obligation to urge the agency to consider less costly alternatives, such as warnings, medical monitoring and screening, respirators, work practice changes, and other market-oriented alternatives that offer more flexibility to regulatees.[93] Some OSHA analysts believe that health scientists and safety engineers tend to emphasize technology and technological feasibility and are generally unreceptive to concepts like cost-benefit analysis.[94] Program office officials recognize that they tend to emphasize health effects over monetary considerations, and they acknowledge that regulatory analysts are less biased in the sense that they are not entirely "wrapped up in the health effects."[95] The health scientists tend to emphasize worst case risk analysis, and they behave more like prosecutors. Sometimes they have been pleasantly surprised when the regulatory analysts demonstrated that the problem before the agency was not as severe as the program office staff thought.[96]

With the abandonment of the formalized team structure, it is clear that the influence of the Policy Directorate has waned somewhat. It is not clear, however, that this was an intended consequence of the move away from the formal team model. Most lower- and midlevel OSHA officials believe that the team concept was abandoned because of the threat that a unified low-level team posed to the decisionmaking discretion of politically appointed officials – the renegade team phenomenon. Still, the effect has been to reduce the role that the Policy Directorate plays in determining the content of the standards.[97] This perhaps unintended consequence was not uniformly lamented in the Health and Safety Standards Directorates.[98] Nevertheless, successful team efforts, like the hazard identification rulemaking, convinced many project officers to attempt to reimplement the team model on an informal basis, even at the risk of yielding decisionmaking turf to the Policy Directorate.

Conclusions

The team approach can ensure that all sources of agency expertise are effectively integrated into the decisionmaking process. In addition, by providing a single place for dividing up research and analysis responsibilities, the team approach can avoid duplication of effort and thereby preserve scarce agency resources. Moreover, the team approach can identify and help avoid conflicts among regulatory programs within the same agency and thereby avoid unnecessary inconsistencies. The team approach can also facilitate management by allowing offices within the agency with responsibilities for different aspects of a single rulemaking effort to coordinate the timing of their efforts. Time is not wasted in sequential referrals from one office to another. Finally, the team model provides a vehicle for effective interchange of professional perspectives. Team meetings can serve as a forum for airing differing views about the assumptions and inferences that the agency should make in its regulatory analysis and rulemaking documents. The product of the interchange can be a synthesis that goes beyond the outlook of any individual member.

The team approach allows regulatory analysts to play a full range of roles. The analysts, who are normally assigned the task of drafting regulatory analysis documents, are able independently to gather and analyze data concerning the costs and benefits of regulatory options. The regulatory analysts are typically involved in the decisionmaking process at the options-identification stage, although the FSIS and OSHA experiences suggest that the regulatory analysts in those agencies are not much more effective in identifying innovative regulatory options than they are under other models. The team model also gives the regulatory analyst an opportunity to play the institutional skeptic and advocate roles. While the team model does not insist that the regulatory analysts criticize the work of other team members, members of the team are expected to offer constructive criticism when copies of studies, memoranda, and rulemaking documents are circulated to them. Similarly, although the team model does not oblige team members to serve as advocates for particular perspectives, it is not uncommon for the representatives of the policy office to become advocates for reduced regulatory burdens and for market-oriented solutions to regulatory problems.

Although spirited debates can break out among team members, the team approach exerts pressure toward resolving differences through compromise. Every member of the team is responsible for producing a product within a specified time frame. If the team fails to achieve consensus and this failure delays the team's effort, the warring participants may be blamed. Indeed, the first question that upper-level decisionmakers in individual offices are likely to put to team representatives when teams fail to reach consensus is, "Did you try to work this out with the other offices?" A team member, or an office, that elevates too many disputes begins to lose its long-term effectiveness.

The team model does, however, have some important disadvantages. The model is very dependent upon high-quality input from all of the relevant offices. Yet, the team leader, who is typically an employee of the program office, has no authority to ensure that high-quality personnel are assigned to his team. In addition, the team leader has few sanctions available for team members who do not attend meetings or who fail to perform assigned duties in a timely fashion.

The team model's great pressure toward consensus can blind the analyst's critical eye. Similarly, the natural tendency to avoid giving offense can reduce the vigor with which the analyst presses for innovative alternatives. The press of deadlines can impel representatives from all of the offices to soften their positions on important regulatory issues in order to get the rule out on time. The team model can thus "reduce policy to its lowest common denominator."[99]

Worse, team members are susceptible to a mind-numbing malady that Professor Janis has labeled "groupthink." According to Professor Janis, "members of any small cohesive group tend to maintain esprit de corps by unconsciously developing a number of shared illusions and related norms that interfere with critical thinking and reality testing."[100] The team model can effectively line up all of the relevant institutional actors behind a single recommendation to the decisionmaker, leaving the agency head with only two realistic options: to accept the staff recommendation or to return to square one. The net result may be that "[w]hen compromise positions reach a high-level executive in a form that suggests a unified, consensual judgment, they can give the ultimate decisionmaker a false sense of security; the policymaker receiving the watered-down proposals may lack an awareness of the potential problems buried within the recommendations."[101]

At the extreme, the team approach can produce such a strong consensus among lower-level team members that it becomes a "renegade team" and literally attempts to impose its views of correct policy upon politically accountable upper-level decisionmakers through leaks to the press and other sabotage techniques. Though this extreme phenomenon is not widely addressed in the public administration literature, it is worthy of serious study as a more general pathology of the bureaucratic process, in which the team model plays a rather prominent role. Although the power of career bureaucrats to co-opt political appointees bent on reorienting bureaucratic norms is well known, the renegade team that literally battles the politically appointed leadership on its own political turf is a much rarer bird. Nevertheless, it did manifest itself in OSHA, an agency in which there was a strong ideological clash between upper-level leadership appointed by a President who ran against "mindless bureaucrats" of whom the OSHA inspector was, in the minds of many small businessmen, the paradigm and lower-level staff committed to interventionist approaches to making the workplace safer who were supported by a powerful constituency in the ranks of organized labor. Whether the OSHA experience is unique is a question for further research. At the very least, it suggests that agency management must be aware of this potential disadvantage of the team model.

The experiences of FSIS and OSHA with the team model demonstrate the attractiveness of that model as a bureaucratic decision-making vehicle. In FSIS, the regulatory analysis requirement pushed the agency away from the hierarchical model. It created a new function – drafting the RIA – which demanded a new kind of expertise, which led to the creation of a new office, which generated the need for a way to integrate its activities into the standard-setting process, which ultimately resulted in the adoption of the team approach. Although OSHA at one time abandoned a very formalized version of the team model, the fact that many project directors in the program offices have returned to the team model on a less formalized basis, despite the threat that that move poses to their own influence, is dramatic testimony to the model's effectiveness.

CHAPTER 15

The adversarial model

One response to the inevitable clash between techno-bureaucratic rationality and comprehensive analytical rationality is to capture the rivalry in an adversarial decisionmaking model. Under this model, each office is responsible for assembling its own information and analyses and for critiquing the information and analyses of the other office. Disagreements over facts, assumptions, inferences and policies are aired in an adversarial fashion, either by memoranda or orally, before the ultimate agency decisionmakers. The National Highway Traffic Safety Administration (NHTSA) in The Department of Transportation (DOT) has adopted a fairly pure version of this adversarial model. Two large offices within NHTSA – the Office of Rulemaking and the Office of Plans and Programs – play large roles in the internal rule development process. The agency leadership has made a conscious effort to play the two offices against each other until fairly late stages of the internal decisionmaking process. Once the head of the agency has decided a question, however, all agency employees are expected to fall in line and provide support for the final decision.

The adversarial model in the National Highway Traffic Safety Administration

NHTSA was established in 1966 to establish safety standards for motor vehicles.[1] The agency was later folded into DOT and was given responsibility for reducing the economic costs of automobile accidents and for promoting fuel conservation.[2] The Office of Vehicle Safety Standards does the vast bulk of the agency's rulemaking work. It is made up of twenty-six Rulemaking Program Directors who prepare the Rulemaking Support Papers that provide the technical basis for the rules that the agency promulgates.[3] The Program Directors are usually professionals with engineering backgrounds, but the office also employs two persons with training in economics.[4]

The Associate Administrator for Plans and Programs is responsible for program evaluation and regulatory analysis. Among other

229

responsibilities, the Office of Plans and Programs (the "plans office") prepares a regulatory analysis document for virtually every rule that the agency promulgates.[5] The office has ten to twelve economists and two to three engineers serving as regulatory analysts.[6]

The decisionmaking process

Rulemaking actions in NHTSA frequently result from petitions to the agency from the automobile industry or other outside groups.[7] In addition, agency employees in any of the Directorates within NHTSA may identify the need for a rule as a result of their day-to-day activities. For example, research carried out at one of the agency's major auto safety research centers may reveal the need to promulgate a new rule. The plans office also has a continuing program of reexamining rules that the agency has already promulgated to see if the predictions and analysis that supported the initial rulemakings are borne out in the real world.[8] Finally, the plans office coordinates the development of the agency's Safety Priorities Plan, which incorporates research priorities and defines the agency's overall regulatory agenda.[9] Nevertheless, the agency has tended to respond to the "squeaky wheels" and to set to one side larger long-term efforts identified in the plan.

The Office of Rulemaking (the "rulemaking office") makes the initial determination whether to initiate a rulemaking based upon a detailed consideration of the information about the relevant topic. For example, a rulemaking office staffer might examine the agency's accident data for evidence of any statistical association between accidents and the subject matter of a petition.[10] Institutional considerations, such as the interest of influential Congressmen, also play a role in deciding which initiatives to pursue.[11] The initiating office prepares a Project Plan Description, which provides a brief statement of the problem, a quick assessment of potential solutions, and a plan of action.[12]

The rulemaking office circulates the project Plan Description to other offices, and the Office of Research and Development (the "research office") prepares a research support plan, which includes a description of the proposed research and a timetable for completion. The plans office notifies the Program Director of any impact assessment data requirements and formulates a schedule for developing the required analyses. The rulemaking office then either revises the Project Plan Description to reflect the comments it has received or explains in a memo the reasons for not incorporating any significant comments and submits the document, along with the information received from the research and plans offices, to the Administrator for approval.[13]

After the Administrator approves the Project Plan Description, the rulemaking office and the research office gather the engineering and statistical information necessary to formulate and support a rule. The two offices attempt to complete the data gathering process within 120 days, but the process often takes somewhat longer than that. On some occasions, it has taken as long as two years.[14]

With the information it has collected, the rulemaking office produces a Draft Rulemaking Support Paper, which includes: (1) an environmental review; (2) a statement of the manner in which the proposed rule meets the relevant statutory criteria; and (3) a discussion of the potential costs, benefits, and "other impacts" of several technical options.[15] The alternatives identified in the Rulemaking Support Paper are generally technical engineering alternatives, rather than broad rulemaking options such as performance standards or statutory amendments.[16] The document represents a synthesis of all of the technical information that the agency has been able to locate on the subject matter.[17] In more recent times, the economic analysis in the Rulemaking Support Paper has not been as extensive as it once was, because the rulemaking office depends more on the plans office to prepare the economic analyses.[18] The ultimate purpose of the Rulemaking Support Paper is to present a "safety rationale" for the agency's proposed action. Because it is intended to be an informal technical document for staff use, it is never made public. It is rarely even seen by the Administrator.[19]

There is usually very little contact between the rulemaking office and the plans office prior to the preparation of the Draft Rulemaking Support Paper. As a general rule, the rulemaking office has defined what it considers to be the relevant options prior to the time that the plans office sees the Rulemaking Support Paper. The analyst who is assigned the rule examines the draft closely to determine whether the Draft Rulemaking Support Paper has asked the right questions.[20] If the analyst identifies places where additional information is necessary and communicates this to the engineers, they redraft the Rulemaking Support Paper to reflect the analyst's input. When the Final Rulemaking Support Paper is finished, the rulemaking office transmits it to the plans office, the Office of Chief Counsel, and other program offices for further review and comment.

The plans office uses the Rulemaking Support Paper, along with other information obtained through its independent literature review, to draft the regulatory analysis document.[21] The Director of the plans office does not assign a single rule to a single regulatory analyst. Instead, a single analyst might be on several "teams" of regulatory analysts working on separate rules. Thus, each regulatory analyst can gain expertise in several areas. In part, this arrangement reflects the Director's desire to foster an interdisciplinary approach to regulatory analysis, and in part, it is compelled by the office's resource constraints.[22] The task of the lower-level regulatory analysts is primarily that of drafting detailed regulatory analysis documents. Although they do not personally participate actively in the agency decisionmaking process,[23] their bosses play important institutional roles.[24]

Just as the Rulemaking Support Paper receives very little input from the plans office, the regulatory analysis documents are drafted entirely independently of the rulemaking office. Because the regulatory analysis document, unlike the Rulemaking Support Paper, eventually becomes a public document, the analysts usually attempt to produce a substantially more detailed analysis of the costs and benefits of a broader range of alternatives. The analysts often read the underlying studies that the rulemaking office relies upon, and they may interpret those studies differently. Although the plans office does not generally perform or contract for empirical research, it frequently conducts independent surveys of the relevant literature and unpublished information to find information that the rulemaking office may have missed. The analysts may also make telephone calls or send written requests to auto manufacturers, health organizations, insurance companies, and other appropriate sources to request data for estimating the costs and benefits of safety technologies. The rulemaking office can in turn comment on the regulatory analysis. Although the engineers seldom comment on the technical economics section of those documents, they frequently comment on other aspects, such as cost and benefit assumptions.[25]

The plans office's separate review function is intended to bring an independent analytical perspective to bear on regulatory issues and to anticipate questions that will arise at the public comment stage. There may, for example, be more than one way to interpret data, and the plans office may interpret them differently from the rulemaking office. In addition, the analysts may identify safety considerations that the engineers did not consider. The analysts believe that one of their roles is to restrain the natural tendency of the engineers to issue rules without a sufficient inquiry into their consequences. This outlook reflects a functional difference between the job of the rulemaking office and the job of the plans office. The engineers measure the engineering effectiveness of various technological alternatives, while the analysts are more interested in lives or dollars saved.[26] Although the analytical process inevitably slows down the rulemaking process (it can take six to eight months to prepare a regulatory analysis document),[27] upper-level decisionmakers believe that it ultimately produces better decisions.[28]

Current and past Administrators have encouraged the plans office to play the role of institutional gadfly and to maintain a sense of skeptical independence from the rulemaking office, so that a wide variety of views is available to higher-level decisionmakers. Because an idea for a rule can germinate within the agency for several years, most upper-level decisionmakers see the value of subjecting the product of that effort to an analysis from a fresh, independent perspective before the agency adopts a public position.[29]

If the analysis does not appear to support the proposed action, the two offices usually meet to discuss differences in analysis or interpretations.[30] The rulemaking office must then attempt to modify the rule to satisfy the plans office within fifteen working days. If the office is unable to develop a mutually acceptable solution, the two offices send a joint memorandum outlining the points of contention to the Administrator for resolution. The Administrator usually pays very close attention to these memoranda.[31]

At this point, the Administrator may call a meeting of the Chief Counsel, the Associate Administrator for Rulemaking, the Associate Administrator for Plans and Programs, and occasionally the Associate Administrator for Research and Development to discuss how the Administrator should decide the unresolved issues. These meetings, which occur no more than three to four times per year, are intended to be adversarial in nature, with each side given time to air its views and to rebut the views of the other side. As we observed in Chapter 5, participants raise fundamental questions, such as whether or not to go forward with a regulation at all. Although it is possible for the two offices to reach an accommodation at this meeting, its adversarial character usually ensures that the meeting will end with one side prevailing over the other.[32]

Once the Administrator has decided an issue, debate within the agency is no longer appropriate, and the parties to the dispute must fall in line behind the Administrator. The rationale and conclusions sections of the Rulemaking Support Paper and the regulatory analysis documents must be amended, if necessary, to reflect the Administrator's decision. The agency's regulatory analysts thus play a "justifier" role at this stage. Although the regulatory analysis documents are not meant to be a "rubber stamp" for the Administrator's decision, their conclusions cannot, in the opinion of upper-level decisionmakers, be inconsistent with the rule. To have the regulatory analysis documents vary significantly from the Administrator's decision would, in their opinion, only confuse the public.[33] Perhaps more importantly, Department attorneys suggest that for the Administrator to choose an option that was not supported by the regulatory analysis document might result in judicial reversal.[34] In practice, there is always enough uncertainty in the calculations that the numbers do not have to be "fudged" for the documents to support the Administrator's decision.[35]

After the issues are resolved, the rulemaking office circulates a final copy of the Rulemaking Support Paper and the impact assessments and submits the package, together with any comments from the other offices, to the Administrator for approval.[36] Any remaining differences are highlighted in a cover memorandum. If the Administrator approves the package, it is transmitted to the Chief Counsel, who prepares the *Federal Register* notice. In addition, the Chief Counsel, in consultation with the rulemaking office, drafts a memorandum to the Administrator summarizing major issues, expected reactions from outside parties, and the pertinent dates.[37]

The plans office occasionally uses the industry comments to ensure that the rulemaking office addresses all relevant considerations in the final rulemaking documents.[38] In the Field of Direct View rulemaking proceeding, for example, the plans office seized upon General Motors' comments that the proposed rule would not appreciably save lives, a position that the office had taken earlier in the intra-agency deliberations, to force the rulemaking office to explain the basis for its disagreement with that position. The plans office then relied heavily on the specific industry comments in the internal debates before the Administrator. Ultimately, the plans office prevailed,[39] and the rule was withdrawn.

The impact of regulatory analysis

The regulatory analysis documents play a very large role in NHTSA, because they are independent products of the agency's regulatory analysts. The documents contain the analysts' independent assessment of the costs and benefits of the alternatives that the rulemaking office proposes, and they often identify options that the engineers either missed or ignored. The regulatory analysis documents almost always analyze the "do nothing" option, an option that the rulemaking office does not often examine in the Rulemaking Support Paper. The process of preparing a regulatory analysis document leads agency personnel to reject at an early stage alternatives that are obviously not cost-effective. The regulatory analysis documents also provide the vehicle for the analysts' input into the intraagency debates that the "adversarial" approach fosters. Finally, for most important regulations, NHTSA's Administrator and the high-level staff do read the regulatory analysis documents, which, unlike the Rulemaking Support Papers, are attached to the Administrator's briefing package.[40]

One former Administrator of NHTSA is convinced that the adversarial use of regulatory analysis leads to more rational decisions.[41] Yet, because of the large uncertainties that becloud many of NHTSAs regulatory issues, a large component of many of the agency's most important rulemaking actions is the policy preference of the Administrator. This may help explain why, despite the efforts of its regulatory analysts, the agency's rulemaking efforts do not always survive judicial review. Reviewing courts have held two of the agency's most important rules to be "arbitrary and capricious" after reviewing the reasoning process revealed in the rulemaking documents and the regulatory analysis documents. The role of judicial review is discussed in greater detail in Chapter 19.

Under NHTSA's "adversarial" decisionmaking process, the plans office is at least an "equal partner," and sometimes it is "more equal" than the rulemaking office. Upper-level agency decisionmakers encourage the analysts to be independent, even when that means disagreeing with the Administrator. The plans office is meant to be a "nay-sayer," forcing the result-oriented rulemaking office to consider the costs as well as the benefits of the regulations that it proposes.[42] Although the workload is great, most analysts are willing to work on weekends to get the job done.[43] This high level of morale may be attributable to the opportunity that the Office gives its professional employees to practice their profession creatively. Obviously, the professionals would not be as dedicated to their task if they believed that high-level decisionmakers were ignoring their input.

On many occasions the rulemaking office's product has changed dramatically as a result of the internal dialogue with the plans office. For example, in the Field of Direct View proceedings, it was largely the concerns that the analysts voiced about the rulemaking office's failure to substantiate the rule's benefits that resulted in its ultimate withdrawal.[44] The plans office has, of course, lost internal battles, and it has produced regulatory analysis documents that appear to undercut agency decisions made on policy grounds.[45] Yet, there is usually room to change the discussion in the conclusion and rationale sections of a regulatory analysis document when it does not seem to support the Administrator's decision, and there are considerable pressures within the agency to "fall in line" behind the Administrator once he or she has decided an issue.

The adversarial model limits the plans office's effectiveness to the extent that it is not involved in the decisionmaking process at an early stage.[46] Even if the analysts take a fresh and independent look at the issues after the Rulemaking Support Paper has been completed, some options can be lost by virtue of the difficulty of going back to the drawing board and studying them. If the analysts object to the failure to include an option in the Rulemaking Support Paper, the rulemaking office can often legitimately complain that the analysts should have voiced their concerns at the time that it was considering options and undertaking research. Still, given current limited resources, it is simply impossible for the plans office to involve itself earlier in the rulemaking process than it does.[47] Moreover, to participate earlier would undermine to some extent the adversarial character of the dialogue between the two offices.

Conclusions

The adversarial model has the capacity to bring comprehensive analytical rationality fully to bear upon agency decisions. The agency analyst independently studies the regulatory problem and prepares a regulatory analysis document that explores a wide range of options, tests each option against the available data, measures the options against preexisting agency policy goals, and assesses the advantages and disadvantages of each option. Most NHTSA regulatory analysis documents are quite comprehensive.

The fact that two separate offices intensely evaluate the existing data and analyses reduces the likelihood of purely technical mistakes.[48] The adversarial model also inhibits the natural tendency of bureaucrats to ignore or belittle information that undercuts their recommendations.[49] The staff in each office can rest assured that if it does not come forward with negative information, its counterpart will. By fostering the broadest possible exchange of information and analysis, the adversarial approach can go a long way toward exposing hidden agendas in both offices. This enhances the accountability of the offices to upper-level decisionmakers and ultimately to the general public. At the same time, it is less likely that the agency will be surprised by the information and arguments of the outside commentators.

The adversarial model also encourages agency analysts to play a policy communication role. Indeed, appropriate regulatory policy is the primary focus of most internal debates. Similarly, the adversarial model maximizes the options available to the upper-level decision-maker. It is highly unlikely that agency analysts will be co-opted by the program office, and innovative options will probably not be rejected out of any perceived need to reach an overall staff consensus. Finally, the adversarial model ensures that the regulatory analyst's market-oriented policy preferences will receive a full airing in the agency's internal debates. If they are effective advocates, the agency's regulatory analysts can become influential determinants of agency policy.

Upper-level decisionmakers in NHTSA believe that the "creative tension" between the program office and the regulatory analysis office is the best way to ensure that the staff-prepared memoranda are not "loaded" in favor of a particular option. They believe that the adversarial process "not only produces the best possible data and analysis, but also provides the Administrator with the most independent and objective advice for arriving at the best possible rulemaking decisions."[50]

The adversarial model, however, has several distinct disadvantages, not the least of which is the duplication of effort that it entails. Each of the two offices performs many of the same data gathering, analysis, and review functions. Moreover, the tendency of the adversarial model to discourage early information-sharing among an agency's program and regulatory analysis offices can result in unnecessary waste of precious analytical and technical resources later in the process. If the regulatory analysis office disagrees with the options that the program office has studied, there is a real possibility that the program office may have to redraft its documents and perhaps even undertake further research, thus delaying the rulemaking efforts. The program office may have to "scramble to catch up with some data on the new option,"[51] or it may simply attempt to amend existing documents to include the new option, thereby increasing the likelihood of technical mistakes.[52] Ironically, a procedure designed to increase accuracy may have precisely the opposite effect.

Although one of the adversarial model's great advantages is its capacity to expand the choices of upper-level decisionmakers, it likewise demands more of their time and effort. The model's encouragement of dissension at low levels means that upper-level decisionmakers must resolve many of the disputes that break out among the adversaries. Because there is no predetermined place in the decision-making process for selecting among regulatory options, disputes requiring upper-level attention can erupt at almost any time. Upper-level decisionmakers must therefore maintain a continuing familiarity with the complex issues in ongoing regulatory proceedings.

The "tension" that the adversarial model generates between the program office and the policy office need not necessarily be "creative." Organizational subunits in large bureaucracies are already prone toward pettiness, "turf consciousness," and personality conflicts. The conscious adoption of an adversarial decisionmaking approach will divert some energies into petty bickering, "one-upsmanship," and other unproductive activities. The disputants may begin to lose sight of the agency's broader goals in their desire to win intra-agency battles and enhance their institutional status. At the same time, the adversarial model poses risks to agency morale. If one of the offices is a more frequent loser of the intra-agency disputes, morale in that office will suffer.

Finally, the output of the adversarial model may depend too much upon the advocacy abilities of the personnel of the various offices. If one of the two offices is blessed with an able advocate for a leader, it may win more regulatory battles for this reason alone. Even better advocates from outside the agency, however, may well reveal the weaknesses in the reasoning or analysis of that office in the public comment process, and the agency may be required to re-work its proposal. On the other hand, upper-level decisionmakers, like good judges, should over time acquire the ability to discount this factor sufficiently to reach sound regulatory decisions, even if it means ruling against the better advocate.

CHAPTER 16

A hybrid model

The Environmental Protection Agency has adopted an intermediate decisionmaking structure that incorporates many of the advantages of both the team and adversarial models and eliminates many of the disadvantages. EPA's Administrator or the Deputy Administrator designates twenty to thirty rules per year for a special "Options Selection-Rejection process." These rules are reviewed on a quarterly basis by the Deputy Administrator and other upper-level decisionmakers. The lower-level decisionmaking process for these special rules adheres to the team model, except that at crucial junctures an Options Review meeting of very high-level agency officials and team members is held to choose which regulatory options the agency will actively pursue throughout the remainder of the rulemaking process.

EPA's organizational structure

The Environmental Protection Agency (EPA) is responsible for administering eight important environmental statutes[1] and portions of several other laws. EPA regulations can cut across several industries and can have profound impacts on whole sectors of the economy. It is consequently one of the most prolific producers of regulatory analysis documents. The agency is run by an Administrator, a Deputy Administrator, two Associate Administrators, and nine Assistant Administrators, four of whom bear responsibility for implementing the agency's regulatory programs.

The Office of Policy, Planning and Evaluation

The Office of Policy, Planning and Evaluation (the "policy office") performs a centralized regulatory analysis review function for the agency and manages the agency decisionmaking process to ensure that agency actions remain on schedule and reflect upper-level policy input. Two of its three suboffices – the Office of Policy Analysis and the Office of Standards and Regulations – play a large role in

239

the day-to-day rulemaking process.[2] The Office of Policy Analysis provides centralized guidance on the content of regulatory analysis documents[3] and represents the policy office in intra-agency debates over the substantive content of rules.[4]

The Office of Policy Analysis occasionally drafts a regulatory analysis document for a program office, and it frequently undertakes special studies related to regulatory analysis, focusing particularly upon benefits analysis. The office's primary functions are to review regulatory analysis documents that analysts in the program offices have drafted and to offer analytical guidance to program offices and work groups. The Regulatory Policy Division of the Office of Policy Analysis consists of twenty-three "lead analysts" who sit on work groups and brief the Assistant Administrator for Policy, Planning and Evaluation for his meetings with high-level agency decisionmakers.[5]

The Office of Standards and Regulations does not generally play a direct role in regulatory analysis drafting and review, but for historical reasons that office provides the lead analyst for rules originating in the Office of Pesticides and Toxic Substances.[6] The office is generally responsible for regulatory "decision management,"[7] making sure that rulemaking initiatives move along on schedule. As related in Chapter 4, the Chemicals and Statistical Policy Division of that office manages statistics and other information relevant to agency rulemakings. The office also has a small regulatory reform staff that is responsible for developing innovative alternatives to existing regulatory approaches. Finally, that office is the designated agency liaison with OMB, although most of the program offices also interact with OMB individually.[8]

EPA decided in the mid-1970s to decentralize its regulatory analysis staff and to give the program offices the primary responsibility for drafting regulatory analysis documents and managing related contracts. Consequently, each of the five program offices discussed here has its own regulatory analysts, and one has three separate groups of regulatory analysts.

The Office of Air Quality Planning and Standards

The Office of Air Quality Planning and Standards (the "air office") promulgates three kinds of rules: National Ambient Air Quality Standards (NAAQS), New Source Performance Standards (NSPS), and National Emission Standards for Hazardous Air Pollutants (NESHAPS). NAAQSs are media-quality-based standards for ubiquitous air pollutants that specify concentrations of pollutant in the ambient air that are sufficiently low to protect the public health and welfare.[9] As noted in Chapter 4, the technical staff and regulatory analysts in the Ambient Standards Branch of the air office prepare a one hundred to two hundred page staff paper for upper-level agency decisionmakers and the Clean Air Scientific Advisory Committee. The staff paper does not contain any information on the costs of implementing alternative standards, because the agency believes that it cannot consider costs in setting primary NAAQSs.[10] The agency has, however, begun to incorporate a benefits analysis into the staff paper as a result of its experience with the particulates NAAQS.[11]

NSPSs are technology-based limitations for emissions from new stationary sources of pollution. The Emissions Standards and Engineering Division of the air office divides an industry into categories and subcategories, surveys existing sources and pilot plants for workable pollution control technologies, and prescribes emissions limitations for new sources reflecting the best available demonstrated control technology. This task calls for a healthy dose of engineering judgment, but cost considerations also play a large role in setting the standards.[12]

NESHAPs are health-based emissions limitations for new and existing sources of hazardous air pollutants.[13] Engineering, cost, and risk considerations are all relevant to NESHAPs.[14] Like the NSPSs, the NESHAPs are initially developed in the Emissions Standards and Engineering Division.

The air office has three groups of regulatory analysts. The Ambient Standards Branch has a staff of two full-time regulatory analysts and several other analysts who devote some time to preparing portions of RIAs for NAAQSs.[15] Six cost engineers and financial analysts in the Cost and Economics section of the Economic Analysis Branch prepare cost analyses and economic impact analyses for NSPSs and NESHAPs.[16] Finally, the Regulatory Impact Section of the Economic Analysis Branch contains four analysts who help prepare regulatory analysis documents for NAAQSs, NSPSs and NESHAPs. This section is the exclusive source of benefits analyses for the air office.

The Office of Toxic Substances

The Office of Toxic Substances (the "toxics office") is responsible for administering the Toxic Substances Control Act, which requires manufacturers to notify EPA prior to marketing new chemicals, empowers EPA to require manufacturers to test such chemicals for toxicity, and requires EPA to remove or place restrictions on existing chemicals if they pose an unreasonable risk to humans or the environment. Although most of the information about new and existing chemicals comes from the manufacturers, the toxics office has a continuing program of evaluating the health effects of existing chemicals on the basis of health and safety studies identified in the literature and elsewhere.[17] The Regulatory Impacts Branch, consisting of fourteen analysts, is responsible for preparing regulatory analysis documents for the office. It spends about $2 million per year for contracts relevant to regulatory analysis.[18]

The Office of Solid Waste

The Resource Conservation and Recovery Act requires EPA's Office of Solid Waste (the "solid waste office") to promulgate regulations identifying the characteristics of hazardous waste and listing particular hazardous wastes. The agency must also promulgate and revise standards for the generation, transportation, storage, and disposal of hazardous wastes.[19] Finally, the agency must promulgate standards for permits for the treatment, storage and disposal of hazardous wastes.[20] Both environmental and cost considerations play a role in these standards, but there is considerable internal debate over their relative weights. Many of the regulations that the agency has promulgated in the past have been promulgated in response to court orders that required the agency to follow fixed rulemaking timetables,[21] and they therefore received exemptions from Executive Order 12,291's RIA requirements. The office's nine regulatory analysts are located in the Economic Analysis Branch, which is allocated approximately $3 million per year for contractor support.[22]

The Office of Drinking Water

The Office of Drinking Water (the "drinking water office") is responsible for writing standards for contaminants in drinking water. New drinking water standards are promulgated as new contaminants are identified, and existing standards are amended as new technologies become available.[23] Both cost and public health considerations are relevant. The office has an informal intelligence network in the field that is constantly on the lookout for new contaminants and new technologies. Its Economic and Policy Analysis Branch devotes three regulatory analysts to preparing regulatory analyses for drinking water standards. The Branch has a budget of $1 million to $1.25 million per year for contractors.[24]

The Office of Water Regulations and Standards

The Office of Water Regulations and Standards (the "water office") devotes the bulk of its regulatory resources to promulgating technology-based effluent guidelines and limitations for new and existing sources of water pollutants. The Effluent Guidelines Division begins the standard-setting process by hiring contractors to categorize the relevant industry, identify pollution control technologies in that industry and industries with similar effluents, and assess the costs of installing available pollution control technologies. The Economic Analysis Staff, a small staff of ten economists, next undertakes a "gross screening" of the technologically feasible options in an attempt to exclude any options that are obviously too costly. The Economic Analysis Staff then directs a contractor to compile necessary economic and financial data, to conduct economic impact assessments, to prepare cost-effectiveness analyses, and, in the case of major rules, to prepare benefits analyses for the remaining technologies.[25] Based on the contractor's reports, the Economic Analysis Staff writes an economic impact analysis and a cost-effectiveness analysis for the standard. The Office has largely delegated the task of preparing benefits analyses to regulatory analysts in the policy office.[26]

The decisionmaking process

Initiation of rulemaking

The most frequent sources of EPA rules are statutory requirements that it promulgate particular rules by specific deadlines and petitions from environmental groups and industry. Rules originate in "lead offices" under the four Assistant Administrators with rulemaking responsibility. The lead office is the primary source of technical expertise on the subject matter of the rules it writes. The regulatory analysts in the lead offices supervise independent contractors, prepare regulatory analysis documents, and occasionally sponsor independent research on issues relevant to their programs. The lead office is also responsible for organizing and chairing the work group, setting the schedule for the rulemaking process, and eliciting the participation of other agency offices and the public. A project officer from the lead office is responsible for managing a regulation's development as it moves through the internal agency procedures.[27]

When a lead office has a choice whether or not to initiate a rule-making effort, it usually assembles a small internal team to make a recommendation to the lead office's Director. Regulatory analysts in the lead office often participate in these informal teams at a very early stage.[28] Most EPA regulatory analysts believe that if they do not become involved in a rule's development at the very early planning and research stage, they cannot be very influential in the rule-making process that follows.[29] The lead office must prepare a "Start Action Request" and submit it to the Office of Standards and Regulations. That office then reviews the Start Action Request and circulates it to the regulatory analysts in the policy office and to the agency's steering committee.[30]

The steering committee has in the past been the primary high-level agency decisionmaking entity. It is composed of representatives of each of the nine Assistant Administrators, the General Counsel, and the two Associate Administrators.[31] The Office of Standards and Regulations chairs the steering committee. The steering committee meets at biweekly intervals and more often as necessary, but much of its business is conducted on the "consent calendar" under which documents are circulated to steering committee members and approved without formal meetings. Most Start Action Requests are decided on the consent calendar.

At the same time that it is reviewing the Start Action Request, the Office of Standards and Regulations must determine whether the action is "major," "significant," or "minor." Major rules are those meeting the definition of major in Executive Order 12,291. A rule is significant if it is not major but nonetheless will have important effects on the environment, public health, or the economy, will present intermedia issues, or will affect the administration or operation of several EPA offices. Minor rules are those that are neither major nor significant. For several programs, these distinctions are relatively unimportant, because the program office prepares a regulatory analysis document for virtually every rule of any consequence that it promulgates.[32]

Superimposed upon this classification scheme is EPA's unique Options Review process, which is designed to facilitate high-level input into the low-level decisionmaking process. Early in the development of a major or significant regulation, the Deputy Administrator designates it for either Level I or Level II Options Review, based upon recommendations from the Assistant Administrators.[33] These designations are made independently of the major and significance determinations. Only about twenty to thirty rules per year are designated for Level I review, while forty to fifty rules per year receive Level II review. Nominations for Level I review are based upon the rule's anticipated cost, the likelihood that it will cause public controversy, its importance to the program, its precedential value, and the probability that it will require the agency to resolve a major policy issue that may have impacts on more than a single program. For example, although a rulemaking dealing with the disposal of sludge in the oceans did not have a sufficient dollar impact to trigger the preparation of an RIA, it was designated for Level I review because it would have required the agency to resolve major issues regarding its posture toward protecting the water quality of oceans versus protecting limited landfill capacity.[34]

The Options Review process for Level I rules is implemented through quarterly planning meetings and more frequent Options Selection-Rejection meetings. The purposes of the quarterly planning meetings are: (1) to give a status overview of all Level I rules; (2) to provide advance notice of rules that will be ripe for an Options Selection-Rejection review during the quarter; and (3) to decide which Assistant Administrators and Regional Administrators should participate in particular Options Review meetings.[35] Additional Options Selection-Rejection meetings are held for individual regulations at crucial decision points.

The purpose of the Options Review process is five-fold. First, upper-level decisionmakers view it as "an institutional mechanism for forcing consideration of a much broader spectrum of approaches to regulatory problems."[36] Second, the process allows high-level policymakers, rather than low-level staff, to narrow the range of options and, as the rulemaking process progresses toward completion, to select the preferred option. A third goal is to make low-level decisionmaking more accountable to high-level politically appointed management. Fourth, it is intended to eliminate the perception on the part of the technical staff in the program offices that the regulatory analysts are officious intermeddlers in the decision-making process. Finally, it gives upper-level management a more direct role in the subtle policymaking that goes on at low levels in the bureaucracy when options are examined and rejected as the staff probes for consensus. In the past, work groups had effectively lined up all of the relevant institutional entities behind a single recommendation to the Administrator, leaving only two options: accepting the recommendation or sending everyone back to "square one." The practical effect of this process was that much agency policy was made at the Branch Chief level. The Options Review process was intended to retain the benefits of the team approach, such as information-sharing and a multidisciplinary perspective, while at the same time enhancing the role of the politically appointed upper-level management in the decisionmaking process.[37]

Conceiving the proposed rule in the work group

By the time that a Start Action Request is approved, the program office has usually defined the regulatory "problem" with some precision and has often arrived at one or more "solutions" to the problem. The regulatory analysts and the scientists and engineers within the program office often debate these issues informally before the office takes an official position.[38] In the Office of Drinking Water, for example, the regulatory analysts are regarded as the resident intellectuals, and the technical staff believes that the regulatory analysts can help identify useful options for resolving some kinds of issues.[39]

In some programs, the regulatory analysts and the technical staff form internal teams to formulate program office positions. In the Office of Toxic Substances, for example, the Director appoints a staff team, consisting of a chemical engineer, a hazard assessment expert, an economist, and an attorney from the Office of General Counsel, to formulate the office's position. This staff team does most of the actual work on rules, and it identifies most of the relevant regulatory options.[40] The technical staffs often value the input of team members from the program office's regulatory analysis branch, because one of their roles is to prevent the program office from being "blind-sided" by policy office analysts in meetings with high-level decisionmakers.[41]

In some programs, however, the technical staff is not as receptive to the input of its regulatory analysts. For example, there was not much coordination in the past between the analysts and the technical staff in the air office in promulgating NAAQSs, partly because of the ambiguous role of cost considerations in promulgating primary NAAQSs. The role of the analysts was historically limited to providing benefits information to other analysts in the Ambient Standards Branch, who reworked it and put it in the regulatory analysis documents without seriously considering it in drafting the standard.[42] In light of its experience with the particulates standard, however, the air office began to rely more heavily upon the benefits analyses that its analysts produced.[43]

Whether or not an internal program office group is appointed, the project officer in the lead office must convene an intra-agency work group shortly after the approval of the Start Action Request.[44] Although the project officer is usually from the technical staff of the lead office, regulatory analysts from the lead office generally attend the work group meetings.[45] The work group is composed of the project officer, the lead analyst from the policy office, a staff attorney from the Office of General Counsel, and usually staff representatives from the Office of Research and Development, the Office of Enforcement and Compliance Monitoring, and a regional office. Other offices may send representatives to work groups that address issues that concern them.[46]

The policy office lacks sufficient personnel to send a lead analyst to every work group meeting for every regulatory program.[47] This leads to friction between the program office and the policy office when that office raises objections or identifies fresh options at the "sign-off" stage very late in the standard-development process. The program offices, with some justification, complain that the policy office should have raised its objections at the work group level. The lead offices are especially reluctant to undertake further analysis at the policy office's request at this late stage, where any additional analysis means additional delay.[48]

The work group is the primary institutional unit for the development of regulations in EPA, and it meets regularly throughout the life cycle of a rule. The functions of the work group are to focus the combined attention of professionals with different perspectives on regulatory problems and to stimulate debate about the appropriate ways to address problems. Members of the work groups do not actually engage in gathering data and drafting documents, tasks that are normally the responsibility of the lead office. Instead, work group members comment upon and critique documents that others draft. Ideally, the interchange of perspectives helps achieve a synthesis that goes beyond the outlook or observations of any individual group member.[49]

Upper-level management input at Options Review meetings

For all Level I rules the lead office must prepare an Options Memorandum for the first Level I Options Review meeting. The precise timing of the first meeting is flexible. It must occur early enough so that options are realistically available, yet it must not occur until after the work group has had an opportunity to analyze the existing data sufficiently to crystallize the thinking of its members. Additional Options Review meetings may be scheduled if other issues needing high-level input arise during the work group's deliberations.[50]

The Options Memorandum must analyze a broad range of options, and consider (in quantitative and monetized terms, if possible) all relevant health and environmental impacts, including primary and secondary impacts, cumulative impacts, and short- and long-term impacts. Implementation issues that must be discussed include the resources required for implementation and enforcement, the enforceability of the options, the degree to which each option allows for flexibility in achieving compliance, and the potential inherent in each option for fraud, waste, or mismanagement in practice. Finally, the Memorandum must assess impacts on other regulatory programs and overall consistency with agency policy and regulatory strategy.[51]

The immediate goal of the Options Review process is to identify several options (perhaps six or seven) that the upper-level policymakers can narrow to a smaller range of options (perhaps three or four) for consideration in detail prior to the publication of the Notice of Proposed Rulemaking. On some occasions, however, the available range of options is quite limited, and the Options Review meeting consists of little more than choosing between the option of going forward with a proposed rule and the option of doing nothing.[52]

Although any member of the work group may suggest options, the lead office in practice identifies most of them, based upon the judgment and prior experience of its scientists and engineers.[53] Options may arise out of informal interchanges between the technical lead office staff and the regulatory analysts in the lead office.[54] The analysts in the lead office can come up with new ways of examining a problem or of looking at options that the scientists and engineers in the office did not envision.[55] In the air office, where the relationship between the regulatory analysts and the technical staff is somewhat distant, the lead office regulatory analysts play only a small role in identifying options.[56]

Once the lead office has identified a set of options, it encourages work group members to comment and to suggest additional options. In practice, work group members are more helpful in reviewing the options that have already been identified than in identifying fresh options. The lead analyst occasionally suggests an option that the lead office has not identified, but the extent to which the policy office devotes time and intellectual effort searching for additional options depends upon the importance of the rule and the need for expedition.[57] The policy office tends to focus its efforts on persuading the lead offices to think more broadly in identifying their own options.[58] On the relatively rare occasions when a program office is unreceptive, the policy office writes its own Options Memorandum for the Options Review meeting.[59]

The first Options Review meeting is devoted to evaluating the options in the Options Memorandum and identifying additional options for further analysis. This meeting is one early forum in which OPA can raise questions about the substantive advantages and disadvantages of the regulatory options that the program office prefers. Because doing nothing is nearly always an option, this meeting also presents an opportunity for the regulatory analysts to question the need for any regulation at all.

In approximately 50 percent of the meetings, the policy office takes a position that varies from that of the program office in "some fairly major way."[60] If the disagreement is strong enough, the policy office drafts a separate memorandum for the meeting that sets out the nature of the disagreement.[61] The debate, however, is rarely acrimonious at this stage. A decision to consider an option further is merely a decision to devote analytical resources to studying that option; it does not mean that the agency must select that particular option. High-level policy office personnel try to avoid putting issues into a win-lose posture, preferring instead to use the Options Review meeting as a "tutorial" in which they insist that the attendees "are sure that they know what they are doing."[62] On the other hand, it is also possible that the lead office has so effectively managed the work group process that the Options Review meeting becomes a "love-in" where no serious debate takes place, but this does not happen very often. The policy office is responsible for drafting a "closure" memorandum to document the results of the meeting. The closure memorandum also serves as a vehicle for raising disagreements for resolution by the Deputy Administrator.[63]

Occasionally, the Options Review meeting reveals gaps in the available information that are so substantial that the Administrator or Deputy Administrator concludes that the work group should undertake additional data-gathering efforts before the upper-level decisionmakers further narrow the options. In these relatively rare instances, the matter is remanded to the lead office, and the Options

Review process goes through another iteration after the work group has assembled further information.[64]

The work group itself serves as the Options Review Committee for Level II rules. Although the work group does not prepare a formal Options Memorandum, the lead office includes a summary of the options that the work group considered and rejected with the final decision package. If a work group member believes that the group has prematurely rejected an option, the member must first attempt to resolve the disagreement with the lead Assistant Administrator. Failing this, the member may communicate the disagreement to the steering committee for resolution by that body. If the steering committee fails to achieve consensus, it refers the matter to the Deputy Administrator and the relevant Assistant Administrators for resolution.[65]

Steering committee and Red Border Review of the decision package

After the Options Review process is completed, the work group settles down to the task of assembling the "Decision Package." In addition to drafts of the proposed preamble and preliminary regulatory analysis document, the Decision Package includes a decision memorandum outlining the options, detailing the pros and cons of each, explaining why and when each option was rejected, summarizing legally proscribed alternatives, and assessing the resources needed to implement the rule. The work group's aim is to achieve consensus on the options that go forward and, if possible, to agree upon a single option to recommend to upper-level decisionmakers for the Notice of Proposed Rulemaking.[66]

After sign-off by the lead office, the Decision Packages for major and significant rules go to the steering committee for final review.[67] The steering committee meeting performs the same function for Level II and other rules that the Options Review meeting performs for Level I rules. Members of the steering committee rarely suggest options that have not already been identified at the work group level, but an office may raise again an option that the lead office rejected at the work group level.[68] The steering committee is more of a reviewing body than an institution for developing different solutions to regulatory problems.[69] In a decision package that raises twelve to fifteen issues, the steering committee may play a significant role in resolving two or three.[70] The steering committee meeting can end with an "agreement to disagree" on an issue, in which case the issue is resolved at the Red Border Review stage.[71]

Red Border Review is the formal senior management review of all decision packages, including those for minor rules. It is normally limited to the Assistant Administrator for Policy, Planning and Evaluation and the General Counsel, although other Assistant Administrators are welcome to participate.[72] Usually at this point the parties to any remaining disputes attempt to resolve as many as possible in informal meetings, often at the Assistant Administrator level.[73] The policy office prepares an action memorandum for Red Border Review that summarizes the important issues and disagreements that arose in the steering committee review.[74]

Response to public comments

The agency procedures for responding to public comments are virtually identical to the procedures governing the preparation of the initial rulemaking and regulatory analysis documents. The project officer in the lead office is responsible for assembling the public comments and breaking them down as far as possible by issue.[75] The agency often hires contractors to read and segregate the comments. The comments are then distributed to the personnel who drafted the portions of the documents that the comments addressed. The regulatory analysts in the lead office occasionally consult the regulatory analysts in the policy office if the comments raise difficult analytical issues.[76] The project officer then calls a work group meeting to discuss how the agency should respond to the comments. The work group attempts to reach consensus on the changes that should be made in light of the public comments.[77] The work group recommendations and dissenting opinions are then forwarded to the steering committee and from there to Red Border Review. Level I rules may be subjected to another Options Review meeting if several alternatives are still available and if upper-level input seems desirable.

The impact of regulatory analysis

The impact of regulatory analysis documents

The agency's RIA Guidelines prescribe a fairly modest role for regulatory analysis documents in the agency's decisionmaking process:

> In view of the limitations of current analytical techniques and the range of factors that may enter into decisionmaking, the RIA is best viewed as a document that organizes information and comprehensively assesses the effects of alternative actions and the tradeoffs among them. The results should identify which regulatory

alternatives are reasonable, while leaving considerable latitude to decisionmakers in selecting the preferred regulatory approach.[78]

In actual practice, the regulatory analysis documents are even less useful than the Guidelines suggest. The completed documents are rarely available until after the work group has completed its work on the rule and has agreed upon a recommendation. Under the agency's typically tight schedules, the members of the work group must make decisions without awaiting the completed document.[79]

Work group members do, however, have access to the preliminary and final contractor and staff reports that form the basis for those documents as soon as they are available to the analysts in the program offices.[80] As work on a document progresses, members of the work group can identify analytical gaps and ask the regulatory analysts in the program office and their contractors to examine particular questions more carefully. When the document evolves in this closely coordinated fashion, it can affect and be affected by how the work group asks and answers important substantive questions, and it can help weed out options that are clearly too expensive.[81] In addition, the summaries of the RIA that accompany the decision package through steering committee and Red Border Review can also have an impact on upper-level decisionmakers.[82]

For many of the agency's programs, it is unclear whether the agency may base its decisions on the kind of cost-benefit analysis that Regulatory Impact Analyses are supposed to provide. For example, the statutory command to set primary NAAQSs at a level that protects the public health with an adequate margin of safety leaves little room for balancing considerations.[83] The agency thus faces a dilemma. Although Congress has made some considerations irrelevant to the standard-setting process, OMB has insisted that those considerations be made part of the regulatory analysis documents. If the Administrator considers the contents of those analysis documents in making substantive decisions, reversal in the appellate courts is possible.

EPA has resolved this dilemma by detaching the regulatory analysis document from the decision package when it goes to the Administrator for signature.[84] This seems disingenuous at best. The evolving contents of the regulatory analysis document are available to the work group, and they are often summarized in the trade press, which the Administrator can read like anyone else. The work group members undoubtedly rely on that information as they brief the First Level Options Review Committee, the steering committee and the Red Border Review Committee. If the considerations explored in a regulatory analysis document are meant to be irrelevant to the agency's decision, it borders on dishonesty to suggest that isolating the ultimate decisionmaker from that document at the critical moment of choice from among two or three narrowly contoured options effectively purges the agency decisionmaking process of those considerations. The institution has considered costs and benefits, and the advice that the Administrator receives orally from subordinates reflects those considerations.[85]

The impact of regulatory analysts in individual program offices

With a few exceptions, the regulatory analysts in the program offices are thoroughly incorporated into the decisionmaking process. In many program offices the regulatory analysis branch is considered the equal of the other branches, and the regulatory analysts participate fully in substantive decisionmaking. In other programs, the role of the regulatory analysts seems limited to that of information-provider.

The Office of Air Quality Planning and Standards. The NAAQS program in the air office has two sets of regulatory analysts. The small staff of analysts in the Ambient Standards Branch is thoroughly incorporated into the decisionmaking process, but it contributes little in the way of innovative options and skeptical review. Its chief function is to manage the outside contractors and to draft the regulatory analysis documents that the Administrator never sees.[86]

The analysts in the Economic Analysis Branch are inclined to be more skeptical and to press market-oriented alternatives, but they have traditionally played only a very limited role in the NAAQS program. Although that Branch supplies the benefits, cost-benefit and economic impact information for RIAs, the analysts in the Ambient Standards Branch have the power to revise its work product.

The regulatory analysts in the Economic Analysis Branch believe that they have sometimes been cut out of the early problem characterization stage of standard development, where they could have had some input into the way that the agency went about gathering data on the benefits of standards. The Economic Analysis Branch analysts feel that by bringing some regulatory analysts into a program office that is dominated by engineers and health scientists and by excluding the regulatory analysts in the Economic Analysis Branch, the Ambient Standards Branch has effectively co-opted the regulatory analysis function. Changes in leadership within the air office and a growing recognition among the technical staff of the virtues of benefits analysis, however, have reduced tensions somewhat.[87]

The Emissions Standards and Engineering Division, by contrast, depends entirely upon the Economic Analysis Branch for virtually all of its analysis on NSPSs and NESHAPs. The Branch primarily analyzes the impact of EPA requirements on profits, jobs, and so on,[88] but it also undertakes an occasional generic benefits assessment.[89] For example, during the promulgation of a NESHAP for maleic anhydride, the regulatory analysts suggested that the engineers consider changing the feedstock for the plants. Although the industry and the agency's engineers first reacted negatively, all but two of the plants in the industry adopted the suggested change in feedstocks within two years, because the change actually proved more profitable than the existing process.[90]

Although the engineers usually defer to the economists in their areas of expertise, they generally regard the Economic Analysis Branch as a provider of information, much like an external contractor, rather than as a powerful decisionmaking entity. Although the analysts rarely play an advocacy role, their analysis of costs, affordability, and general economic impacts of individual standards can as a practical matter determine the choice from among various technological options.[91] The regulatory analysts therefore believe that an important aspect of their role is to educate the engineers about the nature and importance of economic considerations.[92]

The Office of Toxic Substances. The technical staffers and the regulatory analysts in the toxics office appear to have a cordial and mutually supportive relationship. The analysts provide analyses of both the costs and the benefits of several regulatory options, and they usually play a large role in the decisionmaking process. They are full-fledged members of the internal rulemaking teams and are regarded as "very thoughtful." This favorable assessment may stem in part from the technical staff's impression that the regulatory analysts "have a good feel for the limitations of regulatory analysis." Yet, the regulatory analysts are not hesitant to criticize the work of the scientists and engineers, and they have occasionally suggested innovative options to provide "more bang for the buck." Comprehensive analytical rationality is especially appropriate in the toxics office, because the statute requires the agency to engage in cost-benefit balancing in deciding what regulatory actions it should take. The program office is no doubt less resistant to cost-benefit balancing when it is an everyday aspect of decisionmaking.[93]

The Office of Solid Waste. The regulatory analysts in the solid waste office attempt to play at least three roles in the internal decision-

making process. First, they attempt to quantify the cost and affordability considerations that the technical staffs in the office use in
arriving at their "best engineering judgment." Second, they play
the role of "institutional skeptic" by attempting to sharpen the
thinking of the technical personnel and trying to make the regulation drafters aware of a broader range of options. Third, they are
advocates for efficiency and free markets, while at the same time
recognizing that the solutions that the engineers arrive at are not
always inefficient.[94]

In the view of the solid waste office's engineers and scientists, the
most important role of the regulatory analysts is costing out options
that the technical staffs identify. They do not think that regulatory
analysts should play a large role in identifying options, and they believe that benefits analysis is still so rudimentary in the context of
hazardous waste regulation that it cannot have much impact on substantive decisions.[95] Perhaps more than in any other program in
EPA, the analysts in the solid waste office face informational impediments to good analysis; it is undeniably difficult to predict the
health and environmental effects of standards designed to prevent
hazardous wastes from leaching into the environment.[96] Worse yet,
that office faces the most severe time constraints of any office in
EPA.[97] Even the role of the regulatory analysts' economic impact
assessment is limited somewhat by the technical staff's view that cost
considerations cannot count for much in the decisionmaking process
when health concerns are at issue.[98] For this reason, the solid waste
office is universally regarded in the policy office as the program
most resistant to comprehensive analytical rationality.

The Office of Drinking Water. In the drinking water office, the regulatory analysts are regarded as the "office intellectuals." They are
present on all important work groups, and they are frequent contributors of options and cost-benefit analyses. The relationship between the regulatory analysts and the scientists and engineers
appears to be cordial and mutually supportive. According to one
high-level official, the regulatory analysts play a "very important
role" in the office's internal decisionmaking process. The two staffs
appear to be equals in the substantive decisionmaking process.[99]

The Office of Water Regulations and Standards. The regulatory
analysts in the water office play two important roles. First, they play
a "quality control" role in analyzing and critiquing the cost projections of the engineers. Second, they probe the cost data that the
engineers provide with an eye toward reducing the economic impact
of the agency's standards on particularly hard-hit industry segments. This might involve nothing more than exempting particular

segments from the regulation or prescribing a lesser degree of control for those segments.[100] Analysts in the water office believe that their cost-conscious approach is necessary to offset the engineers' fixation on technology.[101] The analysts do not, however, appear to be major participants in the internal decisionmaking process. They have not put much effort into benefits analysis, and they have not played a major role in developing larger innovative options such as the "water bubble." They rarely act as institutional skeptics.

The impact of regulatory analysts in the Office of Policy Analysis

In most regulatory agencies, the central regulatory analysis office might be characterized as a "mini-OMB," but in no other agency does this description apply with greater force than in EPA. The policy office has evolved through several agency reorganizations into a very powerful institutional force. It has been "consciously integrated" into the internal rulemaking process.[102] It participates in every important regulatory decision; it relishes its role of institutional critic and gadfly; it is not hesitant to provide its own information and analysis; it is the chief institutional proponent of market-oriented innovations; and it often has the ear of the two most influential persons in the agency: the Administrator and the Deputy Administrator.

Policy office analysts draft a few regulatory analysis documents and manage economic impact consulting contracts for some programs that lack their own regulatory analysis staffs. Largely for historical reasons, policy office analysts also draft the benefits sections of the RIAs for some programs.[103] In addition, the policy office prepares analyses to support its institutional role on agency work groups. For example, it prepares second-guess analyses that repeat the analyses done by program offices, perhaps under slightly different assumptions, to see if the two offices come up with similar results. It also prepares independent analyses for options that it suggests in work group meetings.[104] Perhaps most importantly, the policy office has prepared Guidelines for the analysts in the program offices to follow in drafting RIAs,[105] and it has an ongoing research program on techniques for assessing costs and benefits of environmental regulations. Finally, policy office personnel are generally available to regulatory analysts in the program offices for consultation on regulatory analysis questions.

The policy office plays a second important role in reviewing and critiquing the regulatory analysis documents that the program offices prepare.[106] In this role the policy office performs a quality control function, and it attempts to ensure some measure of objectivity and consistency.[107] Policy office analysts interact routinely with analysts in the program offices and with their contractors. Although the policy office's role of critic sometimes breeds defensiveness in program office analysts, the relationship on the whole seems supportive and fruitful. This may be explained by the fact that the regulatory analysts share a common outlook. The similarities in approaches that they take to regulatory problems in general may form a common bond that prevents criticism from erupting into acrimony. Indeed, it is not unusual for the regulatory analysts in the program offices to form alliances with their counterparts in the policy office against the technical staff in their own programs.

Policy office analysts also attempt to suggest novel options and innovative regulatory approaches in an effort to counteract the tendency of the technical staff in the program offices to focus upon a single solution to a regulatory problem.[108] Although program office staffers do not always find policy office analysts helpful in identifying realistic options,[109] they concede that they do occasionally suggest new permutations of previously identified options and provide insights into how other programs in the agency handle similar problems.[110] Resource constraints, however, preclude the policy office from participating actively in the standard-setting activities of some programs until relatively late in the process, after significant new options are precluded.[111]

In both its review and participant roles, the policy office attempts to force the program offices to think about what they are doing and why they are doing it.[112] Of all the functions mentioned by policy office personnel, this is the one most intensely and consistently stressed. Policy office analysts refer to the office as the "institutional skeptic," a "devil's advocate," and the "chief critic and reviewer" of the agency's regulatory activities.[113] A former Deputy Assistant Administrator for Policy, Planning and Evaluation opined that policy office analysts should be "pushing decisionmakers' noses in the facts and the principles that are or are not being followed" so that they "know what they are buying into." If this educational effort is reduced to writing and made public in a regulatory analysis document, it has the added value of informing the public of the reasons for and consequences of the agency's decisions, and it thereby enhances public accountability.[114]

There is, of course, a presumption built into this view that the agency decisionmakers do not ordinarily know what they are doing and why they are doing it. This presumption is not lost upon staffers in the program offices, and they do not generally agree. Clearly, this attitude can contribute to an adversarial relationship between the regulatory analysis office and the program offices. Indeed, this presumption is the nub of the differences between the two rulemaking cultures. Without it, the regulatory analyst is little more than an information provider. With it, the regulatory analyst becomes essential to the decisionmaking itself.

Yet, upon closer inspection, it is clear that many policy office analysts view "rational decisionmaking" through their own special lens. They cannot, for example, understand why an engineer would view the installation of an effective pollution reduction technology as an end in-and-of-itself, apart from any measure of the benefits of the pollution removal that will result.[115] But it is unfair to characterize this as a mindless bureaucratic act. The engineer may have devoted considerable attention to the matter and have very comprehensible reasons for viewing the installation of a technology as an end in itself; they are just not reasons that regulatory analysts generally consider valid. More importantly, the engineers' approach is often compelled by the agency's statute, in which case the Office of General Counsel may insist that the analyst's worldview must take a back seat. Program office staffers complain that policy office analysts attempt to second-guess their technical judgments, although they recognize that these judgments often have a large policy component. In addition, program office staffers often view the policy office's insistence upon additional analysis merely as an excuse to delay the issuance of rules.

The view that the policy office is more concerned with substance than analysis has a sound basis. Many regulatory analysts in that office believe that they should play the substantive role of "explicit advocate for efficiency."[116] For example, the policy office engaged in a decade-long battle with the air and enforcement offices over whether the agency should allow an emissions trading idea called the "bubble" for new sources in areas that do not currently meet the National Ambient Air Quality Standards. The policy office argued that it is more efficient to allow companies to offset increased emissions that result from modifications of existing facilities with reductions from other facilities in the same plant, rather than meet technology-based emissions limitations for the entire plant. The air and enforcement offices argued that such bubbles are very difficult to enforce and often represent no net reductions in emissions.[117]

This commitment to efficiency often makes the regulatory analyst an advocate of less regulation as well, because regulatory analysts tend to place relatively more emphasis on efficiency than on public health and environmental protection.[118] The cost-effectiveness cut-off suggested by OMB and EPA regulatory analysts for NESHAPs, for example, derived directly from the subjective value that those offices placed on human life. In the case of the Benzene NESHAP, OMB and EPA's policy office used $1,000,000 for the value of a human life in reaching a cost-effectiveness cutoff of approximately $1,000 per ton for volatile organic carbon compounds.[119] This determination did not address how the agency thought about problems; it was the essence of the public policy choice itself.

For similar reasons, the analysts in the policy office tend to prefer state and local solutions to environmental problems, rather than solutions imposed at the federal level. For example, when the agency was considering a generic rule regulating emissions of several organic chemicals from many different kinds of plants, the program office risk assessments revealed that some plants posed high individual risks in the areas immediately surrounding the plants but relatively low overall risks to the general population. Whereas the air office argued in favor of promulgating a national standard, the policy office preferred leaving the matter to state and local agencies.[120]

The regulatory analysts who stress the policy office's advocacy role recognize that there is a tension between this role and the roles of information provider, neutral reviewer and identifier of innovative options.[121] Because of this role conflict, upper-level decisionmakers generally recognize that the office's "neutral" advice must be taken with a grain of salt.[122] There may also be a conflict between this role and the position adopted by Congress in the agency's statute, thus creating a tension between the policy office and the Office of General Counsel. The agency's attorneys are responsible for ensuring that the agency's rules survive judicial review, and they know that beneficiary groups will not tolerate policy office attempts to elevate efficiency concerns over other statutory goals.

The degree to which the policy office and its predecessors have been influential in determining the agency's substantive output has varied through the years. During the Carter Administration, the office effectively served as a brake upon some of the more radical program office proposals, and it even advanced some significant regulatory reform techniques, such as the much-debated bubble concept for allowing modifications of existing sources of air pollution to avoid new source review. But Administrator Costle was fundamentally a regulator of the techno-bureaucratic stripe.[123] Administrator Gorsuch was an avowed deregulator, and she was willing to listen to agency analysts only to the extent that they confirmed her predisposition not to regulate. Because this was more often the case than not, the policy office was much more powerful during her tenure. Still, many analysts believed that their work product was used not so much as a tool for reaching the best decisions as a way to justify after-the-fact decisions reached on other grounds.

The analysts in the policy office achieved their zenith during the second Ruckelshaus administration. Both the Administrator and his very active deputy were strong proponents of analysis. Even though neither sought explicitly to steer the agency away from regulation, both listened carefully to agency analysts and paid attention to regulatory analysis documents. The program offices were well aware of the fact that the policy office had the ear of the Administrator. During this time, agency analysts were probably its most powerful institutional actors. As one high-level analyst put it: "The culture was very supportive of the second opinion from the policy shop. You got awards for playing that role."[124]

During Administrator Thomas's years, at the end of the Reagan Administration, the analysts slipped a notch in influence. Prior to becoming Administrator, Thomas had been Assistant Administrator for a program office, and he had been on the receiving end of many policy battles with the policy office. Many analysts in the agency feel that although Administrator Thomas still relied heavily upon analysis, he was much more inclined than his predecessor to be persuaded by techno-bureaucratic thinking. Agency analysts began more often to play the part of the "honest broker," attempting to provide an "intellectual predicate" for agency action.[125]

This role change may in the long run enhance the influence of the policy office on the program offices. Although the relationship is still very much adversarial, the honest brokering has dispelled to some degree the program offices' initial distrust of comprehensive analytical rationality. For example, many program officials in the air office initially regarded benefits analysis as a thinly veiled excuse for relieving regulated industries of burdensome pollution control technologies. But the experience with the Lead Phasedown and Particulates RIAs convinced many that benefits analysis could be applied neutrally to support their philosophical positions.[126] If this trend continues, the agency's analysts may become more influential through their ability to persuade the program office staff of the virtues of analysis before matters get elevated to high levels in the agency.

Conclusions

EPA's unique Options Review process has facilitated the incorporation of comprehensive analytical thinking into the agency decision-making process in several ways. First, it retains the team model's capacity to bring different perspectives to bear upon information-gathering and data evaluation. Second, by forcing lower-level staff to analyze a set of realistic options prior to the Options Review meetings, it naturally expands their horizons. Third, by giving the regulatory analysts and the technical staff a day in court before the highest level agency decisionmaker early in the process while many options are still alive, it interjects a creative adversarial note into the agency deliberations thereby reducing the potential for "groupthink."[127] Fourth, the process reduces the risk of alienating the program office staff, because the Deputy Administrator hears both sides of all arguments and often decides issues in the presence of the staff, and not later after an opportunity for "insider" lobbying.[128] Fifth, by forcing all branches of the agency to identify options early in the process, it helps ensure against the "late hit" phenomenon, where one office brings up an option very late in the process and urges the program office to slow down the process while that option is being considered.[129] Finally, to the extent that the Administrator or Deputy Administrator is a proponent of comprehensive analytical rationality, the Options Review process can move the agency toward that way of thinking and away from techno-bureaucratic rationality.

The agency has, however, experienced a few problems with the Options Review process. On some occasions, each side to a debate has read the closure memorandum for an Options Selection-Rejection meeting to seal a victory for its point of view. On other occasions, one office has disagreed with the closure memorandum's interpretation of the outcome of the meeting.[130] The fact that the policy office is charged with drafting the closure memorandum exacerbates the problem, because that office is often an active participant in the debates before the Options Review Committee.

Although the Options Selection-Rejection meeting is very effective in selecting a few options from among the alternatives suggested by the work group, the participants at those meetings rarely identify new options that the work group participants failed to discover. The meeting can result in the selection of variations of one or more of the suggested options,[131] but at times such variations are little more than "window dressing."[132]

The Options Review process may force closure too rapidly on very important issues. A single three hour meeting with the key staff and the Administrator or Deputy Administrator may not be sufficient to air all of the important issues. The Administrator may want time to mull over the arguments pro and con in private or with a few trusted advisors, rather than decide issues with enormous consequences on the spot. The Options Review process is probably not appropriate for "mega-issues."[133]

Finally, the Options Review process demands a lot of the time of the Administrator or the Deputy Administrator. Yet, the key to its success is their willingness and ability to devote the time and intellectual effort necessary to prepare for the sometimes grueling sessions.[134] Absent such dedication, the process will no doubt rapidly devolve to the team model that governs Level II rules.

Despite the problems, the hybrid model appears to be an extremely effective policy communication vehicle and it has forced low-level employees to cast their nets broadly for alternatives to standard ways of writing rules. These considerable virtues warrant the additional high-level time and effort that the process demands.

CHAPTER 17

Selecting the right model

The foregoing analysis of the five most prominent models for structuring regulatory analysis into the decisionmaking process suggests that no single model is best for all regulatory programs. Different agencies have different degrees of discretion; different programs have different levels of complexity; different agency heads have different management styles; and the likelihood of attracting high-quality technical and analytical personnel varies from agency to agency. Hence, rather than attempting to prescribe a single "best" approach to incorporating regulatory analysis, this chapter will focus upon the considerations that might guide a particular agency toward one or another of the available models.

The hierarchical model is well suited for agencies that regulate according to statutes that articulate clear policy goals and provide very little agency discretion. It is probably best adapted to agencies engaged primarily in "economic" regulation where costs and benefits analyses demand the same kind of expertise and can easily be reduced to the same units. The hierarchical model will not be as useful for agencies engaged primarily in social regulation, where gathering information on costs and benefits might require an entirely different mix of training and skills. This may explain why the Food Safety and Inspection Service in USDA, which is one of the few agencies in that department with large consumer protection responsibilities, appears to be evolving away from the hierarchical model that characterizes most of the other agencies in the department.

Because the hierarchical model lacks a designated institutional skeptic, it will function best in a standardized regulatory context in which there are few realistic options and there can be little dispute over the validity of the available information. It is not well suited for regulatory programs that are highly controversial and for which most important rules will be subjected to intense public scrutiny and executive and judicial review. Similarly, the hierarchical model may not work well in programs that must deal with large data gaps and highly uncertain predictive models. In such wide open regulatory contexts, where costs and benefits are not easily reduced to a common coin, the decisionmaking process can usually profit from a healthy debate between the technical staff and the skeptical staff of a separate regulatory analysis office.

The outside advisor model is better adapted to regulatory programs in which information and analysis on costs and benefits is helpful to the decisionmaker on occasion, but rarely outcome-determinative. It is therefore well suited for wealth redistribution programs and statutes that place economic feasibility concerns on a lower plane. The outside advisor model is not well adapted to new or controversial programs in which an analyst could be useful in identifying innovative options that could reduce conflict. Because the analyst in the outside advisor model is not allowed to be an advocate for any particular policy outlook, that model may be most useful in programs where the analyst's market-oriented policy orientation runs counter to statutory directives. The model uses the regulatory analyst's information-analyzing talents without allowing the analyst to advocate policies that would in effect usurp legislative policy prescriptions.

The team and adversarial models are very similar in the extent to which they make use of the analyst's data-gathering abilities. Both models are well suited for bringing comprehensive analytical rationality to bear upon complex regulatory programs in which many perspectives are relevant to the decisionmaking process. They are both useful in programs that require the agency to base its decisions upon a comprehensive assessment of all the relevant information on the costs and benefits of many regulatory options.

The adversarial model may be slightly more effective in using the regulatory analyst in his or her information-provider role, because it allows the analyst to undertake an independent review of the relevant literature and draft a separate document. The regulatory analyst in the team model is expected to provide all available information to the rest of the team members for use in drafting rule-making documents, but the analyst may be inclined to rely upon the program office for most information. A fully independent data-gathering effort by the regulatory analyst under the adversarial approach may turn up more useful information than the team effort.

Both the team and the adversarial models allow the regulatory analyst to play an options-identification role. The adversarial model, however, is structured to guarantee friction when the analyst identifies options. Because of the resource constraints and the structure of the model, the analysts are not likely to suggest innovative options until rather late in the process after the program office has expended considerable effort in identifying, narrowing and analyzing options. If the analyst's options vary significantly from those of the program office, that office is likely to be very resistant to slowing down the process to reanalyze the new options. The result is either a slow process or a process that does not effectively use the options-identification role of the regulatory analysis office.

The team model, by contrast, allows the regulatory analyst to suggest options early in the evolution of a rule, before the program office has settled upon and studied a particular set of options. Because the analyst can approach the options-identification task as a helper, rather than as an adversary, the other members of the team are likely to be more receptive to the analyst's suggestions. There is less chance that the analyst will be forced to elevate a dispute to higher levels in the decisionmaking process.

On the other hand, the team model may reduce the range of options available to the upper-level decisionmakers. The consensus-building process that is inevitably part of the team approach may exclude controversial options before upper-level decisionmakers have had an opportunity to explore them. The adversarial model often insists that upper-level decisionmakers consider a broad range of options in order to resolve disputes between the two offices. Because of its consensus-building tendencies, the team model may not be well suited for strong agency executives who desire to have a significant degree of input into the actual process of defining and rejecting regulatory options. It is better suited to a busy manager who is inclined to trust the technical staff.

The great virtue of the hybrid model is its ability to interject upper-level input into the team setting through the Options Review process. The hybrid model both forces the teams to search for options to traditional approaches and maximizes the discretion of upper-level decisionmakers to select from among those options.

The team, adversarial and hybrid models can more effectively use the regulatory analyst as an institutional skeptic than the outside advisor and hierarchical models. The adversarial model may give the analyst a greater incentive to be critical of the work of the program office staff, but this advantage may come only at a significant loss of institutional harmony and some risk of technical error. The creative tension of the adversarial or hybrid models may dissolve into destructive backbiting.

All three models are also effective vehicles for the regulatory analyst's advocacy role. Under the team model the regulatory analyst has an opportunity to advocate efficient approaches during the team meetings. Similarly, the adversarial model allows the regulatory analyst to argue for efficient options in debates with the program office. The hybrid model encourages consensus-building at team meetings but encourages adversarial debates at the critical high-level Options Review meetings. All three models will be useful in programs in which the ultimate decisionmakers have fairly broad latitude to make decisions based upon a rough balance of costs and benefits.

Because of the team and hybrid models' tendency toward compromise at low bureaucratic levels, however, the adversarial model may result in the clearest articulation of the efficiency considerations involved in a rulemaking effort. The adversarial model may therefore be better suited to an agency that faces complicated regulatory problems about which the clash of competing perspectives could be illuminating to upper-level decisionmakers. The adversary model is resource-intensive, however, and an agency adopting it should be prepared to devote significant resources to the process. The team model may be better suited to an agency that has to reach many important decisions under relatively tight time constraints.

The adversarial and hybrid approaches also presume that upper-level decisionmakers want to be closely involved in important day-to-day decisionmaking and are willing to devote a relatively intense level of continuous attention to important rulemaking efforts. Under the adversarial model, the upper-level decisionmakers must be willing to keep "up to speed" with important rulemaking efforts, and under the hybrid model they must be "quick studies" in preparing for Options Review meetings. The adversarial model may be most appropriate for relatively small agencies that deal with only a few very important and very complicated rulemaking initiatives in a given year. For large agencies whose busy leaders cannot follow carefully the development of rules in subordinate decisionmaking units, the hybrid model may be the better approach. The team model is best for decisionmakers who prefer to delegate authority.

Finally, the team, adversarial and hybrid models can allow the regulatory analysts to become influential determinants of agency policy. Agency analysts are not likely to play that role at all under the outside advisor model. The team model allows representatives from the policy office to participate fully in the deliberations of the subordinate decisionmaking entities. They can advocate that the agency adopt a particular option, and this advocacy can extend to presentations before high-level working groups and before the ultimate decisionmaker. Likewise, regulatory analysts under the adversarial model can advocate particular policies in the internal agency debates that typify that model. The hybrid model gives analysts the opportunity to influence policy at both the team level and the Options Review level.

The team model, however, may give the regulatory analysts more influence upon agency decisions in the long term. The pressure toward compromise and consensus that the team model exerts upon team members ensures that the recommendations of the teams will in the long run reflect to some degree the policy preferences of the agency's regulatory analysts. By contrast, the regulatory analysts may acquire only erratic influence under the adversarial and hybrid models as upper-level decisionmakers who share the perspective of the analysts come and go.

The primary message of Part III is that agency managers must pay attention to agency structure if agency analysts are to function effectively in their assigned roles. Because the internal decisionmaking structure will vary, perhaps considerably, depending upon the roles that upper-level decisionmakers want their regulatory analysts to play, there is no particular structure that is best for all agencies at all times. The foregoing discussion has attempted to identify some considerations that should guide institution builders in structuring regulatory analysis into the decisionmaking process. The ultimate choice belongs to the agency managers.

PART IV

Review of regulatory analysis

CHAPTER 18

Office of Management and Budget review of regulatory analysis

Rather than leaving regulatory analysis entirely to the agencies, Executive Order 12,291 assigned an important review role to the Office of Management and Budget (OMB). It empowered OMB to designate any minor rule as "major" and to waive regulatory analysis requirements for any major rule. OMB was given authority to identify "duplicative, overlapping and conflicting rules" and rules that were "inconsistent with the policies underlying" the Executive Order and to require "appropriate interagency consultation to minimize or eliminate such duplication, overlap, or conflict." Finally, the Executive Order required OMB to "[m]onitor agency compliance" with its requirements and to "advise the President with respect to such compliance."[1] All regulations and all RIAs accompanying major regulations are reviewed by desk officers in OMB's Office of Information and Regulatory Affairs (OIRA), and most RIAs are also reviewed by a separate group of "superanalysts" in OIRA that set the analytical agendas for all executive agencies. Disputes between OMB and the agencies have been resolved by a vague process that includes the White House.[2] In practice, the vast majority of disputes are resolved in the informal give and take of day-to-day interactions.

The relationship between OMB and most executive agencies cannot fairly be characterized as a cooperative pursuit of common ends. To the contrary, it is typically highly adversarial and often acrimonious. According to a former Deputy Administrator of OIRA: "We yell and scream, jump up and down, do whatever we can to get them to listen to us."[3] Disputes between OSHA and OMB have been especially bitter.[4] OMB officials generally regard OSHA as one of the greatest offenders of the principle that comprehensive analytical rationality should govern regulatory decisionmaking, and OSHA officials – at least at the staff and midmanagement levels – almost universally regard OMB as an officious intermeddler. The relationship between EPA and OMB has not been much more harmonious. Although EPA has a reputation for being one of the most analytical agencies in the federal government, OMB personnel feel that too many important EPA decisions lack a sufficient analytical basis.[5]

EPA employees, on the other hand, strongly believe that OMB attempts to usurp the agency's delegated authority. In one extreme instance one hundred EPA professionals signed a letter to the EPA Administrator demanding to know whether "all future decisions on risk control are to be made by OMB in private consultations with special interests who are not identified on the public record."[6]

Of the agencies studied here, only the agencies in DOT seem to have a reasonably amicable relationship with OMB. Most disputes between DOT agencies and OMB involve minor matters and amount to "silly disagreements" that are relatively easily worked out at the staff level. When OMB and DOT have disagreements over regulatory policy, they are almost always resolved at the staff level. The agency staffs generally attempt to accommodate OMB comments and seek to work OMB's concerns into the rulemaking or regulatory analysis documents, rather than delaying the rulemaking effort further.[7] At least in the case of NHTSA, the relative harmony may be attributable to the fact that the head of the agency for much of the Reagan Administration was formerly the desk officer for NHTSA at OMB.

Tiffs between OMB and the agencies frequently break out in the press, and the worst disputes become the subjects of congressional investigations. In part, this poor relationship reflects the reluctance of bureaucrats to be reined in by politically accountable officials. In part, it is a predictable manifestation of institutional "turf battles" between the Director of OMB and Cabinet Secretaries. And in part, it is a battleground in a more profound struggle between Congress and the Executive branch over control over executive agencies. Yet, on a somewhat more abstract plane, it reflects the same clash of rulemaking cultures that was described in Part I.

This chapter will first describe OMB's formal role. Next it will examine several issues over which OMB and the agencies have disagreed in an attempt to convey a feel for the institutional and philosophical posture of OMB analysts in interagency debates. The chapter will then explore some of the advantages and disadvantages of OMB review, and it will conclude with an assessment of the roles that OMB has played in the rulemaking process in EPA, OSHA, and the agencies in DOT and USDA.

OMB's formal role

OIRA has a staff of about forty professionals with training in subjects ranging from math to public policy administration. Fifteen of the forty have backgrounds in public policy and eight have economics and finance backgrounds. The vast majority of OIRA professionals have advanced degrees.[8] The OIRA staff has assumed a general supervisory role over the preparation of regulatory analyses in the executive agencies. In this connection, OIRA analysts read RIAs, challenge assumptions, critique analytical efforts, suggest areas where more data are needed, and generally play on a government-wide level the roles that agency analysts play within their own bureaucracies.[9] During the 1980s OMB also assumed a considerably more controversial substantive role of ensuring that regulations complied with the Reagan Administration's generally antiinterventionist regulatory policies, sometimes with little regard to the agencies' statutory commands. OMB has continued to play a deregulatory role in the Bush Administration.

Although several agency procedural memoranda specify a particular office as the official OMB liaison, in practice interaction occurs at all levels within the agencies.[10] In probing questions about the quality of data or the validity of interpretations, OMB analysts and desk officers usually interact with fairly low-level agency officials; on questions of great moment, higher-level officials in OIRA will meet with high-level agency officials. Yet, although OMB and the agencies have, in practice, reached an accommodation that facilitates informal interaction, this very informality tends to render ambiguous formal lines of authority within agencies, sometimes leading to questions about who is really in charge. This tendency toward erosion of agency autonomy is especially distressing to beneficiaries of regulation who generally perceive OMB to be a politically motivated enemy of congressionally articulated policy goals.

One of the most frustrating aspects of OMB review for agency analysts is the absence of any formal criteria for that review function. Many agency analysts believe that OMB exercises unconstrained discretion to find fault with their analyses, and they often wonder by what criteria a good faith effort to comply with the Executive Order's requirements is judged a "good" or "bad" analysis. A former high-level OIRA official, Mr. Thomas Hopkins, described OMB's analytical review role as follows:

> On the first level, we use common sense. If a reasonably intelligent lay person is reading through the supporting documentation for the rule, could he reach the same result? Is there a reasonably clear documentation of the major effects? If we can't tell what is going on, we send it back. We look for objectives, alternatives, costs, and benefits.

> On the next level (it is like gradually lifting the layers) we ask how confident we can be that the way in which costs and benefits were identified and ascertained is sensible. How does the rulemaking relate to research that we are aware of and other analytical exercises we have seen?
>
> We then do a cost effectiveness check. For example, what is the cost per pound [of a pollutant] removed and how does this compare with other regulations that remove the same pollutant? All of this requires some experience.
>
> Occasionally, we have the luxury of getting into sophisticated issues, such as calculating the discount rate and how sensitive the predictions are to the discount rates. Unfortunately, we do not always have time for this.
>
> We look for instances in which the agency has mixed transfer costs with dead weight efficiency. We check to see whether the valuation techniques hold together.[11]

One upper-level desk officer in OMB, Ms. Gail Coad, said that she looked for "red flags" that indicated the agency had taken a wrong turn.[12] Another analyst reviewed analyses as if they were submissions for publication in a journal; "objectivity" and "reproducibility of results" were the desiderata.[13] Some OMB analysts believe that once agency decisionmakers reach a decision to move forward with a particular version of a rule, the agency's position is set in stone, and agency analysts bend every assumption and inference in the direction necessary to support that outcome.[14] To some extent, then, OMB analysts view their role as acting as a check against the abuse of analysis. There is no easy way to write formal criteria for this role of policing for intellectual honesty. It is rather like the role of the courts in identifying unprotected pornography in First Amendment analysis – they know it when they see it.

Agency experience with OMB review

Because the experience of the executive agencies with OMB review is mixed, it is dangerous to generalize about the role that OMB plays in the analytical process or about the quality of that review. Nevertheless, some issues have emerged with sufficient frequency that the experience of OMB-agency interaction may be mined for some generally applicable observations. The following discussion will examine several controversies between OMB and agencies over analytical methodologies in an attempt to determine the impact that the superanalysts in OMB have had on regulatory analysis in the agencies.

Value of life

Although many agencies are reluctant to put an explicit value on a human life for purposes of cost-benefit calculations, OMB has occasionally delayed agency actions because they implicitly valued human lives too highly. For example, when an OSHA regulation implicitly valued a construction worker's life at $3.5 million, OMB argued that $1 million was more appropriate.[15] OMB has also joined some EPA analysts in arguing that National Emissions Standards for Hazardous Air Pollutants should not be set at a level where the cost per life saved exceeded $400,000.[16] More recently, OMB objected to an EPA rule for hazardous waste incinerators on the ground that it would have cost $288 million for every statistical cancer avoided. OMB argued that $300,000 to $700,000 was a more appropriate measure of people's willingness to pay to avoid the risk of cancer.[17]

Discount rate for valuing the future

A major source of controversy between OMB and the agencies is how the future benefits of regulation should be discounted in cost-benefit analysis. Although it is customary to discount the future benefits of resource projects to present value, we saw in Chapter 9 that many beneficiaries of regulation and even some economists have doubts about the appropriateness of discounting future health and environmental benefits. OMB does not share these doubts, and it has consistently demanded that agencies use a very high 10 percent discount rate for this purpose. OMB has, for example, urged EPA to monetize the lives saved by protections against an environmental carcinogen and to reduce the net benefit to present value across the carcinogen's latency period, even though this greatly reduces the dollar value of such protections."[18]

Uniform carcinogen policy

Nowhere are the uncertainties involved in health and environmental regulations more apparent than in attempts to regulate human exposure to carcinogens. Most observers recognize that policy must fill the factual gaps,[19] but the critical question is *what* policy shall be used. In early 1983, OIRA decided to replace the existing Carter Administration carcinogen policies with a new Reagan Administration carcinogen policy that was less risk averse. The head of OIRA complained that "[w]hen you can measure the risk in terms of one molecule per billion, we can't simply adopt a policy that wherever we find a molecule we will spend whatever is necessary to get rid of it."[20] OMB created a new "risk management group" composed of representatives from several agencies and headed by OMB to review all cancer policies of all agencies. An OMB official said that the primary purpose of the group was to make a value judgment about the carcinogenic risks that were "allowable risks for society." OMB planned to refer all regulations involving carcinogens to the group for advice on whether they complied with the requirements of Executive Order 12,291.[21]

The agencies reacted to the new OMB initiative in late 1983 by forming their own Risk Management Council composed of representatives from five agencies with responsibilities for regulating carcinogens. OMB had the last word, however, soon after the 1984 election when a permanent risk assessment work group that included OMB was formed under the Cabinet Council on Natural Resources and Environment. The dispute was paralleled in the House of Representatives, which was debating whether to exclude OMB from a risk assessment board that would have been established by a pending bill. Officials from EPA and other agencies secretly urged House committee members to exclude OMB from the board.[22]

On the theory that it was better to have "OMB in the tent, pissing out, rather than outside, pissing in,"[23] EPA began to develop less conservative ways to express cancer risks to replace its traditional upper-bound estimates. EPA also agreed to reopen other risk assessment issues, such as whether the linear "one-hit" model for risk extrapolation is the most appropriate model and whether risks can be extrapolated from mouse to man.[24] In the meantime, EPA continued to use conservative assumptions and models in individual rulemaking initiatives.[25] The net result was a draft carcinogen policy that retreated only slightly from the Carter Administration position. OMB held up these rules for months to press its case that they were too risk-averse,[26] and its 1986-7 Regulatory Program publicly blasted EPA for using "conservative assumptions and upper-bound estimates" in its carcinogen risk assessments.[27] OMB was also critical of the agency for stating explicitly that it would "err on the side of public health" in assessing cancer risks.[28]

Although one may quarrel with OMB's attempt to characterize its carcinogen initiative as an effort to establish "scientific" principles, it is hard to fault the effort to achieve the implementation of uniform policies for addressing science/policy questions in all agencies. If the

Reagan Administration wanted to be less risk averse than the Carter Administration, it was free to do so, so long as that did not violate the statutes that the agencies were implementing. For example, many EPA statutes require it to "err on the side of public health," and it would therefore be unlawful for the agency to follow OMB's demand for a different risk assessment policy. The experience also demonstrates that agencies are capable of defending their "turf." Although it is impossible to declare a winner in the battle over carcinogen policy, the experience demonstrates that OMB is not always the powerful engine for social change that regulatory reformers desire and that regulatory beneficiaries fear.

Uniform cost-effectiveness cutoffs for technology-based standards

Invariably, one of the factors in choosing a technology for a technology-based standard is the cost of installing it, but the statutes are generally vague about how much cost is too much. Agencies can facilitate comparisons among industries by calculating the cost-per-ton-of-pollutant-removed for various alternative technologies and comparing that to the cost-per-ton imposed by other technology-based standards. Disputes have arisen, however, when OMB has attempted to use this cost-effectiveness measure more ambitiously to specify more or less uniform "cost-effectiveness cutoffs" for all technology-based standards dealing with a single pollutant. In setting "best conventional control technology" standards under the Clean Water Act, for example, OMB objected to EPA's proposal to use a cutoff of $1.15 per pound of pollutant removed and insisted that the appropriate level was in the $.20 to $.60 range.[29] EPA and OMB have also argued about the "cost-per-ton" cutoff for new source performance standards promulgated under the Clear Air Act. EPA maintained that $2,000 per ton of volatile organics was an appropriate cutoff; OMB argued that $1,000 per ton would be more reasonable.[30] These disputes are not so much about analytical techniques as about the substantive question of how expensive technology-based standards should be.

De minimis risk cutoffs

OMB has consistently attempted to force agencies to adopt what OMB considers to be consistent positions with respect to levels of risk that are deemed acceptable.[31] For example, OMB and EPA have debated whether EPA should establish uniform risk levels for toxic substances below which the agency would not regulate. OMB concluded that EPA uses a de facto cutoff of one-in-a-million for carcinogen risks, refusing to require the installation of risk reduction technologies that would reduce risks below this cutoff.[32] Although Administrator Thomas admonished his staff not to rely upon such rules of thumb to limit regulatory options, OMB insisted that the agency use a one-in-one-hundred-thousand cancer risk cutoff.[33] In objecting to EPA regulations for hazardous waste cleanups, OMB has consistently objected to including one-in-one-hundred-million risks as within the appropriate range of risks for consideration and has insisted that one-in-ten-thousand risks should be considered.[34] Similarly, OMB and the Food and Drug Administration have skirmished over whether FDA should take a *de minimis* approach to regulating carcinogens under the Delaney Clause, which prohibits the deliberate addition to food and cosmetics of substances found to be carcinogenic in laboratory animals.[35] According to OMB and some analysts within FDA, the agency should allow dyes in foods when the assessed risks are small enough, even though this might violate a strict reading of the Delaney Clause. Once again, this position is more substantive than analytical.

"Best case" versus "Worst case" estimates

OMB analysts argue that agencies should use best estimates, reflecting the most likely possibilities, rather than highly unlikely worst case risk estimates on the plausible theory that worse case estimates bias regulations in the direction of greater stringency.[36] In commenting upon EPA's carcinogen assessment guidelines, OMB criticized the agency for adopting the stance that it would "err on the side of public health." OMB urged EPA instead to adopt the position that "[w]hen there is uncertainty in the scientific facts the exposure estimate will characterize this uncertainty" and "[i]n calculating potential risks to the public health and safety, the Agency intends to be realistic in characterizing exposures."[37]

Agency officials responded that responsible government agencies must at least consider the worst case before allowing the public to be exposed to substances that pose such risks. Administrator Ruckelshaus observed that when "reasonable worst case analysis suggests a potential for significant risk, EPA believes the prudent approach is to limit exposure until data necessary to assess risks accurately are developed."[38] Noting that OMB often insists that agencies use worst case estimates for calculating the costs of regulations,[39] some agency analysts wondered about the impartiality of OMB's position.

Advantages and disadvantages of OMB review

The absence of formal criteria for OMB's review function hinders attempts at evaluation. Apart from anecdotal evidence like the foregoing examples, the evaluator is left largely to the opinions of the people in the agencies whose work OMB reviews (an obviously biased source) and outside observers (many of whom also have a stake in the issue). The following discussion of the pros and cons of OMB review will set out the facts and the opinions of those who have spoken on the question and allow the reader to form his or her own conclusions. How one stands on this question depends upon the answers to broader questions of the appropriateness of governmental intervention into private arrangements and the institutional locus of power over regulatory agencies under the constitutional principle of separation of powers.

Advantages of OMB review

Quality control. Frequent readers of RIAs (probably a very tiny class of persons) know that they are quite uneven in quality. Although many represent quite credible attempts to bring comprehensive analytical rationality to bear on rulemaking initiatives, many are mere window dressing. OMB analysts, who review all RIAs, are in an ideal position to perform a valuable quality control function. Because OMB operates at a higher institutional level than analysts in individual agencies, OMB should be able to attract the highest caliber analysts from the top schools of public policy. OMB analysts can be superanalysts, charged with the task of monitoring agency compliance with state-of-the-art analytical techniques.

Coordinating agency approaches to analysis. Regulatory analysis has not yet achieved that professional status where its practitioners follow common norms and adopt uniform approaches to their work. As a consequence, analytical techniques vary from agency to agency. Although centralized review cannot eliminate all inconsistencies among the agencies, it can help achieve a sufficient degree of uniformity that one agency's analysis at least resembles another's. OMB can encourage agencies to use consistent models and to characterize uncertainties in ways that can be compared across agencies. OMB has, for example, attempted to require all agencies to use the same discount rate for reducing future costs and benefits to present value.[40] From its centralized position as reviewer of all agency regulations and analyses, OMB can detect instances in which one agency's requirements needlessly (or even inconsistently) overlap with another agency's requirements.[41] For example, OMB played an intermediary role in a dispute between EPA and NHTSA over whether "on-board" canisters to control gasoline evaporative emissions would increase fire hazards during collisions.[42] Regulatory reformers argue that OMB must be able to resolve unseemly disputes that can arise when one agency's unconstrained pursuit of its statutory goals clashes with another agency's similar pursuit of conflicting goals, even if that means giving OMB the power to elevate one agency's goals over another's.[43] OMB's institutional position at the apex of the federal bureaucracy puts it in a unique position to undertake this coordination function.[44]

Supporting analysts in the agencies. OMB analysts and desk officers can be allies of their kindred spirits in the agencies. For example, the regulatory analysts in the Office of Policy Analysis of EPA have used OMB review as an opportunity to wage anew battles that they lost internally. OMB analysts frequently telephone the lead analysts in EPA for a different view of EPA regulations, and they can use the insights gained from those conversations in OMB's future discussions with EPA program office staff and with upper-level decisionmakers. EPA analysts are acutely aware of the tension that exists between institutional loyalty and professional perspective. Interestingly, EPA once considered including a representative from OMB in its Options Selection-Rejection process as a cure for this potential problem, but rejected that approach because it did not feel it appropriate to give a staff level OMB analyst such a prominent role in EPA's internal decisionmaking process.[45]

Vehicle for presidential policy management. Just as regulatory analysis can provide a vehicle for policy management within agencies, it can help the President manage the executive agencies. Increased presidential control of informal rulemaking has been a fairly common prescription for a whole host of regulatory ills.[46] Although the President is accountable to a national electorate, government bureaucrats are elected by no one. Many therefore believe that the President, who has a broad national policy perspective, should (through OMB) play a large role in determining agency policy.[47]

Writing "better" rules. Some regulatory reformers argue that agencies have promulgated unjustifiable and unworkable rules that do not reflect an appropriate balance between narrow agency goals and broader public ends.[48] Accordingly, OMB's broader "generalist's" perspective can place some realistic constraints on the tendency of agencies to enact bad rules.[49] This argument, however, assumes that interjecting ad hoc, overtly political considerations will result in sounder rules and that there is some agreed-upon measure of "soundness."[50]

Disadvantages of OMB intervention

Analytical quality of OMB review. Although the evaluations of personnel from the agencies whose work OMB analysts review must necessarily be taken with a grain of salt (especially since many decline to speak for attribution on this topic), they are almost uniformly negative.[51] Terms such as "terrible" and "off-the-wall" characterized the comments of OSHA personnel on the quality of OMB review. In one midlevel OSHA employee's opinion, "they [OMB personnel] don't know what they are talking about, and they don't care." One EPA analyst complained that OMB analysts spend too little time with any single regulation to become sufficiently educated to contribute much to the agency's analytical effort.[52] Agency officials frequently observe that OMB analysts lack sufficient expertise to understand highly technical questions that often arise in agency rulemaking.[53] OSHA program office scientists, for example, note that OMB analysts often "venture their opinions on items of industrial hygiene and epidemiology when they are not qualified to be giving opinions."[54] Addressing OMB's attempt to affect agency carcinogen policies, Congressman John Dingell complained about OMB's "extensive effort to second-guess the scientific and technical judgments of federal agencies in the highly complex area of cancer risk assessment."[55]

Not all agency officials, however, are critical of OMB review. A former head of OSHA's policy office considered OMB's input "helpful," and an FSIS analyst conceded that "they can see things that we have blind spots about."[56] An attorney in DOT, who dealt with OMB on a daily basis, observed that OMB desk officers generally had "a good understanding of the Department's problems and needs."[57]

OMB analysts recognize that they do not always have sufficient expertise to understand highly technical scientific considerations, but they respond that they can call on technical experts elsewhere in the Administration, like the President's Office of Science and

Technology Policy.[58] A more persuasive answer may be that if the regulatory analysis documents cannot be understood by the highly trained and experienced analysts in OMB, they are probably too obtuse for public consumption as well.

Delay. Probably the most frequent complaint about OMB review is that it often delays the rulemaking process. Although delay is inherent in any system of institutional review, outside observers share a strong impression that the most serious delays occur with the most important rules.[59] OSHA employees and representatives of organized labor have been especially critical of perceived OMB attempts to affect the substance of rules by threatening to delay them indefinitely.[60] EPA personnel and beneficiary groups have likewise complained about OMB delays.[61] At the end of his tenure at EPA, former Administrator Lee Thomas complained that: "OMB is important but they are more of a pain in the ass because it takes a long, long time to get anything through."[62] Although the average delay caused by OMB is only about four weeks, the fact that OMB can "sit" on the rule for months or even years[63] means that EPA loses credibility with its constituent groups.[64]

Although APHIS, ASCS and FSIS in the Department of Agriculture have experienced few OMB-inspired delays, AMS has had severe problems. OMB personnel have had an intense philosophical antipathy toward AMS marketing orders, and on several occasions OMB prolonged its review of these seasonal orders to such an extent that they never went into effect. Not surprisingly, the affected constituency groups petitioned Congress for relief, and Congress wrote a prohibition on interference with AMS marketing orders into OMB's appropriation.[65]

OMB critics maintain that OMB often holds up rules (sometimes to the eve of judicial and statutory deadlines) in order to extract substantive concessions from agencies.[66] For example, although EPA was under a strict court order to propose a rule for diesel powered trucks, OMB withheld approval up until a week before the deadline, all the time pressing its case that the proposed regulations were unnecessarily stringent.[67] Later, as EPA approached a court-ordered deadline to promulgate the final standard, OMB once again held up approval while it argued its substantive concerns.[68] OMB also held up OSHA's proposed safety standards for grain elevators for more than four months while it pressured the agency on fifteen issues that concerned OMB.[69]

The courts have been unsympathetic to agency claims that OMB review requires an extension of statutory deadlines. In the EPA proceeding on diesel trucks, a federal district judge ordered the agency to issue the proposed rules by a statutory deadline, even if that meant publishing them without OMB review.[70] And in a highly visible case in which OMB review threatened EPA's compliance with a statutory deadline for promulgating hazardous waste regulations, the district court found that "OMB did contribute to the delay in the promulgation of the regulations by insisting on certain substantive changes."[71]

Incoming OMB Director Richard Darman recognized that OMB had held up rules in the past, but he promised to "make things move more quickly." In Congressional testimony, Darman said that he did not approve of using delay as a negotiating tactic.[72] In OMB's defense, however, Darman pointed out that at least some of the delay stemmed from the agencies' failure to answer OMB inquiries about pending rules in a timely fashion. According to former OIRA Director Jay Plager, agencies had been "gaming" OMB by failing to answer OMB questions and then complaining that OMB review was taking too long.[73] In an attempt to place blame for delay on the deserving institution, OMB in 1989 instituted a process whereby its review of a rule would be "suspended," thus tolling any nonstatutory deadlines, while the agency responded to OMB's questions and objections.[74] According to a former head of OIRA, this process was designed as "a way of publicly announcing who has got the ball."[75]

Failure to approve agency surveys. Agency analysts express frustration that OMB insists that agency predictions have a solid empirical basis, while at the same time refusing to approve agency information-gathering efforts. Under the Paperwork Reduction Act, OMB must approve all agency surveys that go out to more than ten private companies.[76] Critics complain that although OMB analysts are not qualified to assess the scientific merits of information-gathering surveys and epidemiology studies, they routinely object to such studies on scientific grounds, sometimes at the behest of regulated industries.[77] For example, when the National Institute for Occupational Safety and Health (NIOSH), which serves as a research arm for OSHA, attempted in 1983 to conduct an epidemiological study on the risk of miscarriages among female users of video display terminals, the company that was to be the subject of the study objected to the scientific adequacy of the inquiries. After hearing the company's arguments, OMB insisted that NIOSH drop the inquiries related to miscarriages.[78] OMB has also rejected agency requests for surveys for assessing the health effects of dioxin, formaldehyde, and methylene choloride.[79] Often the grounds for OMB's objections are highly technical and presume a high level of expertise in epidemiology.[80] In the minds of some, OMB analysts have used this power as a substantive tool to inhibit agency rulemaking indirectly by refusing to approve studies that might yield information that could provide the basis for new regulations.[81] An OMB official acknowledged that "[w]hen you look at practical utility of information and the agency's need for it, you are necessarily looking at . . . substance."[82] In the minds of many observers, OMB's past paperwork reviews have had a "chilling effect" upon the conduct of regulation-related research by federal agencies.[83]

Failure to provide adequate analytical resources. Agency analysts often respond to OMB's criticisms by observing that they could collect better data and craft better analyses if they had more resources. They point out that OMB has steadfastly refused to request additional funding for regulatory analysis.[84] Agency analysts suggest that OMB staffers should direct their complaints about the adequacy of supporting data to the budget officers in OMB. In short, agencies sometimes believe that they are getting mixed signals from OMB.

Reinterpreting agency statutes. OMB analysts have on several occasions been at odds with agency lawyers over the correct interpretation of agency statutes.[85] Because most regulatory statutes have multiple goals and are not written with crystal clarity, agencies often have considerable interpretational leeway. OMB frequently attempts to push agency interpretations as far as possible to the noninterventionist end of the spectrum. For example, OMB analysts disagreed with EPA lawyers about whether regulations promulgated under the strict 1984 Amendments to the Resource Conservation and Recovery Act were more stringent than required by those amendments.[86] OMB's novel interpretation of the Delaney Clause to allow *de minimus* levels of carcinogens in food and cosmetics dyes drew a rebuke from the chairman of the House subcommittee charged with overseeing the implementation of that statute.[87] And in one especially egregious instance, OMB apparently ordered EPA to consider options for stack height requirements (to protect against acid rain) that a federal court of appeals had already declared unlawful in the very rulemaking proceeding at issue.[88] Perhaps because the threat of impartial judicial review looms over both OMB and the agencies, OMB has had very little success in imposing its interpretation of agency statutes on the agencies charged with their implementation, but it continues to try.

Lack of accountability. One of the best rationales for the regulatory analysis requirement is that it informs Congress and the public about the consequences of major regulatory decisions, thereby rendering the agency accountable for its actions. When OMB insists that agencies use assumptions that push analyses in a particular direction, when it delays its review of RIAs as a means of extracting substantive concessions from agencies, and when it simply commands agencies to reach particular substantive results, it should likewise be held accountable for the impacts of its actions. Yet, when OMB plays its superanalyst role in private, it cannot be held accountable for the impact that it has on agency decisionmaking.[89]

On the other hand, the doctrine of executive privilege holds that the President and his aides should be able to engage in candid dialogue with subordinates in the agencies.[90] A past director of OIRA argued that placing the contents of OMB-agency interactions in the public record "would bring the policymaking process to a screeching halt,"[91] and former EPA Administrator Ruckelshaus, in declining to make the contents of oral OMB-EPA communications public, said that "the proper exercise of informal rulemaking authority requires both a full and complete dialog within EPA, and consultation within the executive branch."[92]

There are two responses to the executive privilege argument. First, OMB is not the President and should not be allowed to cloak itself in the mantle of executive privilege. Second, *ex parte* presidential intervention into ongoing public proceedings implicates many countervailing values. The policies underlying executive privilege would not justify a presidential claim to *ex parte* intervention in an FCC licensing proceeding or an NLRB unfair labor practice adjudication.[93] Likewise, they should not prevail over the values of open, accountable and participatory decisionmaking in the rulemaking context.[94]

OMB as a conduit. Perhaps the most damning indictment leveled at OMB by agency officials and regulatory beneficiaries is that OMB sometimes serves as a conduit for relaying information and arguments *ex parte* from the regulated industries to the agency.[95] OMB internal procedures require that OMB must send a copy of all written materials that it receives from outsiders to the relevant agencies, and they preclude face-to-face meetings with outsiders for all but the highest-level officials.[96] OMB officials insist that they have always sent any factual information that they receive directly to the agency for inclusion in record.[97] Yet, a high-level OMB official once boasted that he did not like "to leave fingerprints."[98] A former chief of staff to the EPA Administrator testified to Congress that he was confident that OMB was sending drafts of EPA regulations to industry representatives and receiving their technical comments before EPA had prepared final documents for publication in the *Federal Register.*[99] On at least one occasion, the Deputy Administrator of OIRA personally telephoned two managers of pharmaceutical plants *ex parte* to obtain information relevant to pending EPA water pollution rules for that industry.[100] In one notorious instance, a congressional committee obtained a copy of a telex strongly indicating that OMB had been acting as a conduit for the Canadian government.[101] But the frequency of such secret exchanges of data is unknown.

Clearly, a secret factual record violates the unwritten norms of policy analysis, which stress heavily the "scientific" virtue of open "peer review" of data, as well as the norms of administrative law, which stress public participation in agency decisionmaking. It would be a fraud on the public (and a great discredit to the analytical enterprise) for an agency to offer up for public inspection one administrative record and base its decision on a separate secret record, the contents of which are known only to the regulated industry, the agency, and OMB. Although OMB's past secrecy prevents an accurate assessment of how widespread the "two records" problem has been, the relative dearth of documented cases in the traditionally "leaky" atmosphere of Washington, D.C. lends some comfort to OMB's defenders on this score.

Using analysis as a guise for substantive control. Virtually all representatives of regulatory beneficiaries complain that OMB review is merely a thinly veiled attempt to use analysis as a vehicle for substantive control over the output of the rulemaking process in executive agencies.[102] This assessment is to a surprising degree shared by the program office staffers and even the regulatory analysts in the agencies. Most agency analysts noted that OMB concerns more often go to the agency's substantive policy choices than to the content of the regulatory analysis documents.[103] Many agency scientists and engineers likewise believe that OMB simply brings its different policy perspective to bear on the same data and analysis to reach different substantive conclusions.[104]

There is a strong sense among most agency analysts that a good analysis will not save a decision with which OMB disagrees and a poor analysis will not slow down a decision with which OMB agrees. There are literally hundreds of cases of OMB intervention into agency rulemakings to urge less stringent regulations, and at most a handful of cases of OMB urging the agencies to regulate more stringently.[105] OMB's attempt to stop FSIS from allowing meat producers to delete all reference to mechanically separated meat in meat food products is one of the rare cases in which OMB objected to a regulatory change that was favorable to the regulated industry. Many agency officials perceive that OMB, operating under the guise of a neutral reviewer of regulatory analysis, poses a very real threat to their agencies' decisionmaking authority.

OMB officials respond that they are merely counteracting the bias in the agencies in favor of regulatory solutions to social problems. OMB analysts and desk officers believe they have a responsibility to "rein in" the agencies that would otherwise tend to overregulate society.[106] In this view, the regulatory analysts in OMB must approach regulatory problems from an "efficiency perspective" and be skeptical of regulations and the documents that support them.[107] OMB analysts recognize that the dominant aspect of OMB's review role is determining "whether the [agency's substantive] decision is sensible"[108] and that this raises substantive concerns. OMB officials generally agree that they have a preference against command and control regulation, but argue that this does not necessarily bias them against all regulation – just poorly conceived regulation.[109]

The tension between OMB's role of superanalyst and its roles of enforcer of political accountability and advocate of regulatory relief is central to its relationship with the agencies. The real test of how OMB views its role is when an adequate analysis suggests that a regulation should be more stringent. This has happened on at least two occasions. In the lead phasedown rulemaking discussed in Chapter 3, OMB analysts were apparently persuaded by EPA's reanalysis of the health and economic impacts of various levels of control, although it is possible that they were also swayed by strong pressures from large refiners. When the agency's benefits analysis in the particulates rulemaking, discussed in Chapter 4, suggested that the standard should be made even more stringent, midlevel OMB analysts believed that the analysis should prevail over OMB's general predilection for less stringent regulations. But they were overturned by high-level officials at OMB.

There is a difference between an agency that brings inconsistencies and gaps in analysis to the attention of the relevant agencies and an agency that is itself empowered to resolve inconsistencies by elevating one agency's goals over another's. And an agency that has a mission of advancing its own extrastatutory policy preferences over another agency's statutory goals is an entirely different matter altogether. Many critics of the current OMB review process believe that it more nearly fits the latter description.[110]

Substituting politics for policy. Although policy must admittedly play a large role in regulatory decisionmaking, the delicate balance between expertise and the generalist's perspective may be upset when expert agency decisionmakers must defer to political decisionmakers in the White House.[111] We were rightly repelled to learn during the Watergate investigations that White House political operatives promised to intervene in an ongoing OSHA rulemaking in exchange for a large contribution from the textile industry to the Committee to Re-elect the President.[112] Even when the exchange is not in coin, behind-the-scenes political tradeoffs severely undermine the integrity of the rulemaking process. We may not be shocked, but we are disturbed to learn that a major factor in an important EPA rulemaking was President Carter's need for Senator Byrd's support on the Panama Canal treaty.[113]

Congress, not the President alone, must provide the content of the policies that the agencies apply in individual proceedings. The policy component of regulatory decisionmaking is not the sort of overarching meta-policy that guides foreign policy and important budget decisions. It is, rather, a micropolicy that guides a decisionmaker in deciding which way to lean when the information and arguments on both sides of a regulatory issue appear about equally balanced. This kind of policy judgment is not likely to make its way to a very high position on the President's policy agenda, even in an administration in which government regulation has a high political profile. To the extent that the President delegates his oversight function to OMB, accountability is attenuated, not enhanced.

Opening up OMB-agency interactions

Regulated firms and their attorneys are well aware of the ease with which OMB's analytical review function slides over into substantive review, and they are prepared to beat a path to OMB's door when they lose at the agency level. OMB officials meet frequently with representatives of regulatees (though rarely, if ever, with representatives of beneficiaries and public interest groups) to discuss pending rulemaking initiatives,[114] although OMB analysts insist that these contacts are limited to high-level OMB officials and are not attended by OMB analysts.[115] On some occasions, OMB officials have even circulated draft agency rules to industry representatives and hostile federal agencies for *ex parte* comment before the general public has had an opportunity to see them.[116] Sometimes proposed rules never survive this "first shot," as, for example, when OMB required OSHA to delete its proposed short-term exposure limit for ethylene oxide the day before the proposal was to be sent to the *Federal Register.*[117] A former EPA General Counsel, who now works as a private attorney, suggested that "[a]nybody representing a client who did use [the OMB] route would be damn negligent."[118] Little wonder, then, that agency officials are reluctant to share early drafts of proposed regulations with OMB.

OMB's secret review process had not been in place for long before several key congressmen began to resist this threat to Congress' influence over the regulatory decisionmaking process. OMB's first retreat came in 1982, when it attempted to avoid a full disclosure provision in pending regulatory reform legislation by offering to release the contents of draft rules that had been sent to OMB and any written comments from OMB to the agencies after the rulemaking process had been completed.[119] Because the regulatory reform bill did not pass the House, OMB practices remained unchanged.

The issue remained submerged for several years, only to resurface again in mid-1985 after President Reagan signed Executive Order 12,498, which required all executive regulatory agencies to submit annual regulatory plans to OMB for approval and inclusion in the Administration's Regulatory Program.[120] Responding to this substantial threat to agency autonomy, several key House committee chairmen demanded that agencies submit their plans to Congress at the same time they were submitted to OMB, thus making any OMB-required changes available for public inspection.[121] At the same time, the Environmental Defense Fund initiated a lawsuit challenging an OMB-caused delay in rulemaking. In the preliminary stages of that case, the judge rejected the government's argument that the contents of OMB-EPA communications were privileged and rejected an extraordinary Justice Department request to keep even the plaintiff's complaint secret.[122] The court ultimately ruled that OMB was not authorized to delay rules that were subject to statutory deadlines.[123]

Relations between OMB and key House and Senate Committee chairmen rapidly deteriorated during late 1985, and the Rulemaking Information Act of 1986 was introduced in the House. The bill would have required agencies to maintain a file for every rule that included drafts to OMB, any substantive changes made in response to OMB, and a summary of all written or oral communications between EPA officials and OMB that resulted in recommendations for change in the rule.[124] Although the bill had very little chance of passing over President Reagan's almost certain veto, the House sent a stronger message to OMB during the appropriations process. In April 1986, the chairman of the House Appropriations Committee told the chairman of the Committee on Energy and Commerce that no funds would be appropriated for OIRA until it had been re-authorized by statute. When key senators also supported the attack on OIRA's budget, OMB was ready to concede.

Pursuant to a compromise understanding with Senators Levin and Durenburger, OMB promulgated a memorandum on June 13, 1986, establishing new procedures for OMB review. The memorandum re-affirmed OMB's existing practice of limiting contacts with outsiders to the Administrator and Deputy Administrator of OIRA or some-one specifically designated by one of them and making written ma-terials received by OIRA from any outsiders available for public comment in OMB's reading room. In addition, OMB agreed to make available to interested parties copies of any draft notices sub-mitted to OIRA after the final versions were published in the *Fed-eral Register,* to make available written correspondence between OIRA and the agency head after publication of the relevant notice in the *Federal Register,* to send to any agency that desired them cop-ies of all written materials concerning rules that OIRA received from persons outside the federal government, to advise the agency of all oral communications that high-level OMB officials had with outsiders, and to invite the relevant agency to all scheduled meet-ings with outsiders.[125]

After some initial controversy over the effective date of the change in procedures,[126] the senators were satisfied, but the chair-men of the House committees pursued their defunding efforts from which OIRA emerged damaged but still intact.[127]

The compromise lasted for almost two years. In mid-1988, how-ever, the General Accounting Office found that EPA was doing little to document the changes that OMB demanded in its standards un-der the Clean Air Act.[128] Noting OMB's extreme aversion to putting its comments in writing, some Congressmen concluded that the Pa-perwork Reduction Act should be amended to require that the con-tents of all OMB-agency communications be memorialized and placed in the public record and to place a thirty-day deadline on all OMB reviews.[129] After Congressman Conyers persuaded the House Appropriations Committee to cut off funding for OIRA until Con-gress had enacted legislation reauthorizing the Paperwork Reduction Act, OMB once again was willing to talk compromise.[130] In late 1989, OIRA agreed to formal changes in its rulemaking review process. Among other things, OMB agreed for the first time to put written reasons for any changes that it suggested in the public rulemaking record. It also agreed to establish a formal rulemaking docket at OMB into which it would place the contents of any documents that it received from outsiders. Finally, OMB agreed to complete its reviews within sixty days of a rule's submission, with the possibility of a thirty-day extension.[131]

Conclusions

In delegating decisionmaking authority and policymaking power to regulatory agencies that are not subject to the immediate control of the President and his aides, Congress has determined that narrow "political" concerns should not play a major role in regulatory decisionmaking. The policy that guides administrative decisions should emanate from a statute, not from the President's view of the political needs of the moment. Although the President and his staff have a legitimate and necessary role to play in establishing broad governmental policy (within the usually wide limits established by statute), OMB participation in individual proceedings should be open to public scrutiny. Only in that way can the public evaluate that agency's own performance in the regulatory context.

Although OMB has an important role to play as superanalyst, it should not play the role of superregulator. The President alone has the power to control the agencies through the exercise of his power of persuasion and ultimately through his removal authority. When that power is exercised it should be by the President himself, and not a subordinate institutional entity that is composed largely of practitioners of a single profession.

Although the past secrecy of the OMB review process hinders an assessment of OMB's impact on agency decisionmaking, it is clear that OMB substantially influenced many of the most important rulemaking initiatives of the 1980s.[132] Yet, OMB's effect on day-to-day decisionmaking should not be overstated. It has lost several very visible battles with the executive agencies. Perhaps its greatest influence lies in the invisible battles and in the rules that never get proposed because the agency wants to avoid conflicts with OMB.

CHAPTER 19

Judicial review of regulatory analysis

The two primary sources of regulatory analysis requirements for federal agencies – the Regulatory Flexibility Act (RFA) and the Executive Orders – have envisioned a very modest role for regulatory analysis in judicial review of rulemaking. Both the act and the Executive Orders specifically preclude judicial review of an agency's failure to prepare a regulatory analysis document.[1] Thus, the regulatory analysis requirement varies significantly from the environmental impact statement requirement, which spawned a decade's litigation over threshold questions.[2]

When an agency does prepare a regulatory analysis document, its failure to comply with the criteria specified in the statute and the Executive Orders is likewise not subject to judicial review. In *Small Refiners Lead Phase-Down Task Force v. EPA,*[3] the case in which the lead phasedown rulemaking described in Chapter 3 was reviewed, the court held that although the contents of the RFA could properly be scrutinized by a reviewing court as part of its substantive review function, the failure of an RFA to meet all of the statute's content requirements was not properly subject to judicial review. The court acknowledged that "in an appropriate case" a reviewing court could strike down an agency rule because of a defect in the RFA, but such a case would exist only when the defect was critical to the reviewing court's analysis of the reasonableness of the underlying rule.[4] Assuming that the Regulatory Impact Analysis (RIA), like the RFA, can be useful to the courts' substantive review function, this chapter will explore how the courts can put regulatory analysis documents to their best use.

Regulatory analysis and agency power

The Executive Orders and the RFA did not expand agency power; the source of that power remains in substantive statutes. Hence, the agencies have not been allowed to rely upon the Executive Orders or the RFA to take actions that they are not otherwise empowered to take or to refrain from taking an action that they are required to take.[5]

292

Under the "arbitrary and capricious" test for judicial review of rulemaking, an agency action may be set aside if the agency has "relied on factors which Congress has not intended it to consider."[6] The question then arises whether regulatory analysis documents may lawfully discuss considerations that the agency is by statute prohibited from considering in writing its final rule. Although not many agency statutes preclude the use of regulatory analysis,[7] a few do, either directly or by clear implication.[8] For example, the Supreme Court has held that OSHA may not base its health standards on cost-benefit analysis,[9] and the D.C. Circuit has held that EPA may not consider costs in promulgating National Ambient Air Quality Standards.[10] We have seen that EPA has resolved the contradictory commands by calculating the costs and benefits of regulations in compliance with the Executive Order, but refusing to let the Administrator see the resulting RIA. Yet, the legality of including information on forbidden considerations in regulatory analysis documents should not turn upon whether or not the agency staff has insulated the agency head from the document. One of the affected parties could submit the same information and analysis in a comment to the agency, and the agency would not be subject to reversal for failing to avert its institutional eyes, even though it theoretically could not consider the information. The fact that the origin of the information and analysis is agency staff, rather than an outsider, should not affect the judicial consideration.

The courts probably did not mean to say that agencies may not *consider* precluded considerations; they held that the agencies may not *rely* upon such considerations in reaching a decision. There is, of course, a very fine line between considering an argument and relying upon it. If the agency considered an argument and reached a result consistent with that argument, it cannot be said with any certainty that it did not rely upon that argument. The matter could be resolved somewhat formally, however, by recognizing that the best evidence of the considerations that an agency relied upon is the agency's written statement of basis and purpose, usually published in the preamble to the final rule. A reviewing court may not normally probe the mind of the administrator once the agency has explained itself to the world in writing,[11] and the agency's action must stand or fall on that explanation. A reviewing court might therefore uphold an agency rule if the agency did not rely upon the forbidden consideration in its statement of basis and purpose and if the facts, analysis, and reasons given in the statement of basis and purpose read in light of the rest of the record demonstrated that the agency's rule was not arbitrary and capricious. Conversely, if the agency relied upon a forbidden consideration in its statement of basis and purpose, including any incorporation by reference of the information and analysis in the regulatory analysis document, then the rule would be set aside under this formal approach.

Although the formal approach is probably satisfactory in most cases, there may remain cases in which petitioners can demonstrate that the agency did in fact rely upon forbidden considerations, even though it did not explicitly mention them in drafting its statement of basis and purpose. For example, a party might uncover a "smoking gun" memorandum indicating that the forbidden consideration did in fact play an important role in the agency's decision. When a party can make such a showing, the courts should be attentive and should set aside the agency rule.

Regulatory analysis and rationality review

The Administrative Procedure Act and many agency statutes give the courts a substantive review function. Depending upon the statute, the reviewing court must set aside agency rules that are "arbitrary and capricious" or lack "substantial evidence" on the record as a whole.[12] Whatever the test, the primary function of substantive judicial review is to ensure that the agency rulemaking meets minimum standards of rationality. Under the "arbitrary and capricious" test the court is to "consider whether the decision was based on a consideration of the relevant factors and whether there has been a clear error of judgment."[13] More particularly, a reviewing court must find an agency arbitrary and capricious if: "The agency has relied on factors which Congress has not intended it to consider, entirely failed to consider an important aspect of the problem, offered an explanation for its decision that runs counter to the evidence before the agency, or is so implausible that it could not be ascribed to a difference in view or the product of agency expertise."[14]

Because the primary purpose of the regulatory analysis process is to bring comprehensive analytical rationality to bear upon rulemaking, regulatory analysis should enhance the quality of substantive judicial review. The comprehensive analytical rationality paradigm is not very different from the ideal paradigm of rational legal reasoning. Legal reasoning breaks problems down into their component parts, identifies options (alternate decision rules), measures those options against previously articulated policy goals (e.g., fairness, justice, and efficiency), and chooses the rule that most effectively addresses those goals.[15] Because substantive judicial review focuses upon whether the agency engaged in "reasoned decisionmaking," given the evidence in the rulemaking record, a written regulatory analysis in the rulemaking record that effectively states the agency's regulatory goals, identifies alternatives, provides information and analysis on the advantages and disadvantages of the alternatives, and measures each alternative against the goals should aid the agency substantially in persuading a reviewing court of the rationality of the rulemaking exercise.

A good example of a case in which a well-done RIA helped support a rule on judicial review is *Center for Auto Safety v. Peck*,[16] in which the court upheld NHTSA's standard for automobile bumper crashworthiness. Examining the regulation under the enhanced judicial scrutiny used to review abrupt departures from settled agency policy, the court nevertheless found that the agency was not arbitrary and capricious in reducing the standard's stringency. The court relied heavily upon the agency's 263-page RIA, which comprehensively examined the costs and benefits of nine alternative standards. Indeed, for most of the important issues in that case, the RIA defined the debate. The court focused closely upon the tables in the RIA in rejecting petitioners' arguments that the agency had erroneously calculated the costs and benefits of the new standard and several prominent alternatives. The court finally concluded that although there were numerous uncertainties, imperfections, and even mistakes in the agency's analysis, they were not of such a magnitude as to render the decision arbitrary and capricious.[17]

Conversely, a reviewing court can point to a poorly done regulatory analysis document as evidence of arbitrary and capricious decisionmaking. The court in *Thompson v. Clark*[18] provided an example of an instance in which an inadequate regulatory analysis document could undermine a rule: "For example, if a defective regulatory flexibility analysis caused an agency to underestimate the harm inflicted upon small business to such a degree that, when adjustment is made for the error, that harm clearly outweighs the claimed benefits of the rule, then the rule must be set aside."[19]

The First Circuit Court of Appeals, in *Natural Resources Defense Council, Inc. v. EPA*,[20] relied heavily on the RIA for EPA's regulations governing the disposal of high-level radioactive waste to find that EPA's reasons for limiting the duration of individual protections to 1,000 years was arbitrary and capricious. Similarly, the district court in *Texarkana Livestock Commission v. Dept. of Agriculture*[21] apparently adopted this approach when it examined the analysis that

APHIS prepared to support its conclusion that its brucellosis quarantine regulations would not have a significant impact upon a substantial number of small entities. The fact that the agency could point to no information to support its "no substantial impact" conclusion helped the court conclude that the entire rule was a product of arbitrary and capricious agency action.

Finally, a good regulatory analysis document might undermine a rule that departs too far from the predictions and analysis set out in the document. At the very least, the agency would be required to explain in its preamble any great departure from the regulatory analysis document. All of this should enhance the quality of judicial review and ultimately of the agency's decisionmaking process.[22]

Yet, the mere presence of a regulatory analysis document in the rulemaking record does not guarantee rationality. One of the most comprehensive RIAs ever prepared could not save the agency's decision in *Motor Vehicles Manufacturers' Association v. State Farm Mutual Casualty Co.*,[23] where the Supreme Court reviewed a NHTSA decision to withdraw its "passive restraint" regulations. After studying the matter for almost a decade, the Secretary of Transportation in 1977 issued Modified Standard 208, which required automobile manufacturers to install passive restraints (e.g. automatic seatbelts or airbags) on a phased basis beginning with large automobiles in the 1982 model year and extending to intermediate and small automobiles in the 1983 and 1984 model years. In February 1981, the new Secretary of Transportation reviewed the standard in light of the economic difficulties of the domestic auto industry. After taking public comments and further studying the matter, the agency decided to withdraw the passive restraint requirements. The agency determined that since automobile manufacturers had almost universally elected to install automatic seatbelts rather than airbags and since its RIA predicted that few people would be protected by automatic seatbelts, the standard would not produce significant safety benefits.

The agency noted that manufacturers planned to install detachable automatic seatbelts in 99 percent of all new automobiles. This would meet the 1977 Modified Standard, but it would make it relatively easy for passengers to detach the automatic seatbelts permanently, thus requiring an affirmative action of the passenger to make the seatbelts automatic once again. The agency predicted in the RIA that large numbers of passengers would permanently detach the automatic seatbelts, thereby rendering the standard inefficacious.[24]

The Supreme Court found this reasoning process to be arbitrary and capricious. First, the Court found that the agency arbitrarily failed to consider modifying the standard to require that manufacturers use airbag technologies. Assuming that automatic seatbelts would not significantly enhance safety, the agency made no attempt whatsoever to explain why it concluded that the passive restraint standard should be rescinded altogether. At best, that conclusion would only justify amending the Modified Standard to eliminate the detachable automatic seatbelt option. In no way did it cast doubt on the need for a passive restraint standard or upon the efficacy of the airbag technology.

Despite the extensive analysis in the RIA, the Court also found that the agency too quickly dismissed the safety benefits of automatic seatbelts. The Court agreed with the agency that substantial uncertainties about the efficacy of a regulation could justify its withdrawal, but it was not sufficient for the agency "to merely recite the terms 'substantial uncertainty' as a justification for its actions."[25]

According to the Court, the record contained no direct evidence that an automatic seatbelt requirement would not increase seatbelt usage substantially. The agency's conclusion to the contrary failed to take into account a critical difference between automatic seatbelts and manual seatbelts, viz inertia. The agency had earlier found that inertia operates against the efficacy of the manual seatbelts, because an affirmative act of "buckling up" is required to take advantage of their safety benefits. The Court reasoned that the same inertia would operate in favor of automatic seatbelts, because it would take an affirmative act to detach the seatbelt. The agency also failed adequately to explain why it did not require nondetachable belts, such as "continuous spool" belts. The Court found the agency's primary rationale – that such a requirement might trigger adverse public reaction – to be unsupported by the record and unexplained.[26]

NHTSA's experience with the passive restraint standard indicates that regulatory analysis does not necessarily enhance the quality of the agency's decisions. Indeed, the information in the RIA helped to undermine the agency's decision, because the Court drew on it to reveal the inadequacy of the agency's reasoning process.[27] The passive restraint case may be an instance in which the Administrator failed to use both techno-bureaucratic and comprehensive analytical thinking in reaching a decision that was dominated by irrelevant political considerations.

A good regulatory analysis will reveal both the strengths and the weaknesses of the agency's approach to a problem. It is designed for two primary purposes: (1) to aid upper-level agency decisionmakers in making difficult decisions in areas where information is scarce and inconclusive; and (2) to inform Congress and the public of the goals that the agency is seeking to advance, the prominent alternatives for achieving those goals, the assumptions and inferences underlying the agency's reasoning process, and the data and information available on the relevant issues. Candor is absolutely critical to these functions. Yet, fear of reversal in reviewing courts may induce regulatory analysts and attorneys in agencies to gloss over uncertainties and to paint a prettier picture of the selected alternative than the facts may warrant. Agency analysts are intensely aware of the fact that intelligent lawyers can seize upon any absence of critical data and any apparent gap in the agency's reasoning process to "trash" regulatory analysis documents during judicial review.[28] Agency analysts therefore feel pressure to state conclusions with more confidence than is warranted, to base predictions on single models that lead to predetermined results, and to stress agency "expertise" at all critical junctures. In short, the very fact of judicial review creates pressures on agency analysts to turn regulatory analysis documents into advocacy documents.

This is an unfortunate development for several reasons. First, it will cause agency analysts and other technical staffers to depart from their roles as professional assessors and analyzers of information. There are already sufficient internal pressures operating upon analysts and program office staffers to take adversarial stances with respect to one another. The quality of agency decisionmaking can only suffer if both are encouraged at an early stage of a rule's development to take an adversarial stance with respect to the rest of the world.

Second, if agency analysts take an adversarial approach toward regulatory analysis documents, the public will be less informed about the true basis for agency decisions. When analysts gloss over uncertainties, hide assumptions, and purport to "find" facts that cannot be found, the public never sees the policy considerations that really motivate the analysts. Policy-laden prescriptions appear to be driven by facts accessible only to the experts, and the experts remain unaccountable for the policies that they adopt *sub silentio*. Democratic oversight of important social decisions thereby suffers.

Finally, the quality of judicial review will also suffer. Reviewing judges cannot hope to match wits with agency experts on technical issues of enormous complexity, even with the aid of two or more sets of lawyers. If an agency wants to hide policy judgments behind the veneer of technical expertise, it will probably succeed in most instances, especially if it is possible to conceal its assumptions in a complex mathematical model. Yet, when agencies adopt such a disingenuous approach, the courts are less able to perform their most important substantive review function – viz determining whether the policy considerations underlying the assumptions and inferences that go into agency predictions are consistent with the agency's statute.

The courts can encourage agency candor by resisting attempts by litigants to trash regulatory analysis documents. Because they address questions where information is scarce and uncertainties are plentiful, regulatory analysis documents are especially subject to trashing. A bright lawyer and two or three technical aids can make almost any regulatory analysis document appear absolutely idiotic. But the reviewing courts must recognize that agency analytical efforts are necessarily imperfect and that imperfections do not usually render the agency's final determinations irrational.[29]

For example, in the *Center for Auto Safety* case, discussed previously, the agency virtually ignored the option that was based upon the higher estimate of benefits and lower estimate of costs for the more stringent standard. The petitioners complained that this was irrational, because that was the option most favorable to them and least favorable to the agency's final position. The court, however, was persuaded that the agency's cost and benefit estimates for that option were based upon an extremely unlikely set of assumptions (which, like other assumptions that the agency used in its analysis, the agency clearly articulated) that reduced the probability that those estimates would be borne out in the real world to virtually zero.[30] The court approved the agency's rejection of that option despite the fact that a second rationale for that rejection in the RIA was plainly irrational. Alluding to the relevant passage in the RIA, the court noted that "[t]his passage bears every evidence of having been inserted as a make-weight by someone who had not the slightest idea what he was talking about."[31] Nevertheless, because the rejection of this option was supported in the RIA on the alternative ground of improbability, the court did not seize upon the rejection of that option as a reason to set aside the rule.

If the regulatory analysis enterprise is to achieve its potential, the courts must follow the deferential approach to reviewing regulatory analysis documents outlined in *Center for Auto Safety*. Judicial decisions themselves are subject to trashing by determined critics for failing to engage in tight analysis and for resting upon hidden policy biases. In a democratic society, the only acceptable approach is to lay bare the assumptions that drive decisions and state explicitly the policies that underlie those assumptions. Only then can we engage in democratic dialogue about the wisdom of those policies. Stringent judicial review of the analysis in an agency's regulatory analysis document (which may itself be motivated by the policy preferences of the judges) will only encourage the agency to hide behind a cloak of expertise and thereby stifle legitimate debate over policy.

PART V

Conclusions

CHAPTER 20

Analysis in the modern regulatory state

Regulatory analysis is currently in a state of awkward adolescence. It has emerged from its infancy, but it has not yet matured. It is often noisy and clumsy, and it generally commands little respect. Yet, despite its considerable shortcomings, it has important virtues. Every decisionmaker wants to make rational and informed decisions, and regulatory analysis can be very useful in sorting out the pros and cons of regulatory options. Perhaps more importantly, it can encourage the decisionmaker to articulate policy preferences and demonstrate to the public how those policy preferences were applied in important rulemaking initiatives. Like most adolescents, regulatory analysis also has great potential for the future. If the public, and particularly the beneficiaries of regulation, become convinced that it is not being used cynically to reach particular substantive results, regulatory analysis can become an effective tool for improving regulatory decisions and for enhancing the accountability of the bureaucracies to the public that they serve.

The conclusions of a high-level USDA employee who had an opportunity to observe the regulatory analysis process for many years at close range may provide an apt summary.[1] This employee is enthusiastic about the theoretical value of regulatory analysis, but pessimistic about its current efficacy in the real world. Although some agencies have a strong analytical orientation, he believes that most bureaucrats, like most other other people, are not comfortable with thinking analytically. They bring their individual experience and intuition to bear on a problem, and when they are presented with a regulatory analyst's work product, they immediately search for the bottom line before agreeing with or critiquing that analysis. If they agree with the analyst's preferred option, they do not heavily critique the document. If they do not agree, they critique the analysis and demand greater certainty.

In this employee's experience, some decisionmakers always rely upon analysis, but many do not. The regulatory analysis requirements of the Executive Orders have had little effect on analysis-oriented decisionmakers because they have historically relied upon analysis anyway. Nevertheless, the Executive Orders have created an environment more supportive of analysis. For decisionmakers not already favorably disposed to use analysis, the regulatory analysis documents at best make the decisionmakers modestly more conservative about issuing rules. Whereas decisionmakers in agencies not often subject to judicial review could, prior to the implementation of the regulatory analysis requirements, render decisions without detailed explanations, current decisionmakers must "paper" their decisions with a regulatory analysis document. In many cases the available information is so equivocal that a plausible regulatory analysis document can be written to support any decision that is not completely unreasonable. Only very rarely has this employee seen an "objective analysis" from agencies that were not already favorably disposed to analysis. Nor can this employee think of an instance in which an agency's decision has been turned around by analysis, although he is willing to concede that the inability to "paper over" a previously reached decision with a subsequent regulatory analysis may have shaped some final decisions or stopped some program offices from going forward with some options.

Despite his general pessimism about the current state of regulatory analysis, this employee is optimistic that if the agencies continue to channel resources into the effort, analysis will become an increasingly important factor in federal rulemaking. Citing Food Safety and Inspection Service as an agency in which the analytical perspective has achieved a firm foothold, he feels that the approach of agencies toward regulatory analysis will change as people with nonanalytical perspectives deal more frequently with analytically oriented people and learn that analysis can be of practical use to them. He is also confident that as more efforts are made to produce information on the costs and benefits of regulations, more hard data will be forthcoming. As this happens, "political" or "intuitive" factors will overshadow "technical" factors on fewer occasions.

The USDA official is correct in concluding that the regulatory analysis process can be improved. Many of the limitations of comprehensive analytical thinking can be avoided. For example, the substantial limitations of quantitative techniques in the area of social regulation preclude heavy reliance on them in the decisionmaking process. Quantitative models should not be allowed to oversimplify complex decisionmaking considerations. To avoid this, regulatory analysis documents should state clearly the major nonobvious assumptions that undergird the models that the agency uses. The documents should discuss in qualitative terms important decisionmaking variables that are not subject to quantitative analysis. And when regulatory analysis documents do make quantitative predictions, they should attempt to characterize the uncertainties that are included in the predictions through the use of confidence intervals, multiple assessment models, sensitivity analysis and worst case analysis.

Some of the considerable limitations in the particular variety of regulatory analysis called cost-benefit analysis can be avoided by recognizing that cost-benefit analysis alone cannot dictate regulatory results in most regulatory contexts. It is better used to achieve more modest ends, such as setting agency priorities and structuring agency options. Less ambitious techniques, such as cost-effectiveness analyses, may be more appropriate for rulemaking initiatives that have impacts on health, environmental, historical, artistic, and esthetic values. In addition, since cost-benefit analysis does not necessarily address distributional impacts of regulations, agencies should use other tools to display such impacts for decisionmakers. Finally, when agencies use cost-benefit analysis in regulatory analysis documents, they should be explicit about discount rates, and they should use more than one discount rate to clarify the sensitivity of analytical projections to the discount rate and to make explicit the value that the agency assigns to future benefits.

One of the most highly touted virtues of regulatory analysis is its ability to identify innovative regulatory options. But this potential can only be realized if the regulatory analysis function becomes an integral part of the structure of the internal agency decisionmaking process. Agencies should not begin intensive information-gathering and other analytical efforts on rules until agency technical staff and agency regulatory analysts have attempted to identify a broad range of regulatory options. In addition, agency regulatory analysts should become involved in the decisionmaking process early in the evolution of a rule, before innovative alternatives have been eliminated. Finally, agencies should experiment with a phased system of reducing options. Under a phased system, the agency should identify a large number of options initially for brief study. As options are rejected, the remaining options should be analyzed with greater and greater thoroughness. As resource constraints preclude the agency from considering an option in greater detail, it should list the option in its regulatory analysis document and explain why it did not warrant further study. Yet, even if agencies pay greater attention to enhancing the analysts' options identification role, the absence of strong evidence that analysts have identified innovative options in agencies, such as EPA and NHTSA, in which they have expressly been assigned that role suggests that the gains from restructuring the decisionmaking process with this goal alone in mind may be relatively modest.

Accurate information on the costs and economic impacts of proposed rules is essential to the regulatory analysis process, and the most important source of this information is the regulated industry. Agencies should have the power to obtain this information from the regulated parties. Where it is currently lacking, Congress should give the agencies authority to address requests to parties that are able to provide cost and economic impact information, subject to adequate protections against the disclosure of trade secret and other commercial and financial information. The Office of Management and Budget should coordinate its regulatory analysis review function with its paperwork reduction function to ensure that it approves information-gathering activities that are designed to yield information that it is likely to require later in the review process. In addition, agencies should attempt to coordinate their own sponsored research activities with their regulatory analysis initiatives. To accomplish this, agencies should structure the decisionmaking process to allow regulatory analysts to participate in setting long term research agendas. In particular, they should structure the decisionmaking process to allow a representative from the office responsible for agency-sponsored research to participate at the very early stages when informational needs are defined.

The perception that regulatory analysis is based on biased information poses a serious threat to the analytical exercise. Agencies should attempt to reduce the threat of bias in the sources of the information that they use in preparing regulatory analysis documents. This does not mean that they should automatically ignore or discount the value of information simply because it comes from a source with an interest in the outcome of the rulemaking initiative. They can take less drastic steps to reduce bias including: (1) consulting, whenever possible, multiple sources of information in preparing regulatory analysis documents; (2) carefully citing all information upon which the analysis draws and making the information available for public scrutiny at convenient times and places; and (3) subjecting critical studies to review by acknowledged experts. Finally, agencies can reduce the perception of bias by attempting on a trial basis to engage in cooperative regulatory impact assessment by bringing representatives from all affected parties together to assess the validity of particular studies prior to relying upon those studies in regulatory analysis documents.

Retrospective analyses of the predictions made in previous regulatory analysis documents can provide feedback on the accuracy of agency predictions and thereby enable agencies to enhance the accuracy of future predictions. Retrospective analysis can also be useful in evaluating the value of regulatory analysis to an agency's regulatory effort. To the extent that agencies devote resources to analysis they should likewise devote resources to retrospective analyses of analysis.

Agencies and the reviewing courts can reduce impediments to the effective use of regulatory analysis in the decisionmaking process. Regulatory analysis documents should be made available to Congress and the public, even if they include information or considerations that the agency decisionmaker may not legally rely upon in promulgating a rule. Regulatory analysis documents should consider reasonably available options, even if the agency is not empowered to implement some of those options, and they should be transmitted to agencies or other institutions with power to implement them.

The courts should not overturn a rulemaking effort solely because a regulatory analysis document addresses factors that the agency is by statute forbidden to consider. Instead, they should examine carefully the agency's statement of basis and purpose and any additional evidence that the agency in fact relied on improper considerations in carrying out the substantive judicial review function. In addition, the courts should avoid forcing agencies to use regulatory analysis disingenuously by discouraging litigants from trashing regulatory analysis documents and by being sensitive to the limitations of and impediments to analysis in performing their substantive review functions.

Although the matter is not entirely free from doubt, it is probably a good idea to mix the two cultures of techno-bureaucratic rationality and comprehensive analytical rationality in the internal rulemaking process. Both cultures have unique perspectives to offer to regulatory decisionmakers. The hierarchical model for regulatory analysis preparation is not a useful model for mixing the cultures, and it should not be employed by decisionmakers who want to hear both perspectives. The outside advisor model is likewise not very likely to bring about the clash of cultures that will be useful to agency decisionmakers. The adversarial model more than adequately encourages this sort of cultural conflict, but it poses a very real threat that the conflict will get out of hand, and it is very resource-intensive. The team model is capable of harnessing the conflict, but it may push too hard toward consensus. Nevertheless, it is by far the most frequently invoked model, and it will probably continue to be used in most agencies. Finally, the hybrid model offers an attractive compromise between the adversarial and team models for agencies that have adequate resources and a sufficient upper-level commitment to policy management.

The gravest threat to the entire analytical enterprise is the prevailing belief that it is being used to achieve particular substantive ends. To avoid the suspicion that analysis is being used to advance hidden agendas, agencies should always frankly acknowledge its limitations and publicize the cases in which analyses suggest that the further regulation is warranted. Only if beneficiaries become convinced that analysis is being used fairly in support of protective regulation as well as against it will they begin to accept it as a legitimate decisionmaking tool. It cannot be forced down their throats as an objective alternative to intuitive decisionmaking, because it is not thoroughly objective and it is usually imminently manipulable. At a minimum, OMB communications to the agencies should be reduced to writing and placed in the rulemaking record. Likewise, agencies should not request, and OMB should not grant, exemptions from the regulatory analysis requirements solely because the underlying rules are perceived to be deregulatory in nature.

Implementing the foregoing recommendations may take the agencies a long way toward effectively integrating regulatory analysis into the decisionmaking process. Whether its virtues justify the cost of preparing the documents after the recommendations are implemented is ultimately a question about which reasonable minds can differ. Whether regulatory analysis ultimately matures into a successful tool for achieving sensible regulation or withers away in acrimonious debate is a matter that is largely within the hands of its proponents.

Notes

Introduction

1. Crunden 1982; Gerber 1984; Hofstadter 1955.
2. Hawley, pt. 1; Irons 1982.
3. Vogel 1981.
4. See Vogel 1981; Wilson J. Q. 1980.
5. As with any broad generalizations, there are important exceptions. Joseph Kennedy, a financier, was the first head of the Securities and Exchange Commission, and health professionals have dominated the leadership of the Food and Drug Administration and the Occupational Safety and Health Administration. Nevertheless, it is beyond cavil that lawyers played the predominant institution-building role for most federal agencies.
6. Irons 1982; McCraw 1984, ch. 5.
7. McGarity 1987, 401.
8. See, e.g., Lochner v. New York, 198 U.S. 45 (1905). See generally Jaffe 1939.
9. Panama Refining Co. v. Ryan, 293 U.S. 388 (1935); Schecter Poultry Corp. v. United States, 295 U.S. 495 (1935); Jaffe 1965, ch. 2.
10. The phrase was crafted by Abe Fortas, then one of Frankfurter's "happy hot dogs." Baker 1984, 332. See also Irons 1982, 276–9.
11. See Walters v. National Ass'n of Radiation Survivors, 105 S.Ct. 3180 (1985) ("that day [of Lochner] is fortunately long gone, and with it the condemnation of rational paternalism as a legitimate legislative goal"); Baker 1984, 332; McGarity 1987.
12. See McGarity 1987; Verkuil 1978.
13. Industrial Union Department, AFL-CIO v. American Petroleum Institute, 448 U.S. 607 (1980); Lowi 1987; Schoenbrod 1987; Schoenbrod 1985.

1. Rational analysis as regulatory reform

1. Hamilton 1972; West 1983, 327.
2. Eads and Fix 1982, 120–1.
3. See Kneese and Schultze 1975; Schoenbrod 1983.
4. Andrews 1982, 120; Rourke 1984, 171.
5. For insightful commentary on the concept of culture as applied to regulatory decisionmaking, see Meidinger 1986, 1987.
6. Edwards and Sharkansky 1978, 6–10; Lindblom 1959; Diver 1981; Rodgers 1981; Meidinger 1985, 466–7.
7. For a discussion of the related concept of "technical rationality" outside of the regulatory context, see Dyesing 1962, ch. 1. Dyesing's con-

309

cept of "technical rationality" contains many elements of what I would label "comprehensive analytical rationality."

8. Lynn 1986, 40.
9. See, e.g., Shapiro and McGarity 1989, 15–20.
10. All but one of the OSHA health standards issued during the Reagan Administration were issued as a result of court orders compelling the agency to take action. United Steelworkers of America v. Rubber Mfgs. Ass'n, 783 F.2d 1117 (D.C. Cir. 1986) (benzene); International Union, UAW v. Donovan, 756 F.2d 162 (D.C. Cir. 1985) (formaldehyde); Public Citizen Health Research Group v. Auchter, 702 F.2d 1150 (D.C. Cir. 1983) (ethylene oxide). For an especially egregious case, see Farmworker Justice Fund, Inc. v. Brock, 811 F.2d 613 (D.C. Cir. 1987) (farmworker protection standard delayed fourteen years before court orders its promulgation).
11. Benveniste 1977, 90.
12. See Diver 1981; Rodgers 1981.
13. Edwards and Sharkansky 1978, 7. See also Lindblom 1959, 13; Meltsner 1976, 115–16; Jenkins-Smith 1982; Forester 1984, 23–4; West 1983, 326.
14. Forester 1984, 24.
15. Meltsner 1976, 118; Leman and Nelson 1981, 99.
16. Kelman, S. 1982, 140.

2. Evolution of the regulatory analysis program

1. 42 U.S. Code §§ 4,321 et seq.; Andrews 1982, 122.
2. 42 U.S. Code § 4,332(2)(C).
3. Andrews 1976; Berlin 1970.
4. Crampton and Berg 1973, 516; Strohbehn 1974, 94.
5. Caldwell 1979, 50,004.
6. Caldwell 1979, 50,003; Sax 1973.
7. Andrews 1976, 28; Caldwell 1979, 50,007; Strohbehn 1974, 94; Council on Environmental Quality 1976, 2.
8. Crampton and Berg 1973, 515; Caldwell 1979, 50,006.
9. Council on Environmental Quality 1976, 23.
10. U.S. Congress. House 1976, 506; Quarles 1976, 61.
11. Quarles 1976, 64.
12. Executive Order No. 11,821; Eads and Fix 1984, 50–4.
13. Executive Order No. 11,821 §§ 1, (2)(a), 2(b).
14. Council on Wage and Price Stability Act, Pub. L. No. 93–387, 88 Stat. 750 (1974).
15. OMB 1974; Council on Wage and Price Stability 1976, ii, 5; Comment 1977, 1,143; U.S. Congress. Senate 1978, 78–9.
16. Council on Wage and Price Stability 1976, 33.
17. Ibid., 29; Miller 1977, 18.
18. Council on Wage and Price Stability 1976, v; General Accounting Office 1977, ch. 8.
19. Comment 1977, 1,161–2; Council on Wage and Price Stability 1976,40; DeMuth 1980, 13; Miller 1977, 18; Viscusi 1983b, 163.

20. Executive Order No. 12,044; Eads and Fix 1984, 54–65.
21. Executive Order No. 12,044 § 2(d).
22. Ibid., § 2(c).
23. Ibid., § 3. See Council on Wage and Price Stability 1981.
24. Eads and Fix 1984, ch. 6; Raven-Hansen 1983.
25. Executive Order No. 12,291.
26. Ibid., § 2.
27. Ibid., § 3(c)(2).
28. Ibid., § 3(d).
29. Eads 1981b, 20; Viscusi 1983b, 161–2.
30. Executive Order No. 12,291 § 1(b).
31. Ibid., § 3(b).
32. Ibid., § 6(a)(4).
33. Ibid., §§ 3(b), 6(a)(2).
34. Ibid., § 3(e).
35. Ibid., § 3(f).
36. OMB 1981.
37. Ibid., 2–3.
38. Ibid., 3–4.
39. Ibid., 1989b.
40. Ibid., 1982a, 11.
41. Ibid., 1983, 9.
42. General Accounting Office 1989, App.III.
43. 5 U.S. Code § 601 et seq.
44. Ibid., § 601(6).
45. Small Business Administration 1982.
46. Verkuil 1982, 215–16.
47. 5 U.S. Code § 601.
48. 5 U.S. Code § 602(a)(1). The terms "significant economic impact" and "substantial number" are not defined by the Act.
49. 5 U.S. Code §§ 602(b) and (c), 609.
50. Ibid., § 603.
51. Ibid., § 604.
52. Ibid., § 610.
53. Ibid., § 603(a).
54. Ibid., § 603(b).
55. Ibid., § 603(b).
56. Ibid., § 604(a).
57. Ibid., § 607.
58. Executive Order No. 12,291 § 6(b).
59. OMB 1980.

3. Getting the lead out of gasoline: EPA's lead phasedown regulations

1. Ethyl Corp. v. EPA, 541 F.2d 1, 7 (D.C. Cir. 1976).
2. EPA 1977, ch. 1; Council on Environmental Quality 1981, IV–25.
3. EPA 1977, 1–1 through 1–3; Ethyl Corp. v. EPA, 541 F.2d 1, 8 (D.-C.Cir. 1976).

4. Ethyl Corp. v. EPA, 541 F.2d 1, 9 (D.C. Cir. 1976).
5. 42 U.S. Code § 7545.
6. EPA 1973a.
7. Ethyl Corp. v. EPA, 541 F.2d 1 (D.C. Cir. 1976), *cert. denied,* 426 U.S. 941 (1976)
8. EPA 1973b, 33,741.
9. EPA 1973b.
10. Ibid., 33,739; see Small Refiner Lead Phase-Down Task Force v. EPA, 705 F.2d 506, 512 (D.C. Cir. 1983).
11. Small Refiner Lead Phase-Down Task Force v. EPA, 705 F.2d 506, 512 (D.C. Cir. 1983).
12. 42 U.S. Code § 7,545(g).
13. EPA 1977.
14. Marshall 1982a; Marshall 1982b; *New York Times,* 6 March 1982, p. 29, col. 3.
15. Marshall 1982a; *New York Times,* 6 March 1982, p. 29, col. 3.
16. Marshall 1982b.
17. Ibid.; *New York Times,* 19 February 1982, p. 18, col. 3.
18. Schwartz, J. 1984.
19. Koslowski, Nussbaum, and Kinney 1984; Nussbaum 1983.
20. Weissman 1984.
21. Cannon 1983b; Cockrell 1981.
22. Cannon 1983b.
23. Weissman 1984; Schwartz, J. 1984.
24. SCI, Inc. 1981.
25. Ibid., 2.
26. McGarity 1983b, 159.
27. Schwartz, J. 1981b, 2.
28. Nussbaum 1983; Koslowski, Nussbaum, and Kinney 1984.
29. Nussbaum 1983.
30. Marshall 1982b, 1,375; Schwartz, J. 1984; Weissman 1984; *Inside OMB,* 4 January 1982, p. 4.
31. Nussbaum 1983.
32. Environmental Strategies, Inc. 1982a, 4.
33. Silbergeld 1982, 252.
34. Schwartz, J. 1984.
35. *New York Times,* 18 April 1982, p. L21, col. 1.
36. Environmental Strategies, Inc. 1982a, 1–5.
37. Ibid., 53–4.
38. Ibid., 12–17.
39. Nussbaum 1983; Schwartz, J. 1984.
40. Cannon 1983b.
41. Schwartz, J. 1984; SCI, Inc. 1982a, 8.
42. SCI, Inc. 1982b.
43. Johnson 1982, 2.
44. Schwartz, J. 1984.
45. Weissman, 1984.
46. Ibid.; Nussbaum 1983.

47. EPA 1982e.
48. Ibid., 14.
49. Marshall, 1982a.
50. Schwartz, J. 1984.
51. Demuth 1982a.
52. Schwartz, J. 1984; *Washington Post,* 18 August 1982, p. A15, col. 2; *Inside OMB,* 13 August 1982, p. 5.
53. DeMuth 1982a.
54. EPA 1982c, 1982d.
55. Weissman 1984; Nussbaum 1983.
56. Weissman 1984.
57. *Inside OMB,* 22 October 1982, p. 4; *Inside EPA,* 22 October 1982, p. 3.
58. Weissman 1984.
59. Inside OMB, 8 October 1982, p. 7; Schwartz, J. 1984.
60. Schwartz, J. 1984; Koslowski, Nussbaum, and Kinney 1984.
61. EPA 1982b.
62. EPA 1982f.
63. Small Refiner Lead Phase-Down Task Force v. EPA, 705 F.2d 506 (D.C. Cir. 1983).
64. EPA 1983b.
65. *Washington Post,* 18 February 1990, p. B3, col. 1.
66. Small Refiners Lead Phase Down Task Force v. EPA, 705 F.2d 506 (D.C. Cir. 1983).

4. Getting the dust out of the air EPA's ambient air quality standard for particulate matter

1. 42 U.S. Code § 7,409(d)(1).
2. EPA 1984c.
3. Ibid.
4. Ibid., 10,425.
5. Ibid., 10,426.
6. *Inside EPA,* 25 September 1981, p. 1.
7. *Inside EPA,* 8 October 1982, p. 3.; Stolpman 1982.
8. Stolpman 1982; *Inside EPA,* 15 October 1982, p. 2.
9. Stolpman 1982.
10. Jennings 1983.
11. *BNA Environment Reporter,* 17 September 1982, p. 506.
12. *Inside EPA,* 17 September 1982, p. 1.
13. Ibid., 19 November 1982, p. 6.
14. Ibid., 1 October 1982, p. 2.
15. Ibid., 8 October 1982, p. 1.
16. CONSAD Research Corp. 1983.
17. *Inside EPA,* 21 January 1983, p. 6.
18. *BNA Environment Reporter,* 18 February 1983, p. 1,832.
19. *Inside EPA,* 11 March 1983, p. 11; *BNA Environment Reporter,* 4 March 1983, p. 2,011.
20. *Washington Post,* 24 March 1983, p. C19, col. 4.

21. *Inside EPA*, 25 February 1983, p. 9.
22. Ibid., 22 April 1983, p. 2.
23. *BNA Environment Reporter*, 4 November 1983, p. 1,248.
24. Ibid., 16 December 1983, p. 1,438.
25. American Petroleum Institute v. Costle, 665 F.2d 1,176, 1,185 (D.C. Cir. 1981), *cert. denied*, 102 S.Ct. 1737 (1982); Lead Industries Ass'n. v. EPA, 647 F.2d 1,130 (D.C. Cir.), *cert. denied*, 101 S.Ct. 621 (1980).
26. *Inside EPA*, 17 February 1984, p. 1.
27. *EPA* 1984b.
28. Ibid., 10,412, 10,421.
29. *EPA* 1984a.
30. Ibid., IV–2.
31. Ibid., IV–4.
32. Ibid., VI–3.
33. Ibid., ch. 6.
34. Jennings 1983.
35. American Iron and Steel Institute 1984.
36. American Mining Institute 1984.
37. Thomas 1986.
38. *Inside EPA*, 13 June 1986, p. 1; *BNA Environment Reporter*, 20 June 1986, p. 197.
39. *EPA* 1986, II–2.
40. Ibid., III–2.
41. Ibid. I–1 through I–2.
42. EPA 1987.
43. Basala 1984a.

5. Getting obstructions out of the driver's view: NHTSA's field of direct view regulations

1. NHTSA 1972.
2. NHTSA. Office of Program and Rulemaking Analysis 1981, 1–1.
3. NHTSA 1973.
4. Felrice 1984a.
5. NHTSA 1978.
6. Finkelstein 1977.
7. Ibid.
8. NHTSA. Acting Associate Administrator for Rulemaking 1978.
9. Ibid.
10. Felrice 1984a.
11. NHTSA. Assistant Chief Counsel for Rulemaking 1978.
12. Ibid.
13. NHTSA. Acting Associate Administrator for Plans and Programs 1978.
14. Ibid.
15. NHTSA. Associate Administrator for Research and Development 1979.
16. NHTSA. Associate Administrator for Rulemaking 1980a.
17. NHTSA. Associate Administrator for Rulemaking 1980b.
18. NHTSA 1981d.

19. Ibid.
20. NHTSA. Office of Program and Rulemaking Analysis 1981, VII–1.
21. Ibid., II–1.
22. Ibid.
23. Ibid.
24. Ibid., VII–2.
25. Ibid., IX–1.
26. Hanna, T. 1983; NHTSA 1981a.
27. NHTSA 1981b.
28. NHTSA. Associate Administrator for Rulemaking 1981.
29. Ibid.
30. Felrice 1984a.
31. NHTSA. Associate Administrator for Plans and Programs 1981.
32. Felrice 1984a; Blincoe 1984.
33. Felrice 1984a.
34. Center for Auto Safety 1981.
35. Felrice 1984a.
36. U.S. Congress. Senate 1966.
37. Felrice 1983.
38. Bollier and Claybrook 1986, ch. 8.

6. Getting the bone out of processed meat: FSIS's mechanically separated meat standard

1. FSIS 1981b, 39,283.
2. Ibid., 39,276–7.
3. Ibid., 39,276.
4. Food Safety and Quality Service 1976.
5. Community Nutrition Institute v. Butz, 420 F. Supp. 751 (D.D.C. 1976).
6. FSIS 1982b, 28,216.
7. Ibid. 1978.
8. Pacific Coast Meat Association 1978.
9. FSIS 1981b, 39,279.
10. Marketing Research Services 1981.
11. FSIS 1981b, 39,280.
12. Bullock and Ward 1981.
13. Food Chemical News, 19 January 1981, p. 55–6.
14. Neibrief 1984b.
15. *Washington Post,* 29 March 1981, p. B6, col. 1; Leonard 1984.
16. Houston 1984; Neibrief 1984a, 1984b; McCutcheon 1984.
17. Neibrief 1984b.
18. Updegraff 1984.
19. Ibid.
20. Houston 1984; Neibrief 1984b.
21. Houston 1984.
22. Ibid.
23. Neibrief 1984b.
24. McCutcheon 1984.
25. Neibrief 1984a; Updegraff 1984.

26. McCutcheon 1984.
27. FSIS 1981b, 39,310.
28. Neibrief 1984a.
29. Ibid. 1984b.
30. Leonard 1984; Updegraff 1984.
31. Leonard 1984.
32. Updegraff 1984.
33. FSIS 1981b, 39,284.
34. Ibid.
35. Ibid., 39,291.
36. Ibid., 39,282.
37. Ibid., 39,297.
38. Updegraff 1984.
39. McCutcheon 1982.
40. FSIS 1982a, 28,246.
41. Ibid., 28,226.
42. FSIS 1982a.
43. Community Nutrition Institute v. Block, 749 F.2d 50 (D.C. Cir. 1984).
44. Ibid., 51.
45. FSIS 1988.
46. *New York Times,* 21 September 1988, p. C8, col. 4.
47. *BNA Daily Report for Executives,* 16 September 1988.
48. FSIS 1981a.
49. Updegraff 1984.
50. Arthur D. Little, Inc. 1982.
51. Updegraff 1984; McCutcheon 1984; Lange 1984a.
52. Leonard 1984.
53. McCutcheon 1984.
54. Segal 1984.
55. McCutcheon 1984.
56. Updegraff 1984.

7. Getting information into hazardous workplaces: OSHA's hazard identification regulations

1. Viscusi 1983a; Hadden 1986; Bollier and Claybrook 1986, 154–6.
2. OSHA 1981a.
3. OSHA 1977.
4. Oelinick 1984.
5. Silk 1984.
6. OSHA 1981b.
7. *BNA Occupational Safety and Health Reporter,* 9 April 1981, p. 1,409.
8. *BNA Chemical Regulation Reporter,* 23 May 1980, p. 190; *BNA Occupational Safety and Health Reporter,* 19 February 1981, p. 1,274.
9. *BNA Occupational Safety and Health Reporter,* 28 May 1981, p. 1,560.
10. Silk 1984.
11. Ibid.; Spiller 1984; Wentzler 1984.
12. Wentzler 1984.

13. Ibid.
14. Connerton 1983.
15. OSHA 1982b.
16. Ibid., 12,123.
17. Ibid., 12,102.
18. Ibid., 12,121.
19. Ibid., 12,122.
20. OSHA 1982a, I–3.
21. Ibid., I–6.
22. Ibid., I–9.
23. Ibid., I–17.
24. Ibid., II–30.
25. Wentzler 1984.
26. OSHA 1982a, III–9.
27. Olenick 1984.
28. Wentzler 1984.
29. Interviewee requested anonymity for this observation.
30. OSHA 1982c, F–2.
31. OMB 1982b.
32. De Muth, N.d.
33. OMB 1982b, 2.
34. Ibid., 5.
35. Ibid., 7.
36. Ibid., 8.
37. Ibid., 10.
38. Donovan 1982, Attachment I.
39. Ibid., Attachment I, p. 2.
40. *BNA Occupational Safety and Health Reporter,* 25 March 1982, p. 844.
41. Ibid., p. 845; Connerton 1983.
42. Viscusi, N.d., 3.
43. Ibid., 4.
44. Ibid.
45. Ibid., 5.
46. Ibid., 8.
47. Ibid., 15–19.
48. *Inside OMB,* 26 March 1982, p. 1, 5.
49. *BNA Occupational Safety and Health Reporter,* 18 March 1982, p. 821.
50. Ibid. 25 March 1982, pp. 844, 845.
51. Ibid., p. 844.
52. Silk 1984.
53. Ibid.
54. Ibid.
55. Ibid.
56. OSHA 1983b, 53,342.
57. Ibid., 53,302.
58. Ibid., 53,343.
59. Ibid., 53,312.
60. OSHA 1983a.

61. Ibid., III–13.
62. Ibid., III–15.
63. Silk 1984.
64. United Steel Workers of America v. Auchter, 763 F.2d 728 (3rd Cir. 1985).
65. Ibid., 739.
66. Ibid.
67. OSHA 1987.
68. American Textile Manufacturers Institute v. Donovan, 452 U.S. 490 (1981).
69. Olenick 1984.
70. Silk 1984.
71. Interviewee requested anonymity for this observation.
72. Spiller 1984.
73. Ibid.

8. The virtues of regulatory analysis

1. Benveniste 1977, 15.
2. Lindblom 1968, 13; Meltsner 1976, 154; Edwards and Sharkansky 1978, 7; Shubert 1980; General Accounting Office 1982, 8.
3. Silberman 1980, 39; Gore and Dyson 1984, 4.
4. Lundberg 1964, 20.
5. Diver 1981, 396–9; Delong 1979, 329–38; Andrews 1982, 108–9.
6. Motor Vehicle Manufacturers Ass'n v. State Farm Mutual Casualty Co., 463 U.S. 29 (1983); Citizens to Preserve Overton Park, Inc. v. Volpe, 401 U.S. 402 (1971).
7. U.S. Congress. Senate 1981b, 43; Foster 1980, 959.
8. Rourke 1984, 174; Wildavsky 1979, 9–12.
9. Edwards and Sharkansky 1978, 118; Diver 1981, 415.
10. Hibbert 1984a.
11. Meltsner 1976, 132–33; Eads 1981b.
12. United States Regulatory Council 1981, 18.
13. See, e.g., Luken and Johnson 1984; Miller 1981b, 53; Stockman 1981; Janofsky 1981, 112; Council on Wage and Price Stability 1976.
14. Zeckhauser and Shepard 1981, 92–93.
15. Meltsner 1976, 154; Moore 1980, 24.
16. Luken 1985, 43–4; Berndt 1983.
17. Miller 1981b, 56.
18. Thaler 1983.
19. Sharp 1981; Verkuil 1982; Comment 1977.
20. General Accounting Office 1984.
21. Houston 1984.
22. Ibid.
23. Auchter 1983.
24. Small Business Administration 1985, I–4; idem 1983, I–6.
25. Cole and Tegeler 1980.
26. Small Business Administration 1985, 1.

27. Lange 1984.
28. Rourke 1984, 34–5; Lange 1984; Segal 1984b.
29. Verkuil 1982, 246.
30. Liroff 1982.
31. McGarity 1979.
32. Meltsner 1976, 124–5.
33. Luken 1985, 44–55.
34. Rung 1983.
35. Behn 1981, 199; Horowitz 1970; Seidman 1977.
36. Leoni 1964, 200–1.
37. Regens, Dietz, and Rycroft 1983, 142–3.
38. U.S. Congress. Senate 1978, 77. See also Lindblom 1968, 11.
39. Executive Order 12,291 § 2(b).
40. Lave 1981, 23–5; Mishan 1973; 11–13; Crooke and Herlevson 1982, 26; Luken and Johnson 1984, 3.
41. Andrews 1982, 128.
42. Claybrook 1983, 218; Kennedy, W. 1981.
43. Wentzler 1984; Eisner 1984; Kranidas 1984a; Hitchcock 1983; Goldin and Braslow 1984; Silk 1984; Sessions 1984; Stasikowski 1984; Ruhter 1984; Kuzmack 1984; Shapiro, M. 1984.
44. Hibbert 1984a; Segal 1984; Wentzler 1984.
45. Kennedy, W. 1981.
46. Andrews 1982, 120–1; Office of Management and Budget 1983, 1.
47. Miller 1981b, 10; Weidenbaum 1981, 56; Viscusi 1983, 160.
48. Lave 1981b, 255.
49. Grubb, Whittington, and Humphries 1984; Comment 1977, 1,139; Hopkins 1982, 1; Auchter 1983.

9. Limitations of regulatory analysis

1. Crampton and Berg 1973; Edwards and Sharkansky 1978, x; Banfield 1980, 13.
2. Simon 1945, 79.
3. Bauer 1968, 3–4; Lindblom 1959; Diver 1981; Rodgers 1981; Leman and Nelson 1981, 99.
4. Banfield 1980, 18; Tribe 1974, 1,329; Tribe 1972, 72; Kelman, S. 1981, 41; Sagoff, 1981.
5. Meltsner 1976, 270.
6. Broder and Morrall 1983, 246.
7. Banfield 1980, 12; Benveniste 1977, 17, 85, 87; Bauer 1968, 12; Silberman 1980, 37; Edwards and Sharkansky 1978, 113.
8. Storing 1980, 112; Leman and Nelson 1981, 100.
9. Edwards and Sharkansky 1978, 111; Benveniste 1977, 85.
10. Crampton and Berg 1973, 531.
11. Edwards and Sharkansky 1978, 10; Lange 1984; Hitchcock 1983.
12. Updegraff 1984.
13. Grubb and Whittington 1984.
14. Inside EPA, 11 October 1985, p. 1.

15. 40 Code of Federal Regulations § 1,502.13 (1984).
16. DuPuis 1984.
17. Hurter, Tolley, and Fabian 1982.
18. Latin 1983, 601; U.S. Regulatory Council 1981, 21–2.
19. EPA, 1985, 2–2.3.
20. U.S. Regulatory Council 1981, 23. Connerton and MacCarthy 1982, 11–12; Latin 1983, 601.
21. U.S. Regulatory Council 1981, 22; Litan and Nordhaus 1983, 14; Latin 1983, 601–2; Luken and Miller 1981, 1258.
22. American Textile Manufacturers Institute, Inc. v. Donovan, 452 U.S. 490, 525 n. 43 (1981). Bollier and Claybrook 1986, 148; *Wall Street Journal,* 18 June 1981, p. 21, col. 1.
23. Bollier and Claybrook 1986, 179, 202.
24. U.S. Regulatory Council 1981, 22–3; Merrill 1982, 113; Adkins and Martonick 1986.
25. Latin 1983, 605–7; Shapiro, M. 1984.
26. 44 U.S. Code §§ 3501 et seq.
27. U.S. Congress. House. Committee on the Judiciary 1982, 42–3. See also, Hurter, Tolley, and Fabian 1982, 93–4; Edwards and Sharkansky 1978, 190; Leone and Jackson 1981.
28. U.S. Regulatory Council 1981, 20; General Accounting Office 1984, 11; Latin 1983, 602–3.
29. Viscusi 1983a, 115–16; Vaupel 1981, 12.
30. Braeutigan 1981; Benveniste 1977, 213.
31. Securities and Exchange Commission 1981, 259; Commodity Futures Trading Commission 1981, 878.
32. Federal Communications Commission 1981, 280.
33. Sunstein 1981, 1,275.
34. McGarity 1983b; Weinberg 1972; Lovins 1977, 925; Merrill 1982, ch. 1; Office of Technology Assessment 1981, ch. 3.
35. Fischhoff 1977, 180–3; Yellin 1981.
36. 45 Code of Federal Regulations § 46 (1981); Dyck and Richardson 1967.
37. Alexander 1985; Gelpe and Tarlock 1977.
38. Cranor 1983, 382–96; Latin 1982, 361–4; McGarity 1979, 740–1.
39. Claybrook 1983; Dinman 1983.
40. Baram 1980, 483.
41. Merrill 1982, 58–71.
42. McGarity 1983b, 138; Merrill 1982, 74–82.
43. Conservation Foundation 1984; Cohen 1986.
44. Wilson, R. 1987; President's Commission on Three Mile Island 1979.
45. Costle 1982, 416–17, 420.
46. National Academy of Sciences 1981; Costle 1982, 416–17; Baram 1980, 482; Vaupel 1981, 8.
47. Latin 1983, 606–7.
48. Swartzman 1982, 61–3; Benveniste 1977, 148; Ferguson, 1981; Green and Waitzman 1979; English 1983; Ditlow 1983.
49. Merrill 1982, 116.

50. Breyer 1979, 572; U.S. Congress. Senate 1978, 84–5; Benveniste 1977, 21; *Washington Post,* 4 December 1984, p. G1, col. 1.
51. Connerton and MacCarthy 1982, 19–20.
52. Hammond and Adelman 1978, 119; Merrill Draft 1982, 112.
53. Cannon 1983b; Gass 1984.
54. Ruhter 1984; General Accounting Office 1981a.
55. U.S. Regulatory Council 1981, 21.
56. General Accounting Office 1981, 241.
57. Administrative Conference of the United States 1982.
58. Evans 1981; *BNA Environment Reporter,* 31 October 1981, p. 820; idem, 14 September 1984, p. 769.
59. EPA 1985; Evans 1981, ch. 3; Fischoff 1977, 180–3.
60. Merrill 1982, 89–92; EPA 1985, 2.2–3 through 2.2–4.
61. Comment 1981; Latin 1982, 370–71; Cranor 1983, 381.
62. Fischhoff 1977, 181–2.
63. Leman and Nelson 1981, 111–12.
64. Edwards and Sharkansky 1978, 170, 186; Banfield 1980, 26; Jenkins-Smith 1982, 90; Kranidas 1984; Beliles 1984; Lange 1984.
65. Lave 1982; U.S. Congress. Senate 1978, 77; Benveniste 1977, 6–7.
66. Lave 1982; Merrill 1982, 105–8.
67. Costle 1982, 418.
68. Bollier and Claybrook 1986, 7.
69. Tribe 1972, 96.
70. Mishan 1973, 109; Tribe 1974, 1,318–19; Andrews 1982, 118–19; Rhoads 1985.
71. Storing 1980, 111; U.S. Regulatory Council 1981, 48; Benveniste 1977, 17.
72. Rourke 1984, 175.
73. National Academy of Sciences 1975, 43–4; Hurter, Tolley and Fabian 1982, 92–9.
74. Goldin and Braslow 1984; Nichols 1984; Felrice 1983; Blincoe 1984.
75. Graham and Vaupel 1983, 176; General Accounting Office 1984.
76. Mishan 1973, 142; Lave 1982; Hurter, Tolley and Fabian 1982, 102–4; General Accounting Office 1984, 11–14.
77. I am indebted to Professor Howard Raiffa for this observation.
78. General Accounting Office 1984, 2, 11; Nichols and Zeckhauser 1986, 21, 24.
79. Comment 1981.
80. Hurter, Tolley and Fabian 1982, 103; Depart. of Transportation, 1982, 18–19. More sophisticated techniques such as "Monte-Carlo simulation" can add to the usefulness of sensitivity analysis. EPA 1985, ch. 6.3.3. But more sophisticated techniques, of course, come at greater expense.
81. 40 Code of Federal Regulations § 1,502.22(b); Save Our EcoSystems v. Clark, 747 F.2d 1,240, 1,244 (9th Cir. 1984). But see Robertson v. Methow Valley Citizens Council, 109 S.Ct. 1,835 (1989) (NEPA does not require "worst case" analysis).
82. Fisher 1984; U.S. Regulatory Council 1981, 22–3; EPA 1985, ch. 6.1.
83. Broder and Morrall 1983, 247; Lave 1982, 53–4; Nichols and Zeckhauser 1986; Zeckhauser and Shepard 1976, 36.

84. Meltsner 1976, 20, 269; Majone 1978, 207.
85. Meltsner 1976, 273; Vaupel 1981, 5.
86. Kranidas 1984a; Hitchcock 1983.
87. Cristofaro 1984; Edwards and Sharkansky 1978, 132.
88. U.S. Congress. Senate 1978, 84 (OSHA vinyl chloride standard); Claybrook 1983.
89. Connerton and MacCarthy 1982, 20. See also *BNA Occupational Safety and Health Reporter,* 24 March 1983, pp. 908, 909.
90. Safeer, Weil, and Harris 1983.
91. Goldin and Braslow 1984.
92. Sessions 1984. See also Storing 1980.
93. Hill 1983; Beliles 1984; Wolcott 1984; Fiorino 1983; Felrice 1983a.
94. Meltsner 1976, 293; Lindblom 1968, 108; Ajax 1984a; Wolcott 1984.
95. U.S. Regulatory Council 1981, 51; Council on Wage and Price Stability 1976, 77; Fiorino 1984; Kranidas 1984; Peak 1984; Shapiro, M. 1984.
96. Lindblom 1968, 14. See also, Meltsner 1976, 154; U.S. Regulatory Council 1981, 18.
97. U.S. Congress. House. Committee on Government Operations 1983, 1,178.
98. U.S. Congress. Senate 1981a, 90.
99. General Accounting Office 1982, Table 1.
100. Portney 1984; Miller 1977.
101. Bernstein 1983; Claybrook 1983; Grubb and Whittington 1984, 50; American Bar Association 1981.
102. General Accounting Office 1984, 29–30; Luken 1985b, 45–6; Gore, A. 1981.
103. *Inside EPA,* 4 July 1986, p. 1.
104. Claybrook 1983; Bernstein 1983; Gore A., 1981.
105. Diver 1981, 416–17; Merrill 1982, 105–6; Neely 1985; Kelman, S. 1981b, 33.
106. Andrews 1982, 108.
107. Tribe 1972; Kelman, S. 1982, 34. For comprehensive critiques of cost–benefit analysis as applied to health and environmental decisionmaking, see Green and Waitzman 1979; Self 1975.
108. Lave 1982, 24–5.
109. See, e.g., *BNA Environment Reporter,* 19 July 1985, p. 472 (quantifying damage due to acid rain).
110. General Accounting Office 1984, 2.
111. Arrow 1973.
112. National Academy of Sciences 1975, 39–42; Litan and Nordhaus 1983, 10–11.
113. Lave 1981, 40; U.S. Congress. Senate 1978, 83; Amy 1984, 577.
114. Bailey 1980, 15; Mendeloff 1979, 68–70; Smith 1976, 34–6; Zeckhauser and Shepard 1976, 91.
115. Bailey 1980, 15–16; Smith 1976, 34–6; Zeckhauser and Shepard 1976, 16.
116. Broder and Morrall 1983, 246.
117. *Inside OMB,* 1 February 1982, p. 1.
118. Westman 1977; Linnerooth 1975, 2–14.

119. Burness, et al. 1983.
120. Schultz, et al. 1983.
121. Turner 1979, 414; Heller 1976, 409.
122. Hurter, Tolley, and Fabian 1982, 92–3; Turner 1979.
123. Schultz, et al. 1983.
124. *New York Times,* 26 June 1985, p. 1, col. 2.
125. Vaupel 1981, 15; Sagoff 1986, 68–73; Connerton and MacCarthy 1982, 15.
126. Linnerooth 1975, 3–6.
127. Sagoff 1986, 69.
128. Linnerooth 1975, 12–14; Graham and Vaupel 1983.
129. Graham and Vaupel 1983, 177.
130. Linnerooth 1975, 14–16; Storr 1969.
131. Linnerooth 1975, 16.
132. Viscusi 1983a, 94–5; Sagoff 1986, 69; Schelling 1968, 127; Connerton and MacCarthy 1982, 16–17.
133. Schelling 1968, 148.
134. See Bailey 1980, 31; Viscusi 1983a, 94–6.
135. Viscusi 1983a, 99; Connerton and MacCarthy 1982, 16 (range from $170,000 to over $3 million); Graham and Vaupel 1983, 177 (range from $500,000 to $8 million for willingness to pay measured by questionnaires and from $300,000 to $3.5 million for willingness to pay as measured by risk premiums for hazardous jobs); EPA 1983, 11 ($400,000 to $7,000,000 for value of life determined from wage rate studies).
136. Department of Transportation 1982, App. 3, A–7.
137. *BNA Occupational Safety and Health Reporter,* 9 January 1986, p. 871.
138. Podberesky 1984a; *BNA Product Safety and Liability Reporter,* 20 November 1981, p. 804; EPA 1983, 11.
139. Ajax 1984a.
140. *Inside EPA,* 11 October 1985, p. 1.
141. Tolchin and Tolchin 1983, 129–33.
142. *U.S. News & World Report,* 19 September 1985, p. 58.
143. *BNA Product Safety and Liability Reporter,* 28 February 1986.
144. Ibid., 14 March 1986, p. 171.
145. *BNA Chemical Regulation Reporter,* 17 Sept. 1982, p. 737; Green and Waitzman 1979, 40.
146. General Accounting Office, 1984, 1; Edwards and Sharkansky 1978, 197; Rodgers 1980, 197–8; Baram 1980, 483; Massachusetts Institute of Technology Center of Policy Alternatives 1980, 19.
147. Connerton and MacCarthy 1982, 16; Settle and Weisbrod 1977, 28–31.
148. Vaupel 1981, 13–16; Adams 1974, 624.
149. Fischhoff 1977, 186; Settle and Weisbrod 1977, 32; Edwards and Sharkansky 1978, 188; Kelman, S. 1979; Sunstein 1981, 1276.
150. Settle and Weisbrod 1977, 31.
151. Okun 1975, 21; Kelman, S. 1982; Sagoff 1986, 72.
152. Kelman, S. 1982, 144.
153. Samuels 1979, 305.

154. Calabrese, G. 1979, 27.
155. Zeckhauser and Shepard 1976, 107–9.
156. Kennedy 1981, 388; National Legal Aid and Defender Association 1981; Kelman, S. 1982, 144–5.
157. McGarity 1983b, 172.
158. Kennedy 1981, 308; Heller 1976, 441–3.
159. Kelman, S. 1981b, 37–8.
160. Thaler 1981.
161. Hurter, Tolley, and Fabian 1982, 92. Vaupel 1981, 15; Kneese and D'Arge 1981; Harrison 1981, 186–7.
162. Pope 1979, 44–5.
163. Fried 1978; Tribe 1972, 88–9; Sagoff 1986, 32–8.
164. Tribe 1972; Schwartz, B. 1985.
165. Sagoff 1986, 88; Kelman, S. 1981b, 35.
166. Kelman, S. 1982, 145.
167. Sagoff 1986.
168. Bollier and Claybrook 1986, 200–1.
169. Ibid., 201.
170. Rhoads 1985, 815.
171. Baram 1980, 486; Rodgers 1980, 196; Grubb and Whittington 1984, 35–6; Merrill 1982, 118; Russell 1986.
172. McGarity 1983b, 188; Rodgers 1980, 198; Fisher 1984; National Academy of Sciences 1975, 42–3; Meltsner 1976, 147.
173. Heller 1976, 462; Massachusetts Institute of Technology Center for Policy Alternatives 1980, 18; Baram 1980, 486 n. 47; Rodgers 1980, 196.
174. Sagoff 1982, 300.
175. Russell 1986.
176. *New York Times*, 17 April 1985, p. B28, col. 1.
177. Kneese and Schultz 1975, 28; Freeman, Haveman, and Kneese 1973, 81; Rodgers 1980, 194; Mishan 1973, 13; Sagoff 1982, 290; Tribe 1972, 71; Mazur 1985.
178. Leman and Nelson 1981, 106; Verdier 1984, 430; Russell 1986; Vaupel 1981, 2.
179. Harrison 1981; 178–9.
180. Calabrese, E. 1978; National Academy of Sciences 1975, 42–3; Friedman 1981.
181. Vaupel 1981, 14–15.
182. Peskin 1978, 144.
183. Harrison 1981, 189.
184. Grubb and Whittington 1984, 31.
185. Goodin and Wilenski 1984, 512, 515.
186. Sagoff 1986, 68.
187. Costle 1982, 421; Leman 1982; Amy 1984, 587; Graham and Vaupel 1983, 177; Sagoff 1986, 73.
188. Amy 1984, 587; Tribe 1972, 85.
189. Weidenbaum 1981; National Association of Manufacturers 1981b; Business Round Table 1981b.

190. Lave 1981, 25; General Accounting Office 1984, 7; Crooke and Herlevson 1982, 26; Edwards and Sharkansky 1978, 198; Stokey and Zeckhauser 1978, 158; Turner 1979, 417; Connerton and MacCarthy 1982, 8.
191. Kasper 1977, 1014; Andrews 1982, 108–9.
192. Quoted in Harrison 1981, 213.
193. Nichols 1984; General Accounting Office 1984, 2; Connerton and MacCarthy 1982, 9.
194. Levin 1983; Lave 1981, 19–21; General Accounting Office 1984, 21; Costle 1982, 417; Luken and Johnson 1984, 3; Neely 1985, 497; EPA 1983a, 18–19.
195. Amy 1984, 581–2; Rein 1976, 29.
196. U.S. Regulatory Council 1981, 25; *Congress Watch* 1981, 420.
197. Raiffa 1968; Fischhoff 1977, 187.
198. Rourke 1984, 150–4; West 1983, 326, 331.
199. West 1983, 331; Leman and Nelson 1981, 102.
200. Rein 1976, ch. 2.
201. *Washington Post,* 22 March 1983, p. A1, col. 1; *Pesticide and Toxic Chemical News,* 5 October 1983, p. 5.
202. *Washington Post,* 5 May 1979, p. A1, col. 5.
203. Rein 1976, 17; Amy 1984, 577–8.
204. Tribe 1972, 105; see also West and Cooper 1985, 204.
205. Tribe 1972, 71.
206. Andrews 1982, 107, 123; Jenkins-Smith 1982, 90; Edwards and Sharkansky 1978, 9, 197; Meltsner 1976, 253; Nager 1982, 41; West 1983, 331, Connerton and MacCarthy 1982, 25; Amy 1984, 578.
207. Jennings 1983; Lange 1984; Felrice 1983a.
208. Sevin 1986.
209. *Inside EPA,* 30 September 1983, p. 1; idem, 23 March 1984, p. 1.
210. Hitchcock 1983; Felrice 1983a.
211. Grubb and Whittington 1984, 42; Meltsner 1976, 202.
212. General Accounting Office 1984, v.
213. Luken 1983; Campbell 1984; Bender 1984; Basala 1984a.
214. Sax 1973, 248; Crampton and Berg 1973, 516.
215. Caldwell 1982. This is true even though the Supreme Court has held that the courts may not substantively review agency actions for failure to comply with NEPA's substantive mandates. Strycker's Bay Neighborhood Council v. Karlen, 444 U.S. 223 (1980).
216. Fiorino 1983; Cristofaro 1984; Updegraff 1984; Leman and Nelson 1981, 105.
217. Vogt 1984; Beliles 1984; Cristofaro 1984; Peak 1984.
218. May 1986; Banfield 1980, 3; Forester 1984, 23, 27.
219. General Accounting Office 1984, 15.
220. Kelman, S. 100–7.
221. American Textile Manufacturers Inst. v. Donovan, 452 U.S. 490 (1981).
222. Lead Industries Association v. EPA, 647 F.2d 1,130 1,148–51 (D.C. Cir. 1980); American Petroleum Institute v. Costle, 609 F.2d 20 (D.C. Cir. 1979).

223. Cannon 1983a; Luken 1983; Nichols 1984; Basala 1984a.
224. *BNA Environment Reporter*, 2 May 1986, p. 4; Thomas 1986.
225. U.S. Regulatory Council 1981, 21.
226. Campbell 1984.
227. General Accounting Office 1984, 18; Blum 1980.
228. Verkuil 1982, 247–8; Fiorino 1983.
229. 40 Code of Federal Regulations § 1,502.14 (1984); Natural Resources Defense Council, Inc. v. Morton, 458 F.2d 827 (D.C. Cir. 1972).
230. Bonine and McGarity 1984, 147.
231. Eads 1981; Sunstein 1981, 1280.
232. Claybrook 1980; Ditlow 1983; Jordan 1983.
233. OMB 1982a; Leonard 1984.
234. Lash, Gillman and Sheridan 1984, p. 72; Hill 1983; Bernstein 1983; Leonard 1984.
235. U.S. Congress. House. Committee on the Judiciary 1983, 1182, 1595–7, 1615–18.
236. Executive Order No. 12,291 § 8(b). The Regulatory Flexibility Act apparently does not exempt deregulatory rules. Verkuil 1982, 243.
237. Ottinger 1983; Bingham 1983; Durkin 1983.
238. Zeisel 1981.
239. Cates 1979; Fredrickson 1982.

10. Regulatory analysis in the real world

1. Dewhurst 1983; Bender 1984.
2. Rosera 1984; Walker 1983.
3. Gessel 1983.
4. Anselmo 1983.
5. Anselmo 1983; Gessel 1984b.
6. Segal 1984b.
7. Hibbert 1984a.
8. FAA 1982; Safeer, Weil, and Harris 1983.
9. FAA 1981.
10. Ibid., i.
11. Safeer, Weil, and Harris 1983.
12. Ibid.
13. Faberman 1984; Hawkins 1984.
14. Kranidas 1984a.
15. Felrice 1983a; Blincoe 1984; Podberesky 1984a.
16. Kranidas 1984c.
17. Ibid. 1984a; Hitchcock 1983.
18. Steed and Jones 1983; Hitchcock 1983; Jones, E. 1984.
19. Krieger 1980; Eckhardt 1980.
20. Felrice 1983.
21. Eisner 1983.
22. Podberesky 1983.
23. Industrial Union Department, AFL-CIO v. American Petroleum Institute, 448 U.S. 607 (1980).

24. American Textile Manufacturers Institute v. Donovan, 452 U.S. 490 (1981).
25. Ibid.
26. Goldin and Braslow 1984; idem, 1985.
27. Beliles 1984; Goldin and Braslow 1985; Hanna F. 1984.
28. Goldin and Braslow 1984; Wentzler 1984; Silk 1984; Beliles 1984.
29. EPA 1983, 11.
30. Ibid. N.d.d, 2.
31. Basala 1986; Thomas 1986.
32. Fiorino 1983; General Accounting Office 1984, 25–7.
33. Sessions 1984.
34. EPA N.d.d, 3; Blum 1980; Wehe 1984.
35. EPA N.d.d, 3.
36. Luken 1984a, 3; Campbell 1984.
37. Sessions 1984; Stasikowski 1984; General Accounting Office 1984, 27–8.
38. Cristofaro 1986; Sessions 1984.
39. Sessions 1984; Cristofaro 1984; Basala 1984a; Thomas 1984a; Shapiro, M. 1984; Stasikowski 1984; Kuzmack 1984; Ruhter 1984; DuPuis 1984.
40. EPA N.d.b, I–6.
41. Sessions 1984; Stasikowski 1984; Ruhter 1984; Kuzmack 1984.
42. Sessions 1984; Shapiro, M. 1984.
43. DuPuis 1984; Shapiro, M. 1984.
44. Shapiro, M. 1984; Kuzmack 1984.
45. Basala 1984; Shapiro, M. 1984; Ruhter 1984; Vogt 1984; Kuzmack 1984; DuPuis 1984.
46. Kuzmack 1984.
47. Vogt 1984.
48. Kuzmack 1984.

11. Roles for the regulatory analyst

1. Updegraff 1984; Segal 1984a; Anselmo 1984a; Viscusi 1983b, 164.
2. Meltsner 1976, 11; Benveniste 1984.
3. Jenkins-Smith 1982.
4. Benveniste 1977; Meltsner 1976, 10–13.
5. Downs 1966.
6. Meltsner 1976, 16.
7. Jenkins-Smith 1982, 92–5.
8. Meltsner 1976, 261, 293; Benveniste 1977, 90.
9. Meltsner 1976, 55.
10. *Wall Street Journal*, 9 October 1981, p. 4, col. 2 (relating a decision-making session of the Federal Communications Commission).
11. Foster 1980; Behn 1981, 216; Horowitz 1970, 340; Benveniste 1977, 55.
12. Foster 1980, 960; Jones 1977, 177.
13. Benveniste 1977, 93; Meltsner 1976, 261, 293.
14. Goldin and Braslow 1985; Leman and Nelson 1981, 113–14; Behn 1981; Foster 1980.

15. Kelman, S. 1981a, 95–9.
16. Lindblom 1968, 33.
17. Edwards and Sharkansky 1978, 119, 248; Jenkins-Smith 1982, 89.
18. Meltsner 1976, 284.
19. Miller 1977, 14; Rourke 1984, 95.
20. Meltsner 1976, 7; Kelly 1984.
21. Benveniste 1977, 90.
22. Meltsner 1976, 210; Benveniste 1977, 159.
23. Meltsner 1976, 261; Nichols 1984; Silk 1984.
24. Thomas 1984a.
25. Ibid.; Silk 1984.

12. The hierarchical model

1. Vitiello 1983.
2. USDA 1983a, 4.
3. Barr 1983; Neibrief 1984b; Lange 1984.
4. Meyerson 1984; Bjorlie 1984; Dewhurst 1983.
5. Clemans 1984a.
6. Bender 1984.
7. Toomey 1984.
8. 5 U.S. Code §§ 556, 557 (1982).
9. Toomey 1983.
10. Borovies 1984.
11. Toomey 1983.
12. Meyerson 1984; Toomey 1983.
13. *Inside the Administration*, 7 September 1984, p. 3.
14. Walker 1983, 1984a.
15. Rosera 1984.
16. Walker 1984a.
17. Bjorlie 1983; Walker 1983.
18. Rosera 1984; Walker 1984b.
19. Rosera 1984.
20. Walker 1984b.
21. Ibid. 1984a.
22. Rosera 1984; Walker 1984a.
23. Edwards and Sharkansky 1978, 133.

13. The outside advisor model

1. Anselmo 1983.
2. Gessel 1984a.
3. Anselmo 1984a; Gessel Interview, 1983.
4. Anselmo 1984a.
5. Gessel 1983; Anselmo Interview, 1983.
6. Gessel 1984a; Anselmo Interview, 1984a.
7. Anselmo 1984b.
8. APHIS, Directive 114.3.

9. Anselmo 1984a.
10. Anselmo 1984a.
11. Anselmo 1983.
12. Gessel 1984b.
13. Gessel 1984b.
14. Gessel 1983; Gessel 1984b.
15. Anselmo 1983; Anselmo 1984b.
16. Anselmo 1983.
17. Anselmo 1983.
18. Gradick 1984.
19. Gessel 1983.
20. Safeer, Weil & Harris 1983.
21. Faberman 1984.
22. Safeer, Weil, & Harris 1983.
23. Faberman 1984.
24. Murdock & Faberman 1983; Faberman 1984.
25. Podberesky 1983; Safeer, Weil & Harris 1983.
26. Faberman 1984; Hawkins 1984.
27. FAA 1982.
28. Safeer, Weil & Harris 1983.
29. Hawkins 1984; Safeer, Weil & Harris 1983.
30. Safeer, Weil & Harris 1983.
31. Hawkins 1984.
32. Murdock and Faberman 1983.
33. Faberman 1984; Hawkins 1984.
34. Safeer, Weil & Harris 1983.
35. Ibid.
36. Murdock & Faberman 1983.
37. Hawkins 1984.
38. Faberman 1984.

14. The team model

1. See, 21 U.S. Code §§ 451 et seq. and 601 et seq. (1982).
2. Segal 1984.
3. Glavin 1986; Segal 1986.
4. Hibbert 1984a.
5. Lange 1984b.
6. Hibbert 1984a; FSIS 1985.
7. Lange 1984; McCutcheon 1984.
8. USDA 1983a.
9. Houston 1984.
10. Ibid.
11. McCutcheon 1984; Lange 1984.
12. Houston 1984.
13. FSIS 1985.
14. Glavin 1986; Segal 1986.
15. Hibbert 1984a.

16. Glavin 1986.
17. Segal 1984a.
18. Hibbert 1984a.
19. Segal 1984a.
20. McCutcheon 1984; Segal 1984a.
21. Glavin 1986.
22. Segal 1986.
23. Hibbert 1984a.
24. Glavin 1986; Segal 1986.
25. Hibbert 1984b.
26. McCutcheon 1984.
27. Ibid.
28. Houston 1984.
29. Occupational Safety and Health Act of 1970, 29 U.S. Code § 651 et seq; Rothstein 1983; Ashford 1976; Mendeloff 1979.
30. McGarity 1983a.
31. Atamik 1984.
32. Weber 1983; Goldin and Braslow 1984.
33. Connerton 1983; R. Shapiro 1984.
34. Department of Labor 1981a, 1981b, 1982.
35. OSHA 1982.
36. Gordon 1986; Wrenn 1986.
37. Wrenn 1986.
38. Wrenn 1986; Gordon 1986.
39. OSHA 1982.
40. Ibid., III–4, III–8.
41. Ibid., V–7.
42. Ibid., V–6.
43. Strobel 1984.
44. Beliles 1984.
45. OSHA 1982, III–15.
46. Gordon 1986; B. White 1986.
47. Frodyma 1986.
48. White, B. 1986.
49. Silk 1984; F. White 1986; Adkins and Martonik 1986.
50. White, F. 1986.
51. Sevin 1986; Stein 1986; Silk 1986; Harwood 1986; F. White 1986; B. White 1986; Adkins and Martonik 1986; Gordon 1986.
52. See, e.g., Organized Migrants in Community Action v. Brennan, 520 F.2d 1,161 (D.C. Cir. 1975).
53. Administrative Conference of the United States 1987.
54. Department of Labor 1981.
55. Beliles 1984; Strobel 1984.
56. Adkins and Martonik 1986; Sevin 1986; Harwood 1986.
57. Harwood 1986.
58. Beliles 1984; Gass 1984a; Goldin and Braslow 1984; Weber 1983.
59. Frodyma 1986.
60. Gass 1984a; Stein 1986; Harwood 1986.
61. Gass 1984a.

62. Ibid.
63. Harwood 1986; Stein 1986.
64. Gass 1984a.
65. Goldin and Braslow 1984.
66. American Textile Manufacturers Institute v. Donovan, 452 U.S. 490 (1981).
67. Adkins and Martonik 1986.
68. Gass 1984a; Silk 1986; Beliles 1984; F. Hanna 1984; Weber 1983.
69. Goldin and Braslow 1984; Wentzler 1984.
70. Gass 1984a; Beliles 1984; Wentzler 1984.
71. Silk 1986; Gass 1984a.
72. Goldin and Braslow 1984; Gordon 1986.
73. Goldin and Braslow 1984; Gass 1984a; Adkins and Martonik 1986; Gordon 1986.
74. Gass 1984a; Henshel 1986.
75. Beliles 1984; Gass 1984a; Goldin and Braslow 1984.
76. Stein 1986; Harwood 1986; Adkins and Martonik 1986.
77. Burkley 1983.
78. Goldin and Braslow 1985.
79. Beliles 1984.
80. Goldin and Braslow 1984; Strobel 1984.
81. Beliles 1984; Gordon 1984.
82. Goldin and Braslow 1984; Stein 1986.
83. Silk 1986.
84. Beliles 1984; Wentzler 1984.
85. Gass 1984a.
86. Goldin and Braslow 1984; Wentzler 1984.
87. Braslow 1986.
88. Silk 1984; Beliles 1984; Gass 1984a; Harwood 1986; Goldin and Braslow 1984.
89. Wentzler 1984; Beliles 1984.
90. Silk 1984; Beliles 1984; Gass 1984a.
91. Silk 1984.
92. Harwood 1986.
93. Goldin and Braslow 1984; Frodyma 1986; Henshel 1986.
94. Goldin and Braslow 1984.
95. Gass 1984a; Harwood 1986.
96. Gass 1984a.
97. Braslow 1986.
98. Sevin 1986.
99. Meltsner 1976, 243.
100. Janis 1972, 35–6.
101. Edwards and Sharkansky 1978, 128.

15. The adversarial model

1. National Traffic Motor Vehicle Safety Act of 1966, 15 U.S. Codes §§ 1,381 et seq. (1982).
2. 15 U.S. Code §§ 1,901 et seq. (1982).

3. Hitchcock 1984.
4. Ibid.
5. Felrice 1983; Kranidas 1984a; Berndt 1983.
6. Kranidas 1984a.
7. Steed and Jones 1983.
8. Felrice 1983; Kranidas 1984a.
9. NHTSA 1977, Attachment 1, p. 1.
10. Hitchcock 1983.
11. Felrice 1986.
12. Kranidas 1984b.
13. Blincoe 1984; Kranidas 1984b.
14. Hitchcock 1984; Steed and Jones 1983.
15. NHTSA 1977, Attachment 2, p. 2; Hitchcock 1983.
16. Hitchcock 1983.
17. Felrice 1984.
18. Ibid.
19. Steed and Jones 1983; Hitchcock 1983.
20. Steed and Jones 1983; Felrice 1984; Hitchcock 1983.
21. Kranidas 1984b.
22. Kranidas 1984a; Blincoe 1984.
23. Blincoe 1984; Warlick 1984.
24. Felrice 1983b; Kranidas 1984b; Steed and Jones 1983.
25. Felrice 1984a; Hitchcock 1983; Kranidas 1984a; Blincoe 1984; Steed
    and Jones 1983.
26. Blincoe 1984.
27. Blincoe 1984; Felrice 1984; Jones, E. 1984; Kranidas 1984a; Kranidas
    1984c.
28. Felrice 1984a; Kranidas 1984b; Claybrook 1980.
29. Kranidas 1984a; Felrice 1984a; Felrice 1983; Steed and Jones 1983;
    Claybrook 1980.
30. Blincoe 1984; Kranidas 1984b.
31. Steed and Jones 1983; Claybrook 1980.
32. Steed and Jones 1983; Felrice 1983a; Kranidas 1984a.
33. Steed and Jones 1983.
34. Eisner and Podberesky 1984.
35. Felrice 1983a; Felrice 1984b.
36. NHTSA 1977.
37. Ibid.
38. Felrice 1984.
39. Ibid. 1983a.
40. Ibid.; Steed and Jones 1983.
41. Steed and Jones, 1983.
42. Felrice 1986; Felrice 1983a.
43. Blincoe 1984; Kranidas 1984a.
44. Felrice 1983a; Steed and Jones 1983.
45. Felrice 1983a; Steed and Jones 1983.
46. Felrice 1983a.
47. Ibid.

48. Blincoe 1984.
49. Edwards and Sharkansky 1978, 129.
50. Berndt 1983.
51. Kranidas 1984a.
52. Hitchcock 1983.

16. A hybrid model

1. National Environmental Policy Act of 1969, 42 U.S. Code § 4,321 et seq. (1982); Clean Air Act, 42 U.S. Code § 7,401 et seq. (1982); Federal Water Pollution Control Act, 33 U.S. Code § 1,251 et seq. (1982); Resource Conservation and Recovery Act of 1976, 42 U.S. Code § 6,901 et seq. (1982); Toxic Substances Control Act, 15 U.S. Code § 2,601 et seq. (1982); Federal Insecticide, Fungicide, and Rodenticide Act, 7 U.S. Code § 136 et seq. (1982); Safe Drinking Water Act, 42 U.S. Code § 300F et seq. (1982); and Comprehensive Environmental Response, Compensation, and Liability Act of 1980, 42 U.S. Code § 9,601 et seq. (1982).
2. Sheehan 1986.
3. Kelly 1984.
4. Fiorino 1984a.
5. Sessions 1984; Luken 1984; Cristofaro 1984.
6. Jennings 1983.
7. Fiorino 1983.
8. Fiorino 1983, 1986; Kelly 1984.
9. 42 U.S. Code §§ 7,408(a)(1), 7,409(d)(1) (1982)
10. Thomas 1986; Basala 1984a; General Accounting Office 1984, 15–16; EPA 1984b, 10,409. See American Petroleum Institute v. Costle, 665 F.2d 1176, 1185 (D.C. Cir. 1981), cert. denied, 192 S. Ct. 1737 (1982); Lead Industries Association v. EPA, 647 F.2d 1130 (D.C. Cir.), cert. denied, 101 S. Ct. 621 (1980).
11. Thomas 1986.
12. 42 U.S. Code § 7,411 (1982); Ajax 1984a.
13. Ibid. § 7,412(b)(1)(B) (1982).
14. McGarity 1983b, 202.
15. Thomas 1984b, 1986.
16. Basala 1984b; Wehe 1984.
17. Stasikowski 1984.
18. Shapiro, M. 1984.
19. 42 U.S. Code §§ 6,921–4 (1982).
20. Ibid. § 6,925 (1982).
21. Ruhter 1984; Tonetti 1984. See Illinois v. Gorsuch, 530 F. Supp. 340 (D.D.C. 1981).
22. Ruhter 1984.
23. 42 U.S. Code §§ 300f–300g (1982).
24. Kuzmack 1986, 1984; Vogt 1984.
25. Luttner 1986; EPA N.d.c., V–4.
26. DuPuis 1984.

27. Alm 1984b, 3.
28. Shapiro, M. 1984; Kuzmack 1984; Tonetti 1984; Ajax 1984a; Wehe 1984.
29. Shapiro, M. 1984; Basala 1984a; Kuzmack 1984.
30. Alm 1984b, 4–5.
31. Ibid., 4.
32. Kuzmack 1984; Vogt 1984; Shapiro, M. 1984; Stasikowski 1984; Basala 1984a; Ajax 1984a; Cristofaro 1984.
33. Alm 1983.
34. Sessions 1984; Cristofaro 1984; Fiorino 1984a.
35. Alm 1983, 2.
36. Wolcott 1984.
37. Wolcott 1984; Fiorino 1984a.
38. Ruhter 1984; Shapiro, M. 1984; Kuzmack 1984.
39. Vogt 1984; Kuzmack 1984.
40. Stasikowski 1984.
41. Ruhter 1984.
42. Basala 1984a.
43. O'Connor 1984; Basala 1984a; Thomas 1984b.
44. Alm 1984b.
45. Basala 1984a; Shapiro, M. 1984; Ruhter 1984. One exception is the Office of Drinking Water, whose regulatory analysts rarely attend work group meetings. Kuzmack 1984.
46. Alm 1984, 4.
47. Cristofaro 1984.
48. Ibid.; Ajax 1984a; DuPuis 1984.
49. Kuzmack 1984.
50. Sessions 1984.
51. Alm 1984a, 5–6.
52. Fiorino 1983; Ruhter 1984.
53. Tonetti 1984; Ruhter 1984.
54. Shapiro, M. 1984; Ruhter 1984; Kuzmack 1984.
55. Shapiro, M. 1984; Tonetti 1984; Ruhter 1984.
56. Basala 1984a.
57. Cristofaro 1984; Napolitano 1984; Nichols 1984.
58. Cristofaro 1984; Sessions 1984.
59. Cristofaro 1984; Sessions 1984.
60. Sessions 1984; Morgenstern 1986; Campbell 1986; *Inside EPA,* 8 June 1984, p 11. (Detailing dispute between policy office and program office on options for reducing airborne exposure to acrylonitrile.)
61. Sessions 1984.
62. Campbell 1986.
63. Alm 1984b, 7.
64. Fiorino 1983; Wolcott 1984.
65. Alm 1984b, 7.
66. Ruhter 1984; Stasikowski 1984; Vogt 1984; Kuzmack 1984.
67. Alm 1984b, 8.
68. Fiorino 1983; Cristofaro 1984; Sessions 1984; Napolitano 1984; Ajax 1984a; Shapiro, M. 1984; Ruhter 1984.

69. Sessions 1984; Ajax 1984a; Ruhter 1984; Campbell 1986; Luttner 1986; Ruhter 1986.
70. Sessions 1984.
71. Cristofaro 1984.
72. Alm 1984b, 9.
73. DuPuis 1984; Cristofaro 1986.
74. Alm 1984b, 8–9.
75. Fiorino 1983; Ajax 1984a.
76. Luken 1984b.
77. Cristofaro 1984.
78. EPA 1983, 20.
79. Fiorino 1983; Thomas 1984a; Kuzmack 1984; Cristofaro 1984; Ruhter 1984.
80. Stasikowski 1984; Shapiro, M. 1984; Ruhter 1984; Thomas 1984a.
81. Ajax 1984a; Shapiro, M. 1984; Stasikowski 1984; Sessions 1984.
82. Sessions 1984; DuPuis 1984; Cannon 1983b; Kuzmack 1984; Cristofaro 1984; Fiorino 1983; Wolcott 1984.
83. General Accounting Office 1984, 15–16; Cristofaro 1984; Thomas 1986.
84. EPA 1984b, 10,421; Basala 1986; Campbell 1984; Thomas 1986.
85. Luken 1984a; Nichols 1984.
86. Thomas 1986, 1984a.
87. Basala 1986; Thomas 1986.
88. Wehe 1984; EPA N.d.b., II–15.
89. EPA N.d.b., II–16.
90. Basala 1984a.
91. Ajax 1984a, 1984b.
92. Wehe 1984.
93. Stasikowski 1984; Shapiro, M. 1984.
94. Ruhter 1984.
95. Tonetti 1984.
96. Morgenstern 1986.
97. Campbell 1986.
98. Tonetti 1984.
99. Vogt 1984; Kuzmack 1984.
100. DuPuis 1984.
101. Luttner 1986.
102. Sessions 1984.
103. Luken 1984a.
104. Cristofaro 1986.
105. EPA 1983a.
106. Luken 1983; Jennings 1983; Sessions 1984.
107. Basala 1984a; Sessions 1984; Wolcott 1984.
108. Fiorino 1983; Wolcott 1984; Jennings 1983.
109. Tonetti 1984; Ajax 1984a; Stasikowski 1984; Vogt 1984.
110. Stasikowski 1984; Tonetti 1984.
111. Ajax 1984a; Kuzmack 1984; Tonetti 1984; Cristofaro 1984; Nichols 1984.
112. Fiorino 1983; Cannon 1983b; Campbell 1984; Wolcott 1984.

113. Wolcott 1984; Stasikowski 1984; Fiorino 1983.
114. Campbell 1984.
115. Ibid.
116. Ibid.; Wolcott 1984; Cannon 1983a.
117. See generally *BNA Environment Reporter*, 26 July 1985, p. 503. For more on the "bubble" policy, see Doniger 1984; Meidinger 1985.
118. Campbell 1984; Sessions 1984; Wolcott 1984.
119. *Inside EPA*, 27 April 1984, p. 1.
120. *BNA Chemical Regulation Reporter*, 12 June 1987, p. 565.
121. Campbell 1984.
122. Wolcott 1984.
123. Costle 1982.
124. Morgenstern 1986.
125. Campbell 1986.
126. Ibid.
127. Jennings 1986; Campbell 1986.
128. Wolcott 1984; Campbell 1986.
129. Campbell 1986.
130. Wolcott 1984.
131. Ibid.; Fiorino 1983.
132. Stasikowski 1984; Ruhter 1986.
133. Campbell 1986; Ruhter 1986.
134. Campbell 1986; Morgenstern 1986.

18. Office of Management and Budget review of regulatory analysis

1. Executive Order 12,291 § 6.
2. West and Cooper 1985.
3. *BNA Environment Reporter*, 7 March 1986, p. 2,050.
4. See, e.g., *Washington Post*, 11 November 1984, p. A15, col. 3; *BNA Occupational Safety and Health Reporter*, 4 August 1983, p. 211; U.S. Congress. House. Committee on Government Operations 1982.
5. Fraas 1984.
6. *BNA Chemical Regulation Reporter*, 22 February 1985, p. 1,380; *Pesticide and Toxic Chemical News*, 20 February 1985, p. 39.
7. Podberesky 1983.
8. General Accounting Office 1989, App. II.
9. Fraas 1984.
10. *Inside the Administration*, 12 September 1985, p. 4 (statement of EPA Administrator Lee Thomas).
11. Hopkins 1983. See also West and Cooper 1985, 201–3.
12. Coad 1983.
13. Fraas 1984.
14. Morrall 1983.
15. *Wall Street Journal*, 24 October 1984, p. 14, col. 2; *U.S. News & World Report*, 16 September 1985, p. 58.
16. *Inside EPA*, 7 June 1985, p. 1.

17. *BNA Daily Report for Executives*, 5 June 1989.
18. U.S. Congress. House Committee on Energy and Commerce 1985, 4.
19. McGarity 1979.
20. *BNA Environment Reporter*, 14 January 1983, p. 1,574.
21. *Inside EPA*, 8 April 1983, p.1; *Inside the Administration*, 17 June 1983, p. 14.
22. *Inside EPA*, 14 September 1984, p. 1.
23. *Inside the Administration*, 4 January 1984, p. 1.
24. *Inside EPA*, 24 August 1984, p. 1.
25. Ibid., 20 June 1986, p. 1.
26. Ibid., 11 July 1986, p. 1.
27. *Pesticide and Toxic Chemical News*, 13 August 1986, p. 31.
28. *BNA Environment Reporter*, 29 August 1986, p. 627.
29. *Inside EPA*, 24 April 1981, p. 1–2.
30. Ibid., 13 January 1984, p. 7; *Inside EPA*, 22 June 1984, p. 1; *BNA Daily Report for Executives*, 5 January 1989.
31. *BNA Environment Reporter*, 18 August 1989, p. 685.
32. Ibid. (statement of Sheldon J. Plager, Director of OIRA).
33. Stanfield 1986a, 391; *Inside EPA*, 28 March 1986, p. 11; *BNA Environment Reporter*, 4 April 1986, p. 2,158.
34. *BNA Daily Report for Executives*, 8 May 1989.
35. Sun 1985; Kosterlitz 1985, 1,568.
36. OMB 1986; *BNA Occupational Safety and Health Reporter*, 1 August 1985, p. 207.
37. *BNA Environment Reporter*, 29 August 1986, p. 627.
38. *Pesticide and Toxic Chemical News*, 21 December 1983, p. 4.
39. *Inside EPA*, 12 October 1984, p. 11; Sessions 1984.
40. Grubb and Whittington 1984.
41. Cutler and Johnson 1975, 1,406; Gray 1982, 863; Shane 1981, 1,245; Bruff 1979, 454–6.
42. *BNA Daily Report for Executives*, 16 December 1988.
43. Strauss and Sunstein 1986, 189; De Muth and Ginsburg 1986.
44. Bruff 1979, 462.
45. Wolcott 1984; Sessions 1984.
46. Eads and Fix 1984, ch. 5; De Muth and Ginsburg 1986, 1,075–80; Pierce 1985, 507–8; Strauss and Sunstein 1986, 206–7.
47. Bruff 1979, 454, 461–2; Cutler and Johnson 1975, 1,405–6, 1,411; Harter 1986, 562–3; Byse 1977, 164; Pierce 1985, 520–1; Strauss and Sunstein 1986, 190.
48. Bruff 1979, 455; Cutler and Johnson 1975, 1,405–6; DeMuth and Ginsburg 1986, 1,080–2.
49. Bruff 1979, 456; West and Cooper 1985, 206.
50. Morrison 1986, 1070.
51. Thomas 1984a; Ruhter 1984; Kuzmack 1984; Cannon 1983b; Luken 1983; Ajax 1984a; Stasikowski 1984; Vogt 1984.
52. Kuzmak 1984.
53. *Washington Post National Weekly Edition*, 21 April 1986, p. 33, col. 1; *BNA Product Safety and Liability Reporter*, 14 February 1986, p. 108; *In-*

side the Administration, 16 May 1985, p. 5; Washington Post National Weekly Edition, 28 July 1986, p. 31.

54. Harwood 1986. See also Washington Post National Weekly Edition, 28 July 1986, p. 31.
55. Pesticide and Toxic Chemical News, 18 June 1986, p. 34; Inside EPA, 20 June 1986, p. 1. See also Olson 1984, 14; Nager 1982, 41.
56. Goldin and Braslow 1984; Hibbert 1984b.
57. Eisner 1983.
58. Hopkins 1983.
59. Olson 1984, 6; Houck 1987, 542–3.
60. Washington Post, 11 November 1984, p. A15, col. 3; Washington Post, 1 August 1983, p. A12, col. 1; BNA Occupational Safety and Health Reporter, 15 February 1984, p. 993; BNA Occupational Safety and Health Reporter, 4 November 1982, p. 438; U.S. Congress. House Committee on the Judiciary 1982.
61. Wolcott 1984; Cristofaro 1984; Stasikowski 1984; Vogt 1984; Tonetti 1984; Kuzmack 1984; Luken 1983.
62. BNA Environment Reporter, 9 December 1988, p. 1,617.
63. Inside OMB, 16 July 1982, p. 8; Inside EPA, 22 March 1985, p. 12; Inside EPA, 20 April 1984, p. 4.
64. Cristofaro 1984; Vogt 1984.
65. Inside the Administration, 7 September, 1984, p. 3.
66. Houck 1987, 542–3.
67. Inside EPA, 12 October 1984, p. 9.
68. New York Times, 8 March 1985, p. 10, col. 2; Inside EPA, 8 March 1985, p. 1; Wall Street Journal, 11 March 1985, p. 8, col. 3.
69. Inside the Administration, 23 September 1983, p. 8.
70. Natural Resources Defense Council, Inc. v. Ruckelshaus, 14 E.L.R. 20,817 (1984).
71. Environmental Defense Fund, Inc. v. Thomas, 627 F. Supp. 566 (D.D.C. 1986).
72. Washington Post, 4 July 1989, p. A21, col. 1; BNA Daily Report for Executives, 25 May 1989.
73. Environmental Forum, July/August, 1989, p. 27 (interview with Sheldon J. Plager).
74. Ibid.; Washington Post, 4 July 1989, p. A21 col. 1.
75. Environmental Forum, July/August, 1989, p. 30 (interview with Sheldon J. Plager).
76. 44 U.S. Code § 3,512.
77. Bollier and Claybrook 1986, 196; Holden 1984, 934.
78. Wall Street Journal, 5 February 1984, p. 21, col. 4; BNA Occupational Safety and Health Reporter, 24 September 1986, p. 422.
79. BNA Occupational Safety and Health Reporter, 16 January 1986, p. 884 (dioxin); BNA Chemical Regulation Reporter, 5 August 1983, p. 662 (formaldehyde); Inside the Administration, 21 September 1984, p. 4 (methylene chloride); BNA Environment Reporter, 6 December 1985, p. 1519 (methylene chloride).
80. BNA Chemical Regulation Reporter, 5 August 1983, pp. 662, 663.

81. Bollier and Claybrook 1986, 196; Holden 1984; Morrison 1984, 220.
82. *Washington Post,* 4 January 1984, p. A15, col. 3 (statement of Robert Bedell).
83. *The Washington Times,* 26 October 1989, p. D5.
84. Luken 1983; General Accounting Office 1982, 29–30.
85. *Inside the Administration,* 8 March 1985, p. 3.
86. *BNA Environment Reporter,* 4 April 1986, p. 2,158; *Inside EPA,* 18 April 1986, pp. 5, 6.
87. *Wall Street Journal,* 5 June 1985, p. 64, col. 1.
88. *Inside EPA,* 15 March 1985, p. 9.
89. Morrison 1986, 1,070; Eads and Fix 1984, 111; Houck 1987, 21; Olson 1984, 14.
90. Verkuil 1980, 958–60; Strauss 1984, 595.
91. *Inside OMB,* 10 September 1982, p. 9.
92. *Inside EPA,* 4 May 1984, p. 4.
93. Verkuil 1980, 255.
94. McGarity 1987.
95. Olson 1984, 61; Eads and Fix 1984, 137; West and Cooper 1985, 202.
96. OMB 1989b, 537.
97. Miller 1981b.
98. *Washington Post,* 10 July 1981, p. A21, col. 2 (quoting OIRA official Jim Tozzi).
99. *Washington Post,* 28 September 1983, p. A1, col. 2 (quoting former EPA official John E. Daniel).
100. *Washington Post,* 26 November 1982, p. A15, col. 2.
101. *Inside the Administration,* 15 May 1986, p. 6–7.
102. Houck 1987, 540; Olson 1984, 42–50.
103. Sessions 1984; Ajax 1984a; Ruhter 1984; Cannon 1983b; Luken 1983; Thomas 1984a.
104. Ajax 1984a; Stasikowski 1984.
105. Lash, Gillman, Sheridan 1984, 72; Houck 1987, 542–3; Olson 1984, 64–73.
106. Morrall 1983.
107. Ibid.; Hopkins 1983.
108. Fraas 1983.
109. Ibid.; *Inside EPA,* 28 May 1982, p. 3; idem, 11 June 1982, p. 1.
110. Lash, Gillman, and Sheridan 1984; Tolchin and Tolchin 1983, ch. 2; Morrison 1986, 1,067; Olson 1984.
111. Olson 1984, 14; Strauss 1984, 640–66.
112. Ashford 1976, 543.
113. *Washington Post,* 5 May 1971, p. A1, col. 5.
114. Olson 1984, 57; Eads and Fix 1984, 137; Houck 1987, 542–3; U.S. Congress. Senate Committee on Environmental and Public Works 1986.
115. Hopkins 1983.
116. Olson 1984, 48; Houck 1987, 543; *Inside EPA,* 4 May 1984, p. 4.
117. Public Citizen Health Research Group v. Tyson, 796 F.2d 1,479, 1,507 (D.C. Cir. 1986).
118. *Washington Post,* 26 November 1982, p. A15, col. 2.

119. *Inside OMB*, 8 October 1982, p. 7.
120. Rosenfield 1987.
121. *Inside the Administration*, 12 April 1985, p. 1.
122. Ibid., 22 August 1985, p. 8; idem, 1 November 1985; *New York Times*, 20 November 1985.
123. Environmental Defense Fund v. Thomas, 627 F. Supp. 566 (D.D.C. 1985).
124. *Inside EPA*, 31 January 1986, p. 5; *BNA Environment Reporter*, 31 January 1986, p. 1,807.
125. Gramm 1986.
126. *BNA Occupational Safety and Health Reporter*, 17 July 1986, p. 148; *Inside EPA*, 25 July 1986, p. 14; *Inside the Administration*, 7 August 1986, p. 7; *BNA Occupational Safety and Health Reporter*, 7 August 1986, p. 261; *Inside the Administration*, 14 August 1986, p. 3.
127. *Inside the Administration*, 3 July 1986, p. 2; *BNA Environment Reporter*, 8 August 1986, p. 533.
128. General Accounting Office 1988; *Inside EPA*, 3 June 1988, p. 13.
129. *BNA Antitrust and Trade Regulation Reporter*, 12 October 1989, p. 504.
130. *BNA Daily Report for Executives*, 26 July 1989.
131. *BNA Washington Insider*, 28 November 1989.
132. West and Cooper 1985, 205; Houck 1987, 539–45.

19. Judicial review of regulatory analysis

1. The Regulatory Flexibility Act provides that "any determination by an agency concerning the applicability of this [Act] to any action of the agency shall not be subject to judicial review." 5 U.S. Code § 611(1). The D.C. Circuit has held that this provision means what it clearly says. Thompson v. Clark, 241 F.2d 401 (D.C. Cir. 1984). Executive Order 12,291 provides that it is "not intended to create any right or benefit, substantive or procedural, enforceable as law by a party against the United States, its agencies, its officers, or any person." Executive Order 12,291 § 9. See Michigan v. Thomas, 805 F.2d 176 (8th Cir. 1986); Raven-Hansen 1983.
2. Anderson 1974; McGarity 1977.
3. 705 F.2d 506 (D.C. Cir. 1983).
4. Ibid., 538–9. See also Thompson v. Clark, 741 F.2d 401, 405 (D.C. Cir. 1984).
5. Environmental Defense Fund, Inc. v. Gorsuch, 713 F.2d 802 (D.C. Cir. 1983); National Resources Defense Council, Inc. v. EPA, 683 F.2d 752 (3d Cir. 1982). See also Center for Science in the Public Interest v. Dept. of the Treasury, 573 F. Supp. 1,168 (D.D.C. 1983), appeal dismissed, 727 F.2d 1,161 (D.C. Cir. 1984).
6. Motor Vehicle Manufacturers Institute v. State Farm Mutual Casualty Co., 463 U.S. 29 (1983).
7. Neely 1985.
8. Silverglade 1984.

9. American Textile Manufacturers Institute v. Donovan, 452 U.S. 490 (1981).
10. Lead Industries Association v. EPA, 647 F.2d 1,130, 1,148–51 (D.C. Cir. 1980); American Petroleum Institute v. Costle, 609 F.2d 20 (D.C. Cir. 1979).
11. Camp v. Pitts, 411 U.S. 138 (1973).
12. 5 U.S. Code § 706; Clean Air Act, § 307 (d)(9), 42 U.S. Code § 7607 (d)(9).
13. Bowman Transportation, Inc. v. Arkansas-Best Freight System, 419 U.S. 281, 285 (1974); Citizens to Preserve Overton Park v. Volpe, 401 U.S. 402, 416 (1971).
14. Motor Vehicle Manufacturer's Institute v. State Farm Mutual Casualty Co., 463 U.S. 29 (1983).
15. One primary difference between legal reasoning and policy analysis would appear to be the heavy focus of legal reasoning upon precedent and reasoning by analogy. Policy analysis does not place nearly as much emphasis upon drawing governing principles from previous decisions. A second major difference is the failure of legal reasoning, despite the heroic efforts of some scholars, to rely as extensively on economic analysis.
16. 751 F.2d 1,336 (D.C. Cir. 1985).
17. See also Natural Resources Defense Council, Inc. v. Thomas, 805 F.2d 410 (D.C. Cir. 1986) (court relies on RIA in upholding EPA's rules for emissions from heavy duty motor vehicles); South Carolina ex rel Tindall v. Block, 717 F.2d 874 (4th Cir. 1983) (court relies heavily upon Regulatory Impact Assessment and Regulatory Flexibility Analysis in concluding that rule requiring fifty-cent deduction from the proceeds of all commercially sold milk not arbitrary and capricious).
18. 741 F.2d 401 (D.C. Cir. 1984).
19. Ibid., 405.
20. 824 F.2d 1258 (1st Cir. 1987).
21. 613 F. Supp. 271, 277 (S.D. Tex. 1985).
22. See, e.g., Reynolds Metals Co. v. EPA, 760 F.2d 549 (4th Cir. 1985) (well-performed economic impact and cost-effective analyses aid regulation survive judicial review under arbitrary and capricious test).
23. 463 U.S. 29 (1983).
24. Federal Register 53,419 (1981).
25. 463 U.S. at 52.
26. Ibid., at 56–7.
27. Ibid., at 53 n. 16, 54 n. 18–19, 56 n. 20.
28. Council on Wage and Price Stability and Office of Management and Budget 1976, 26.
29. American Textile Manufacturers Institute v. Donovan, 452 U.S. 490, 528 (1981) (cautioning the reviewing courts not to let an agency's candor about the uncertainties that it faces enhance the stringency of judicial review); Latin 1982, 381–6.
30. Center for Auto Safety v. Peck, 751 F.2d 1,336, 1,365–6 (D.C. Cir. 1985).
31. Ibid., 1,366.

20. Analysis in the modern regulatory state

1. This employee requested anonymity, but his observations demonstrated such keen insight into the practical workings of the regulatory agencies that the paraphrases of his remarks in the text are almost verbatim quotes. I regret his request for anonymity, because I think that he deserves credit for his insights. Nevertheless, I shall honor that request.

Bibliography

Ackerlow, Charles. 1982. Testimony. U.S. Congress. Senate. Committee on the Judiciary. Subcommittee on Regulatory Reform. Committee on Small Business. Subcommittee on Government Regulation and Paperwork. *Regulatory Flexibility Act: Joint Hearings.* 62 97th Cong., 2d sess., 1982.

Ackerman, B. A., and W. T. Hassler, 1981. *Clean Coal – Dirty Air.* New Haven, Conn.: Yale University Press.

Adams, J. G. U. 1974. ". . . And How Much for Your Grandmother." *Environmental Policy* 6:619.

Adkins, Charles, Director, Health Standards Directorate, OSHA; and John Martonik, Deputy Director, Health Standards Directorate, OSHA. 1986. Interview with author. Washington, D.C., 26 September.

Administrative Conference of the United States. 1982. "Recommendation 82-5." Code of Federal Regulations 1: § 305.82-5.

Administrative Conference of the United States. 1987. *Report from the Office of the Chairman to the Assistant Secretary for Occupational Safety and Health, Occupational Safety and Health Administration on OSHA Rulemaking Procedures.* Consultants' report prepared by Thomas O. McGarity and Sidney A. Shapiro.

Ajax, Robert L., Chief, Standards Development Branch, Emissions Standards and Engineering Division, Office of Air Quality Planning and Standards, Office of Air and Radiation, EPA. 1984a. Telephone interview with author, 13 July.

1984b. Letter to author. 22 August.

Alexander, M. 1986. "Ecological Consequences of Genetic Engineering: Reducing the Uncertainties." *Issues in Science and Technology* 1:57.

Allen, W. H. 1980. "The 'Revolving Door' – Should It Be Stopped?" *Administrative Law Review.* 32:383.

Alm, Alvin, Deputy Administrator, EPA. 1983. *Memorandum to Assistant Administrators and General Counsel on Options Selection/Rejection Process.* 4 November.

1984a. *Memorandum to Assistant Administrators, General Counsel, Inspector General, Assistant Administrators, Regional Administrators and Staff Office Directors on Criteria and Guidelines for Reviewing Agency Actions.* 30 January.

1984b. *Memorandum to Assistant Administrators, General Counsel, Inspector General, Associate Administrators, Regional Administrators, and Staff Office Directors on Procedures for Regulation Development and Review.* 21 February.

343

American Iron and Steel Institute. 1984. The Need To Revise the National Ambient Air Quality Standards for Particulate Matter. Comments submitted to EPA in connection with the particulates rulemaking.

N.d. Comments on proposed revisions to 40 CFR, Pts. 50, 53, and 58. Comments submitted to EPA.

American Mining Institute. 1984. Testimony to U.S. Environmental Protection Agency on Proposed Revisions to the National Ambient Air Quality Standards for Particulate Matter.

Amy, D. J. 1984. "Why Policy Analysis and Ethics Are Incompatible." *Journal of Policy Analysis and Management* 3:573.

Anderson, F. 1973. *NEPA and the Courts.* Baltimore: Johns Hopkins University Press.

1974. "The National Environmental Policy Act." In *Federal Environmental Law.* Edited by E. Dolgin and T. Guilbert. St. Paul, Minn.: West Publishing Co.

Andrews, R. N. L. 1976. "NEPA in Practice: Environmental Policy or Administrative Reform." In *Workshop on the National Environmental Policy Act,* 94th Cong., 2d sess., 1976, Serial 94-E.

1982. "Cost Benefit Analysis as Regulatory Reform." In *Cost–Benefit Analysis and Environmental Regulations: Politics, Ethics, and Methods.* Edited by D. Swartzman, R. Liroff, and K. Crooke. Washington, D.C.: Conservation Foundation.

Anselmo, Rita, Policy Analyst, Policy Analysis and Program Evaluation Staff, Animal and Plant Health Inspection Service, USDA. 1983. Telephone interview with author, 5 May.

1984a. Telephone interview with author, 3 May.

1984b. Telephone interview with author, 21 May.

APHIS. 1982. *APHIS Directive 114.3.* 19 October.

Arrow, K. 1973. "The Theory of Discrimination." In *Discrimination in Labor Markets.* Edited by D. Ashenfelter and A. Rees. Princeton, N.J.: Princeton University Press.

Arthur D. Little, Inc. 1982. *Assessment of the Market Research Services Summary Report on Focus Groups Concerning Mechanically Processed Meat Product.* Report prepared for FSIS.

Ashford, N. A. 1976. *Crisis in the Workplace.* Cambridge, Mass.: MIT Press.

Atamik, Pat, Administrative Officer, Directorate of Technical Support, OSHA, DOL. 1984. Telephone interview with author, 23 July.

Auchter, Thorne, Assistant Secretary for Occupational Safety and Health, DOL. 1985. Testimony. U.S. Congress House. Committee on the Judiciary. Subcommittee on Administrative Law and Governmental Relations. *Hearings on H.R. 2327.* 455 98th Cong., 1st sess., 1983.

Bailey, M. J. 1980. *Reducing Risks to Life.* Washington, D.C.: American Enterprise Institute.

Baker, L. 1984. *Brandeis and Frankfurter: A Dual Biography.* New York: Harper & Row.

Banfield, E. C. 1980. "Policy Science as Metaphysical Madness." In *Bureau-*

crats, *Policy Analysts, Statesmen: Who Leads?* Edited by R. Goldwin. Washington, D.C.: American Enterprise Institute.

Baram, M. S. 1980. "Cost–Benefit Analysis: An Inadequate Basis for Health, Safety and Environmental Regulatory Decisionmaking." *Ecology Law Quarterly* 8:473.

Bardach, E., and R. A. Kagan. 1981. *Going by the Book: The Problem of Regulatory Unreasonableness.* Philadelphia: Temple University Press.

Barr, Terry, Office of the Assistant Secretary for Economics, USDA. 1983. Telephone interview with author, 3 May.

Basala, Allen, Chief, Regulatory Impact Section, Economic Analysis Branch, Strategies and Air Standards Division, Office of Air Quality Planning and Standards, Office of Air and Radiation, EPA. 1984a. Telephone interview with author, 29 May.

1984b. Letter to author, 21 August.

1985. Telephone interview with author, 1 May.

1986. Telephone interview with author, 12 November.

Bauer, R. 1968. "The Study of Policy Formation: An Introduction." In *The Study of Policy Formation.* Edited by R. Bauer and K. Gergen. New York: Free Press.

Baybrook, T., and C. Lindblom. 1963. *Strategy of Decision: Policy Evaluation as a Social Process.* New York: Free Press.

Beck, Eckardt, Assistant Administrator for Water and Waste Management, EPA. 1980. Testimony. U.S. Congress. House. Committee on Interstate and Foreign Commerce. Subcommittee on Oversight and Investigations. *Hearings on Cost–Benefit Analysis: The Potential for Conflict of Interest.* 483 96th Cong., 2d sess., 1980.

Beliles, Robert P., Office of Risk Assessment, Directorate of Health Standards Programs, OSHA, DOL. 1984. Telephone interview with author, 23 July.

Senior Scientist, Carcinogen Assessment Group, Office of Research and Development, EPA. 1986. Telephone interview with author, 21 October.

Behn, E. D. 1981. "Policy Analysis and Policy Politics." *Policy Analysis* 7:199.

Bender, Miriam, Office of General Counsel, USDA. 1984. Telephone interview with author, 15 March.

Benne, R. 1981. *The Ethic of Democratic Capitalism.* Philadelphia: Fortress Press.

Bennett, Kathleen, Assistant Administrator for Air and Radiation, EPA. 1982. *Memorandum to the Administrator on Lead Phasedown – Action Memorandum.* 27 July 1982. Reprinted in Bureau of National Affairs. *Environment Reporter,* 20 August 1982, 541.

Benveniste, G. 1977. *The Politics of Expertise.* San Francisco: Boyd & Fraser Publishing Co.

1984. "On a Code of Ethics for Policy Experts." *Journal of Policy Analysis and Management* 3:561.

Berg, Richard, Executive Director, Administrative Conference of the United States. 1981. Testimony. U.S. Congress. House. Committee on the Judiciary. Subcommittee on Administrative Law and Governmental Regulations. *Hearings on Regulatory Procedures Act of 1981.* 75 97th Cong., 1st sess., 1981.

Berlin, Edward, Counsel, Environmental Defense Fund. 1970. Testimony. U.S. Congress. House. Committee on Merchant Marine and Fisheries. Subcommittee on Fisheries and Wildlife Conservation. *Hearings on Administration of the National Environmental Policy Act.* 1,104 91st Cong., 2d sess., 1970.

Berndt, Frank, Chief Counsel, NHTSA. 1983. Testimony. U.S. Congress. House. Committee on the Judiciary. Subcommittee on Administrative Law and Governmental Relations. *Hearings on H.R. 2327.* 247 98th Cong., 1st sess., 1983.

Bernstein, Joan, former General Counsel, EPA. 1983. Testimony. U.S. Congress. House. Committee on the Judiciary. Subcommittee on Administrative Law and Governmental Relations. *Hearings on H.R. 2327.* 50 98th Cong., 1st sess., 1983.

Biemiller, Andrew J., Director, Department of Legislation, AFL-CIO. 1977. Testimony. U.S. Congress. House. Committee on Banking, Finance and Urban Affairs. Subcommittee on Economic Stabilization. *Hearings on Amendments to the Council on Wage and Price Stability Act.* 196 95th Cong., 1st sess., 1977.

Bingham, Eula, former Assistant Secretary, Occupational Safety and Health, DOL. 1983. Testimony. U.S. Congress. House. Committee on the Judiciary. Subcommittee on Administrative Law and Governmental Relations. *Hearings on H.R. 2327.* 351 98th Cong., 1st sess., 1983.

Bjorlie, Wayne, Office of Budget and Program Analysis, USDA. 1983. Telephone interview with author, 5 May.
1984. Telephone interview with author, 1 May.

Blincoe, Larry, Office of Program and Rulemaking Analysis, Office of Plans and Programs, NHTSA, DOT. 1984. Telephone interview with author, 10 April.

Blum, Barbara, former Deputy Administrator, EPA. 1980. Testimony. U.S. Congress. House. Committee on Interstate and Foreign Commerce. Subcommittee on Oversight and Investigations. *Hearings on Cost–Benefit Analysis: The Potential for Conflict of Interest.* 690 96th Cong., 2d sess., 1980.

Bollier, D., and J. Claybrook. 1986. *Freedom From Harm.* Washington, D.C.: Public Citizen.

Bonine, J., and T. McGarity. 1984. *The Law of Environmental Protection.* St. Paul, Minn.: West Publishing Co.

Borovies, John, Dairy Division, AMS, USDA. 1984. Telephone interview with author, 4 May.

Braeutigam, R. 1981. "The Deregulation of Natural Gas." In *Case Studies in Regulation Revolution and Reform.* Edited by L. Weiss and M. Klass. Boston: Little, Brown.

Braslow, Larry, Chief of Economics, Office of Regulatory Analysis, Directorate of Policy, OSHA. 1986. Telephone interview with author, 24 October.

Breyer, S. 1979. "Analyzing Regulatory Failure: Mismatches, Less Restricted Alternatives and Reform." *Harvard Law Review* 92:549.

Broder T. E., and J. F. Morrall. 1983. "The Economic Basis for OSHA's and EPA's Generic Carcinogen Regulations." In *What Role for Government? Lessons from Policy Research.* Edited by R. Zeckhauser and D. Leebart. Durham, N.C.: Duke University Press.

Bruff, H. 1979. "Presidential Power and Administrative Rulemaking." *Yale Law Journal* 88:451.

——— 1984. "Presidential Management of Agency Rulemaking." *George Washington Law Review* 27:533.

Bruff, H., and E. Gellhorn. 1977. "Congressional Control of Administrative Regulation: A Study of Legislative Vetoes." *Harvard Law Review* 90:1,369.

Bullock, J. B., and C. E. Ward. 1980. "Economic Impacts of Regulations on Mechanically Deboned Red Meats." *Federal Register* 46:39,339.

Burkley, Dianne, Special Assistant to the Solicitor for Regulatory Affairs, Office of the Solicitor, DOL. 1983. Interview with author. Washington, D.C., 19 May.

Burness, et al. 1983. "Valuing Policies Which Reduce Environmental Risk." *Natural Resources Journal* 23:675.

Business Roundtable. 1979. Testimony. U.S. Congress. House. Committee on the Judiciary. Subcommittee on Administrative Law and Government Relations. *Hearings on the Regulatory Reform Act of 1979.* 1,975 96th Cong., 1st and 2d sess., 1979.

——— 1981a. Testimony. U.S. Congress. House. Committee on the Judiciary. Subcommittee on Administrative Law and Governmental Relations. *Regulatory Procedures Act of 1981: Hearings on H.R. 746.* 302 97th Cong., 1st sess., 1981.

——— 1981b. Testimony. U.S. Congress. Senate. Committee on Governmental Affairs. *Hearings on Regulatory Reform Legislation of 1981.* 188 97th Cong., 1st sess., 1981.

Byse, C. 1977. "Comments on a Structural Reform Proposal: Presidential Directive to Independent Agencies." *Administrative Law Review* 28:157.

Calabrese, E. 1978. *Pollutants and High Risk Groups.* New York: Wiley.

Calabrese, Guido, Dean, Yale Law School. 1979. Testimony. U.S. Congress, House. Committee on Interstate and Foreign Commerce. Subcommittee on Oversight and Investigations and Subcomm. on Consumer Protection and Finance. *Joint Hearings on the Use of Cost–Benefit Analysis by Regulatory Agencies.* 27 96th Cong., 1st sess., 1979.

Caldwell, L. 1979. "Is NEPA Inherently Self-Defeating?" *Environmental Law Reporter* 9:50,001.

——— 1982. *Science and the National Environmental Policy Act.* University of Alabama Press.

Campbell, John, Deputy Assistant Administrator for Policy, Planning and

Evaluation, EPA. 1984. Interview with author. Washington, D.C., 29 June.

Cannon, Joseph, Associate Administrator for Policy and Resource Management, EPA. 1983. Testimony. U.S. Congress. House. Committee on the Judiciary. Subcommittee on Administrative Law and Governmental Relations. *Hearings on H.R. 2327.* 600 98th Cong., 1st sess., 1983.

   1983. Interview with author. Washington, D.C., 18 May.

Carter, J. 1978. "Improving Government Regulation." *Weekly Compilation of Presidential Documents* 14:561.

Cates, C. 1979. "Beyond Muddling: Creativity." *Public Administration Review* 39:527.

Center for Auto Safety. Comments to Docket 70-07 Notice 12, Federal Motor Vehicle Safety Standard No. 1228, Fields of Direct View. 22 October 1981.

Chemical Manufacturers Association. 1982. Comments on OSHA Hazard Communication Standard. Comments submitted to OSHA.

Claybrook, Joan, Administrator, NHTSA. 1980. Testimony. U.S. Congress. House. Committee on Interstate and Foreign Commerce. Subcommittee on Oversight and Investigations. *Hearings on Cost–Benefit Analysis: The Potential for Conflict of Interest.* 763 96th Cong., 2d sess., 1980.

Claybrook, Joan, former Administrator, NHTSA. 1983. Testimony. U.S. Congress. House. Committee on the Judiciary. Subcommittee on Administrative Law and Governmental Relations. *Hearings on H.R. 2327.* 111 98th Cong., 1st sess., 1983.

Clemans, Sid, Chief, Legislative, Regulatory, and Automated Systems, Office of Budget and Program Analysis, USDA. 1984a. Telephone interview with author, 4 May.

   1984b. Letter to author, 10 August.

   1984c. Telephone interview with author, 14 August.

Coad, Gail, Office of Information and Regulatory Affairs, OMB. 1983. Interview with author. Washington D.C., 8 March.

Cohen, Y. 1986. "Organic Pollutant Transport." *Environmental Science and Technology* 20:538.

Cole, R. J., and P. D. Tegeler. 1980. *Government Requirements of Small Business.* Lexington, Mass.: Lexington Books.

Comment. 1977. "The Inflation Impact Statement Program: An Assessment of the First Two Years." *American University Law Review* 26:1138.

   1981. "The Significant Risk Requirement in OSHA Regulation of Carcinogens." *Stanford Law Review* 33:551.

Commodity Futures Trading Commission. 1981. Testimony. U.S. Congress. House. Committee on the Judiciary. Subcommittee on Administrative Law and Governmental Relations. *Regulatory Procedures Act of 1981: Hearings on H.R. 746.* 878 97th Cong., 1st sess., 1981.

Congressional Research Service. 1983. *A Review of Risk Assessment Methodologies.* Report prepared for the Subcommittee on Science, Research and Technology, transmitted to the House Committee on Science, Research and Technology. 98th Cong., 1st sess., 1983.

Congress Watch. 1981. Testimony. U.S. Congress. House. Committee on the Judiciary. Subcommittee on Administrative Law and Governmental Relations. *Regulatory Procedures Act of 1981: Hearings on H.R. 746.* 422 97th Cong., 1st sess., 1981.

Connerton, Marguerite, Senior Economist, Office of Regulatory Economics and Policy Analysis, Office of Policy, DOL. 1983. Interview with author. Washington, D.C., 17 May.

Connerton, Marguerite, and M. MacCarthy. 1982. *Cost–Benefit Analysis & Regulation: Expressway to Reform or Blind Alley?* Washington, D.C.: Center for National Policy.

CONSAD Research Corp. 1983. Preliminary Comments on Mathtech, Inc. Report on Benefits Analysis of Alternative National Ambient Air Quality Standards for Particulate Matter.

Conservation Foundation. 1984. *Issue Report on Cross-Media Pollutants.* Washington, D.C.: Conservation Foundation.

Costle, D. M. 1982. "Environmental Regulation and Regulatory Reform." *Washington Law Review* 57:409.

Council on Environmental Quality. 1976. *Environmental Impact Statements: An Analysis of Six Years' Experience by Seventy Federal Agencies.*

1981. *Chemical Hazards to Human Reproduction.*

Council on Wage and Price Stability. 1981. *A Review of the Regulatory Interventions of the Council on Wage and Price Stability, 1974–1980.*

Council on Wage and Price Stability and Office of Management and Budget. 1976. *An Evaluation of the Inflation Impact Statement Program.*

Crampton, R. C., and R. K. Berg. 1973. "On Leading a Horse to Water: NEPA and the Federal Bureaucracy." *Michigan Law Review* 71:511.

Crandall, R. W. 1980. "Alternatives to the Administration's Initiatives." In *Reforming Regulation,* edited by T. Clark, M. Kosters and J. Miller. Washington, D.C.: American Enterprise Institute.

Cranor, C. F. 1983. "Epidemiology and Procedural Protections for Workplace Health in the Aftermath of the Benzene Case." *Industrial Relations Law Journal* 5:372.

Cristafaro, Alex, Chief, Air Economics Branch, Economic and Regulatory Analysis Division, Office of Policy Analysis, Office of Policy Planning and Evaluation, EPA. 1984. Telephone interview with author, 24 and 25 May.

1986. Telephone interview with author, 3 November.

Crooke, K. G., and N. B. Herlevsen. 1982. "Environmental Cost–Benefit Analysis: The Illinois Experience." In *Cost–Benefit Analysis and Environmental Regulations: Politics, Ethics, and Methods.* Edited by D. Swartzman, R. Liroff, and K. Crooke. Washington, D.C.: Conservation Foundation.

Crunden, R. 1982. *Ministers of Reform.* New York: Basic.

Cutler, L. N., and D. R. Johnson. 1975. "Regulation and the Political Process." *Yale Law Journal* 84:1395.

DeLong, J. V. 1979. "Informal Rulemaking and the Integration of Law and Policy." *Virgnia Law Review* 65:257.

1981. "Defending Cost–Benefit Analysis." *Regulation* (March/April):39.

DeMuth, C. C. 1980a. "The White House Review Programs." *Regulation* (January/February):13.

1980b. "The Regulatory Budget." *Regulation* (March/April):29.

1982a. Letter to Joseph A. Cannon, 30 August.

1982b. Letter to Joseph A. Cannon, 10 October.

N.d. *Memorandum for Members of the Presidential Task Force on Regulatory Relief on OSHA's "Hazard Communication" Proposal.*

DeMuth C. C., and D. H. Ginsburg. 1986. "White House Review of Agency Rulemaking." *Harvard Law Review* 99:1075.

Department of Health and Human Services. 1983. Testimony. U.S. Congress. House. Committee on the Judiciary. Subcommittee on Administrative Law and Governmental Relations. *Hearings on H.R. 2327.* 1,900 98th Cong., 1st sess., 1983.

Department of Labor. 1981a. *Memorandum on Departmental Decisionmaking Procedures – Overall Policies.* 23 October.

1981b. *Memorandum on Policy Review and Coordinating Committee Operating Procedures.* 29 November.

1982. *Memorandum on Improving the Management and Policy Processes Within the Department.* 17 November.

N.d. *Preliminary Regulatory Impact Analysis on Proposed Office of Federal Contract Compliance Regulations.*

Department of Transportation. Office of the Secretary. 1979. "Improving Government Regulations: Regulatory Policies and Procedures." *Federal Register* 44:11,034.

Office of Industry Policy. Office of the Assistant Secretary for International Affairs. 1982. *Guidance for Regulatory Evaluations: A Handbook for DOT Benefit Cost Analysis.*

Derthick, M., and P. J. Quirk. 1985. *The Politics of Deregulation.* Washington, D.C.: Brookings Institution Press.

Dewhurst, Steven, Director, Office of Budget and Policy Analysis, USDA. 1983. Testimony. U.S. Congress. House. Committee on the Judiciary. Subcommittee on Administrative Law and Governmental Relations. *Hearings on Regulatory Reform Act.* 526 98th Cong., 1st sess., 1983.

Dinman, Bertram, Vice President for Health and Safety, Aluminum Company of America. 1983. Testimony. U.S. Congress. House. Committee on the Judiciary. Subcommittee on Administrative Law and Governmental Relations. *Hearings on H.R. 2327.* 357 98th Cong., 1st sess., 1983.

Ditlow, Clarence, Director, Center for Auto Safety. Testimony. U.S. Congress. House. Committee on the Judiciary. Subcommittee on Administrative Law and Governmental Relations. *Hearings on H.R. 2327.* 224 98th Cong., 1st sess., 1983.

Diver, C. J. 1981. "Policymaking Paradigms in Administrative Law." *Harvard Law Review* 95:414.

Doniger, D. D. 1984. Natural Resources Defense Council, Inc. Statement on the Proposed Revisions to the National Ambient Air Quality Standards for Particulate Matter. 30 April.

1985. "The Dark Side of the Bubble." *Environmental Forum* (July):32.

Donovan, Raymond, Secretary of Labor. 1982. *Memorandum for the Vice President and Members of the President's Task Force on Regulatory Relief on OSHA's Proposed Hazard Communication Standard.* 18 January.

Dorfman, N. S., and A. Snow. 1975. "Who Will Pay for Pollution Control? The Distribution by Income of The Burden of the National Environmental Protection Program, 1972–1980." *National Tax Journal* 28:101.

Downs, A. 1966. *Inside Bureaucracy.* Boston: Little, Brown.

Dunlop, J. 1980. *Business and Public Policy.* Cambridge, Mass.: Harvard University Press.

Dupuis, Lewis, Chief, Economic Analysis Staff, Office of Analysis and Evaluation, Office of Water Regulations and Standards, Office of Water, EPA. 1984. Telephone interview with author, 31 May.

Durkin, Edward, Food and Beverage Trades Dept., AFL-CIO. 1983. Testimony. U.S. Congress. House. Committee on the Judiciary. Subcommittee on Administrative Law and Governmental Relations. *Hearings on H.R. 2327.* 429 98th Cong., 1st sess., 1983.

Dyck, A. J., and H. W. Richardson. 1967. "The Moral Justification for Research Using Human Subjects." In *Use of Human Subjects in Safety Evaluation of Food Chemicals: Proceedings of a Conference.* Washington, D.C.: National Academy of Sciences National Research Council.

Dyesing, P. 1962. *Reason in Society.* Urbana: University of Illinois Press.

Eads, G. 1981a. "The Benefits of Better Benefits Estimation." In *The Benefits of Health and Safety Regulation.* Edited by A. Ferguson and E. LeVeen. Cambridge, Mass.: Ballinger.

1981b. "Harnessing Regulation: The Evolving Role of White House Oversight." *Regulation* (May/June):18.

Eads, G., and M. Fix. 1984. *Relief or Reform? Reagan's Regulatory Dilemma.* Washington, D.C.: Urban Institute Press.

Eagleton, Thomas. 1981. Testimony. U.S. Congress. House. Committee on the Judiciary. Subcomm. on Administrative Law and Governmental Relations. *Regulatory Procedures Act of 1981: Hearings on H.R. 746.* 8 97th Cong., 1st sess., 1981.

Eckhardt, Robert. 1980. Statement. U.S. Congress. House. Committee on Interstate and Foreign Commerce. Subcommittee on Oversight and Investigations. *Hearings on Cost–Benefit Analysis: The Potential for Conflict of Interest.* 19 96th Cong., 2d sess., 1980.

Economic Regulatory Administration. 1979. "Establishment of Mandatory Production Levels for Middle Distillates." *Federal Register* 44:46,246.

Edwards, G., and I. Sharkansky. 1978. *The Policy Predicament.* San Francisco: Freeman.

Eisner, Neil, Assistant General Counsel for Regulation and Enforcement, DOT. 1983. Telephone interview with author, 6 May.

Eisner, Neil, and Samuel Podberesky. Deputy Assistant General Counsel for Regulation and Enforcement, DOT. 1984. Interview with author. Washington, D.C., 16 November.

English, James, Office of General Counsel, United Steelworkers. 1983. Testimony. U.S. Congress. House. Committee on the Judiciary. Subcommittee on Administrative Law and Governmental Relations. *Hearings on H.R. 2327.* 369 98th Cong., 1st sess., 1983.

Environmental Strategies, Inc. 1982a. "Summary of Comments on the Environmental Protection Agency's February 22, 1982 Proposal on Regulation of Fuel and Fuel Additives (Lead Phasedown)." Mimeo.

1982b. "Summary of Comments on the Environmental Protection Agency's August 27, 1982 Proposal on Regulation of Fuel and Fuel Additives (Lead Phasedown)." Mimeo.

EPA. 1973a. "Regulation of Fuels and Fuel Additives." *Federal Register* 38:1254.

1973b. "Regulation of Fuel and Fuel Additives: Control of Lead Additives in Gasoline." *Federal Register* 38:33,734.

1977. *Air Quality Criteria for Lead.*

1982a. *Initial Regulatory Flexibility Analysis for Lead Phasedown Proposal.*

1982b. *Final Regulatory Flexibility Analysis for Lead Phasedown Regulations.*

1982c. "Projections of Total Lead Usage Under Alternative Lead Phasedown Programs." Mimeo.

1982d. "Projections of Total Lead Usage Under the Lead Phasedown Regulation." Mimeo.

1982e. "Regulation of Fuel and Fuel Additives: Withdrawal of Proposed Rule." *Federal Register* 47:38,070.

1982f. "Regulation of Fuels and Fuel Additives: Final Rule." *Federal Register* 47:49,322.

1983a. Guidelines for Performing Regulatory Impact Analysis.

1983b. "Regulation of Fuel and Fuel Additives: Final Rule." *Federal Register* 48:5,724.

1984a. *Preliminary Regulatory Impact Analysis, National Ambient Air Quality Standards for Particulate Matter.*

1984b. "Proposed Revisions to the National Ambient Air Quality Standards for Particulate Matter." *Federal Register* 49:10,408.

1984c. "Addendum 1 – Executive Summary – Review of the National Ambient Air Quality Standards for Particulate Matter: Assessment of Scientific and Technical Information—OAQPS Staff Paper." *Federal Register* 49:10,423.

Strategies and Air Standards Division. Economic Analysis Branch. 1985. *Analytical Methods Manual.*

1986. *Regulatory Impact Analysis of the National Ambient Air Quality Standards for Particulate Matter – Second Addendum.*

1987. "Revisions to the National Ambient Air Quality Standards for Particulate Matter." *Federal Register* 52:24,634.

EPA. Task Force on Analytic Resources. N.d.a. "Case Study on the Inorganic Chemicals Industry Effluent Guideline (Phase I)." Mimeo.

N.d.b. "Case Study on the NSPS for the Coil Coating Industry." Mimeo.

N.d.c. "Case Study Studies, Executive Summary." Mimeo.

N.d.d. "Memorandum to the Deputy Administrator." Mimeo.

Evans, J., 1981. "Precision and Decision: The Regulatory Use of Air Quality Impact Modeling." Mimeo.

Executive Order No. 11,821, 3 Code of Federal Regulations 926 (1971–5 Comp.).

Executive Order No. 12,044, 3 Code of Federal Regulations 152 (1979).

Executive Order No. 12,291, 3 Code of Federal Regulations 127 (1982).

FAA. 1981. Office of Aviation Policy and Plans. *Economic Values for Evaluation of Federal Aviation Administration Investment and Regulatory Programs.*

1982. Office of Aviation Policy and Programs. *Economic Analysis of Investment and Regulatory Decisions – A Guide.*

Faberman, Edward P. 1983. See Murdock.

Deputy Chief Counsel and Acting Chief Counsel, Federal Aviation Administration, DOT. 1984a. Telephone interview with author, 6 June.

Acting Chief Counsel and Deputy Chief Counsel, Federal Aviation Administration, DOT. 1984b. Letter to author, 29 August.

Fairfax, S. 1978. "A Disaster in the Environmental Movement." *Science* 199:743.

Federal Communications Commission. 1981. Testimony. U.S. Congress. House. Committee on the Judiciary. Subcommittee on Administrative Law and Governmental Relations. *Regulatory Procedures Act of 1981: Hearings on H.R. 746.* 280 97th Cong., 1st sess., 1981.

Federal Energy Regulatory Administration. 1982. "High Cost Gas Produced from Tight Formations: Final Rule." *Federal Register* 47:53,342.

Feldstein, M. 1982. "Distributional Preferences in Public Expenditure Analysis." In *Redistribution Through Public Choice.* Edited by H. Hochman and G. Peterson. New York: Columbia University Press.

Felrice, Barry, Associate Administrator for Plans and Programs, NHTSA, DOT. 1983a. Interview with author. Washington, D.C., 18 May.

1983b. Telephone interview with author, 2 August.

Associate Administrator for Rulemaking, NHTSA, DOT. 1984a. Telephone interview with author, 11 April.

1984b. Letter to author, 23 August.

1986. Telephone interview with author, 25 November.

Ferguson, A. 1981. "Statement." In *The Benefits of Health and Safety Regulation.* Edited by A. Ferguson and E. LeVeen. Cambridge, Mass.: Ballinger.

Finkelstein, Michael M., Associate Administrator for Rulemaking, NHTSA, DOT. 1977. *Memorandum to Associate Administrator for Planning and Evaluation on Proposed NPRM on Fields of Direct View.* 2 June.

Fiorino, Daniel, Acting Director, Regulation and Enforcement Management Division, Office of Standards and Regulations, Office of Policy Planning and Evaluation, EPA. 1983. Telephone interview with author, 8 February.

1984. Telephone interview with author, 23 May.

Fischhoff, B. 1977. "Cost–Benefit Analysis and the Art of Motorcycle Maintenance." *Policy Sciences* 8:177.

Fisher, A. 1984. "An Overview and Evaluation of EPA's Guidelines for Conducting Regulatory Impact Analysis." In *Environmental Policy Under Reagan's Executive Order: The Role of Benefit Cost Analysis.* Edited by V. K. Smith. Chapel Hill: University of North Carolina Press.

Food and Drug Administration. 1983. Testimony. U.S. Congress. House. Committee on the Judiciary. Subcommittee on Administrative Law and Governmental Relations. *Hearings on H.R. 2327.* 1,658 98th Cong., 1st sess., 1983.

Food Safety and Quality Service. 1976. "Standards and Labeling Requirements for Tissues from Ground Bone: Proposed Rulemaking." *Federal Register* 42:54,437.

Ford, G. 1974. "President's Address to Joint Session of Congress." *Weekly Compilation of Presidential Documents* 10:1,239.

Forester, J. F. 1984. "Bounded Rationality and the Politics of Muddling Through." *Public Administration Review* 44:23.

Foster, J. F. 1980. "An Advocate Role Model for Policy Analysis." *Policy Studies Journal* 8:958.

Fraas, Arthur, Office of Information and Regulatory Affairs, OMB. 1983. Interview with author. Washington, D.C., 19 May.

Fredrickson, H. G. 1982. "The Recovery of Civicism in Public Administration." *Public Administration Review* 42:501.

Freeman, A., R. Haveman, and A. Kneese. 1973. *The Economics of Environmental Policy.* New York: Wiley.

Fried, C. 1978. *Right and Wrong.* Cambridge, Mass.: Harvard University Press.

Friedman, R. 1981. *Sensitive Populations and Environmental Standards.* Washington, D.C.: Conservation Foundation.

Frodyma, Frank, Policy Directorate, OSHA. 1986. Telephone interview with author, 26 September.

FSIS. 1978. "Mechanically Processed (Species) Product: Standards and Labeling Requirements: Final Rule." *Federal Register* 43:23,416.

———. 1981a. "Questionnaire, WB Research." *Federal Register* 46:39,316.

———. 1981b. "Standards and Labeling Requirements for Mechanically Processed (Species) Product and Products in Which It Is Used: Proposed Rule." *Federal Register* 46:39,274.

———. 1982a. *Regulatory Analysis of Amendments to the Regulations for Mechanically Separated (Species).*

———. 1982b. "Standards and Labeling Requirements for Mechanically Separated (Species) and Products in Which It Is Used: Final Rule." *Federal Register* 47:28,214.

———. 1985. *FSIS Directive 1232.1. Docket Management Procedures.*

———. 1988. "Labeling of Meat Products under Certain Circumstances That Contain Mechanically Separated (Species): Proposed Rule." *Federal Register* 53:35,089.

Garland, M. B. 1985. "Deregulation and Judicial Review." *Harvard Law Review* 98:505.

Gass, Arthur, Office of Risk Reduction Technology, Directorate of Health Standards Programs, OSHA, DOL. 1984a. Telephone interview with author, 23 July.

1984b. Telephone interview with author, 17 September.

General Accounting Office 1977. *Delays in Setting Workplace Standards for Cancer-Causing and Other Dangerous Substances.*

1980. *Government Earns Low Marks on Proper Use of Consultants.*

1981a. Testimony. U.S. Congress. Senate. Committee on Governmental Affairs. *Hearings on Regulatory Reform Legislation of 1981.* 255 97th Cong. 1st sess., 1981.

1981b. Testimony. U.S. Congress. Senate. Committee on Governmental Affairs. Subcomm. on Federal Expenditures, Research and Rules. *Hearings on the Consultant Reform and Disclosure Act of 1981.* 19 97th Cong., 1st sess., 1981.

1982. *Improved Quality, Adequate Resources, and Consistent Oversight Needed if Regulatory Analysis is to Help Control Costs of Regulations.*

1984. *Cost–Benefit Analysis Can Be Useful in Assessing Environmental Regulations, Despite Limitations.*

1988. *Air Pollution: Better Internal Controls Needed to Insure Complete Air Regulation Dockets.*

1989. *Regulatory Review: Information on OMB's Review Process.*

Gelpe, M. R., and A. D. Tarlock. 1974. "The Uses of Scientific Information in Environmental Decisionmaking." *Southern California Law Review* 48:371.

Gerber, L. 1984. *The Limits of Liberalism.* New York: New York University Press.

Gessel, Thomas, Director, Regulatory Coordination Staff, APHIS, USDA. 1983. Telephone interview with author, 4 May.

1984a. Telephone interview with author, 21 May.

1984b. Telephone interview with author, 17 August.

Glavin, Margaret, Director, Standards and Labelling Division, Meat and Poultry Inspection Technical Services Staff, FSIS, USDA. 1986. Telephone interview with author, 24 November.

Goldin, Anthony, Director, Directorate of Policy, and Larry Braslow, Chief of Economics, Office of Regulatory Analysis, Directorate of Policy, OSHA, DOL. 1984. Telephone interview with author, 26 July.

1985. Letter to Author, 9 April.

Goodin, R. E., and P. Wilenski. 1984. "Beyond Efficiency: The Logical Underpinnings of Administrative Principles." *Public Administration Review* 44:512.

Gordon, Charles, Office of the Solicitor, DOL. 1986. Telephone interview with author, 13 October.

Gore, A. 1981. Statement. U.S. Congress. House. Committee on Energy and Commerce. Subcommittee on Oversight and Investigations. *Hearings on Role of OMB in Regulation.* 70 97th Cong., 1st Sess., 1981.

Gore, W. J., and J. W. Dyson. "Introduction." In *The Making of Decisions: A*

Reader in Administrative Behavior. Edited by W. Gore and J. Dyson. London: Collier-MacMillan.

Gradick, David, Deputy Director, Budget and Accounting Division, APHIS, USDA. 1984. Telephone interview with author, 8 January.

Graham, J. D., and J. W. Vaupel. 1983. "The Value of a Life: What Difference Does It Make?" In *What Role for Government? Lessons from Policy Research.* Edited by R. Zeckhauser and D. Leebart. Durham, N.C.: Duke University Press.

Gramm, Wendy. 1986. *Memorandum for the Heads of Departments and Agencies Subject to Executive Orders 12291 and 12478 on Additional Procedures Concerning OIRA Review Under Executive Order Nos. 12291 and 12498.* 13 June.

Gray, C. Boyden, Staff Director, Vice President's Task Force on Regulatory Relief. 1981. Testimony. U.S. Congress. Senate. Committee on Governmental Affairs. *Hearings on Regulatory Reform Legislation of 1981.* 6 97th Cong., 1st sess., 1981.

——— 1982. "Presidential Involvement in Informal Rulemaking." *Tulane Law Review* 56:863.

Green, M., and N. Waitzman. 1979. *Business War on the Law: An Analysis of the Benefits of Federal Health/Safety Enforcement.* Washington, D.C.: Corporate Accountability Project.

Grubb, W. N., D. Whittington, and M. Humphries, M. 1984. "The Ambiguities of Cost-Benefit Analysis: An Evaluation of Regulatory Impact Analyses Under Executive Order 12291." In *Environmental Policy Under Reagan's Executive Order: The Role of Benefit Cost Analysis.* Edited by V. K. Smith. Chapel Hill: University of North Carolina Press.

Hadden, S. G. 1986. *Read the Label: Reducing Risk by Providing Information.* Boulder, Co.: Westview.

Hamilton, R. W. 1972. "Procedures for the Adoption of Rules of General Applicability: The Need for Procedural Innovation in Administrative Rulemaking." *California Law Review* 60:1276.

Hammond, A., and K. Adelman. 1978. "Science, Values and Human Judgment." In *Judgment and Decision in Public Policy Formation.* Boulder, Col.: Westview Press.

Hanna, Favez, Director, Office of Risk Reduction Technology, Directorate of Health Standards Programs, OSHA, DOL. 1984. Telephone interview with author, 19 July.

Hanna, Thomas, Motor Vehicle Manufacturers Association. 1983. Testimony. U.S. Congress. House. Committee on the Judiciary. Subcommittee on Administrative Law and Governmental Relations. *Hearings on H.R. 2327.* 195 98th Cong., 1st sess., 1983.

Harris, Herbert. 1980. Testimony. U.S. Congress. House. Committee on Interstate and Foreign Commerce. Subcommittee on Oversight and Investigations. *Hearings on Cost–Benefit Analysis: The Potential for Conflict of Interest.* 7 96th Cong. 2d sess., 1980.

Harris, Ken. *See* Safeer.

Harrison, D. 1981. "Distributional Objectives in Health and Safety Regulation." In *The Benefits of Health and Safety Regulation.* Edited by A. Ferguson and E. LeVeen. Cambridge, Mass.: Ballinger.

Harter, P. 1986. "Executive Oversight of Rulemaking: The President Is No Stranger." *American University Law Review* 36:357.

Harwood, Susan, Office of Risk Assessment, Health Standards Directorate, OSHA. 1986. Telephone interview with author, 21 October.

Havemann, R. H. 1975. "Agencies Slow in Producing Inflation Impact Statements." *National Journal* 7:892.

Hawkins, Joseph, Regulatory Analysis Branch, Systems Analysis Division, Office of Aviation Policy and Plans, FAA, DOT. 1984. Telephone interview with author, 5 June.

Hawley, E. W. 1966. *The New Deal and the Problem of Monopoly.* Princeton, N.J.: Princeton University Press.

Hazleton, J. 1978. "Post Hearing Comment on Proposed Generic Regulation of Occupational Carcinogens." Submitted to OSHA in connection with the generic carcinogen rulemaking proceedings. Mimeo. 10 October.

Heller, T. C. 1976. "The Importance of Normative Decisionmaking: The Limitations of Legal Economics as a Basis for a Liberal Jurisprudence – As Illustrated by the Regulation of Vacation Home Development." *Wisconsin Law Review,* 385.

Henshel, George, Office of the Solicitor, DOL. 1986. Telephone interview with author, 28 October.

Hibbert, Robert, Director, Standards and Labeling Division, Meat and Poultry Inspection Technical Services, FSIS, USDA. 1984a. Telephone interview with author, 5 April.

1984b. Telephone interview with author, 24 May.

Hill, Jerry, former Assistant Secretary of Agriculture, USDA. 1983. Testimony. U.S. Congress. House. Committee on the Judiciary. Subcommittee on Administrative Law and Governmental Relations. *Hearings on H.R. 2327.* 533 98th Cong., 1st sess., 1983.

Hitchcock, Ralph, Director, Office of Vehicle Safety Standards, Office of Rulemaking, NHTSA, DOT. 1983. Interview with author. Washington, D.C., 19 May.

Hofstadter, R. 1955. *The Age of Reform.* New York: Knopf.

Holden, C. 1984. "Congress to Investigate Charges That OMB is Obstructing Data Collection." *Science* 234:934.

Hopkins, Thomas D., Deputy Administrator for Regulatory and Statistical Analysis, OIRA, OMB. 1982. Statement. In Department of Transportation, *Seminar on Executive Order 12291 and OMB Regulatory Impact Analysis Guidance.*

1983. Interview with author. Washington, D.C., 17 May.

Horowitz, A. 1970. "Social Science Mandarins: Policymaking as a Political Formula." *Policy Sciences* 1:339.

Houck, O. A. 1987. "President X and the New (Approved) Decisionmaking." *American University Law Review* 36:535.

Houston, Donald, Administrator, FSIS, USDA. 1984. Telephone interview with author, 23 April.

Hurter, A. P., G. S. Tolley, and R. G. Fabian. 1982. "Benefit–Cost Analysis and the Common Sense of Environmental Policy." In *Cost–Benefit Analysis and Environmental Regulations: Politics, Ethics, and Methods.* Edited by D. Swartzman, R. Liroff, and K. Crooke. Washington, D.C.: Conservation Foundation.

Institute for Public Interest Representation. 1981. Testimony. U.S. Congress. Senate. Committee on Governmental Affairs. *Hearings on Regulatory Reform Legislation of 1981.* 263 97th Cong., 1st sess., *1981.*

Interagency Regulatory Liaison Group. 1979, 1980. "Scientific Bases for Identification of Potential Carcinogens and Estimation of Risk." *Federal Register* 44;39,858, 45:5,009.

Irons, P. H. 1982. *The New Deal Lawyers.* Princeton, N.J.: Princeton University Press.

Jackson, Shelton, Chief, Policy Analysis Division, Office of Economics, Office of Policy and International Affairs, DOT. Telephone interview with author, 5 June 1984.

Jaffe, L. L. 1939. "Invective and Investigation in Administrative Law." *Harvard Law Review* 52:1,201.

1965. *Judicial Control of Administrative Action.* Boston: Little, Brown.

Janis, I. L. 1972. *Victims of Groupthink: A Psychological Study of Foreign Policy Decisions and Fiascoes.* Boston: Houghton Mifflin.

Janofsky, L., President, American Bar Association. 1981. Testimony. U.S. Congress. House. Committee on the Judiciary. Subcommittee on Administrative Law and Governmental Relations. *Regulatory Procedures Act of 1981: Hearings on H.R. 746.* 103 97th Cong., 1st sess., 1981.

Jenkins-Smith, H. C. 1982. "Professional Roles for Policy Analysts: A Critical Assessment." *Journal of Policy Analysis and Management* 2:88.

Jennings, Al, Director, Chemicals and Statistical Policy Division, Office of Standards and Regulations, Office of Policy and Program Planning, EPA. 1983. Interview with author. Washington, D.C., 18 May.

Johnson, E. 1983. " 'Agency 'Capture:' The 'Revolving Door' Between Regulated Industries and Their Regulating Agencies." *University of Richmond Law Review* 18:95.

Johnson, William, SCI, Inc. 1982. *Memorandum to Joel Schwartz on Urban Areas in Which Small Refiners Are an Important Factor in Gasoline Supply.* 25 March.

Jones, C. D. 1977. *An Introduction to the Study of Public Policy.* North Scituak, Mass.: Duxbury Press.

Jones, Erika. 1983. *See* Steed.

Special Counsel to the Administrator, NHTSA, DOT. 1984. Telephone interview with author, 20 August.

Jones, G. R., et al. 1975. "A Method for the Quantification of Aesthetic Values for Environmental Decision Making." *Nuclear Technology* 25: 682.

Jordan, William, Union of Concerned Scientists. 1983. Testimony. U.S. Congress. House. Committee on the Judiciary. Subcommittee on Administrative Law and Governmental Relations. *Hearings on H.R. 2327.* 558 98th Cong., 1st sess., 1983.

Kasper, R. 1977. "Cost–Benefit Analysis in Environmental Decision-Making." *George Washington Law Review* 45:1013.

Kelly, Thomas, Program Division, Office of Systems and Evaluation, Office of Policy Planning and Evaluation, EPA. 1984. Telephone interview with author, 21 May.

Kelman, M. 1979. "Choice and Utility." *Wisconsin Law Review* 769.

Kelman, S. 1981a. *What Price Incentives?* Boston: Auburn House.

   1981b. "Cost–Benefit Analysis: An Ethical Critique." *Regulation* (January/February):33.

   1982. "Cost–Benefit Analysis and Environmental, Safety, and Health Regulation: Ethical and Philosophical Considerations." In *Cost–Benefit Analysis and Environmental Regulations: Politics, Ethics, and Methods.* Edited by D. Swartzman, R. Liroff, and K. Crooke. Washington, D.C.: Conservation Foundation.

Kennedy, D. 1981. "Cost–Benefit Analysis of Entitlement Problems: A Critique." *Stanford Law Review* 33:387.

Kennedy, William F., Business Roundtable. 1981. Testimony. U.S. Congress. Senate. Committee on the Judiciary. Subcommittee on Regulatory Reform. *Hearings on Regulatory Reform Act – S. 1080.* 2 97th Cong., 1st sess., 1981.

Kinney, Robert. *See* Koslowski.

Kleindorfer, P. R. 1981. Statement. In *The Benefits of Health and Safety Regulation.* Edited by G. Ferguson and E. LeVeen. Cambridge, Mass.: Ballinger.

Kleindorfer, P. R., and H. K. Kunreuther. 1981. "Descriptive and Prescriptive Aspects of Health and Safety Regulation." In *The Benefits of Health and Safety Regulation.* Edited by G. Ferguson and E. LeVeen. Cambridge, Mass.: Ballinger.

Knetsch, J. L., and J. A. Sinden. 1984. "Willingness to Pay and Compensation Demanded: Experimental Evidence of an Unexpected Disparity in Measures of Value." *Quarterly Journal of Economics* 99:507.

Kneese A. V., and R. C. D'Arge. 1981. "Benefit Analysis and Today's Regulatory Problems." In *The Benefits of Health and Safety Regulation.* Edited by G. Ferguson and E. LeVeen. Cambridge, Mass.: Ballinger.

Kneese, A. V., and C. Schultz. 1975. *Pollution, Prices, and Public Policy.* Washington, D.C.: Brookings Institution Press.

Kolb, Jeff, Benefits Branch, Economic Analysis Division, Office of Policy Analysis, Office of Policy, Planning and Evaluation, EPA. 1983. Telephone interview with author, 28 July.

Koslowski, Richard, Barry Nussbaum, and Robert Kinney, Field Operations and Support Division, Office of Mobile Sources, Office of Air Noise and Radiation, EPA. 1984. Telephone interview with author, 12 January.

Kosterlitz, J. 1985. "Reagan Is Leaving His Mark on the Food and Drug Administration." *National Journal* 17:1,568.

Kranidas, Ellen, Acting Associate Administrator for Plans and Programs, NHTSA, DOT. 1984a. Telephone interview with author, 13 June.

1984b. Telephone interview with author, 16 August.

1984c. Letter to author, 25 September.

Krieger, H. L., Director, Federal Personnel and Compensation Division, General Accounting Office. 1980. Statement. U.S. Congress. House. Committee on Interstate and Foreign Commerce. Subcommittee on Oversight and Investigations. *Hearings on Cost–Benefit Analysis: The Potential for Conflict of Interest.* 19 96th Cong., 2d sess., 1980.

Kuzmak, Arnold, Director, Office of Program Development and Evaluation, Office of Drinking Water, Office of Water, EPA. 1984a. Telephone interview with author, 22 May.

1984b. Letter to author, 27 August.

1986. Telephone interview with author, 18 November.

Lange, Loren, Deputy Director, Policy and Program Planning Staff, FSIS, USDA. 1984a. Telephone interview with author, 13 March.

1984b. Letter to author, 21 August.

Lash, J., K. Gillman, and D. Sheridan. 1984. A *Season of Spoils: the Reagan Administration's Attack on the Environment.* New York: Pantheon.

Latin, H. A. 1982. "The 'Significance' of Toxic Health Risks: An Essay on Legal Decisionmaking Under Uncertainty." *Ecology Law Quarterly* 10:339.

1983. "The Feasibility of Occupational Health Standards: An Essay on Legal Decisionmaking Under Uncertainty." *Northwestern University Law Review* 78:583.

Lave, Lester B., Brookings Institution. 1979. Testimony. U.S. Congress, House. Committee on Interstate and Foreign Commerce. Subcommittee on Oversight and Investigations and Subcommittee on Consumer Protection and Finance. *Joint Hearings on the Use of Cost–Benefit Analysis by Regulatory Agencies.* 20 96th Cong., 1st sess., 1979.

1981a. *The Strategy of Social Regulation.* Washington, D.C.: Brookings Institution Press.

1981b. Testimony. U.S. Congress. Senate. Committee on Governmental Affairs. *Hearings on Regulatory Reform Legislation of 1981.* 254 97th Cong., 1st sess., 1981.

1982. "Introduction." In *Quantitative Risk Assessment in Regulation.* Edited by L. Lave. Washington, D.C.: Brookings.

Leape, J. P. 1980. "Quantitative Risk Assessment in Regulation of Environmental Carcinogens." *Harvard Environmental Law Review* 4:86.

Leman, C. K. 1982. "Some Benefits and Costs of the Proliferation of Analysis." In *Natural Resources Budgeting.* Prepared for the 4th Annual Research Conference of the Association for Public Policy Analysis and Management, October 23–30, 1982.

Leman, C. K., and R. H. Nelson. 1981. "Ten Commandments for Policy Economists." *Journal of Policy Analysis and Management* 1:97.

Leonard, Thomas, OIRA, OMB. 1984. Telephone interview with author, 16 April.

Leone, R. A., and J. E. Jackson. 1981. "The Political Economy of Federal Regulatory Activity: The Case of Water Pollution Controls." In *Studies in Public Regulation*. Edited by G. Fromm. Cambridge, Mass.: MIT Press.

Leoni, B. 1964. "The Meaning of 'Political' in Political Decisions." In *The Making of Decisions: A Reader in Administrative Behavior*. Edited by W. Gore and J. Dyson. London: Collier-MacMillan.

Levin, H. M. 1983. *Cost-Effectiveness: A Primer*. Beverly Hills, Calif.: Sage.

Lindblom, C. E. 1959. "The Science of 'Muddling Through.' " *Public Administration Review* 19:79.

1968. *The Policy Making Process*. Englewood Cliffs, N.J.: Prentice-Hall.

Linnerooth, J. 1975. "The Evaluation of Life-Saving: A Survey." International Institute for Applied Systems Analysis. Mimeo.

1978. "Reevaluating the Value of Life." Paper presented to the Joint Operations Research Society of America/The Institute of Management Sciences Conference, Los Angeles, November 13–15, 1978.

Liroff, R. 1982. "Cost–Benefit Analysis in Federal Environmental Programs." In *Cost–Benefit Analysis and Environmental Regulations: Politics, Ethics, and Methods*. Edited by D. Swartzman, R. Liroff, and K. Crooke. Washington, D.C.: Conservation Foundation.

Litan, R., and W. Nordhaus. 1983. *Reforming Federal Regulation*. New Haven, Conn.: Yale University Press.

Lovins, A. B. 1977. "Cost–Risk Benefit Assessments in Energy Policy." *George Washington Law Review* 45:911.

Lowi, T. J. 1987. "Two Roads to Serfdom: Liberalism, Conservatism and Administrative Power." *American University Law Review* 36:295.

Luken, Ralph, Benefits Grants Chief, Economic Analysis Division, Office of Policy Analysis, Office of Policy and Program Evaluation, EPA. 1983. Interview with author. Washington, D.C., 18 May.

1984a. "The Emerging Role of Benefit–Cost Analysis in the Regulatory Process at EPA." Mimeo, July.

1984b. Letter to author, 22 August.

1985a. Telephone interview, 25 May.

1985b. "Benefit–Cost Analysis at EPA." *The Environmental Forum* (October):42.

Luken, Ralph and E. Johnson. 1984. "The Emerging Role of Benefit-Cost Analysis in the Regulatory Process, at EPA." (Unpublished manuscript dated July 1984.)

Luken, Ralph and S. G. Miller. 1981. "The Benefits and Costs of Regulating Benzene." *Journal of the Air Pollution Control Association* 31:1,254.

Lundberg, C. C. 1964. "Administrative Decisions: A Scheme for Analysis." In *The Making of Decisions: A Reader in Administrative Behavior*. Edited by W. Gore and J. Dyson. London: Collier-MacMillan.

Luttner, Mark, Chief, Economic Analysis Staff, Office of Analysis and Evaluation, Office of Water Regulations and Standards, Office of Water, EPA. 1986. Telephone interview with author, 13 November.

Lynn, F. M. 1986. "The Interplay of Science and Values in Assessing and

Regulating Environmental Risks." *Science, Technology, and Human Values* 11:40.

Majone, G. 1978. "Technology Assessment in a Dielectic Key." *Public Administration Review* 38:52.

Marketing Research Services. 1981. "Consumer Focus Groups Concerning Mechanically Processed Meat Product (1980)." *Federal Register* 46:39,309.

Marshall, E. 1982a. "White House Steps into Lead Fight." *Science* 217:807.

1982b. "EPA May Allow More Lead in Gasoline." *Science* 215:1,375.

Martonik, J. *See* Adkins.

Massachusetts Institute of Technology. Center for Policy Alternatives. 1980. Benefits of Environmental, Health, and Safety Regulation. Prepared for U.S. Congress. Senate. Committee on Governmental Affairs. 96th Cong., 2d sess., 1980.

May, P. 1986. "Politics and Policy Analysis." *Political Science Quarterly* 101:109.

Mazmanian, D. A., and J. N. Clark. 1979. *Can Organizations Change?: Environmental Protection, Citizen Participation, and the Army Corps of Engineers.* Washington, D.C.: Brookings Institution Press.

Mazur, A. 1985. "Bias in Risk–Benefit Analysis." *Technology in Society* 7:25.

McCraw, T. K. 1984. *Prophets of Regulation.* Cambridge, Mass.: Harvard University Press.

McCutcheon, John, Director, Policy and Program Planning Staff, FSIS, USDA. 1984. Telephone interview with author, 14 March.

1982. *Memorandum to Donald L. Houston.* 21 June.

McGarity, T. O. 1977. "The Courts, The Agencies and NEPA Threshold Issues." *Texas Law Review* 55:801.

1979. "Substantive and Procedural Discretion in Administrative Resolution of Science Policy Questions: Regulating Carcinogens in EPA and OSHA." *Georgetown Law Journal* 77:729.

1983a. "OSHA's Generic Carcinogen Policy: Rulemaking under Scientific and Legal Uncertainty." In *Law and Science in Collaboration.* Edited by D. Nyhart and M. Carrow. Lexington, Mass.: Lexington Books.

1983b. "Media Quality, Technology and Cost–Benefit Balancing Strategies for Health and Environmental Regulation." *Law and Contemporary Problems* 46:159.

1986. "Regulatory Reform in the Reagan Era." *Maryland Law Review* 45:253.

1987. "Presidential Control of Regulatory Agency Decisionmaking." *American University Law Review* 36:443.

McGarity, T. O., and E. P. Schroeder. 1981. "Risk-Oriented Employment Screening." *Texas Law Review* 59:999.

McGarity, T. O., and S. A. Shapiro. 1980. "The Trade Secret Status of Health and Safety Testing Data: Reforming Agency Disclosure Policies." *Harvard Law Review* 93:837.

Meidinger, E. 1985. "On Explaining the Development of 'Emissions Trading' in U.S. Air Pollution Regulation." *Law and Society* 7:447.

1986. Regulatory Culture, Draft Working Paper, Baldy Center for Law and Social Policy, Buffalo, N.Y.

1987. Regulatory Culture and Democratic Theory, Draft Working paper, Baldy Center for Law and Social Policy, Buffalo, N.Y.

Meltsner, A. 1976. *Policy Analysts and the Bureaucracy.* Berkeley and Los Angeles: University of California Press.

Mendeloff, J. 1979. *Regulating Safety: An Economic and Political Analysis of Occupational Safety and Health Policy.* Cambridge, Mass.: MIT Press.

Merrill, R. 1982. Federal Regulation of Cancer-Causing Chemicals. Report to the Administrative Conference of the United States, Washington, D.C.

Meyerson, Jon, Office of Budget and Policy Analysis, USDA. 1984. Telephone interview with author, 2 May.

Miller, J. 1977. "Lessons of the Economic Impact Statement Program." *Regulation* (July/August):14.

Administrator, OIRA, OMB. 1981a. Testimony. U.S. Congress. Senate. Committee on the Judiciary. Subcommittee on Regulatory Reform. *Hearings on Regulatory Reform Act – S. 1080.* 165 97th Cong., 1st sess., 1981.

1981b. Testimony. U.S. Congress. Senate. Committee on Governmental Affairs. *Hearings on Regulatory Reform Legislation of 1981.* 10 97th Cong., 1st sess., 1981.

Mishan, E. 1971. "Evaluation of Life & Limb: A Theoretical Approach." *Journal of Political Economy* 79:687.

1973. *Economics for Social Decisions: Elements of Cost–Benefits Analysis.* New York: Praeger.

1981. "Distributive Implications of Economic Controls." In *The Benefits of Health and Safety Regulation.* Edited by G. Ferguson and E. LeVeen. Cambridge, Mass.: Ballinger.

Moore, M. H. 1980. "Statesmanship in a World of Particular Substantive Choices." In *Bureaucrats, Policy Analysts, Statesmen: Who Leads?* Edited by R. Goldwin. Washington, D.C.: American Enterprise Institute.

Morgan, T. D. 1980. "Appropriate Limits on Participation by Former Agency Officials in Matters Before the Agency." *Duke Law Journal* 1980:1.

Morgenstern, Richard, Acting Director, Office of Policy Analysis, Office of Policy, Planning and Evaluation, EPA. 1986. Telephone interview with author, 7 November.

Morrall, John, OIRA, OMB. 1983. Interview with author. Washington, D.C., 17 May.

1984. Telephone interview with author, 24 September.

Morrison, Alan B., Public Citizen Litigation Group. 1979. Testimony. U.S. Congress. Senate. Committee on the Judiciary. Subcommittee on Administrative Practice and Procedure. *Hearings on Regulatory Reform.* 419 96th Cong., 1st sess., pt. 2, 1979.

1984. Testimony. U.S. Congress. Senate. Committee on Governmental Affairs. Subcommittee on Information Management and Regulatory Affairs. *Hearings on the Paperwork Reduction Act Amendments of 1984.* 228 98th Cong., 2d sess., 1984.

1986. "OMB Interference with Agency Rulemaking: The Wrong Way to Write a Regulation." *Harvard Law Review* 99:1,059.

Mudge, Shaw. 1982. Testimony. U.S. Congress. Senate. Committee on the Judiciary. Subcommittee on Regulatory Reform. Committee on Small Business. Subcommittee on Government Regulation and Paperwork. *Regulatory Flexibility Act: Joint Hearings.* 56 97th Cong., 2d sess. 1982.

Murdock III, J. E., Acting Deputy Administrator and Chief Counsel, and E. Faberman, Deputy Chief Counsel, FAA, DOT. Interview with author. 1983. Washington, D.C., 18 May.

Nager, G. D. 1982. "Bureaucrats and the Cost–Benefit Chameleon." *Regulation* (September/October):37.

Napolitano, Sam, Chief, Hazardous Waste Branch, Regulatory Policy Division, Office of Policy Analysis, Office of Policy, Planning and Evaluation, EPA. 1984. Telephone interview with author, 24 May.

National Academy of Science. Institute of Medicine. 1981. *Costs of Environment-Related Health Effects.*

National Research Council. 1975. *Decision Making for Regulating Chemicals in the Environment.*

1983. *Risk Assessment in the Federal Government: Managing the Process.*

National Association of Manufacturers. 1981. Testimony. U.S. Congress. House. Committee on the Judiciary. Subcommittee on Administrative Law and Governmental Relations. *Regulatory Procedures Act of 1981: Hearings on H.R. 746.* 560 97th Cong., 1st sess., 1981.

National Council of Professional Services Firms. 1981. Testimony. U.S. Congress. Senate. Committee on Governmental Affairs. Subcommittee on Federal Expenditures, Research and Rules. *Hearings on the Consultant Reform and Disclosure Act of 1981.* 82 97th Cong., 1st sess., 1981.

National Foundation of Independent Businesses. 1982. Testimony. U.S. Congress. Senate. Committee on the Judiciary. Subcommittee on Regulatory Reform. Committee on Small Business. Subcommittee on Government Regulation and Paperwork. *Regulatory Flexibility Act: Joint Hearings.* 63 97th Cong., 2d sess., 1982.

National Food Processors Association. 1981. Testimony. U.S. Congress. House. Committee on the Judiciary. Subcommittee on Administrative Law and Governmental Relations. *Regulatory Procedures Act of 1981: Hearings on H.R. 746.* 837 97th Cong., 1st sess., 1981.

National Legal Aid and Defenders Association. 1981. Testimony. U.S. Congress. House. Committee on the Judiciary. Subcommittee on Administrative Law and Governmental Relations. *Regulatory Procedures Act of 1981: Hearings on H.R. 746.* 690 97th Cong., 1st sess., 1981.

Neely, A. S. 1985. "Statutory Inhibitions to the Application of Principles of Cost/Benefit Analysis in Administrative Decision Making." *Duquesne Law Review* 23:489.

Neibrief, Judith. Special Assistant to the Administrator, FSIS, USDA. 1984a. Telephone Interview with author, 12 March.

1984b. Telephone interview with author. 19 April.

NHTSA. 1972. "Fields of Direct View: Proposed Motor Vehicle Safety Standard." *Federal Register* 37:7,210.

1973. "Motor Vehicle Safety Standards: Further Notice on Visibility Standard." *Federal Register* 38:6,194.

1977. *Order 800-1, Rulemaking Procedures: Motor Vehicle Standards.* 2 February.

1978. "Fields of Direct View: Motor Vehicle Safety Standard: Notice of Proposed Rulemaking and Invitation for Applications for Financial Assistance in the Preparation of Comments." *Federal Register* 43:51,677.

Acting Associate Administrator for Plans and Programs. 1978. *Memorandum to Assistant Chief Counsel for Rulemaking on OCC Questions on the Fields of Direct View Proposal.* 17 August.

Acting Associate Administrator for Rulemaking. 1978. *Memorandum to National Highway Traffic Administrator on Fields of Direct View and Rearview Mirrors.* 17 July.

Assistant Chief Counsel for Rulemaking. 1978. *Memorandum to Acting Associate Administrator for Rulemaking and Acting Associate Administrator for Planning and Programming on Fields of Direct View.* 10 August.

Associate Administrator for Plans and Programs. 1981. *Memorandum to Associate Administrator for Rulemaking on Revocation of Standard No. 1289 for Passenger Cars.* 4 June.

Associate Administrator for Research and Development. 1979. *Memorandum to Associate Administrator for Rulemaking on Accident Statistics to Support Rulemaking, CAO Request #3.* 23 August.

Associate Administrator for Rulemaking. 1980a. *Memorandum to Associate Administrator for Plans and Programs on Regulatory Analysis for "Fields of Direct View."* 8 December.

Associate Administrator for Rulemaking. 1980b. *Memorandum on Response to P&P's Draft Memo of December 16, 1980, regarding FMUSS No. 128, Fields of Direct View.* 17 December.

Associate Administrator for Rulemaking. 1981. *Memorandum to Addressees on Petitions for Reconsiderations, "Fields of Direct View," FMVSS No. 128.* 17 March.

1981a. "Federal Motor Vehicle Standards; Fields of Direct View." *Federal Register* 46:21,203.

1981b. "Federal Motor Vehicle Safety Standards; Fields of Direct View; Response to Petitions for Reconsideration." *Federal Register* 46:32,254.

1981c. "Federal Motor Vehicle Safety Standards: Occupant Crash Protection." *Federal Register* 46:53,419.

1981d. "Fields of Direct View: Final Rule." *Federal Register* 46:40.

Office of Program and Rulemaking Analysis. 1981. "Fields of Direct View." *Regulatory Evaluation.* (FMVSS 128).

Nichols, Albert, Acting Director, Economic Analysis Division. Office of Policy Analysis, Office of Policy, Planning and Evaluation, EPA. 1984. Telephone interview with author, 22 May.

Nichols, Albert and R. Zeckhauser. 1986. "The Perils of Prudence." *Regulation* (November/December):15.

Note. 1970. "Implementation of the Environmental Impact Statement." *Yale Law Journal* 88:596.

Note. 1986. "Executive Orders 12,291 and 12,498: Usurpation of Legislative Power or Blueprint for Legislative Reform?" *George Washington Law Review* 54:512.

Nussbaum, Barry, Fuels Branch Chief, Field Operations and Support Division, Office of Mobile Sources. Office of Air, Noise and Radiation, EPA. 1983. Telephone interview with author, 31 October.

1984. See Koslowski.

O'Connor, John, Director, Strategies and Air Standards Division, Office of Air Quality Planning and Standards Division, Office of Air Quality Planning and Standards, Office of Air and Radiation, EPA. 1984. Telephone interview with author, 24 August.

Oelinick, Arthur, Department of Environmental and Industrial Health, University of Michigan. 1984. Telephone interview with author. 18 April.

Office of Science and Technology Policy. 1985. "Chemical Carcinogens; A Review of the Science and Its Associated Principles." *Federal Register* 50:10,372.

Office of Technology Assessment. 1981. *Technologies for Determining Cancer Risks from the Environment.*

1982. *The Role of Genetic Testing in the Prevention of Occupational Disease.*

Okun, A. 1975. *Equality and Efficiency: The Big Tradeoff.* Washington, D.C.: Brookings Institution Press.

Olson, E. D. 1984. "The Quiet Shift of Power: Office of Management and Budget Supervision of Environmental Protection Agency Rulemaking Under Executive Order 12291." *Virginia Journal of Natural Resources Law* 4:1.

OMB. 1974. Circular Number A-107, 28 January.

1980. *Incorporating Regulatory Flexibility into the Regulatory Process: Interim Guidance.* December.

1981. *Interim Regulatory Impact Assessment Guidance,* 12 July.

1982a. *Executive Order 12,291 on Federal Regulation: Progress During 1981.*

1982b. "A Critical Review of OSHA's Proposed Hazard Communication Regulation." Mimeo. 7 January.

1983. *Executive Order 12,291 on Federal Regulation: Progress During 1982.*

1986. *The Regulatory Program of the United States Government.*

1989a. *Final Regulatory Impact Assessment Guidance.* Reprinted in OMB 1989b, App. V.

1989b. *The Regulatory Program of the United States Government.*

OSHA. 1977. "Hazardous Materials Labeling: Advance Notice of Proposed Rulemaking." *Federal Register* 42:4,412.

1981a. "Hazard Identification: Notice of Public Rulemaking and Public Hearings." *Federal Register* 46:4,412.

1981b. "Hazard Identification: Withdrawal of Proposed Rule." *Federal Register* 46:12,214.

1982a. *Draft Regulatory Impact and Regulatory Flexibility Analyses of The Hazard Communication Standard.*

1982b. "Hazard Communication: Notice of Public Rulemaking and Public Hearings." *Federal Register* 47:12,092.

1982c. *Instruction RUL. 1.* 1 March.

1983a. *Final Regulatory Impact and Regulatory Flexibility Analyses of The Hazard Communication Standard.*

1983b. "Hazard Communication: Final Rule." *Federal Register* 48:53,280.

1983c. Testimony. U.S. Congress. House. Committee on the Judiciary. Subcommittee on Administrative Law and Governmental Relations. *Hearings on H.R. 2327.* 2,015 98th Cong., 1st sess., 1983.

1987. "Hazard Communication: Final Rule." *Federal Register* 52:31,852.

Ottinger, Richard. 1983. Statement. U.S. Congress. House. Committee on the Judiciary. Subcommittee on Administrative Law and Governmental Relations. *Hearings on H.R. 2327.* 476 98th Cong., 1st sess., 1983.

Pacific Coast Meat Association. 1979. "Citizen Petition." *Federal Register* 46:39,278.

Peak, John, Legislative and Regulatory Coordination Staff Director, Office of Industry Policy, Office of the Assistant Secretary for Policy and International Affairs, DOT. 1983. Telephone interview with author, 9 May.

1984. Telephone interview with author, 5 June.

Peskin, H. M. 1978. "Environmental Policy of the Distribution of Benefits and Costs." In *Current Issues in U.S. Environmental Policy.* Edited by P. Portney, et al. Baltimore: Johns Hopkins University Press.

Pierce, R. J. 1985. "The Role of Constitutional and Political Theory in Administrative Law." *Texas Law Review* 64:469.

Podberesky, Samuel, Deputy Assistant General Counsel for Regulation and Enforcement, DOT. 1983. Interview with author. Washington, D.C., 20 May.

1984a. Telephone interview with author, 4 April.

1984b. Interview with author. Washington, D.C., 27 April.

1984c. *See* Eisner 1984.

Pope, C. 1979. "Problems in the Toxic Substance Area." In *Toxic Substances: Decisions and Values.* Washington, D.C.: Technical Information Project.

Portney, P. 1984. "The Benefits and Costs of Regulatory Analysis." In *Environmental Policy Under Reagan's Executive Order: The Role of Benefit Cost Analysis.* Edited by V. K. Smith. Chapel Hill: University of North Carolina Press.

President's Commission on Three Mile Island. 1979. *Report of the President's Commission on Three Mile Island: The Need for Change: The Legacy of TMI.*

Quarles, J. 1976. *Cleaning Up America: An Insider's View of the Environmental Protection Agency.* Boston: Houghton Mifflin.

Former Deputy Administrator, EPA. 1979. Testimony. U.S. Congress. Senate. Committee on Environment and Public Works. Subcommittee on Environmental Pollution. *Hearings.* 61 96th Cong., 1st sess., 1979.

Raiffa, H. 1968. *Decision Analysis: Introductory Lectures on Choices Under Uncertainty.* Reading, Mass.: Addison-Wesley.

Raven-Hansen, P. 1983. "Making Agencies Follow Orders: Judicial Review of Agency Violation of Executive Order 12,291." *Duke Law Journal* 1983:285.

Regens, J. L., T. M. Deitz, and R. W. Rycroft. 1983. "Risk Assessment in the Policy-Making Process: Environmental Health and Safety Protection." *Public Administration Review* 43:137.

Regens, J. L., and T. M. Rycroft. 1986. "Measuring Equity in Regulatory Policy Implementation." *Public Administration Review* 46:423.

Rein, M. 1976. *Social Science and Public Policy.* New York: Viking-Penguin.

Rhoads, S. E. 1985. "Do Economists Overemphasize Monetary Benefits?" *Public Administration Review* 45:815.

Richardson, Russell, Chairman, Committee on Contracting Out. 1981. Testimony. U.S. Congress. Senate. Committee on Governmental Affairs. Subcommittee on Federal Expenditures, Research and Rules. *Hearings on the Consultant Reform and Disclosure Act of 1981.* 57 97th Cong., 1st sess., 1981.

Rodgers, W. H. 1980. "Benefits, Costs and Risks: Oversight of Health and Environmental Decisionmaking." *Harvard Environmental Law Review* 4:191.

———. 1981. "Judicial Review of Risk Assessments: The Use of Decision Theory in Unscrambling the Benzene Decision." *Environmental Law Review* 11:301.

Rosenfield, A. 1987. "Presidential Policy Management of Agency Rules Under Executive Order 12498." *Administrative Law Review* 37:63.

Rosera, Gene, Commodity Analysis Division, Commodity Operations, ASCS, USDA. 1984. Telephone interview with author, 1 May.

Rothstein, M. 1983. *Occupational Safety and Health Law.* St. Paul, Minn.: West.

Rourke, F. E. 1984. *Bureaucracy, Politics, and Public Policy.* Boston: Little, Brown.

Ruhter, Dale, Chief Economic Analysis Branch, Waste Management and Economics Division, Office of Solid Waste, Office of Solid Waste and Emergency Response, EPA. 1984. Telephone interview with author, 10 July.

———. 1984b. Letter to author, 25 July.

———. 1985a. Telephone interview with author, 8 January.

———. 1985b. Telephone interview with author, 20 November.

Rung, C. F., 1983. "Risk Assessment and Environmental Benefits Analysis." *Natural Resources Journal* 23:683.

Russell, M. 1986. " 'Discounting Human Life' (or, the Anatomy of a Moral–Economic Issue)." *Resources* 82:8.

Safeer, Harvey, Norman Weil, and Ken Harris. Office of Aviation Plans and Programs, FAA, DOT. 1983. Interview with author, 18 May.

Sagoff, M. 1981. "Economic Theory and Environmental Law." *Michigan Law Review* 79:1,414.

1982. "We Have Met the Enemy and He Is Us, or Conflict and Contradiction in Environmental Law." *Environmental Law* 12:283.

1986. "The Principles of Federal Pollution Control Law." *Minnesota Law Review* 71:19.

Samuels, S. 1979. "The Role of Scientific Data in Health Decisions." *Environmental Health Perspectives* 32:301.

Sax, J. L. 1973. "The (Unhappy) Truth About NEPA." *Oklahoma Law Review* 26:239.

Schelling, T. C. 1968. "The Life You Save May Be Your Own." In *Problems in Public Expenditure Analysis.* Edited by S. Chase. Washington, D.C.: Brookings Institute Press.

Schoenbrod, D. 1983. "Goals Statutes and Rules Statutes: The Case of the Clean Air Act." *UCLA Law Review* 30:740.

1985. "The Delegation Doctrine: Could the Court Give It Substance?" *Michigan Law Review* 83:1223.

1987. "Separation of Powers and the Powers That Be: The Constitutional Purposes of the Delegation Doctrine." *American University Law Review* 36:355.

Schroeder, C. H. 1986. "Rights Against Risks." *Columbia Law Review* 86:495.

Schultz, George, Director, Office of Management and Budget. *Memorandum to Heads of Departments and Agencies,* 5 October 1971.

Schultz, W., et al. 1983. "The Economic Benefits of Preserving Visibility in the National Parklands of the Southwest." *Natural Resources Journal* 23:149.

Schwartz, B. 1985. "Cost–Benefit Analysis in Administrative Law: Does It Make Priceless Procedural Rights Worthless? *Administrative Law Review* 37:1.

Schwartz, Joel, Office of Policy and Resource Management, Office of Policy, Planning and Evaluation, EPA. 1981a. *Memorandum on "Gasoline Lead Analysis" from Joel Schwartz to Marty Wagner, George Sugiyama, Rob Weissman and Richard Koslowski.* 6 November.

1981b. *Memorandum on "Economic Analysis of Gasoline Lead Use" to Addressees,* 30 November.

1984. Telephone interview with author, 5 January.

Schwartzman, D. 1982. "Cost–Benefit Analysis in Environmental Regulation: Sources of the Controversy." In *Cost–Benefit Analysis and Environmental Regulations: Politics, Ethics, and Methods.* Edited by D. Swartzman, R. Liroff, and K. Crooke. Washington, D.C.: Conservation Foundation.

SCI, Inc. 1981. "Potential for Cost Reduction and Energy Savings Realized through Modification of Lead Phasedown Regulation." Mimeo.

SCI, Inc. 1982a. "Three Alternative Limitations on the Use of Lead Additives in Gasoline." Mimeo.

SCI, Inc. 1982b. "Estimates of Refiners' Cost Changes if Lead Regulations

370   **Bibliography**

Are Applicable Only to Leaded Grades of Gasoline Instead of to the Total Pool." Mimeo.

Securities and Exchange Commission. 1981. Testimony. U.S. Congress. House. Committee on the Judiciary. Subcommittee on Administrative Law and Governmental Relations. *Regulatory Procedures Act of 1981: Hearings on H.R. 746.* 259 97th Cong., 1st sess., 1981.

Segal, Judith, Director, Policy and Program Planning Staff, FSIS, USDA. 1984a. Telephone interview with author, 15 March.

1984b. Telephone interview with author, 2 May.

1984c. Telephone interview with author, 21 May.

1986. Telephone interview with author, 25 November.

Seidman, D. 1977. "The Politics of Policy Analysis." *Regulation* (July/August):22.

Self, P. 1975. *Econocrats and the Policy Process: The Politics and Philosophy of Cost–Benefit Analysis.* London: Macmillan Press.

Sessions, Stuart, Acting Director, Regulatory Policy Division, Office of Policy Analysis, Office of Policy, Planning and Evaluation, EPA. 1984. Telephone interview with author, 29 May.

Settle, R., and D. Weisbrod. 1977. Governmentally-Imposed Standards: Some Normative Aspects. Institute for Research on Poverty Discussion Paper No. 439-77.

Sevin, Imogene, Health Standards Directorate, OSHA. 1986. Telephone interview with author, 5 November.

Shane, P. M. 1981. "Presidential Regulatory Oversight and the Separation of Powers: The Constitutionality of Executive Order No. 12,291." *Arizona Law Review* 23:1,235.

Shapiro, Michael, Acting Director, Economics and Technology Division, Office of Toxic Substances, Office of Pesticides and Toxic Substances, EPA. 1984a. Telephone interview with author, 23 and 24 May.

1984b. Letter to author, 13 August.

Shapiro, Robert, Special Assistant to the Solicitor of Labor for Regulatory Affairs, DOL. 1984. Telephone interview with author, 8 January.

Shapiro, S. A. and T. O. McGarity. 1989. "Reorienting OSHA: Regulatory Alternatives and Legislative Reform." *Yale Journal on Regulation* 6:1.

Sharp, Steven, General Counsel, Federal Communications Commission. 1981. Testimony. U.S. Congress. House. Committee on Small Business. Subcommittee on Export Opportunities and Special Small Business Problems. *Hearings on Oversight of Regulatory Flexibility Act (Part 1).* 285 97th Cong., 1st sess., 1981.

Shaw, B., and A. Wolfe. 1982. "A Legal and Ethical Critique of Cost–Benefit Analysis in Public Law." *Houston Law Review* 19:899.

Sheehan, Eileen, Program Evaluation Division, Office of Management Systems and Evaluation, Office of Policy, Planning and Evaluation, EPA. 1984. Telephone interview with author, 26 July.

Shiffrin, S. 1983. "Liberalism, Radicalism and Legal Scholarship." *UCLA Law Review* 30:1,103.

Shubert, G. H. 1980. "Policy Analysis and Public Choice." In *Bureaucrats, Policy Analysts, Statesmen: Who Leads?* Edited by R. Goldwin. Washington, D.C.: American Enterprise Institute.

Silbergeld, Ellen, Staff Scientist, Environmental Defense Fund. 1982. Testimony. U.S. Congress. House. Committee on Government Operations. *Hearings on Lead in Gasoline: Public Health Needs.* 244 97th Cong., 2d sess., 1982.

Silberman, L. H. 1980. "Policy Analysis: Boon or Curse for Politicians." In *Bureaucrats, Policy Analysts, Statesmen: Who Leads?* Edited by R. Goldwin. Washington, D.C.: American Enterprise Institute.

Silk, Jennifer, Directorate of Health Standards Programs, OSHA, DOL. 1984. Telephone interview with author, 30 April.

—— 1986. Telephone interview with author, 24 October.

Silverglade, B. 1984. "Judicial Control of Regulatory Action Based on Cost–Benefit Analysis." *Administrative Law Review* 36:387.

Simon, H. A. 1945. *Administrative Behavior A Study of Decisionmaking Processes in Administrative Organizations.* New York: Macmillan.

Small Business Administration. Office of Advocacy. 1977. *The Study of Small Business.*

—— Chief Counsel for Advocacy. 1982. Testimony. U.S. Congress. Senate. Committee on the Judiciary. Subcommittee on the Regulatory Reform. Committee on Small Business. Subcommittee on Government Regulation and Paperwork. *Regulatory Flexibility Act: Joint Hearings.* 25 97th Cong., 2d sess., 1982.

—— 1983. *Annual Report of the Chief Counsel for Advocacy on the Implementation of the Regulatory Flexibility Act.*

—— 1985. *Annual Report of the Chief Counsel for Advocacy on the Implementation of the Regulatory Flexibility Act.*

Small Business Legislative Council. 1982. Testimony. U.S. Congress. Senate. Committee on the Judiciary. Subcommittee on Regulatory Reform. Committee on Small Business. Subcommittee on Government Regulation and Paperwork. *Regulatory Flexibility Act: Joint Hearings* 58 97th Cong., 2d sess., 1982.

Smith, R. S. 1976. *The Occupational Safety and Health Act: Its Goals and Its Achievements.* Washington, D.C.: American Enterprise Institute.

Spiller, Nathan, Office of the Solicitor, DOL. 1984. Telephone interview with author, 19 April.

Stanfield, R. 1986a. "EPA Administrator Lee Thomas Is More a Manager than a Policy Maker." *National Journal,* 15 January.

—— 1986b. "The Ozone Deadline." *National Journal,* 13 September.

Starr, C. 1969. "Social Benefit Versus Technological Risks." *Science* 165: 1,232.

Stasikowski, Margaret, Acting Director, Chemical Control Division, Office of Toxic Substances, Office of Pesticides and Toxic Substances, EPA. 1984. Telephone interview with author, 11 July.

Steed, Dianne, Administrator, National Highway Traffic Safety Administration, DOT, and Erika Jones, Special Counsel to the Administrator, NHTSA, DOT. 1983. Interview with author. Washington, D.C., 19 May.

Stein, Edward, Health Standards Directorate, OSHA. 1986. Telephone interview with author, 21 October.

Stockman, David. 1981. *Memorandum to the Heads of Executive Departments and Agencies.* 11 June. Reprinted in U.S. Congress. Senate. Committee on Governmental Affairs. *Hearings on Regulatory Reform Legislation of 1981.* 83 97th Cong., 1st sess., 1981.

Stokey, E., and R. Zeckhauser. 1978. *A Primer for Policy Analysis.* New York: Norton.

Stoplman, Paul, Special Assistant to the Director, Office of Policy Analysis, Office of Policy, Planning and Evaluation, EPA. 1982. *Memorandum to Al Jennings, Acting Director, Office of Standards and Regulations,* 30 September.

Storing, H. J. 1980. "American Statesmanship: Old and New." In *Bureaucrats, Policy Analysts, Statesmen: Who Leads?* Edited by R. Goldwin. Washington, D.C.: American Enterprise Institute.

Strauss, P. L. 1984. "The Place of Agencies in Government: Separation of Powers and the Fourth Branch." *Columbia Law Review* 84:573.

Strauss, P. L. and C. R. Sunstein. 1986. "The Role of the President and OMB in Informal Rulemaking." *Administrative Law Review* 38:181.

Strobel, Gary, Special Assistant to the Assistant Secretary for Regulatory Affairs, OSHA, DOL. 1984. Telephone interview with author, 23 July.

Strohbehn, E. L. 1974. "Perspective: NEPA's Impact on Federal Decisionmaking: Examples of Noncompliance and Suggestions for Change." *Ecology Law Quarterly* 4:93.

Sun, M. 1985. "Food Dyes Fuel Debate Over Delaney." *Science* 229:739.

Sunstein, C. R. 1981. "Cost–Benefit Analysis and the Separation of Powers." *Arizona Law Review* 23:1,267.

Thaler, R. H. 1981. Precommitment and the Value of a Life. Paper presented at the Geneva Conference on the Value of Life and Safety, Geneva, March 30–April 1, 1981.

1983. "Illusions & Mirages in Public Policy." *The Public Interest,* (Fall):60.

Thomas, Henry C., Ambient Standards Branch, Strategies and Air Standards Division, Office of Air Quality Planning and Standards, Office of Air and Radiation, EPA. 1984a. Telephone interview with author, 25 May.

1984b. Use of Quantitative Analysis in the NAAQS Review Process. Paper presented at the 77th Annual Meeting of the Air Pollution Control Association, San Francisco, June 1984.

1984c. Telephone interview with author, 24 July.

1984d. Letter to author, 16 August.

1986. Telephone interview with author, 7 November.

Tolchin, M. 1979. "Presidential Power and the Politics of RARG." *Regulation* (July/August):44.

Tolchin, S. J. and M. Tolchin. 1983. *Dismantling America: The Rush to Deregulate.* Boston: Houghton Mifflin.

Tonetti, Robert, Land Disposal Branch, Waste Management and Economics Division, Office of Solid Waste, Office of Solid Waste and Emergency Response, EPA. 1984. Telephone interview with author, 26 July.

Toomey, James, Regulation Review Staff Officer, Market Research and Development Division, Marketing Program Operations, AMS, USDA. 1983. Telephone interview with author, 6 May.

1984. Telephone interview with author, 1 May.

Tribe, L. H. 1972. "Policy, Science: Analysis or Ideology?" *Philosophy and Public Affairs* 2:66.

1973. "Technology Assessment and the Fourth Discontinuity: The Limits of Instrumental Rationality." *Southern California Law Review* 46:617.

1974. "Ways Not to Think About Plastic Trees: New Foundations for Environmental Law." *Yale Law Journal* 83:1,315.

Turner, R. 1979. "Cost–Benefit Analysis – A Critique." *Omega* 7:411.

U.S. Congress. House. Committee on Merchant Marine and Fisheries. 1970. Subcommittee on Fisheries and Wildlife Conservation. *Hearings on Administration of the National Environmental Policy Act.* 91st Cong., 2d sess., 1970.

1976. Committee on Interstate and Foreign Commerce. Subcommittee on Oversight and Investigation. *Federal Regulatory [sic] and Regulatory Reform.* 94th Cong., 2d sess., 1976. H. Doc. No. 134.

Committee on the Judiciary. 1979. Subcommittee on Administrative Law and Government Relations. *Hearings on the Regulatory Reform Act of 1979.* 96th Cong., 1st and 2d sess., 1979.

Committee on Interstate and Foreign Commerce. 1979. Subcommittee on Oversight and Investigations and Subcommittee on Consumer Protection an Finance. *Joint Hearings on the Use of Cost–Benefit Analysis by Regulatory Agencies.* 96th Cong., 1st sess., 1979.

Committee on Interstate and Foreign Commerce. 1980. Subcommittee on Oversight and Investigations. *Hearings on Cost–Benefit Analysis: The Potential for Conflict of Interest.* 96th Cong., 2d sess., 1980.

Committee on Government Operations. 1980. *Paperwork Reduction Act of 1980: Hearings on H.R. 641.* 96th Cong., 2d sess., 1980.

Committee on Interstate and Foreign Commerce. 1980. Subcommittee on Oversight and Investigations. *Report on Cost–Benefit Analysis: Wonder Tool or Mirage?* 96th Cong., 2d sess., 1980.

Committee on Energy and Commerce. 1981. Subcommittee on Oversight and Investigations. *Hearings on Role of OMB in Regulation.* 97th Cong., 1st sess., 1981.

Committee on the Judiciary. 1981. Subcommittee on Administrative Law and Governmental Relations. *Regulatory Procedures Act of 1981: Hearings on H.R. 746.* 97th Cong., 1st sess., 1981.

Committee on Small Business. 1981. Subcommittee on Export Opportunities and Special Small Business Problems. *Hearings on Oversight of Regulatory Flexibility Act (Part 1).* 97th Cong., 1st sess., 1981.

Committee on Agriculture. 1982. Subcommittee on Department Operations, Research, and Foreign Agriculture. *Staff Report on Regulatory Pro-*

cedures and Public Health Issues in the EPA's Office of Pesticide Programs. 97th Cong., 2d sess., 1982.

Committee on Government Operations. 1982. *Hearings on Office of Management and Budget Control of OSHA Rulemaking.* 97th Cong., 2d sess., 1982.

Committee on the Judiciary. 1982. *Regulatory Procedure Act of 1982.* 97th Cong., 2d sess., 1982. H. Rept. 97–435.

Committee on Government Operations. 1983. *OMB Interference with OSHA Rulemaking, Thirtieth Report by the House Committee on Government Operations.* 98th Cong., 1st sess., 1983.

Committee on the Judiciary. 1983. Subcommittee on Administrative Law and Governmental Relations. *Hearings on H.R. 2327.* 98th Cong., 1st sess., 1983.

Committee on Energy and Commerce. 1985. Subcommittee on Oversight and Investigations. *Report on EPA's Asbestos Regulations: Case Study on OMB Interference in Agency Rulemaking.* 99th Cong., 1st sess., 1985.

U.S. Congress. Senate. 1966. S. Rept. 89–1301. 89th Cong., 2d sess., 1966.

1981a. S. Rept. 97–284. 97th Cong., 1st sess., 1981.

1981b. S. Rept. 97–305. 97th Cong., 1st sess., 1981.

Committee on Governmental Affairs. 1978. *Study on Federal Regulation, Report of the Senate Committee on Governmental Affairs.* 96th Cong., 1st sess., 1978. S. Doc. 13. Vol. 6.

Committee on Environment and Public Works. 1979. Subcommittee on Environmental Pollution. *Hearings on Executive Branch Review of Environmental Regulations.* 96th Cong., 1st sess., 1979.

Committee on the Judiciary. 1979. Subcommittee on Administrative Practice and Procedure. *Hearings on Regulatory Reform.* 96th Cong., 1st sess., pt. 2, 1979.

Committee on Governmental Affairs. 1981a. *Hearings on Regulatory Reform Legislation of 1981.* 97th Cong., 1st sess., 1981.

Committee on Governmental Affairs. 1981b. Subcommittee on Federal Expenditures, Research and Rules. *Hearings on the Consultant Reform and Disclosure Act of 1981.* 97th Cong., 1st sess., 1981.

Committee on the Judiciary. 1981. Subcommittee on Regulatory Reform. *Hearings on Regulatory Reform Act – S. 1080.* 97th Cong., 1st sess., 1981.

Committee on the Judiciary. 1982. Subcommittee on Regulatory Reform. Committee on Small Business. Subcommittee on Government Regulation and Paperwork. *Regulatory Flexibility Act: Joint Hearings.* 97th Cong., 2d sess. 1982.

Committee on Governmental Affairs. 1984. Subcommittee on Information Management and Regulatory Affairs. *Hearings on the Paperwork Reduction Act Amendments of 1984.* 98th Cong., 2d sess., 1984.

Committee on Environment and Public Works. 1986. *Staff Report on Office Management and Budget Influence on Agency Regulations.* 99th Cong., 2d sess., 1986.

USDA. 1983a. *Departmental Regulation No. 1512-1, USDA Regulatory Decisionmaking Requirements,* 15 December.

1983b. Testimony. U.S. Congress. House. Committee on the Judiciary. Subcommittee on Administrative Law and Governmental Relations. *Regulatory Reform Act of 1983: Hearings on H.R. 232.* 256 98th Cong., 1st sess., 1983.

U.S. Regulatory Council. 1981. *A Survey of Ten Agencies' Experience with Regulatory Analysis.*

Updegraff, Gail, Deputy Director, Policy and Program Planning Staff, FSIS. USDA. 1984. Telephone interview with author, 13 March.

Urkowitz, A. G. and R. E. Laessing. 1982. "Assessing the Believability of Research Results Reported in the Environmental Health Matrix." *Public Administration Review.* 42:427.

Vaupel, J. W. 1981. "On the Benefits of Health and Safety Regulation." In *The Benefits of Health and Safety Regulation.* Edited by G. Ferguson and E. LeVeen. Cambridge, Mass.: Ballinger.

Verdier, J. M. 1984. "Advising Congressional Decision-Makers: Guidelines for Economists." *Journal of Policy Analysis and Management* 3:421.

Verkuil, P. R. 1978. "The Emerging Concept of Administrative Procedure." *Columbia Law Review* 78:258.

1980. "Jawboning Administrative Agencies: Ex Parte Contacts by the White House." *Columbia Law Review* 80:943.

1982. "A Critical Guide to the Regulatory Flexibility Act." *Duke Law Journal,* 213.

Viscusi, W. K. 1983a. *Risk By Choice: Regulating Health and Safety in the Workplace.* Cambridge, Mass.: Harvard University Press.

1983b. "Presidential Oversight: Controlling the Regulators." *Journal of Policy Analysis and Management* 2:157.

N.d. "Analysis of OMB and OSHA Evaluations of the Hazard Communication Proposal." Mimeo.

Vitiello, Daniel, Policy and Program Planning Staff, FSIS, USDA. 1983. Telephone interview with author, 3 May.

Vogel, D. 1981. "The 'New' Social Regulation in Historical and Comparative Perspective." In *Regulation in Perspective.* Edited by T. K. McGraw. Cambridge, Mass.: Harvard University Press.

Vogt, Craig, Deputy Director, Criteria and Standards Division, Office of Drinking Water, Office of Water, EPA. 1984. Telephone interview with author, 26 June.

Wald, P. M. 1983. "Judicial Review of Economic Analysis." *Yale Journal on Regulation* 1:43.

Walker, Larry, Director, Regulatory Impact and Executive Correspondence Staff, Program Planning and Development, ASCS, USDA. 1983. Telephone interview with author, 5 May.

1984a. Telephone interview with author, 1 May.

1984b. Telephone interview with author, 15 August.

Warlick, Carol, Office of Planning and Analysis, Office of Plans and Programs, NHTSA, DOT. 1984. Telephone interview with author, 9 April.

Weber, M. E., Office of Regulatory Analysis, Directorate of Technical Support, OSHA, DOL. 1983. Telephone interview with author, 10 May.

Wehe, Al, Cost and Economics Section, Economic Analysis Branch, Strategies and Air Standards Division, Office of Air and Radiation, EPA. 1984. Telephone interview with author, 26 July.

Weidenbaum, Murray L. 1981. Testimony. U.S. Congress. Senate. Committee on Governmental Affairs. *Hearings on Regulatory Reform Legislation of 1981.* 43 97th Cong. 1st sess., 1981.

Weidenbaum, Murray L., and R. DeFina. 1978. *The Cost of Federal Regulation of Economic Activity.* Washington, D.C.: American Enterprise Institute.

Weil, Norman. *See* Safeer.

Weinberg, A. 1972. "Science and Trans-Science." *Minerva* 10:209.

Weissman, Robert, Special Assistant to the Director, Mobile Source Division, EPA. 1984. Telephone interview with author, 6 January.

Wentzler, Nancy, formerly Office of Regulatory Analysis, Directorate of Policy, OSHA, DOL. 1984. Telephone interview with author, 18 April.

West, W. F. 1983. "Institutionalizing Rationality in Regulatory Administration." *Public Administration Review* 43:326.

West, W. F., and J. Cooper. 1985. "The Rise of Administrative Clearance." In *The Presidency and Public Policy Making.* Edited by G. Edwards, S. Shull, and N. Thomas. Pittsburgh, Penn.: University of Pittsburgh Press.

    1989. "Legislative Influence v. Presidential Dominance: Competing Models of Bureaucratic Control." *Political Science Quarterly* 104:581.

Westman, W. E. 1977. "How Much Are Nature's Services Worth?" *Science* 197:960.

White, Barry, Director, Safety Standards Directorate, OSHA. 1986. Interview with author. Washington, D.C., 26 September.

White, Frank. Deputy Assistant Secretary, OSHA. 1986. Interview with author. Washington, D.C., 26 September.

Wichelman, A. F. 1976. "Administrative Agency Implementation of the National Environmental Policy Act of 1969: A Conceptual Framework for Explaining Deferential Response." *Natural Resources Journal* 16:263.

Wildavsky, A. 1979. *Speaking Truth to Power: The Art and Craft of Policy Analysis.* Boston: Little, Brown.

Wilson, J. Q. 1980. *The Politics of Regulation.* New York: Basic.

Wilson, R. 1987. "A Visit to Chernobyl." *Science* 236:1,636.

Wines, M. 1982. "Automobile Bumper Standard Crumples as Cost–Benefit Analysis Falls Short." *National Journal,* 15:145.

Wolcott, Robert, Special Assistant to the Deputy Administrator, EPA. 1984. Interview with author. Washington, D.C., 27 June.

Wrenn, Grover, Environ Corp. 1986. Telephone interview with author, 23 October.

Wright, Mike, United Steelworkers of America. 1986. Telephone interview with author, 24 October.

Yellin, J. 1981. "High Technology and the Courts: Nuclear Power and the Need for Institutional Reform." *Harvard Law Review* 94:489.

Zeckhauser, R. Z., and D. S. Shepard. 1976. "Where Now for Saving Lives?" *Law and Contemporary Problems* 40:5.

   1981. "Principles for Saving and Valuing Lives." In *The Benefits of Health and Safety Regulation.* Edited by A. Ferguson and E. LeVeen. Cambridge, Mass.: Ballinger.

Zeisel, H. 1981. "Social Science Hubris? A Review of Lindblom and Cohen's Usable Knowledge." *American Bar Foundation Research Journal,* 273.

Index